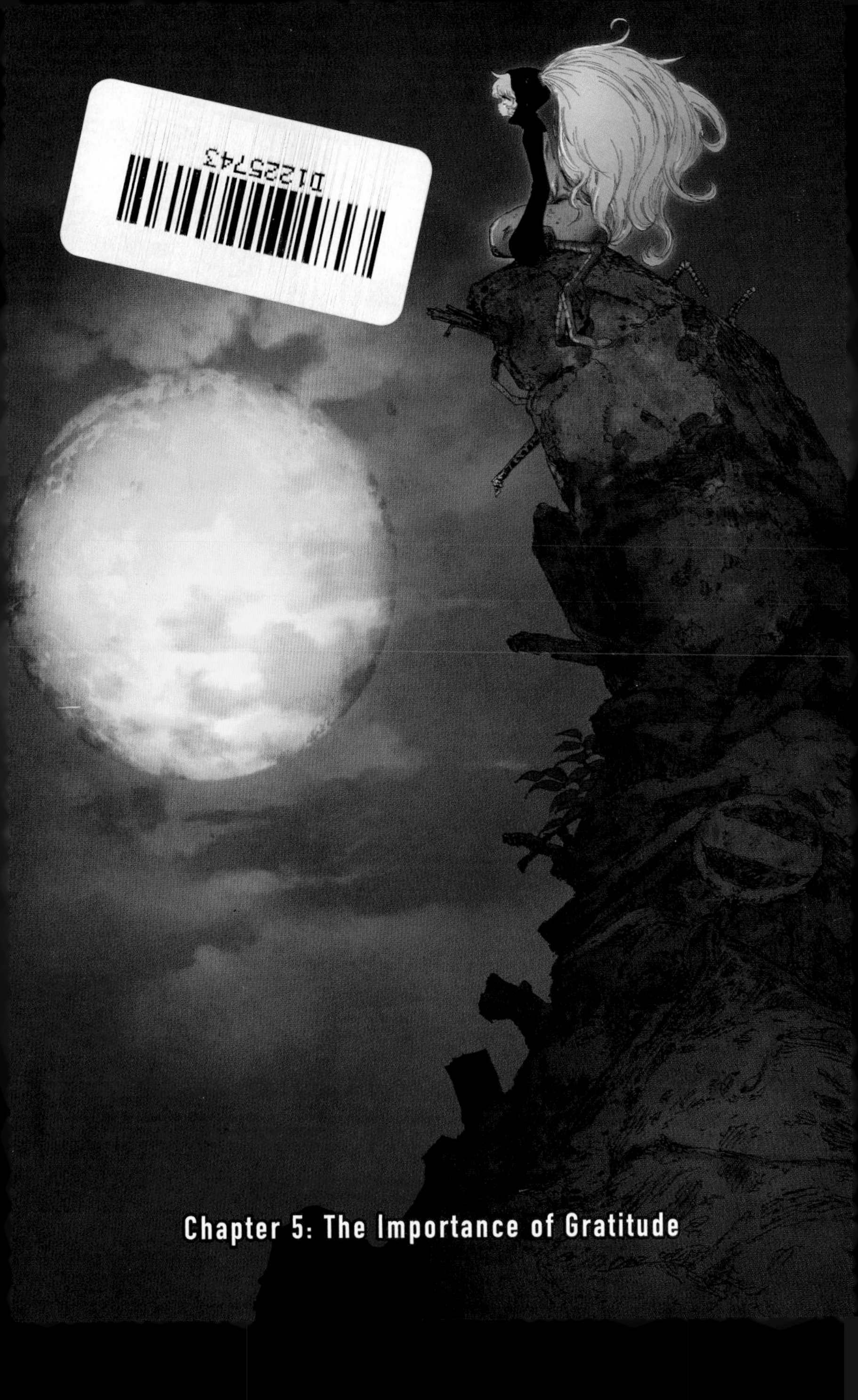

Chapter 5: The Importance of Gratitude

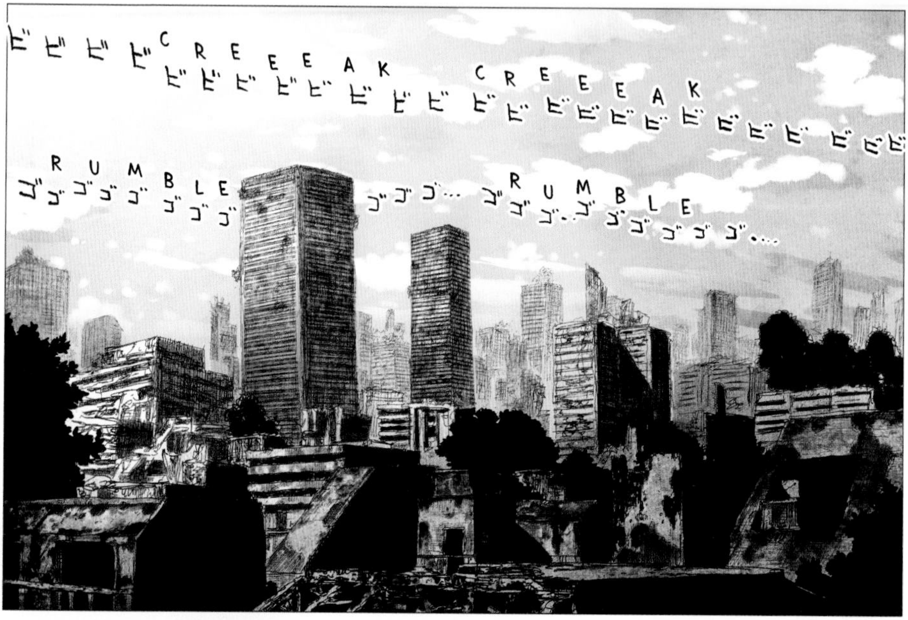
CREEEAK
CREEEAK
RUMBLE
RUMBLE

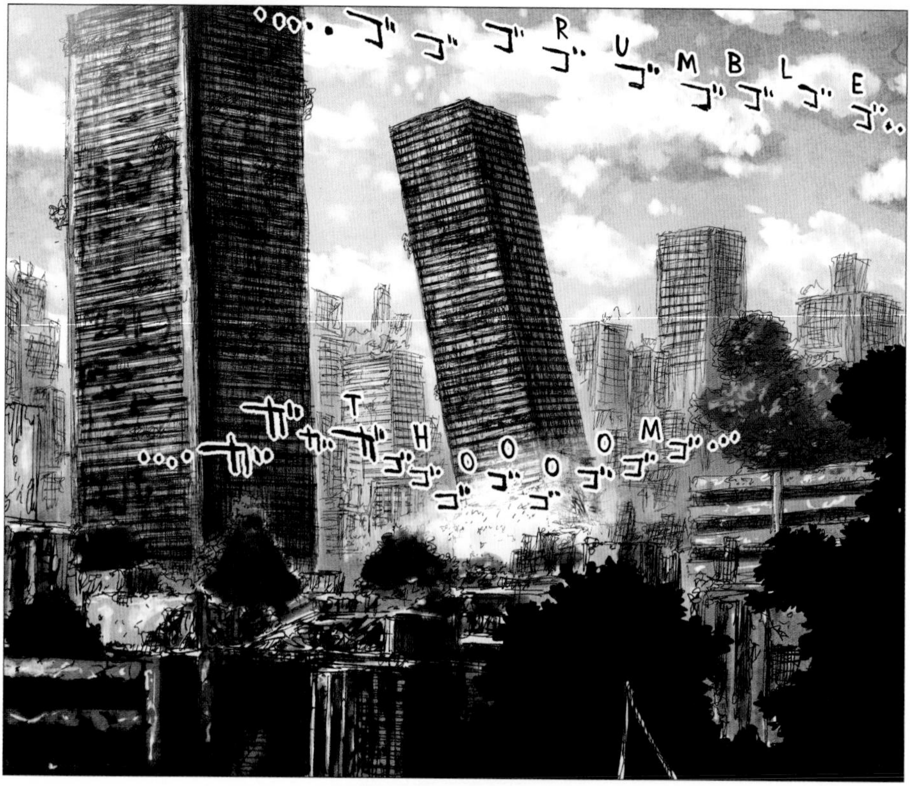
RUMBLE
THOOOM

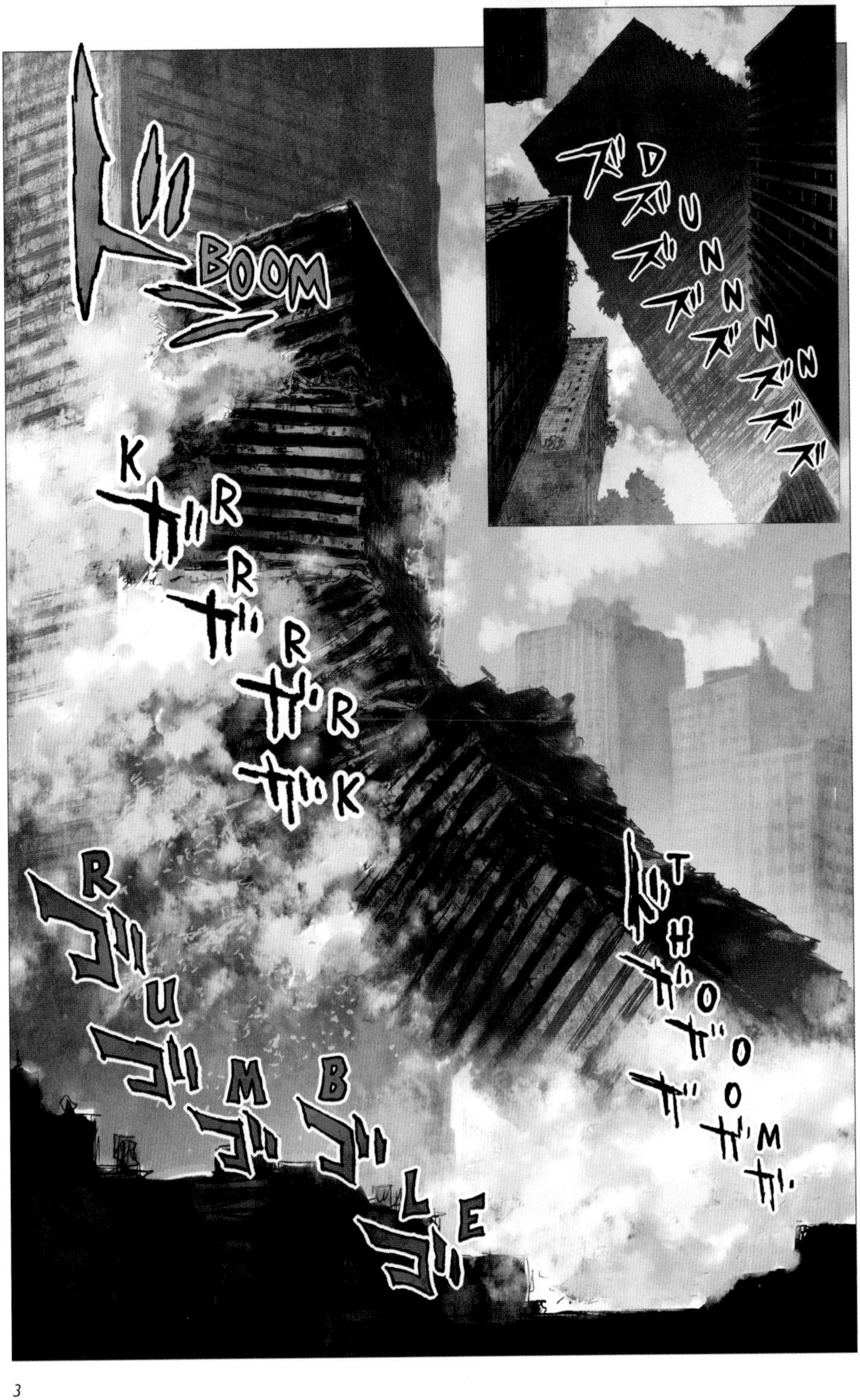
DUNNNN
BOOM
KRRRK
THOOOM
RUMBLE

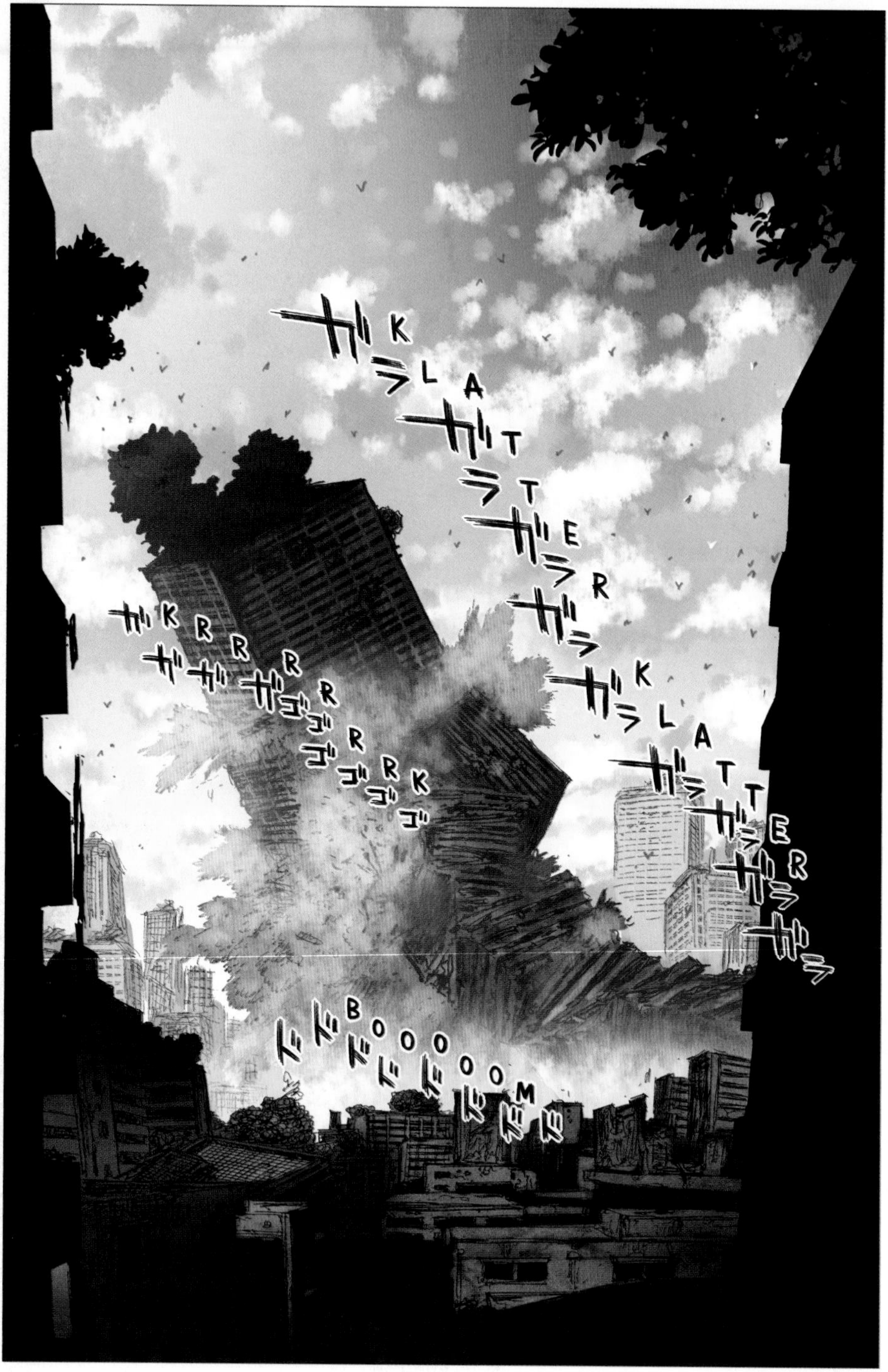
KLATTER
KLATTER
KRRRRRRK
BOOOOM

2

ippatu

TSUGUMI PROJECT

Contents

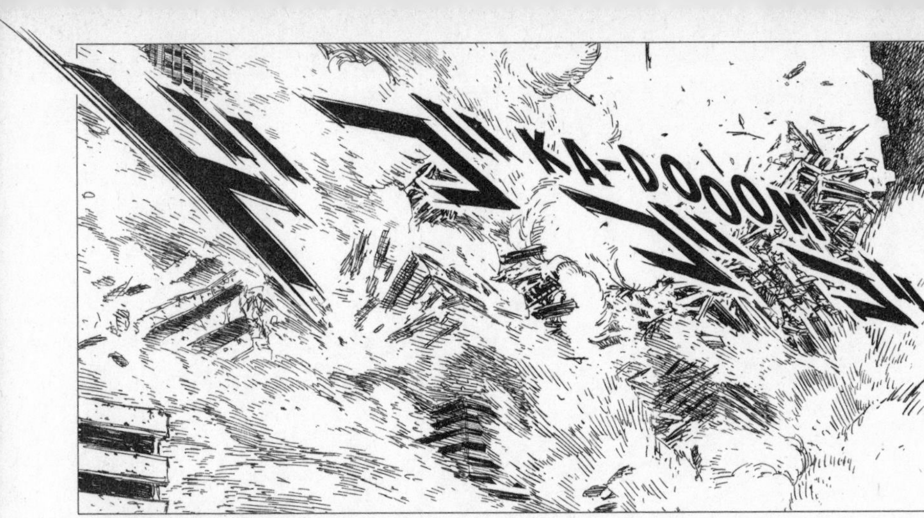
KA-DOOOM
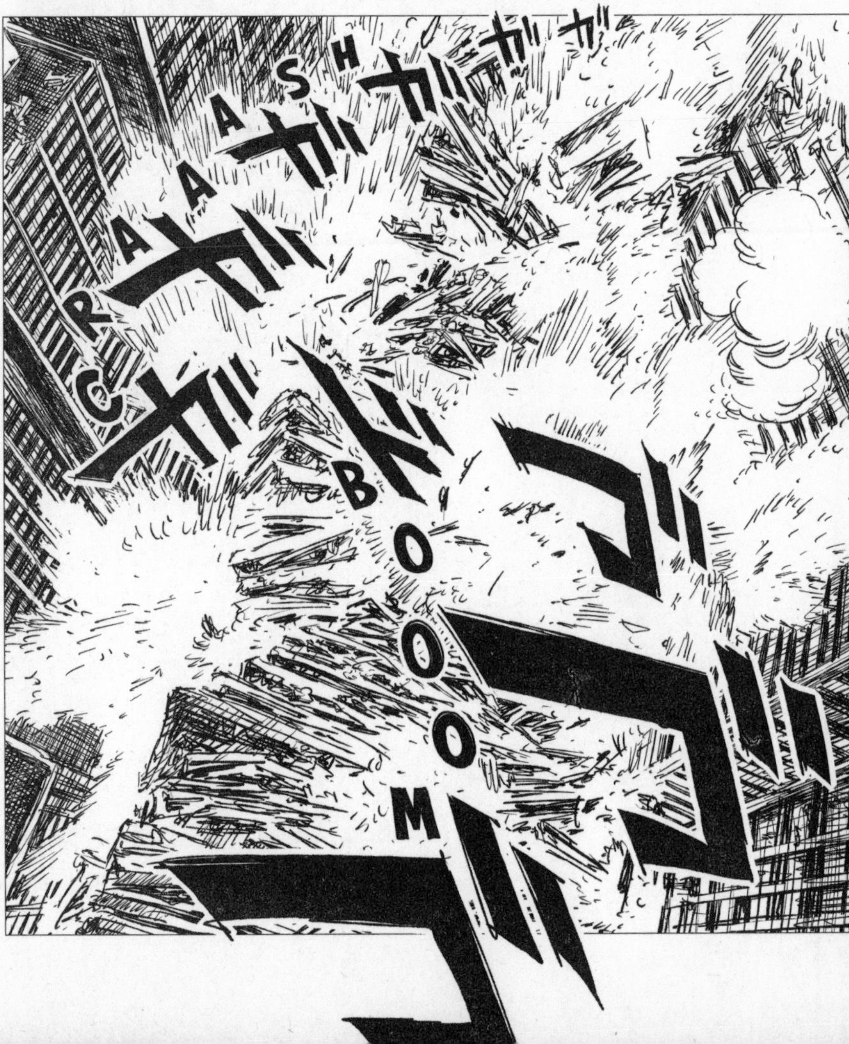
CRAASH
BOOOM

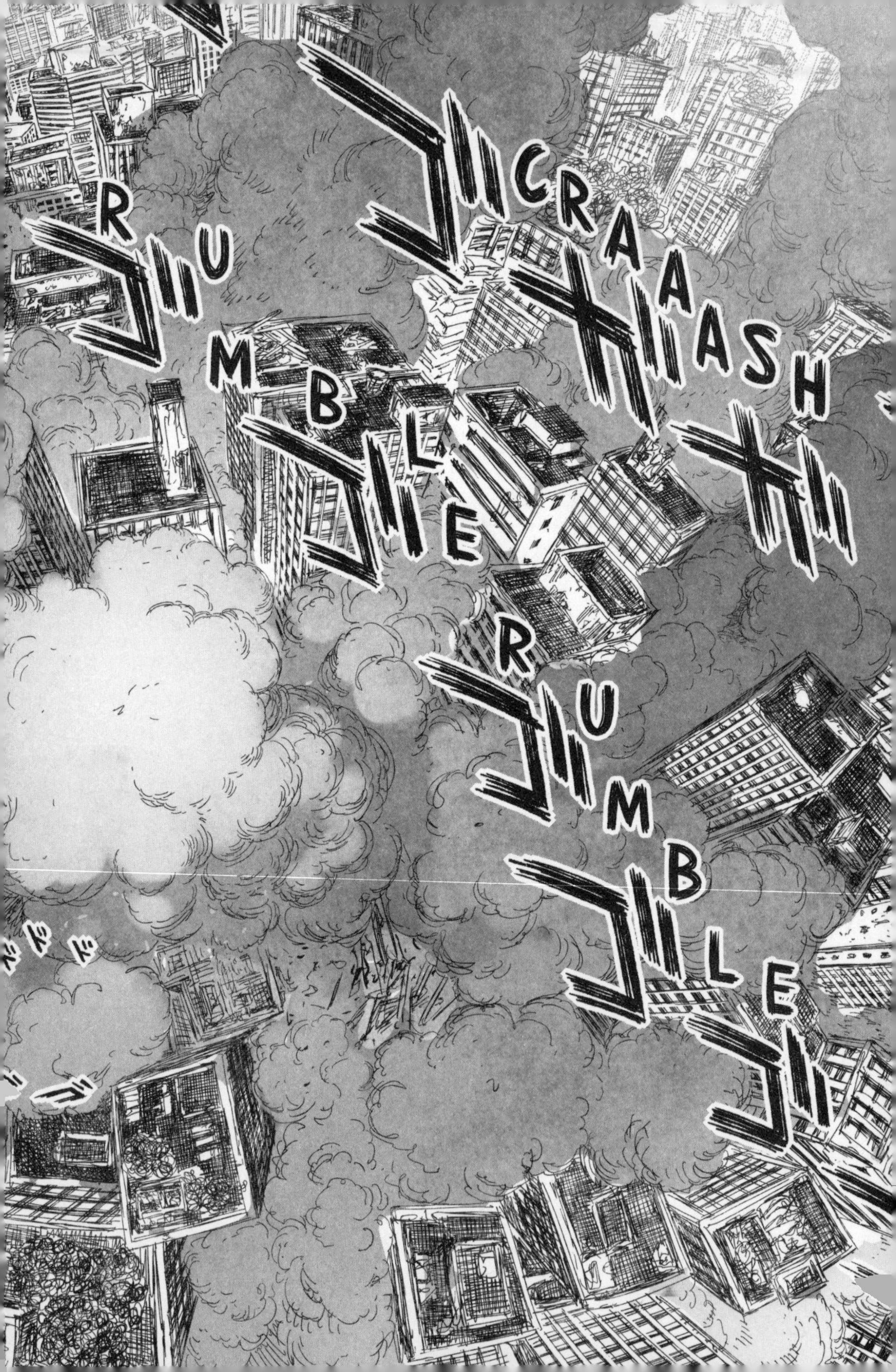
CRAAASH
RUMBLE
RUMBLE

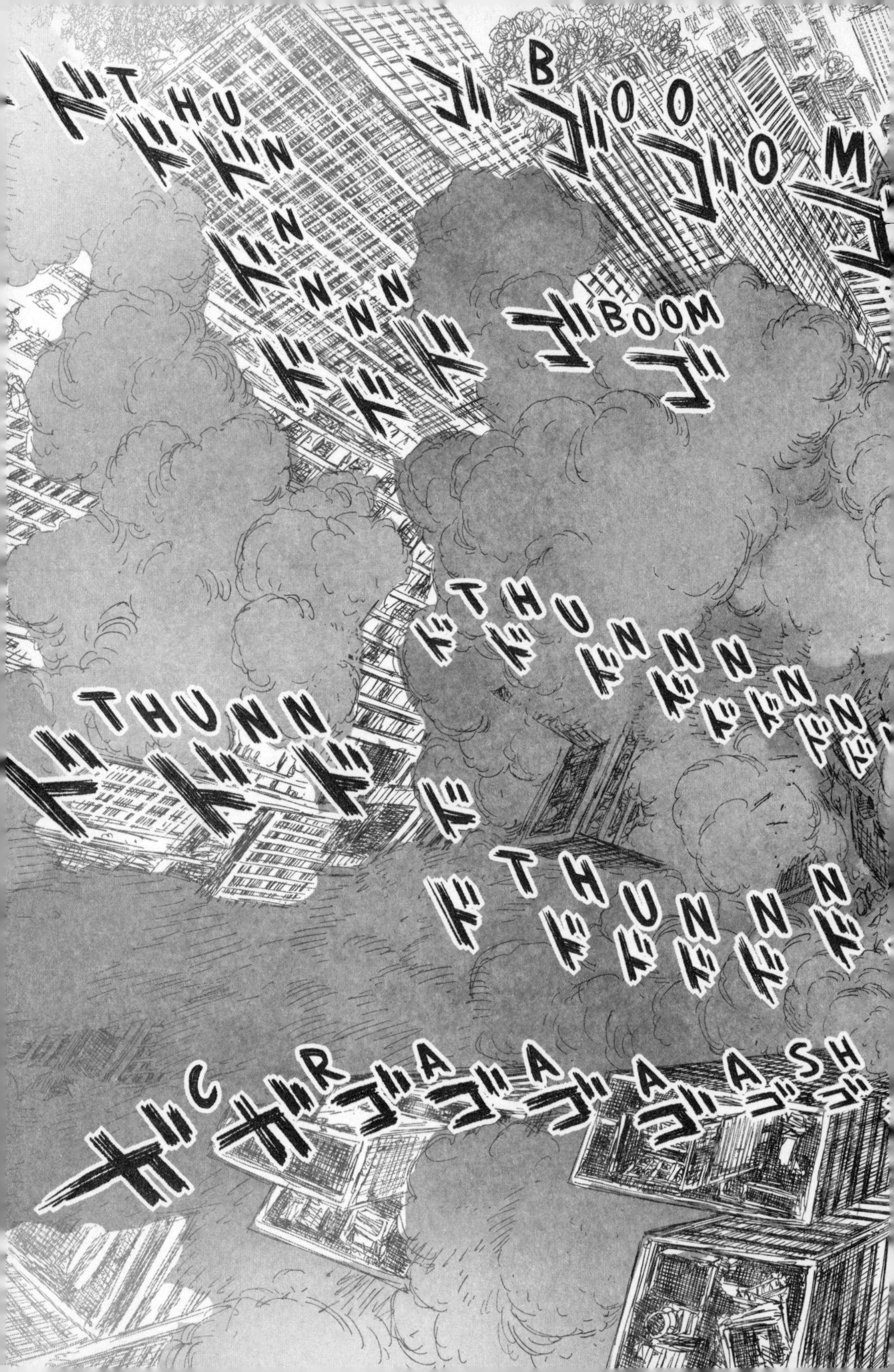
BOOOM
THUNNNN
BOOM
THUNNNN
THUNN
THUNNN
CRAAASH

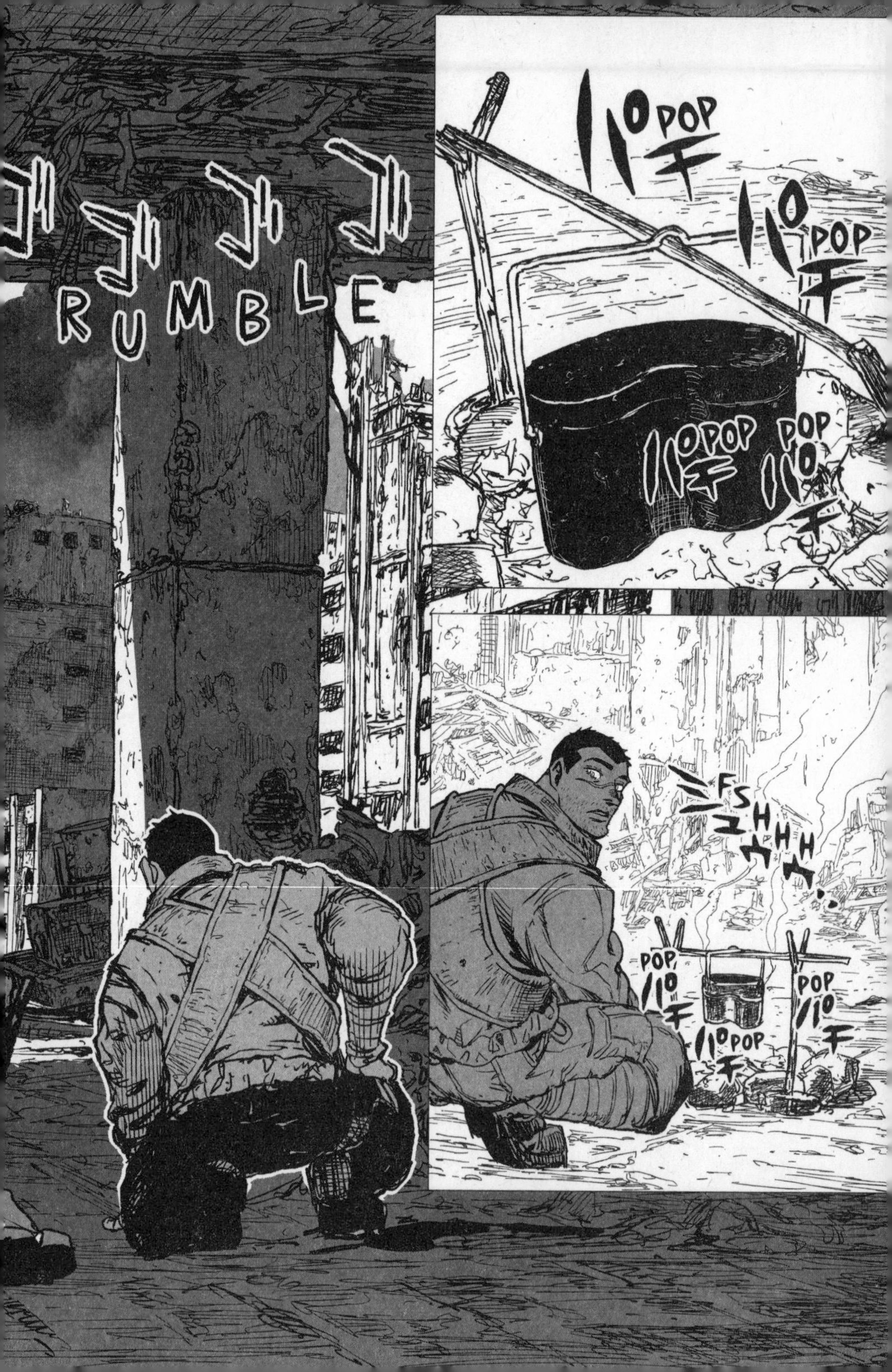
パチ POP
パチ POP
パチ POP
パチ POP
シュウウ FSHHH
パチ POP
パチ POP
パチ POP
ゴゴゴゴ RUMBLE

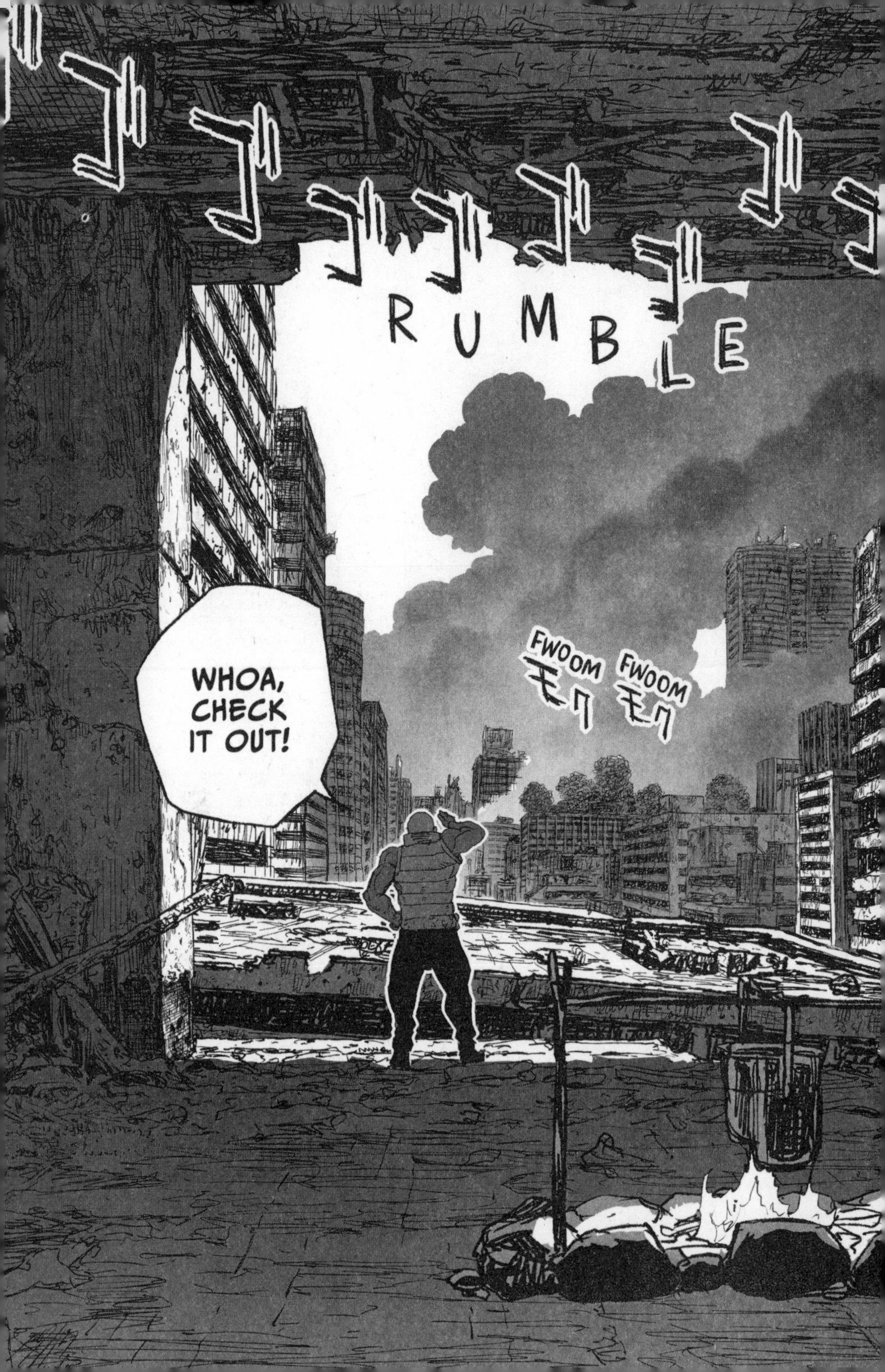
ゴゴゴゴゴゴゴ
RUMBLE
FWOOM FWOOM
モクモク
WHOA, CHECK IT OUT!

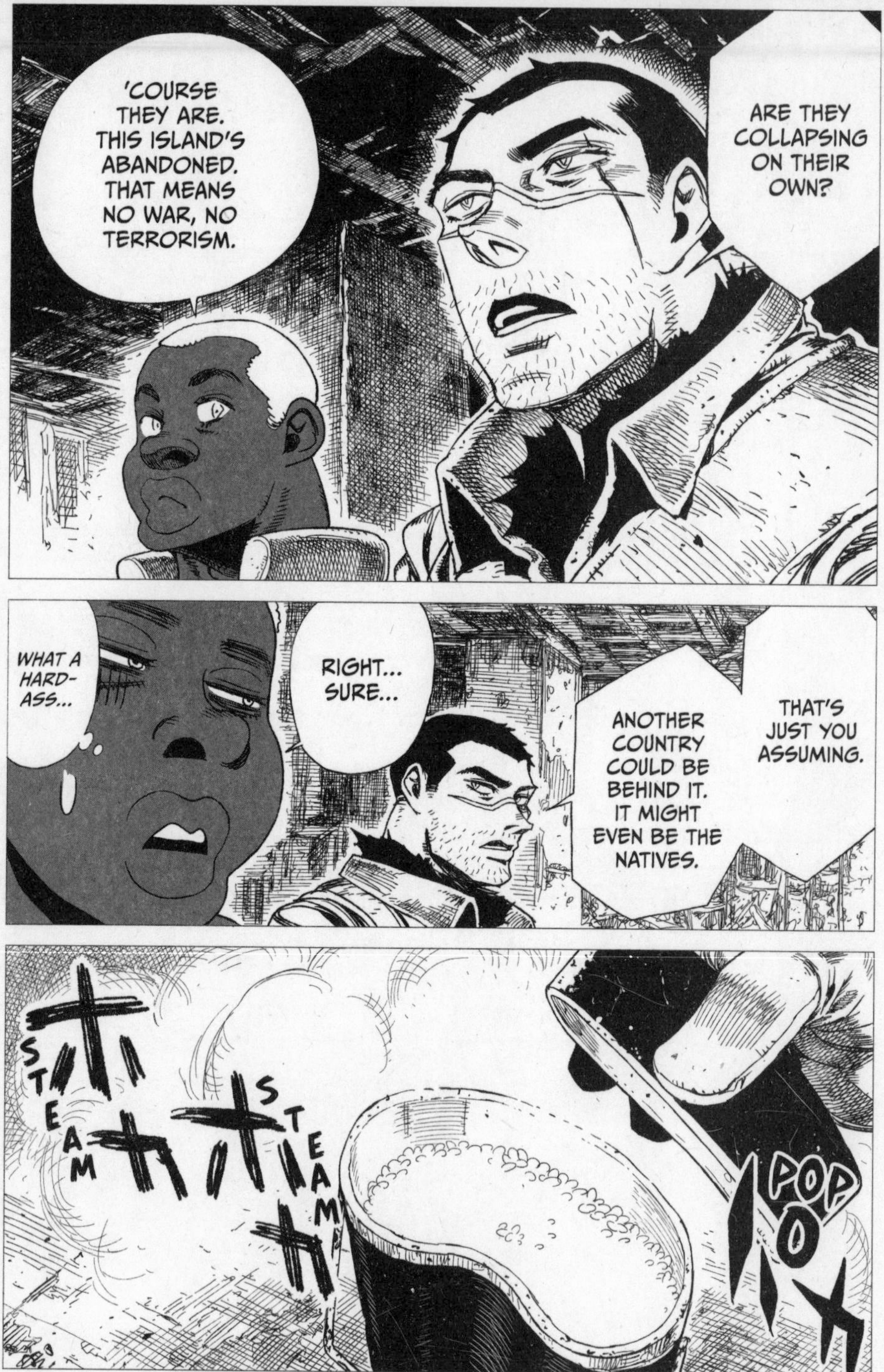
ARE THEY COLLAPSING ON THEIR OWN?
'COURSE THEY ARE. THIS ISLAND'S ABANDONED. THAT MEANS NO WAR, NO TERRORISM.
THAT'S JUST YOU ASSUMING.
ANOTHER COUNTRY COULD BE BEHIND IT. IT MIGHT EVEN BE THE NATIVES.
RIGHT... SURE...
WHAT A HARD-ASS...
POP
STEAM
STEAM

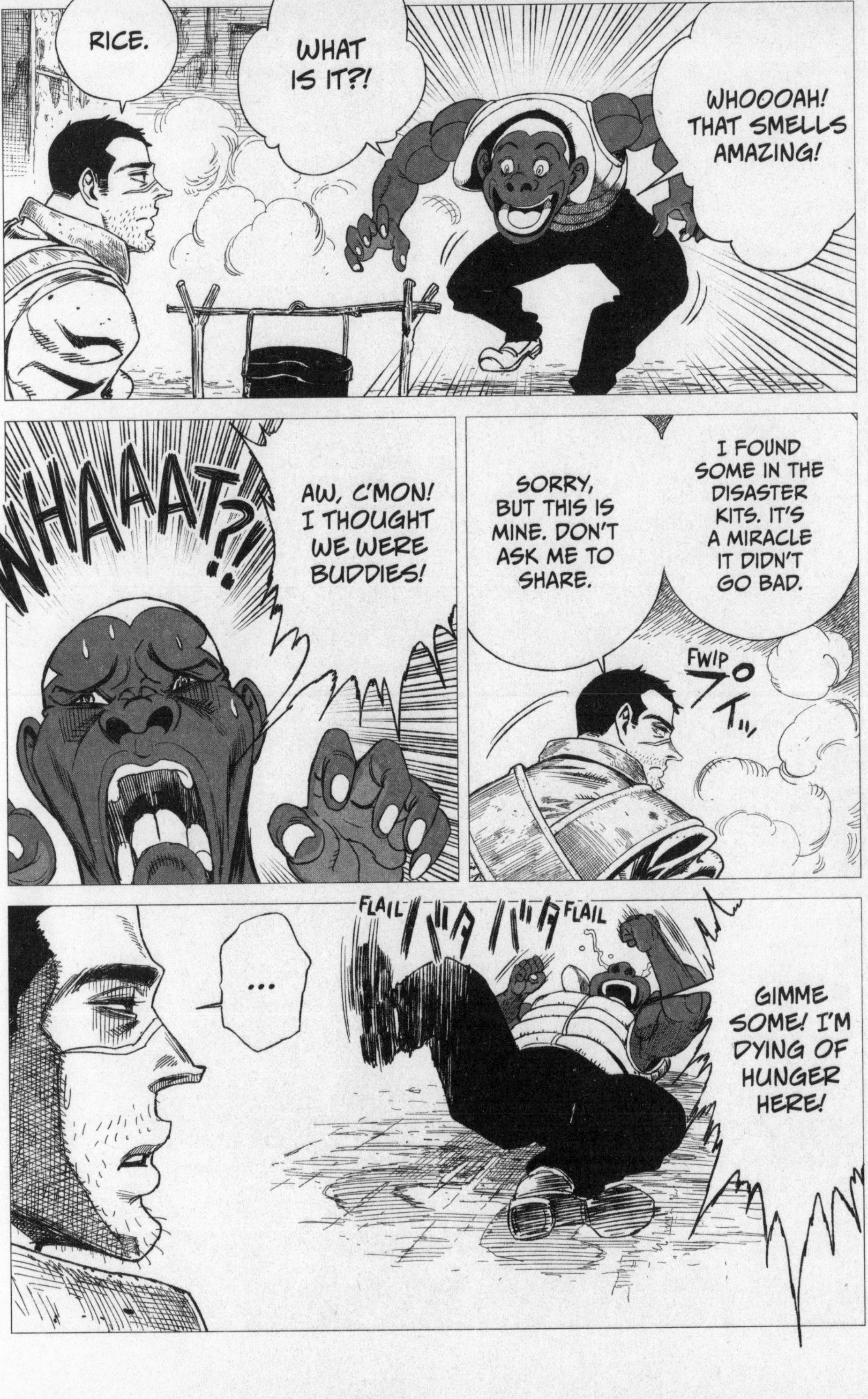
WHOOOAH! THAT SMELLS AMAZING!
WHAT IS IT?!
RICE.
I FOUND SOME IN THE DISASTER KITS. IT'S A MIRACLE IT DIDN'T GO BAD.
SORRY, BUT THIS IS MINE. DON'T ASK ME TO SHARE.
FWIP
WHAAAT?!
AW, C'MON! I THOUGHT WE WERE BUDDIES!
GIMME SOME! I'M DYING OF HUNGER HERE!
FLAIL
FLAIL
...

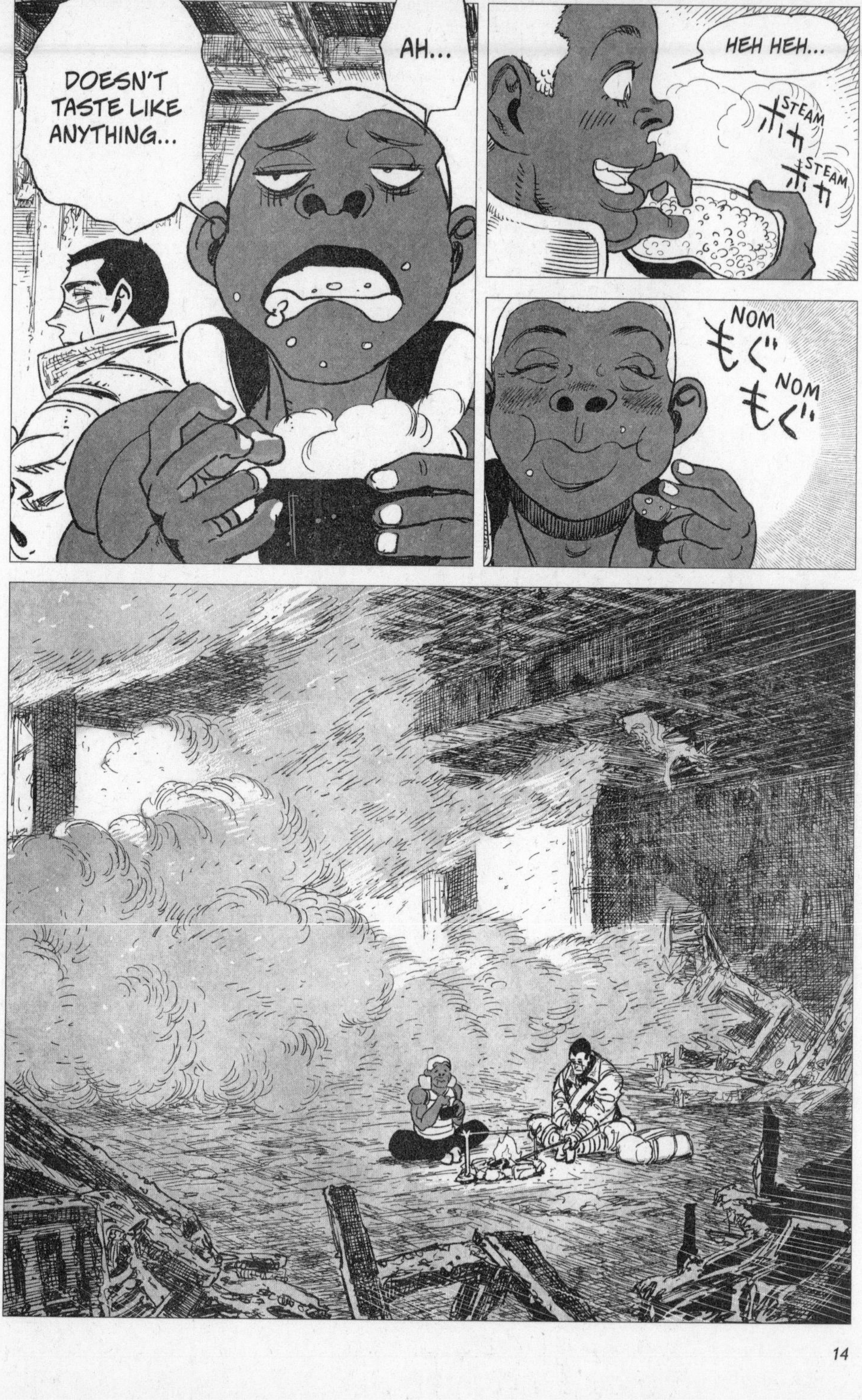
HEH HEH...
STEAM ホカ
STEAM ホカ
NOM もぐ
NOM もぐ
AH...
DOESN'T TASTE LIKE ANYTHING...

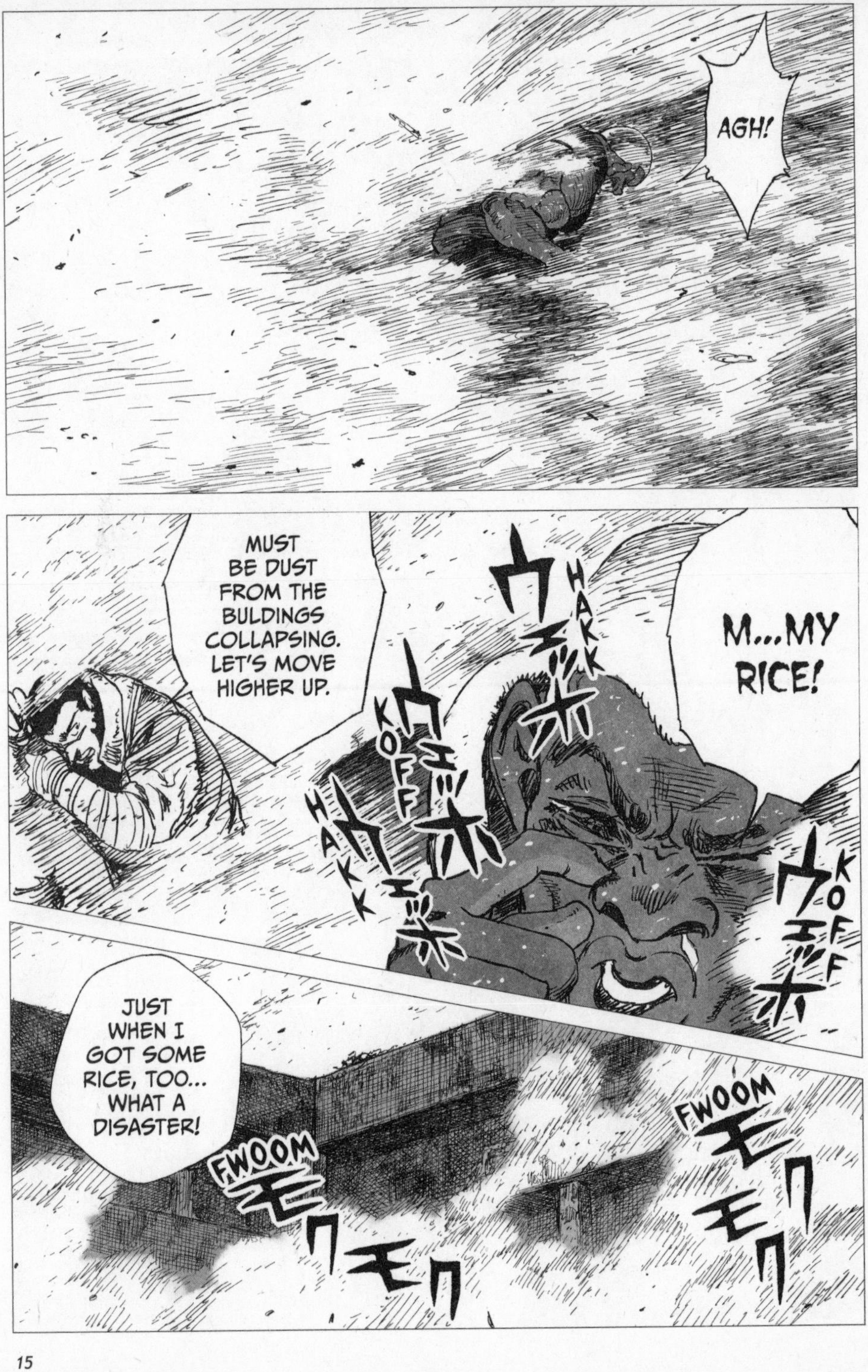
AGH!
M...MY RICE!
HAKK
KOFF
HAKK
KOFF
MUST BE DUST FROM THE BULDINGS COLLAPSING. LET'S MOVE HIGHER UP.
FWOOM
FWOOM
JUST WHEN I GOT SOME RICE, TOO... WHAT A DISASTER!

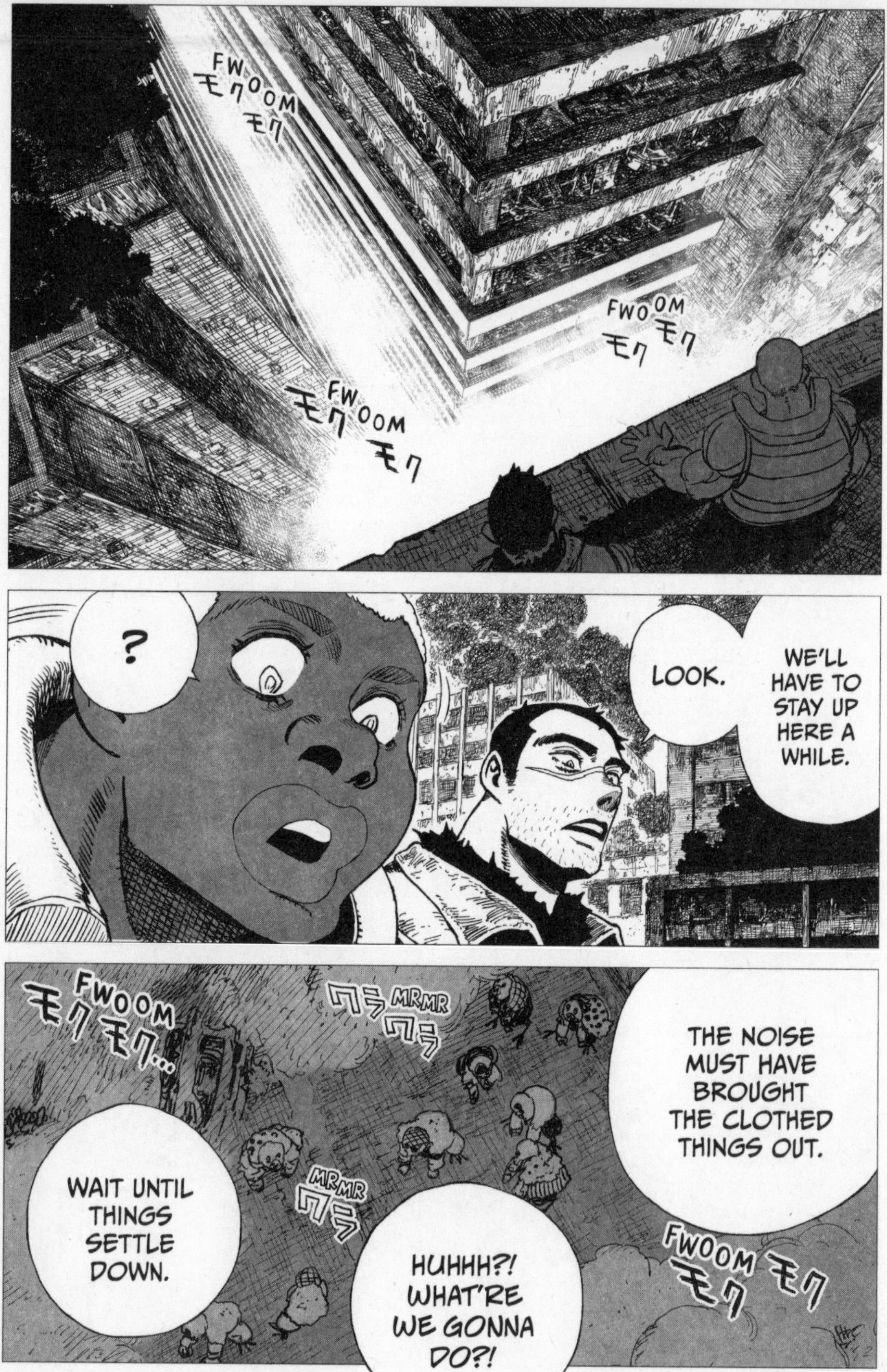
FWOOM モクモク
FWOOM モクモク
FWOOM モクモク
WE'LL HAVE TO STAY UP HERE A WHILE.
LOOK.
?
THE NOISE MUST HAVE BROUGHT THE CLOTHED THINGS OUT.
FWOOM モクモク
MRMR ワラワラ
FWOOM モクモク…
MRMR ワラ
HUHHH?! WHAT'RE WE GONNA DO?!
WAIT UNTIL THINGS SETTLE DOWN.

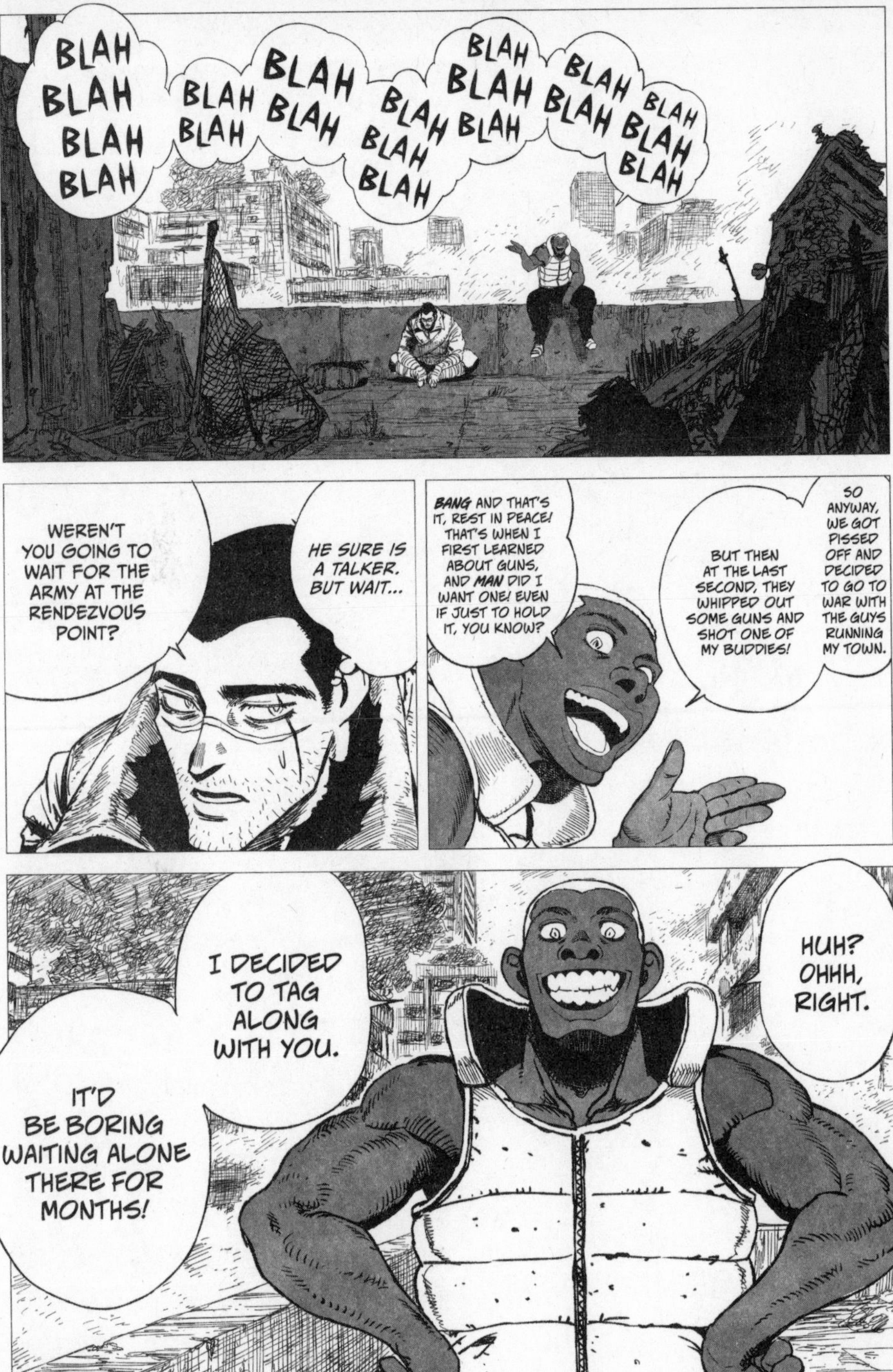
BLAH BLAH BLAH
BLAH BLAH BLAH
BLAH BLAH BLAH
BLAH BLAH BLAH
BLAH BLAH
BLAH BLAH
BLAH BLAH BLAH BLAH
SO ANYWAY, WE GOT PISSED OFF AND DECIDED TO GO TO WAR WITH THE GUYS RUNNING MY TOWN.
BUT THEN AT THE LAST SECOND, THEY WHIPPED OUT SOME GUNS AND SHOT ONE OF MY BUDDIES!
BANG AND THAT'S IT, REST IN PEACE! THAT'S WHEN I FIRST LEARNED ABOUT GUNS, AND MAN DID I WANT ONE! EVEN IF JUST TO HOLD IT, YOU KNOW?
HE SURE IS A TALKER. BUT WAIT...
WEREN'T YOU GOING TO WAIT FOR THE ARMY AT THE RENDEZVOUS POINT?
HUH? OHHH, RIGHT.
I DECIDED TO TAG ALONG WITH YOU.
IT'D BE BORING WAITING ALONE THERE FOR MONTHS!

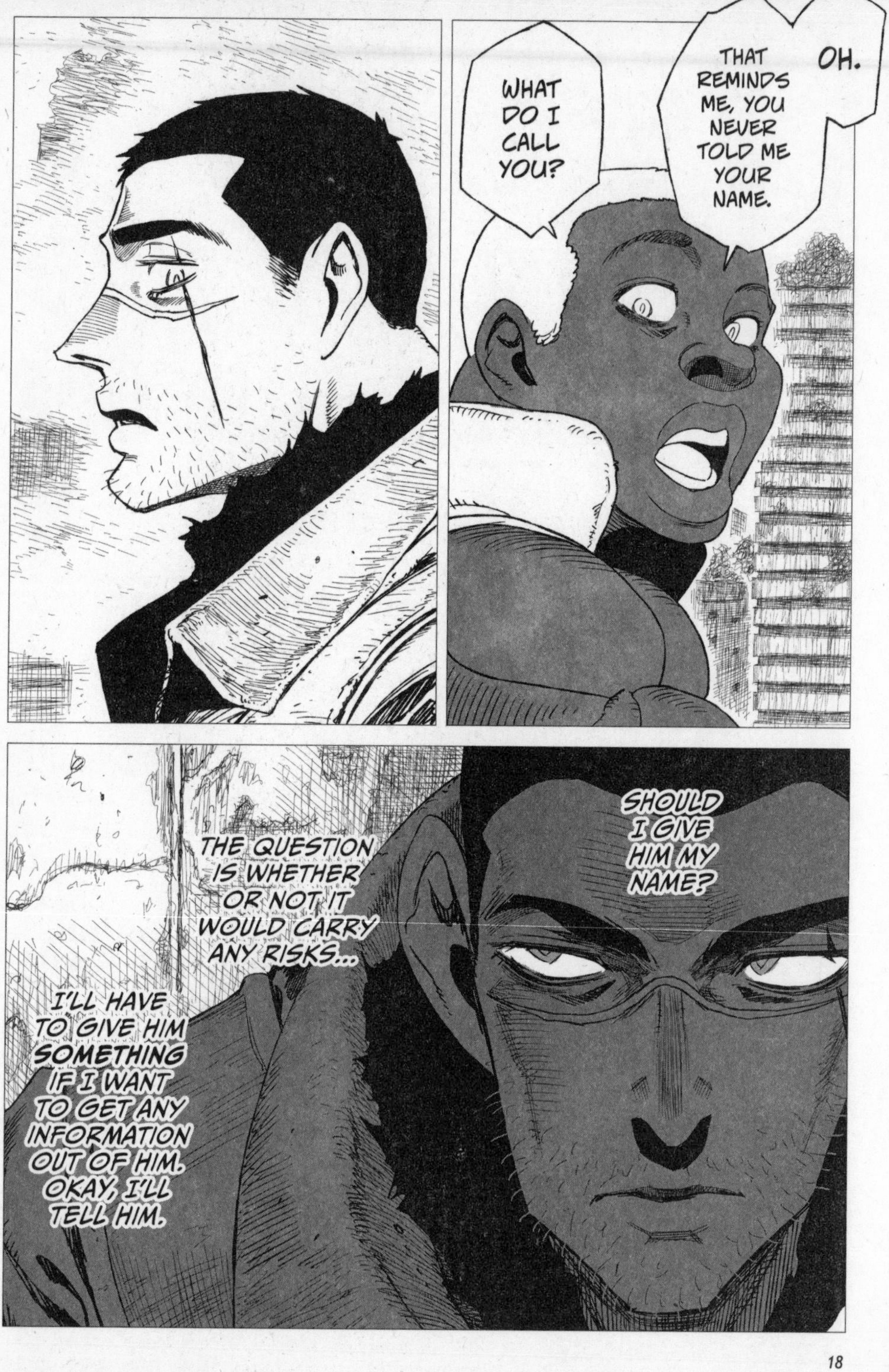
OH.
THAT REMINDS ME, YOU NEVER TOLD ME YOUR NAME.
WHAT DO I CALL YOU?
SHOULD I GIVE HIM MY NAME?
THE QUESTION IS WHETHER OR NOT IT WOULD CARRY ANY RISKS...
I'LL HAVE TO GIVE HIM SOMETHING IF I WANT TO GET ANY INFORMATION OUT OF HIM. OKAY, I'LL TELL HIM.

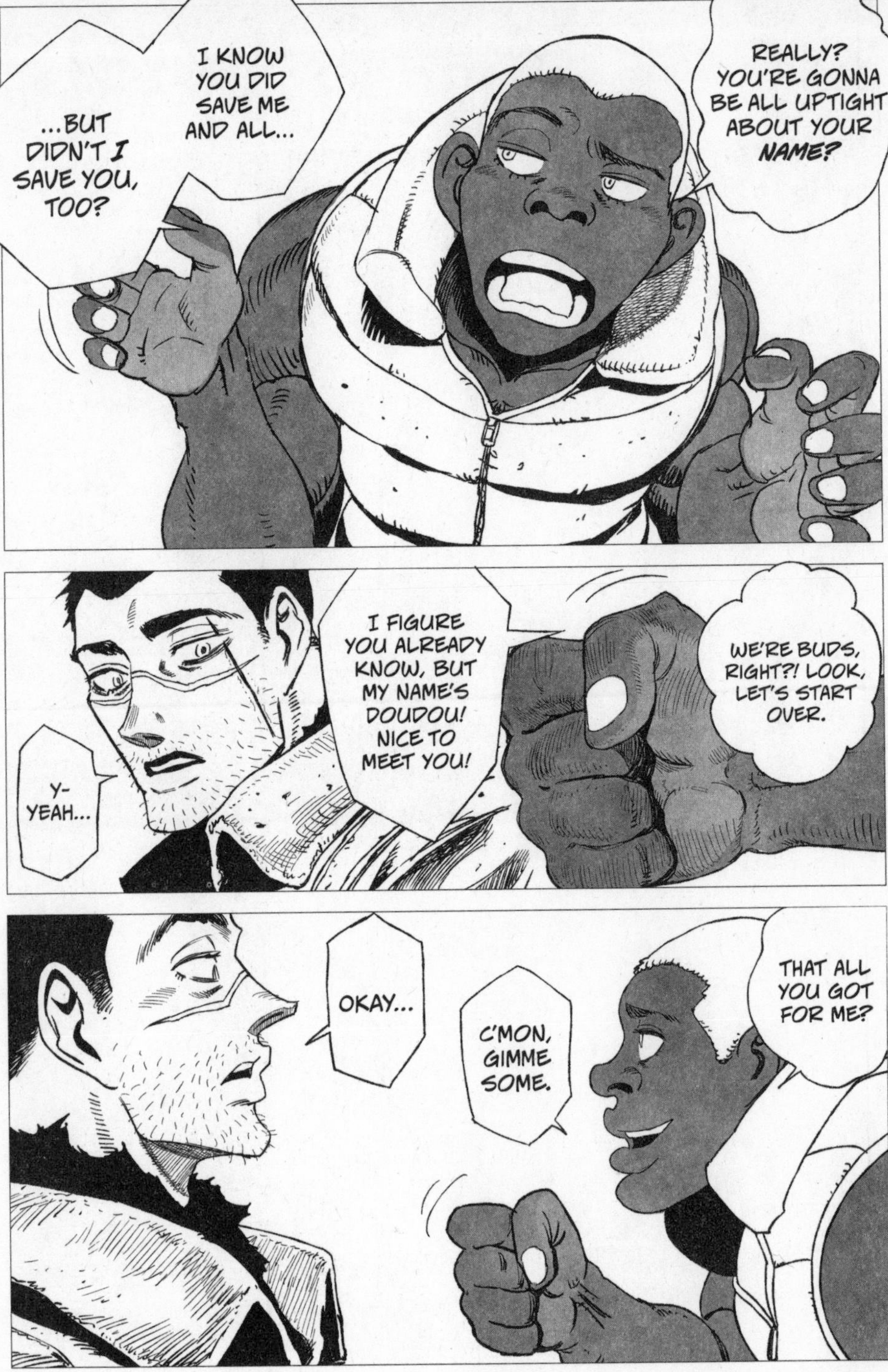
REALLY? YOU'RE GONNA BE ALL UPTIGHT ABOUT YOUR *NAME?*
I KNOW YOU DID SAVE ME AND ALL...
...BUT DIDN'T *I* SAVE YOU, TOO?
WE'RE BUDS, RIGHT?! LOOK, LET'S START OVER.
I FIGURE YOU ALREADY KNOW, BUT MY NAME'S DOUDOU! NICE TO MEET YOU!
Y-YEAH...
THAT ALL YOU GOT FOR ME?
C'MON, GIMME SOME.
OKAY...

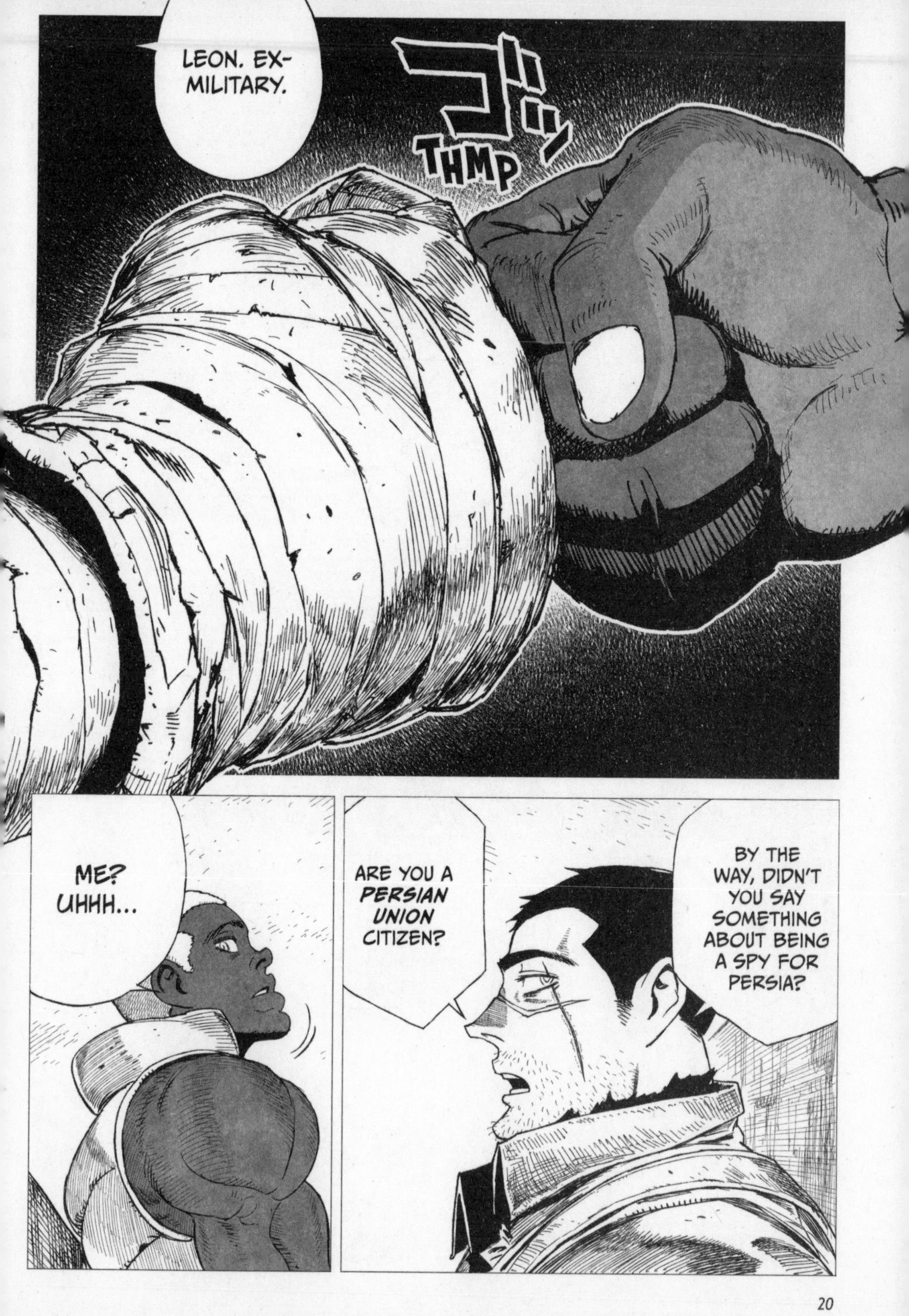
LEON. EX-MILITARY.
ゴッ
THMP
BY THE WAY, DIDN'T YOU SAY SOMETHING ABOUT BEING A SPY FOR PERSIA?
ARE YOU A *PERSIAN UNION* CITIZEN?
ME? UHHH...

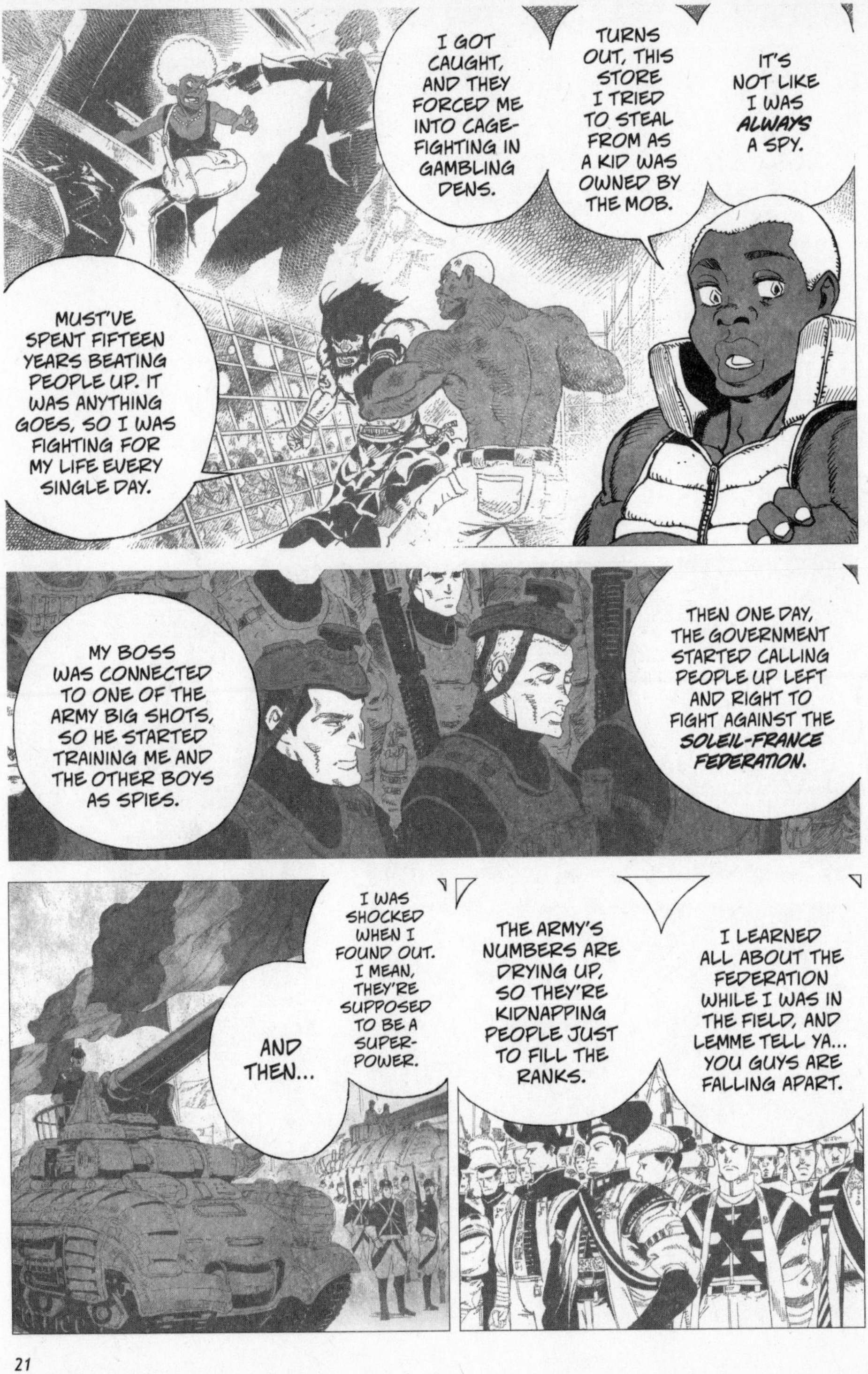
IT'S NOT LIKE I WAS ***ALWAYS*** A SPY.
TURNS OUT, THIS STORE I TRIED TO STEAL FROM AS A KID WAS OWNED BY THE MOB.
I GOT CAUGHT, AND THEY FORCED ME INTO CAGE-FIGHTING IN GAMBLING DENS.
MUST'VE SPENT FIFTEEN YEARS BEATING PEOPLE UP. IT WAS ANYTHING GOES, SO I WAS FIGHTING FOR MY LIFE EVERY SINGLE DAY.
THEN ONE DAY, THE GOVERNMENT STARTED CALLING PEOPLE UP LEFT AND RIGHT TO FIGHT AGAINST THE ***SOLEIL-FRANCE FEDERATION.***
MY BOSS WAS CONNECTED TO ONE OF THE ARMY BIG SHOTS, SO HE STARTED TRAINING ME AND THE OTHER BOYS AS SPIES.
I LEARNED ALL ABOUT THE FEDERATION WHILE I WAS IN THE FIELD, AND LEMME TELL YA... YOU GUYS ARE FALLING APART.
THE ARMY'S NUMBERS ARE DRYING UP, SO THEY'RE KIDNAPPING PEOPLE JUST TO FILL THE RANKS.
I WAS SHOCKED WHEN I FOUND OUT. I MEAN, THEY'RE SUPPOSED TO BE A SUPER-POWER.
AND THEN...

...I WENT AND GOT MYSELF KIDNAPPED.
I'M ON DEATH ROW, SO IT WAS EITHER DIE OR JOIN THIS WEAPON-FINDING UNIT.
SO THAT'S WHAT HAPPENED... IF I WAS INNOCENT, THEN I GUESS I WAS TECHNICALLY KIDNAPPED, TOO...
THAT'S SOME LIFE STORY, THOUGH. IT CAN'T HAVE BEEN EASY LIVING LIKE THAT FROM SUCH A YOUNG AGE...
FRANCE... THOSE DIRTY BASTARDS...
CLENCH
I'M STARTING TO DOUBT WHETHER THEY'LL REALLY PARDON US, EVEN IF WE DO FINISH THE MISSION...

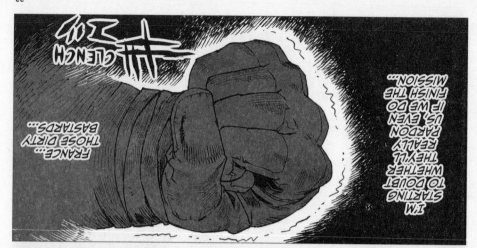

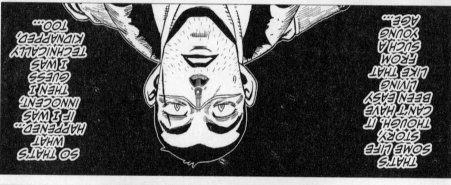

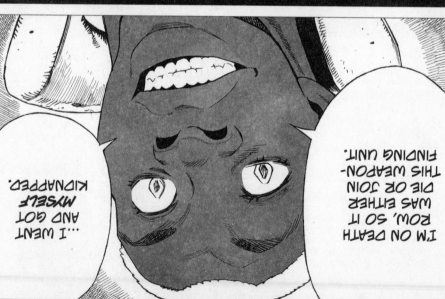

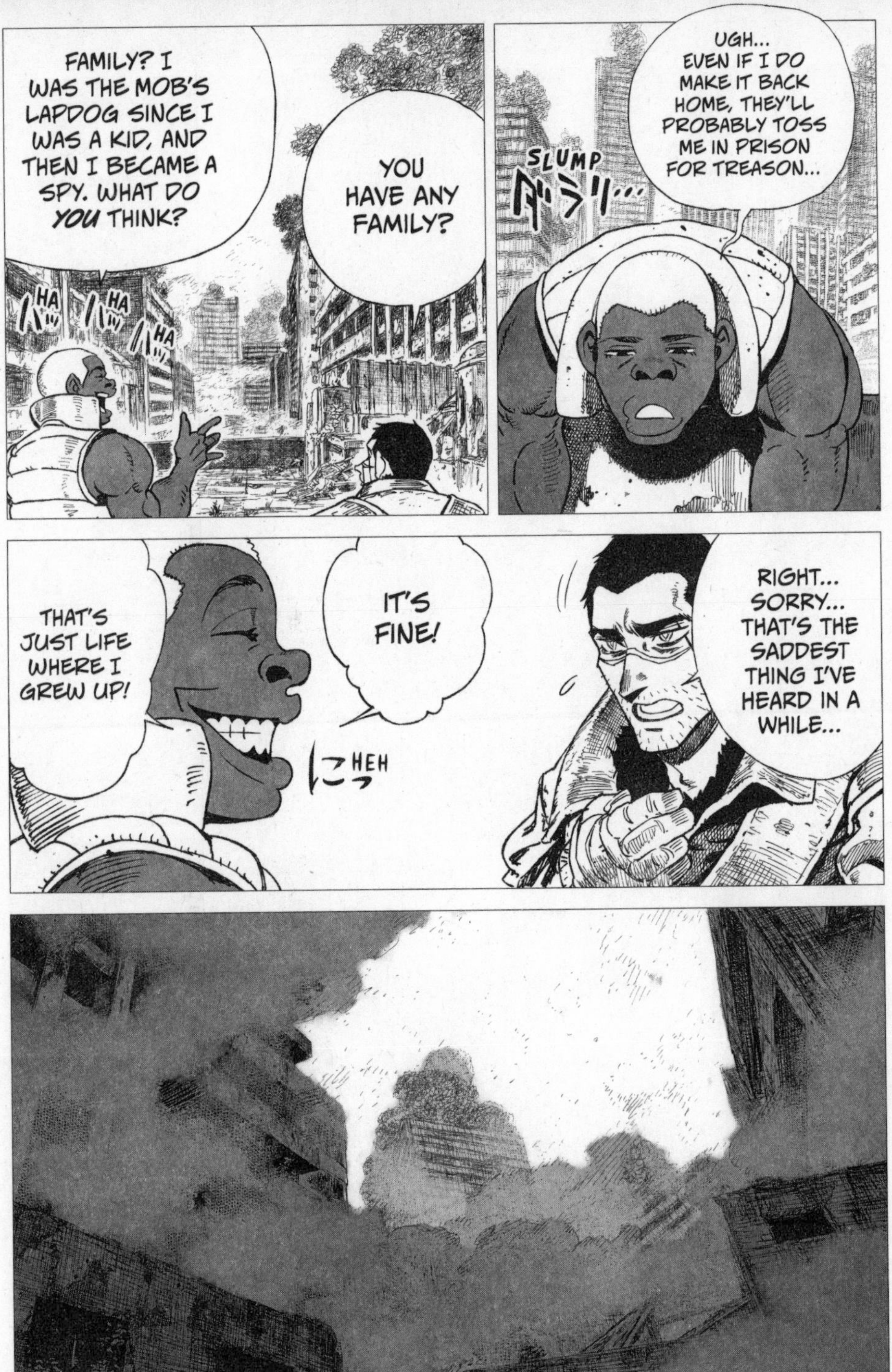
UGH... EVEN IF I DO MAKE IT BACK HOME, THEY'LL PROBABLY TOSS ME IN PRISON FOR TREASON...
SLUMP
YOU HAVE ANY FAMILY?
FAMILY? I WAS THE MOB'S LAPDOG SINCE I WAS A KID, AND THEN I BECAME A SPY. WHAT DO *YOU* THINK?
HA HA HA
RIGHT... SORRY... THAT'S THE SADDEST THING I'VE HEARD IN A WHILE...
IT'S FINE!
HEH
THAT'S JUST LIFE WHERE I GREW UP!

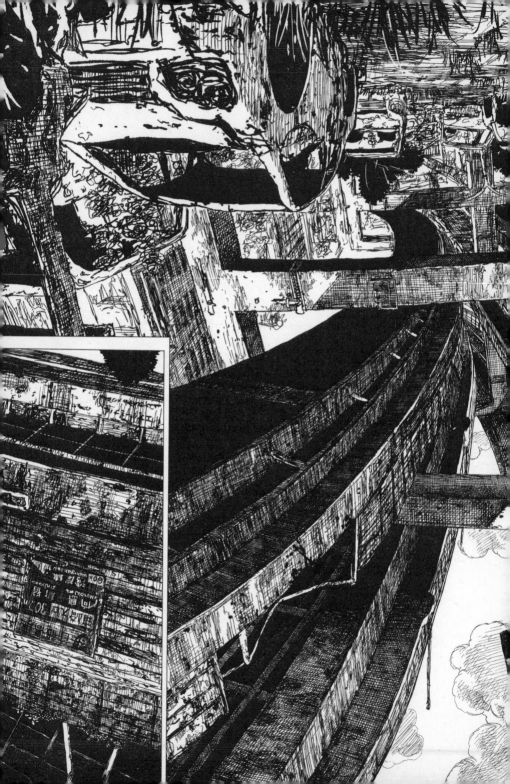

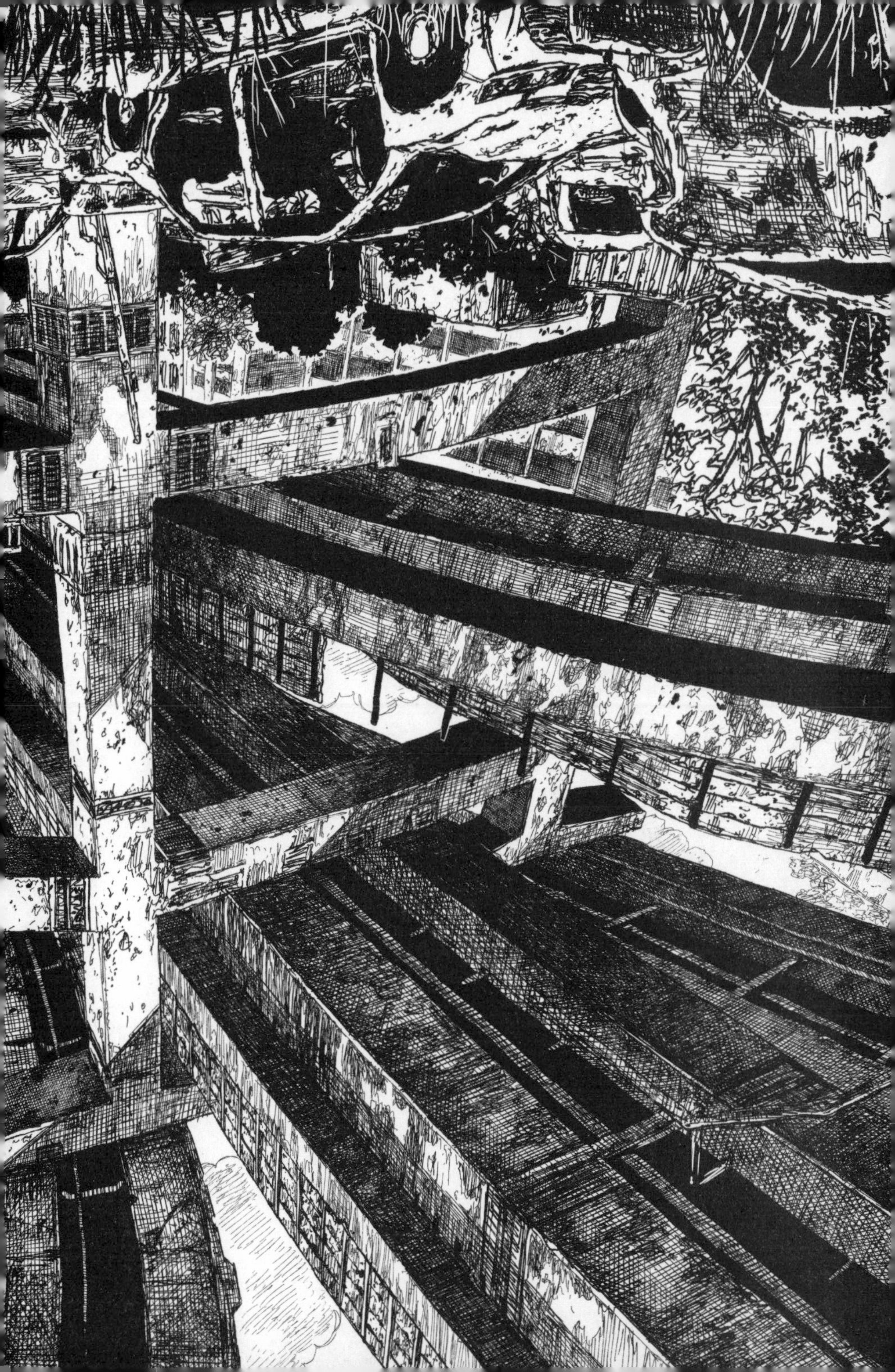

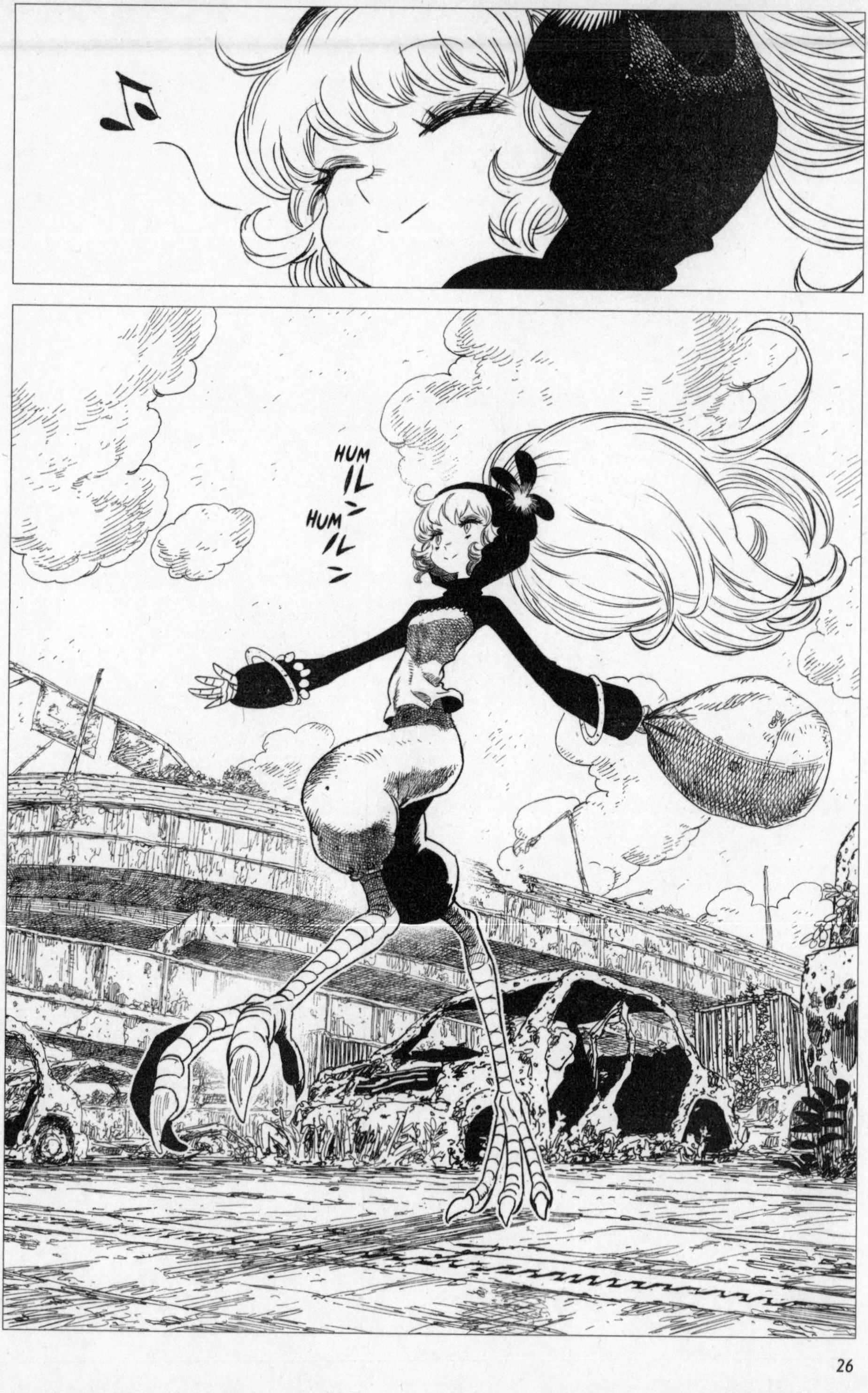
HUM
HUM

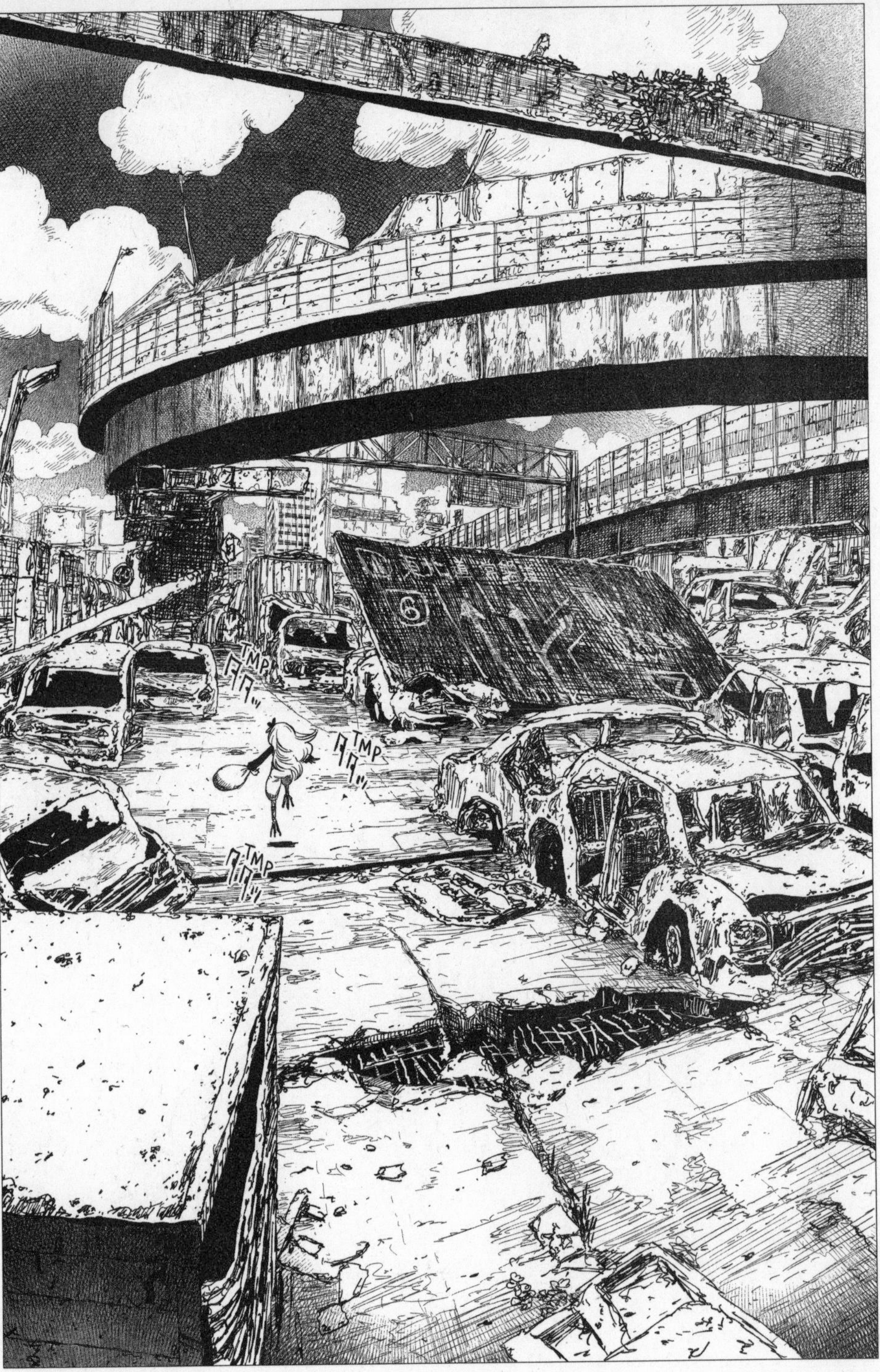
TMP
タタッ
TMP
タタッ
TMP
タタッ

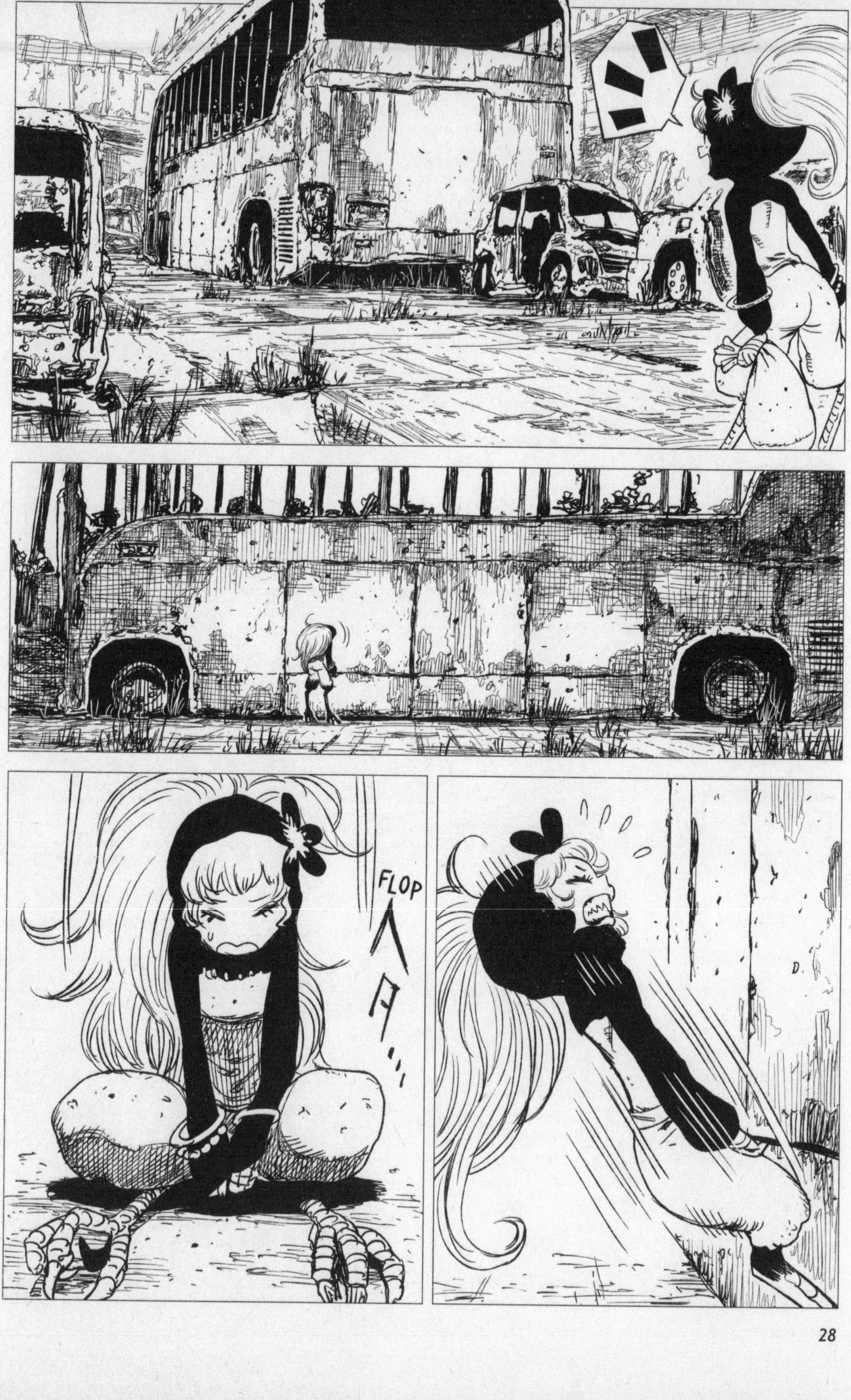
FLOP
ヘタ…

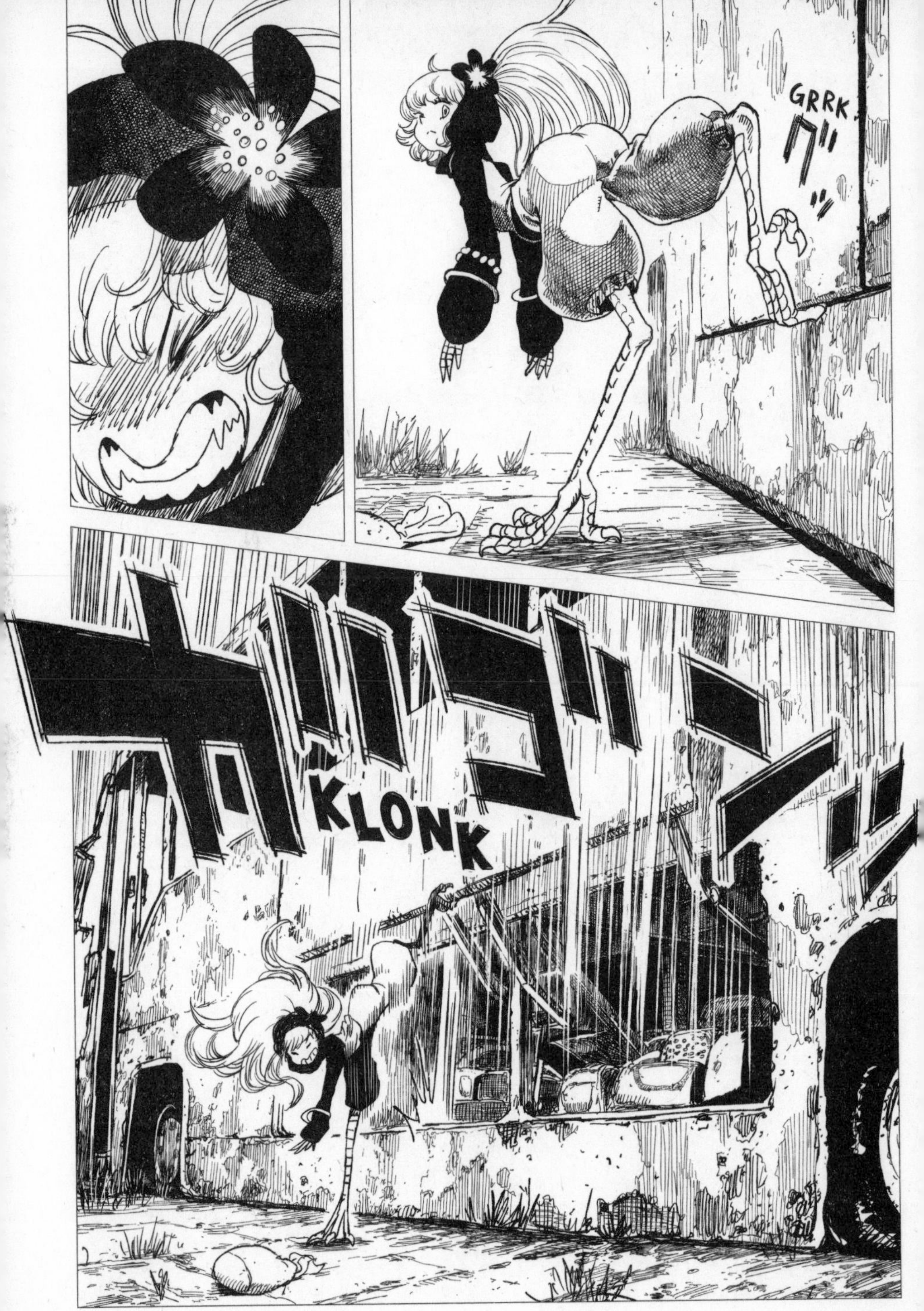
GRRK
KLONK

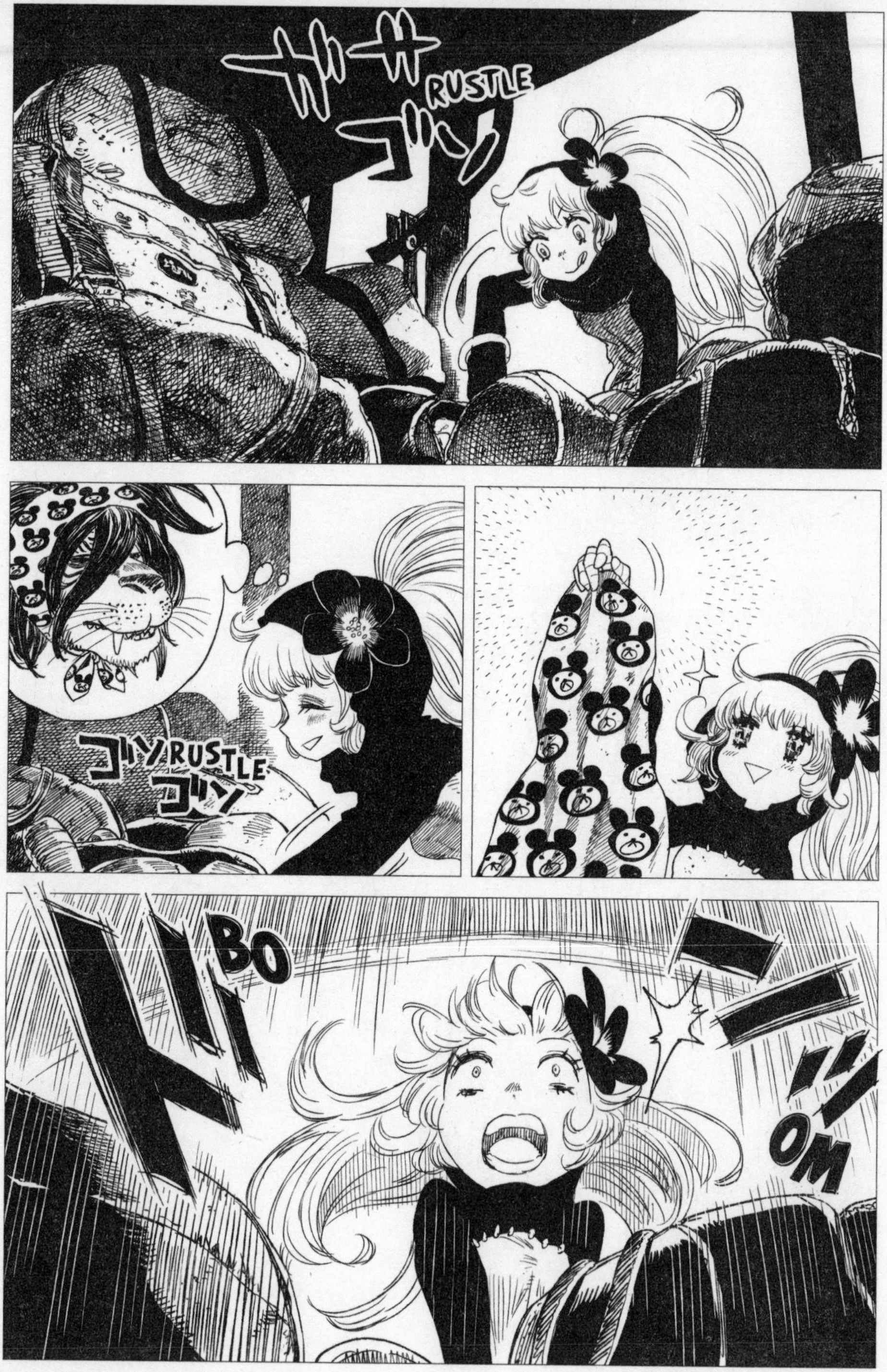
ガサ RUSTLE
ゴソ
ゴソ RUSTLE ゴソ
BO
OM

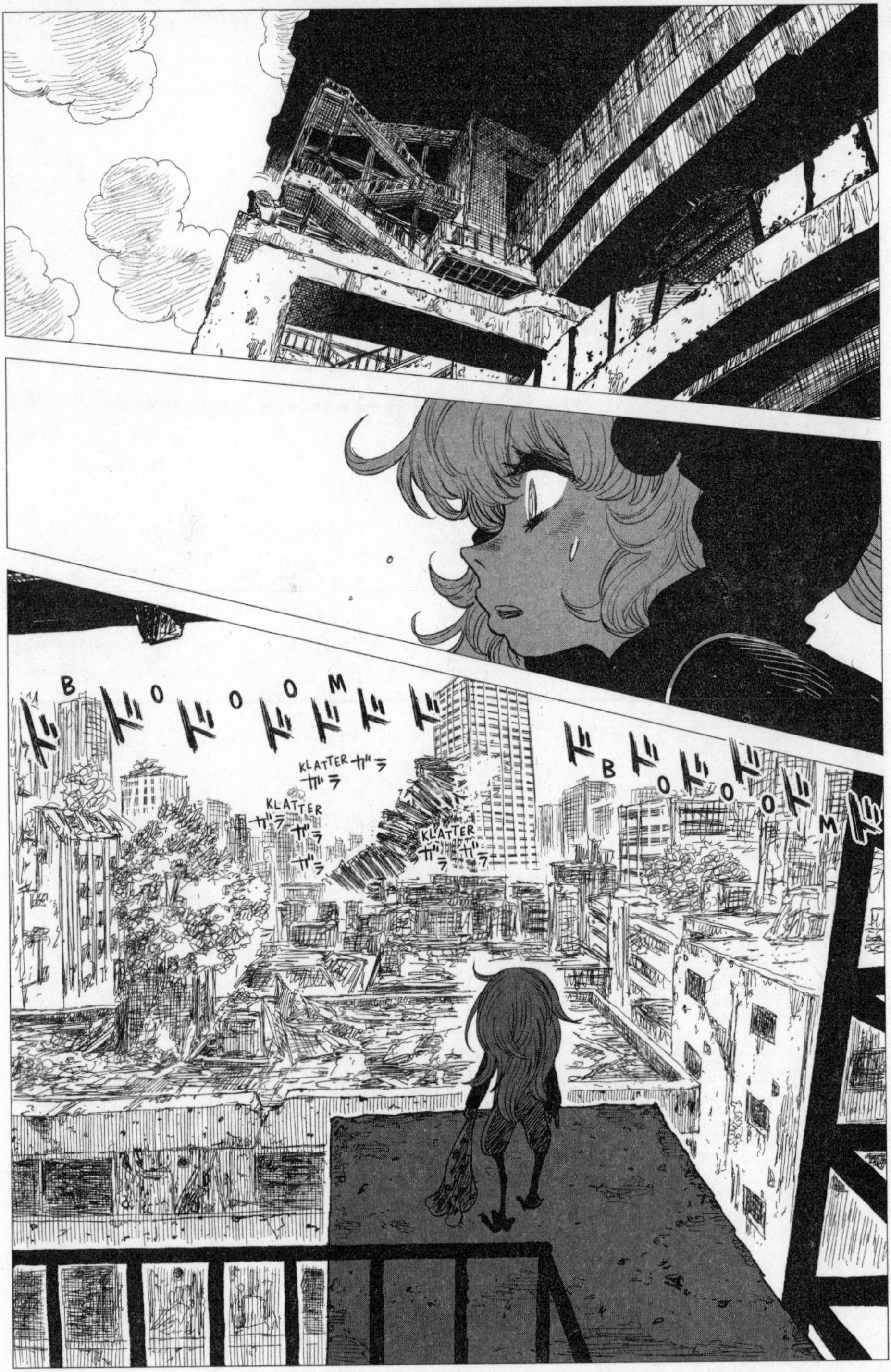
BOOOM ドドドドドド
BOOOM ドドドドドド
KLATTER ガラガラ
KLATTER ガラガラガラ
KLATTER ガラガラ

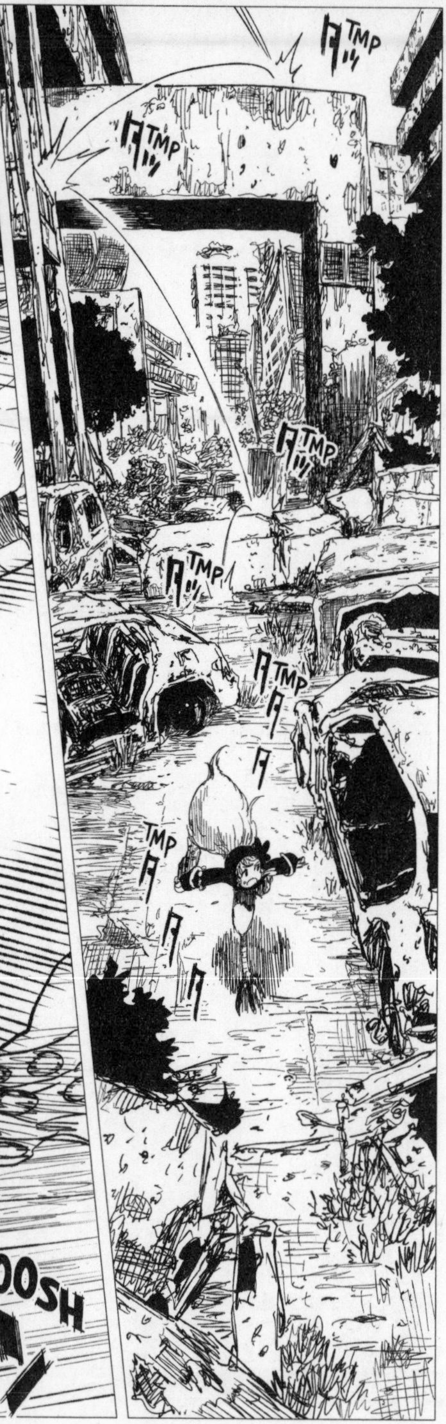
TMP
TMP
TMP
TMP
TMP
TMP
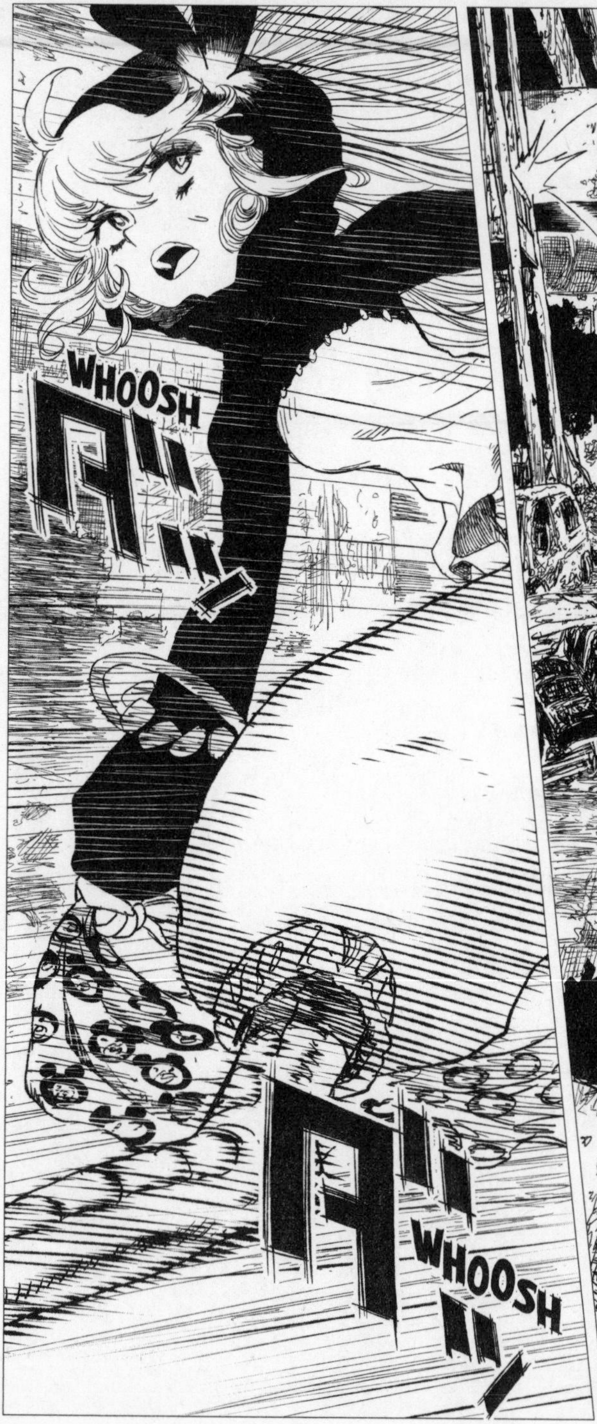
WHOOSH
WHOOSH

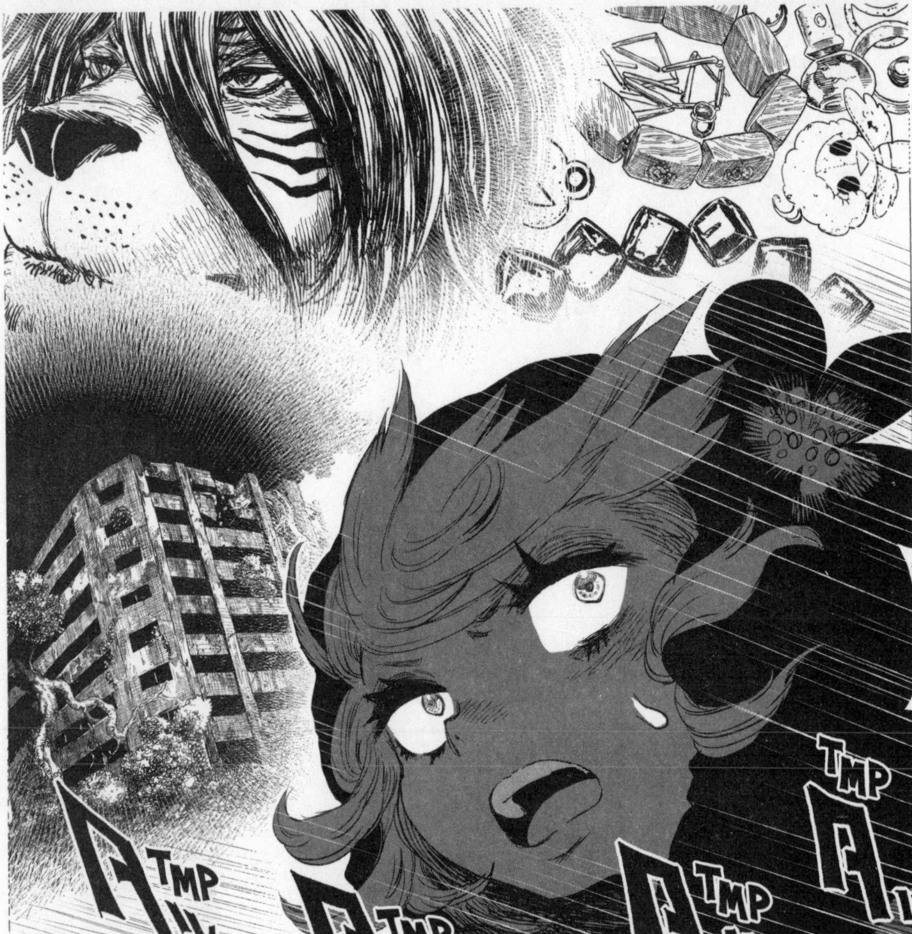
TMP
TMP
TMP
TMP

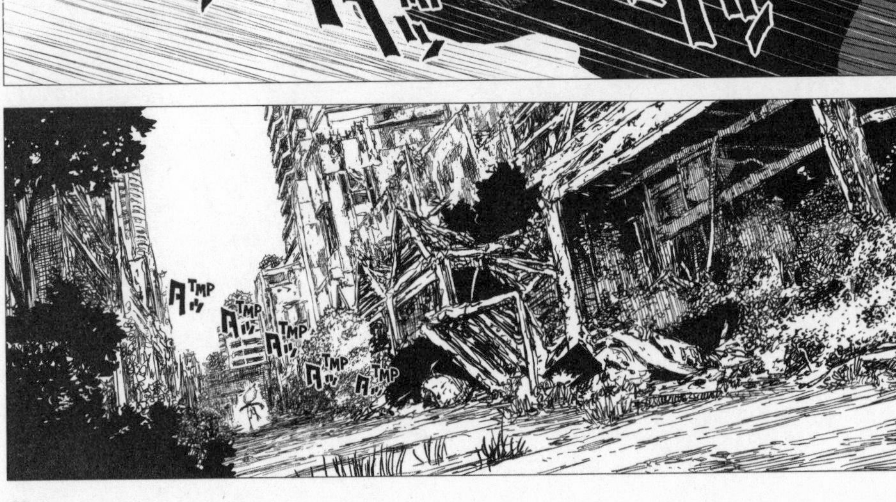
TMP
TMP
TMP
TMP
TMP

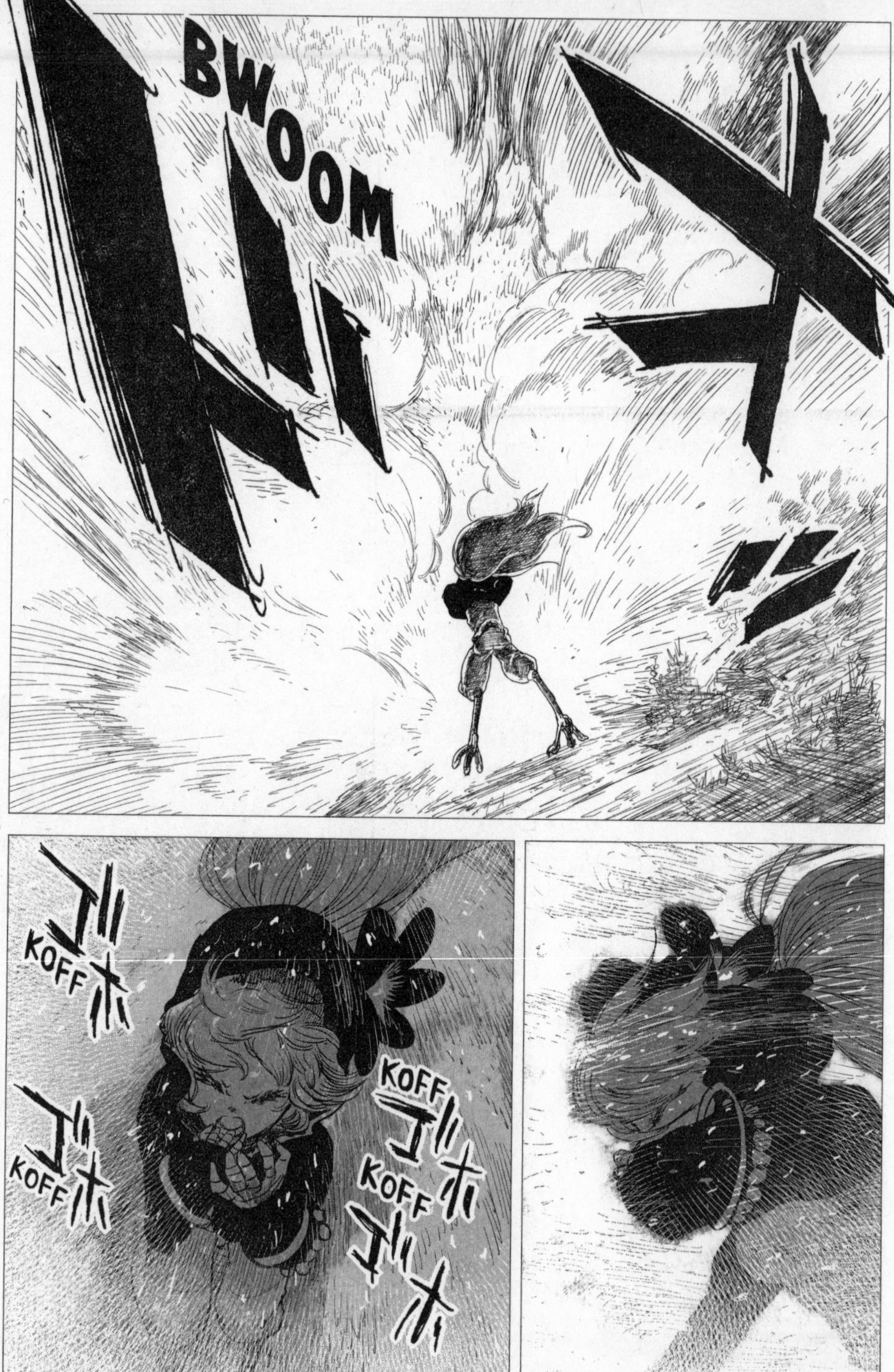
BWOOM
KOFF
KOFF
KOFF
KOFF

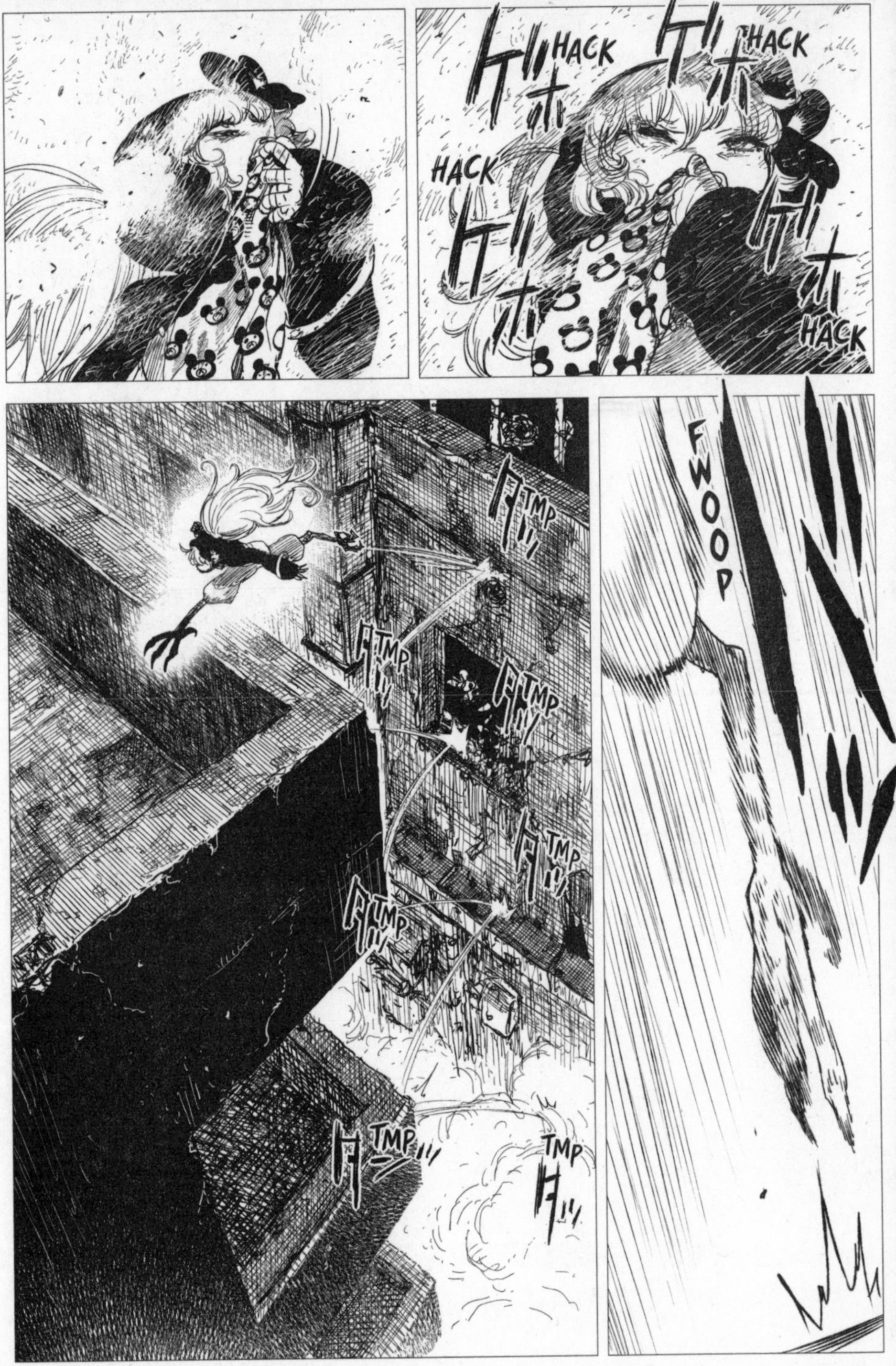
HACK
HACK
HACK
HACK
FWOOP
TMP
TMP
TMP
TMP
TMP
TMP
TMP

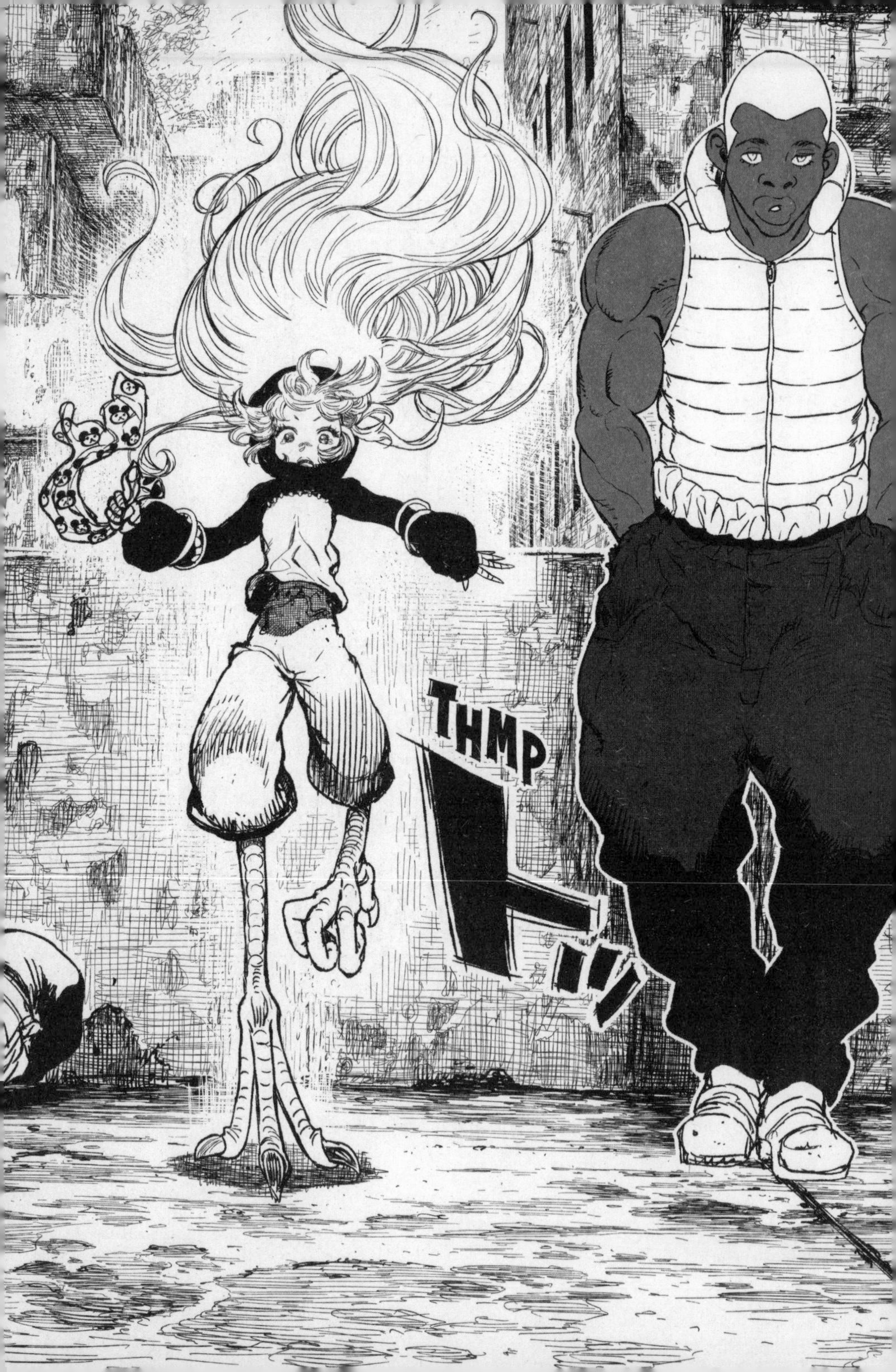
THMP

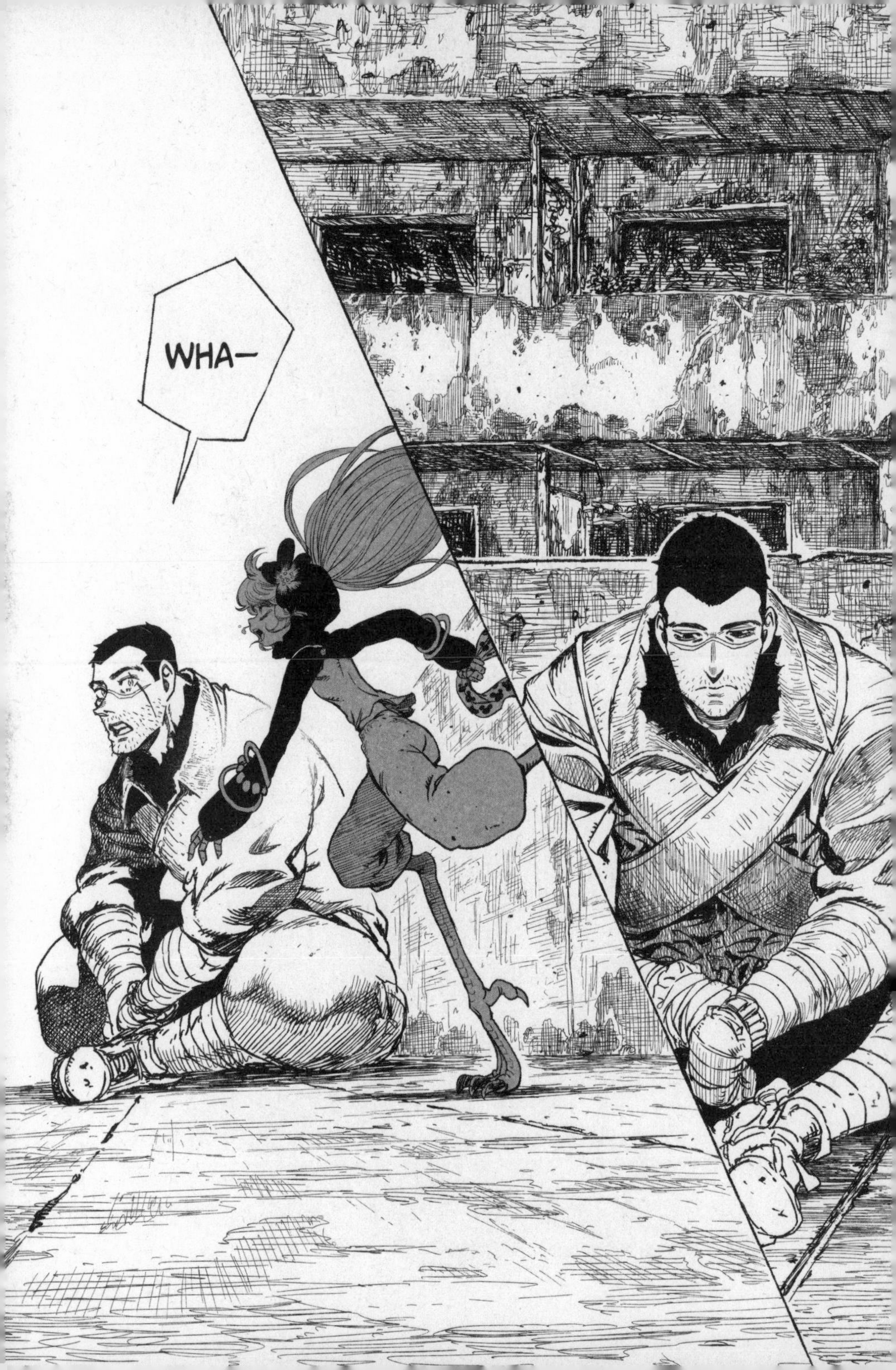
WHA–

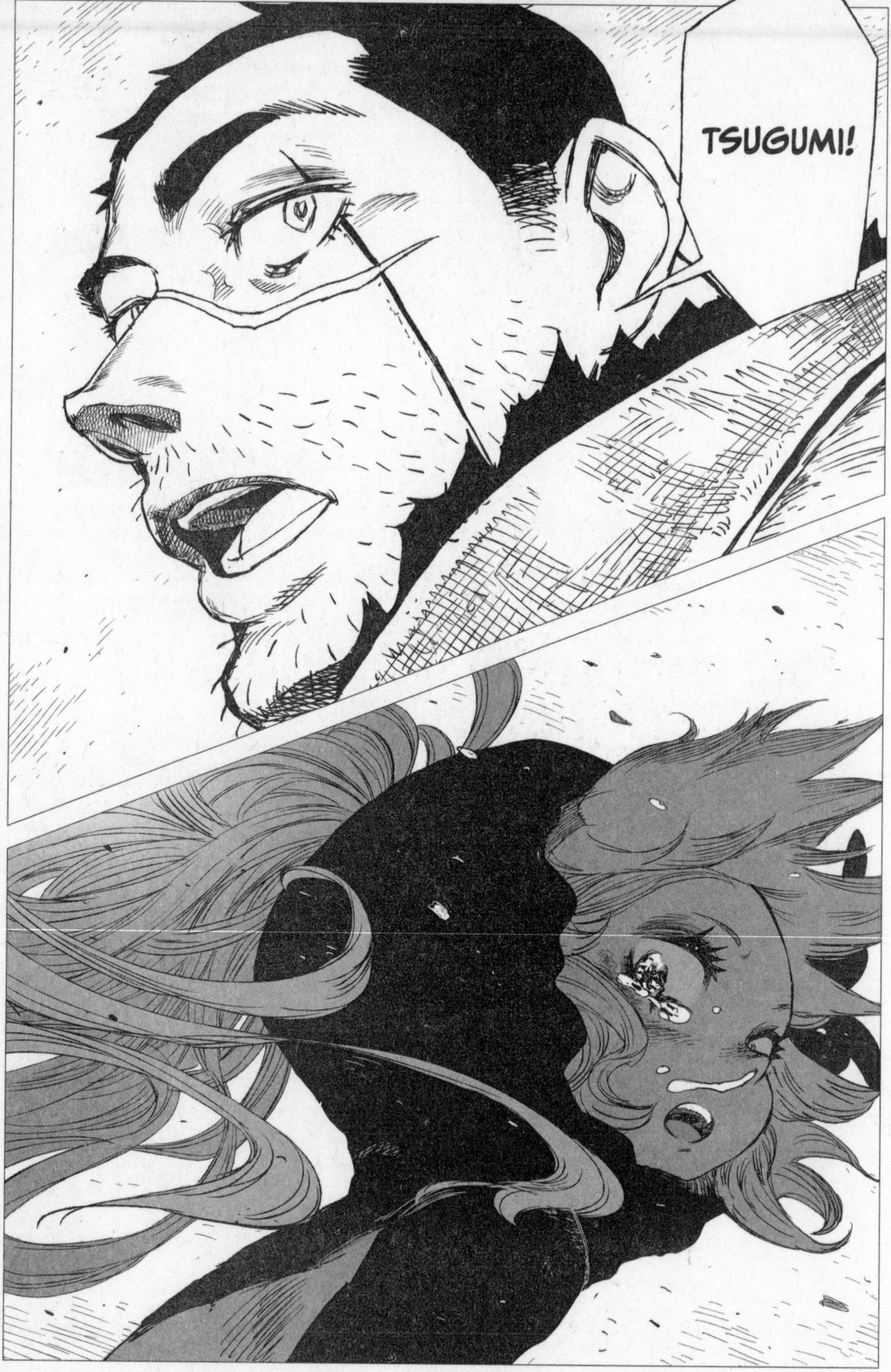
TSUGUMI!

SHE'S CRYING?!

DID SOMETHING HAPPEN?

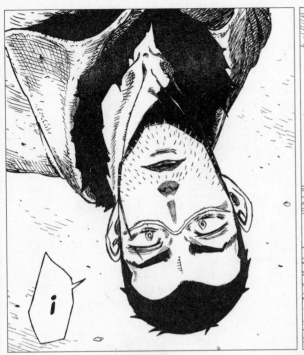

!

LE...

"NO..."

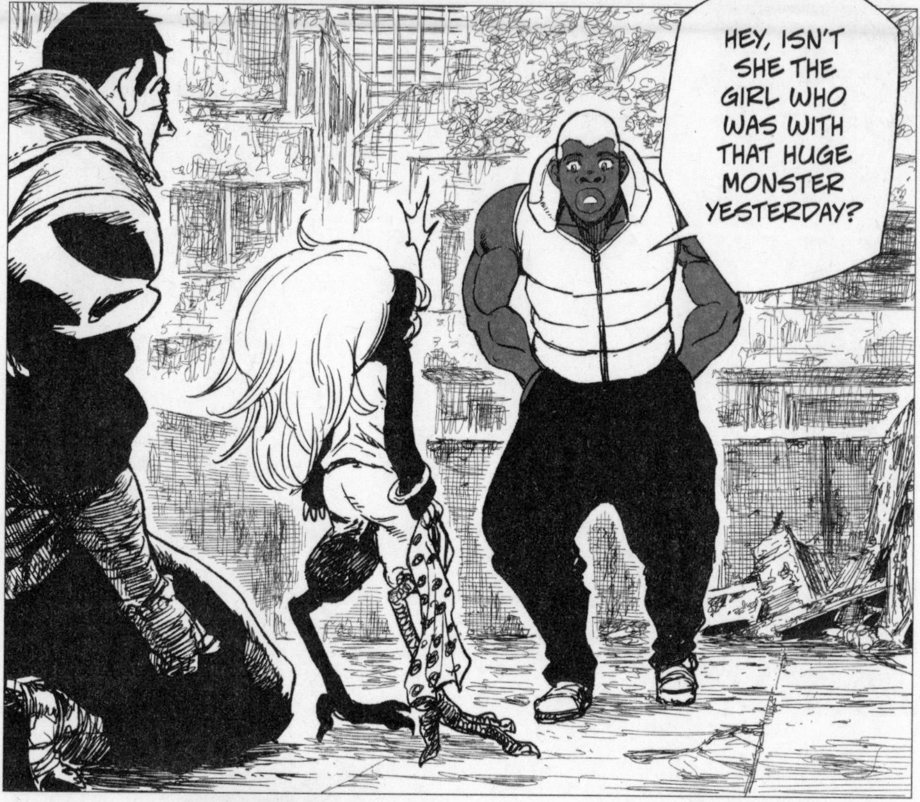
HEY, ISN'T SHE THE GIRL WHO WAS WITH THAT HUGE MONSTER YESTERDAY?

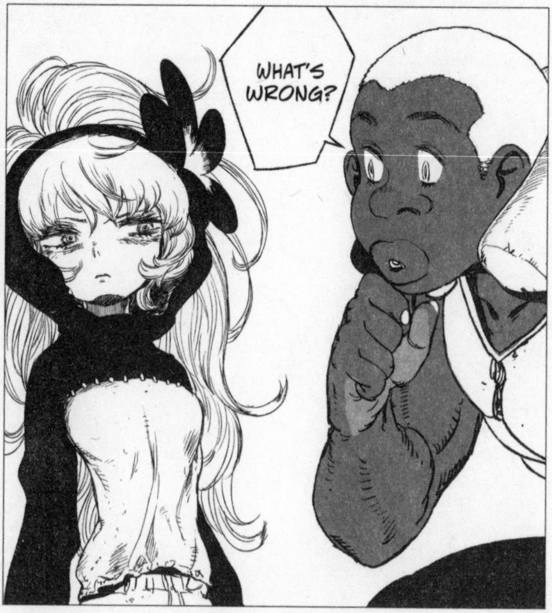
WHAT'S WRONG?

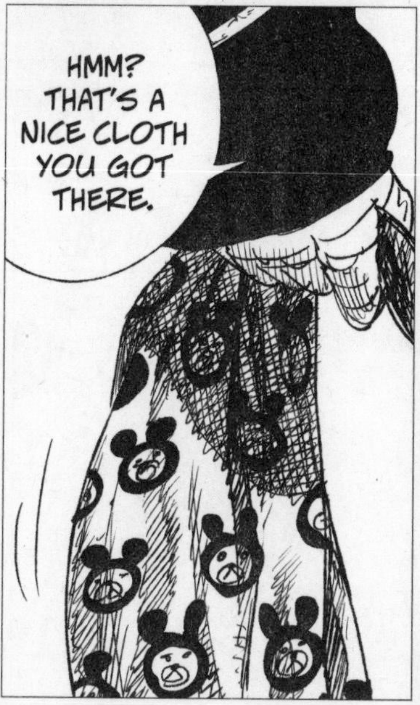
HMM? THAT'S A NICE CLOTH YOU GOT THERE.

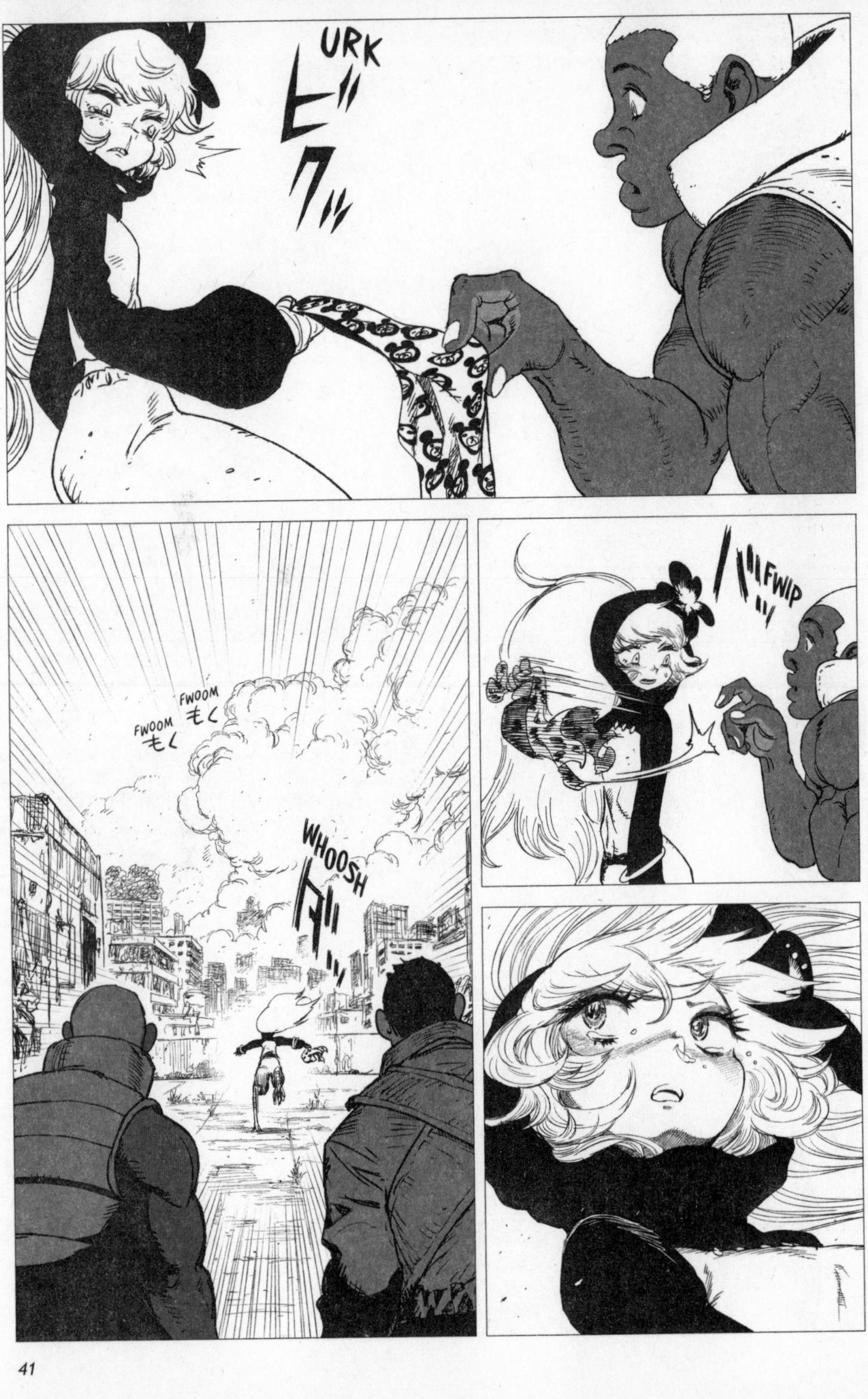
URK
ビクッ
FWIP
WHOOSH
ダッ
FWOOM もく
FWOOM もく

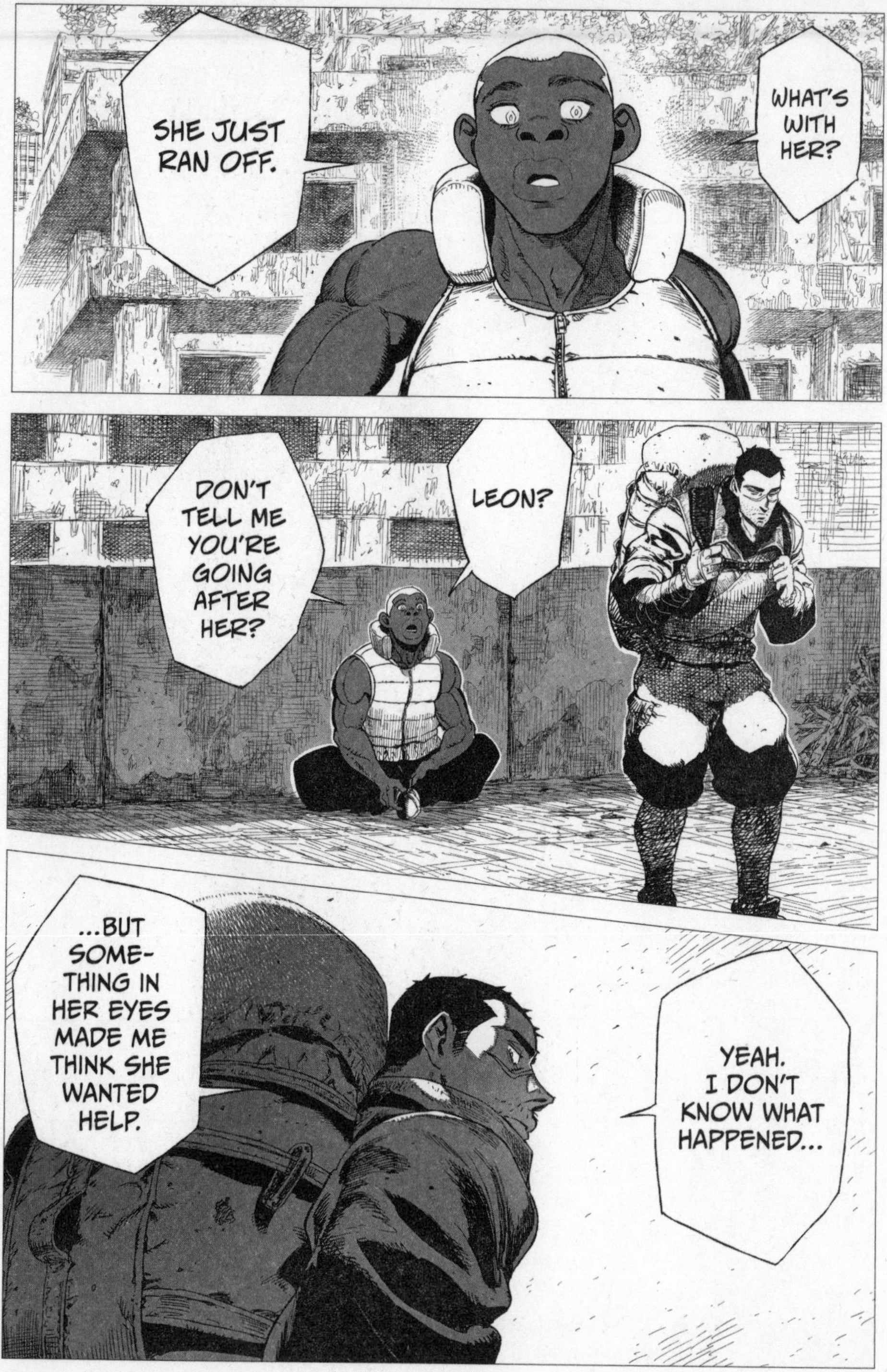
WHAT'S WITH HER?
SHE JUST RAN OFF.
LEON?
DON'T TELL ME YOU'RE GOING AFTER HER?
YEAH. I DON'T KNOW WHAT HAPPENED...
...BUT SOME-THING IN HER EYES MADE ME THINK SHE WANTED HELP.

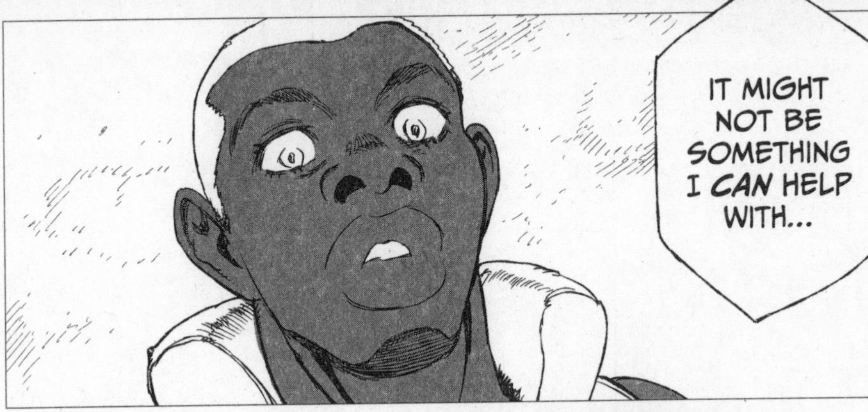
IT MIGHT NOT BE SOMETHING I *CAN* HELP WITH...

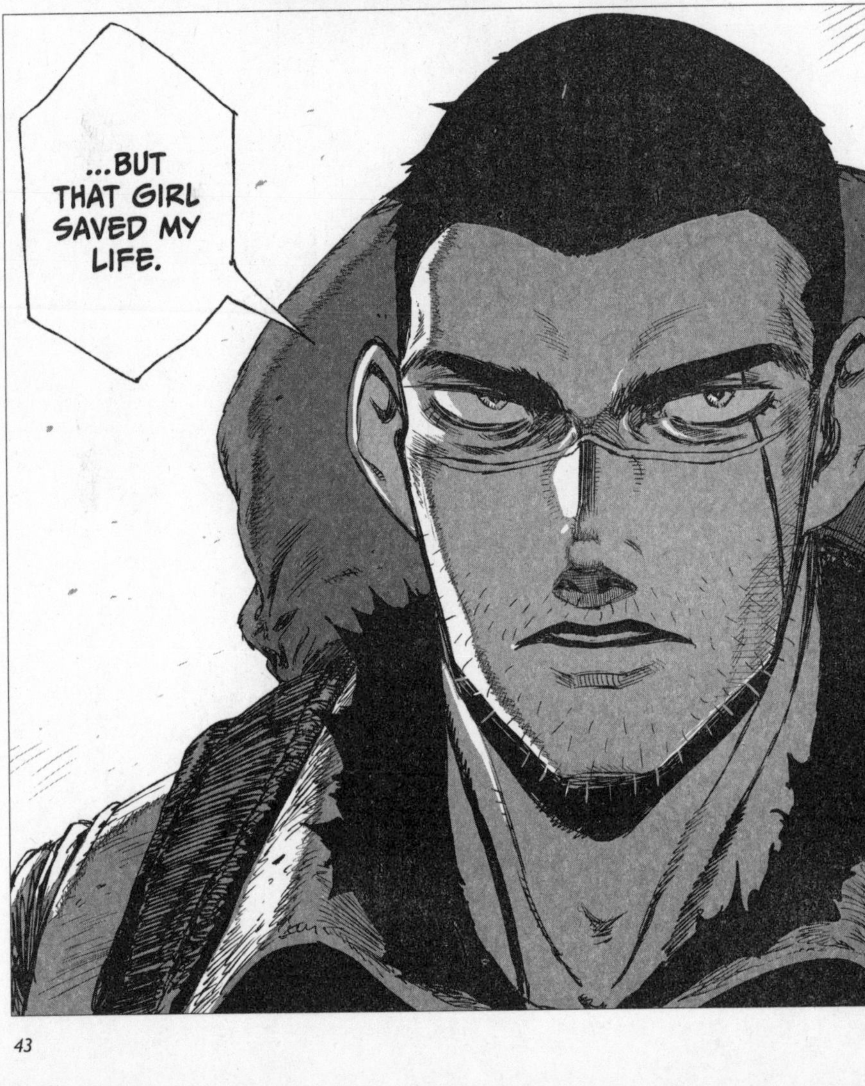
...BUT THAT GIRL SAVED MY LIFE.

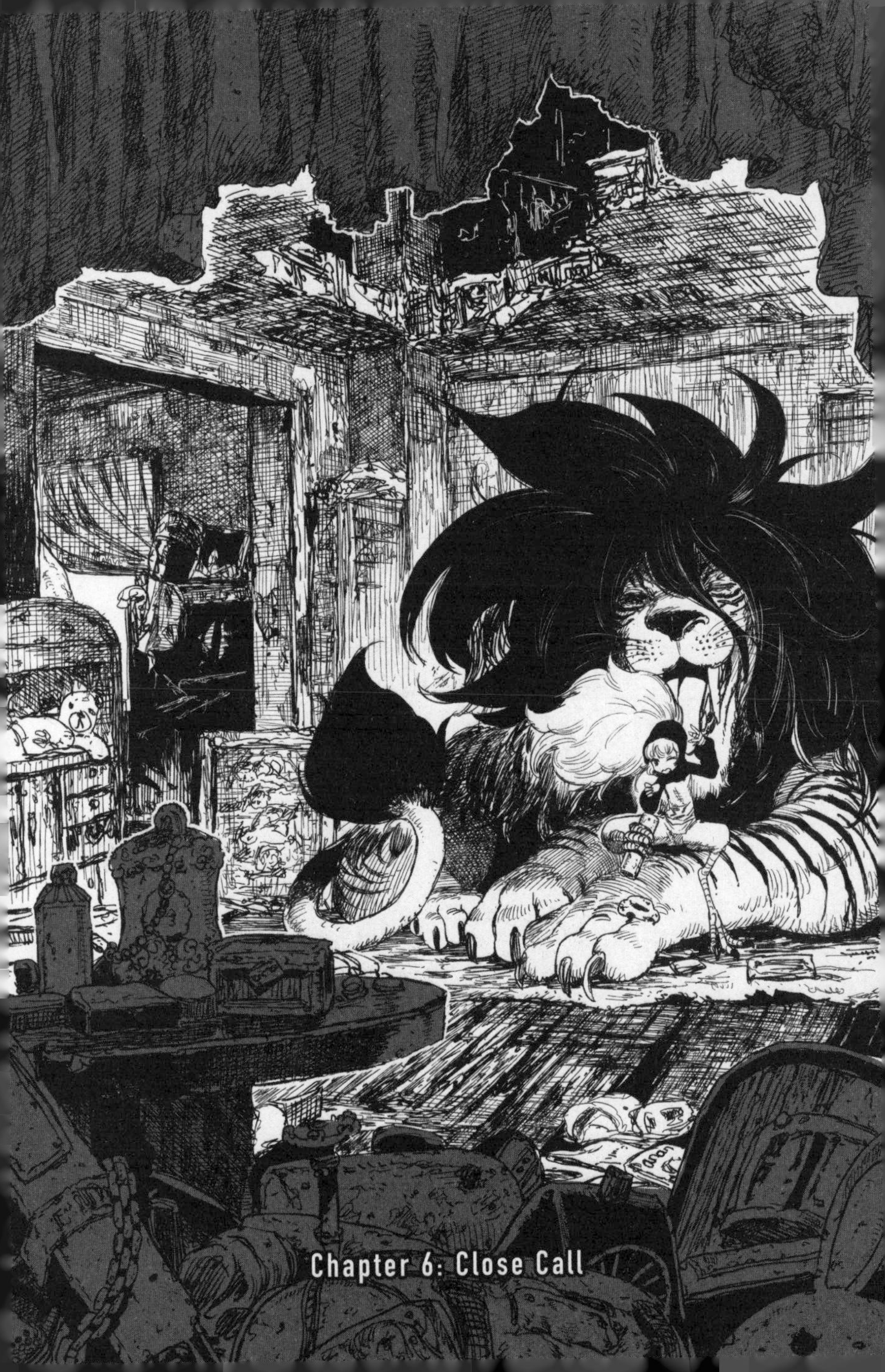
Chapter 6: Close Call

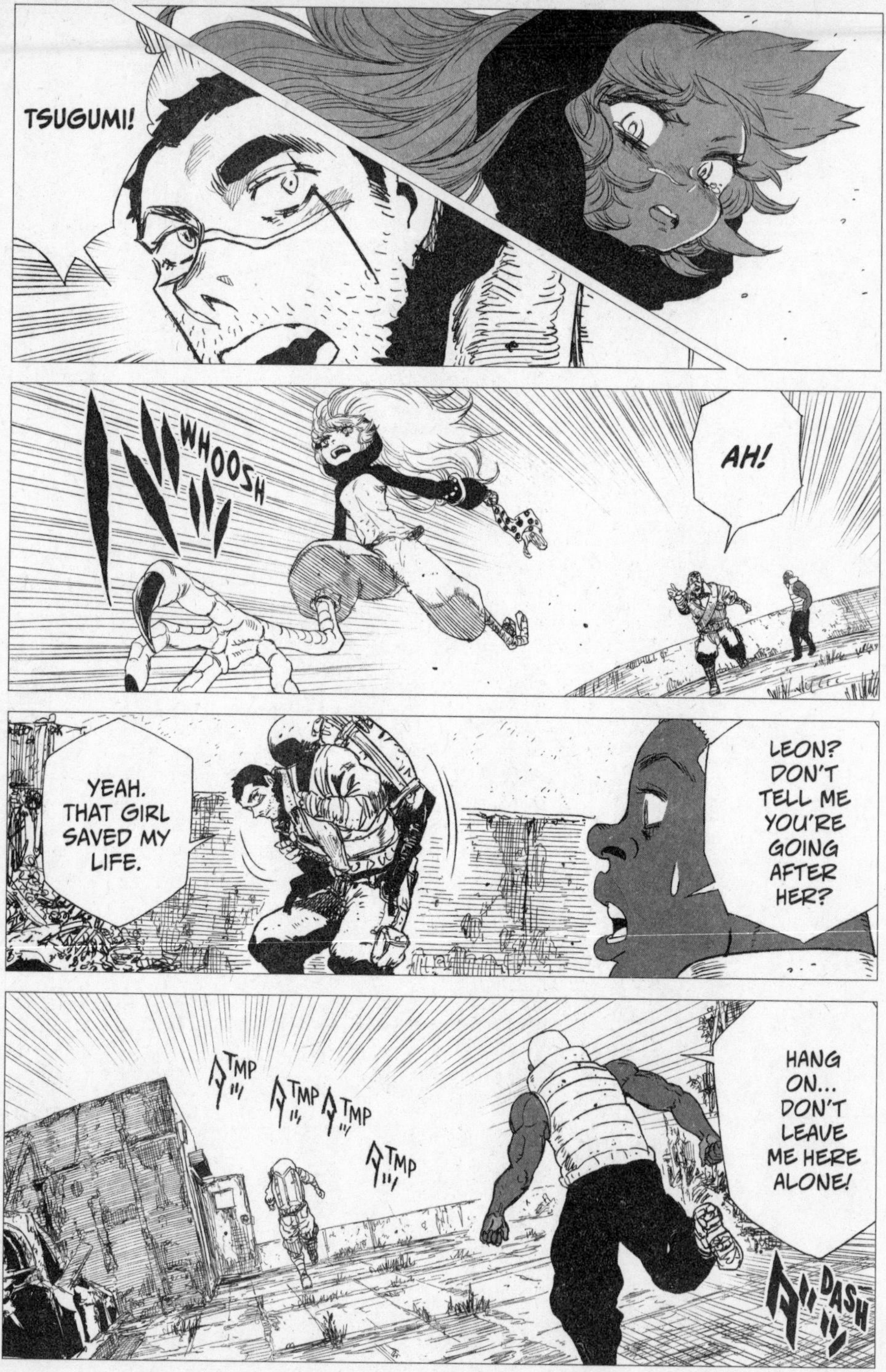
TSUGUMI!
AH!
WHOOSH
LEON? DON'T TELL ME YOU'RE GOING AFTER HER?
YEAH. THAT GIRL SAVED MY LIFE.
HANG ON... DON'T LEAVE ME HERE ALONE!
TMP
TMP
TMP
TMP
DASH

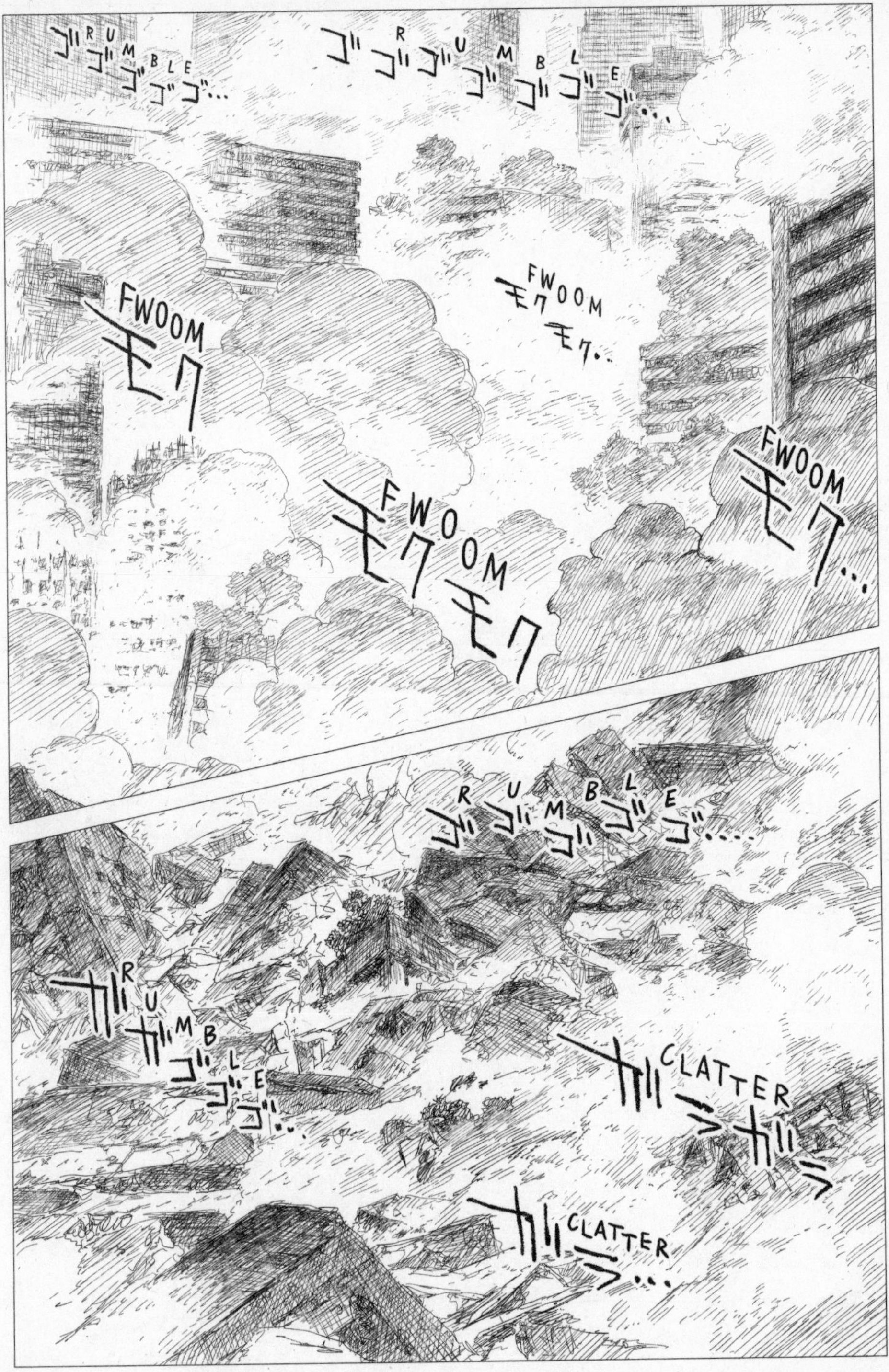

ゴゴゴゴゴゴゴ…
RUMBLE
ゴゴゴゴ…
RUMBLE
モク…
FWOOM
モクモク
FWOOM
モクモク…
FWOOM
モク
FWOOM
ゴゴゴゴ…
RUMBLE
ガラガラ
CLATTER
ガラ…
CLATTER
ガガゴゴ…
RUMBLE

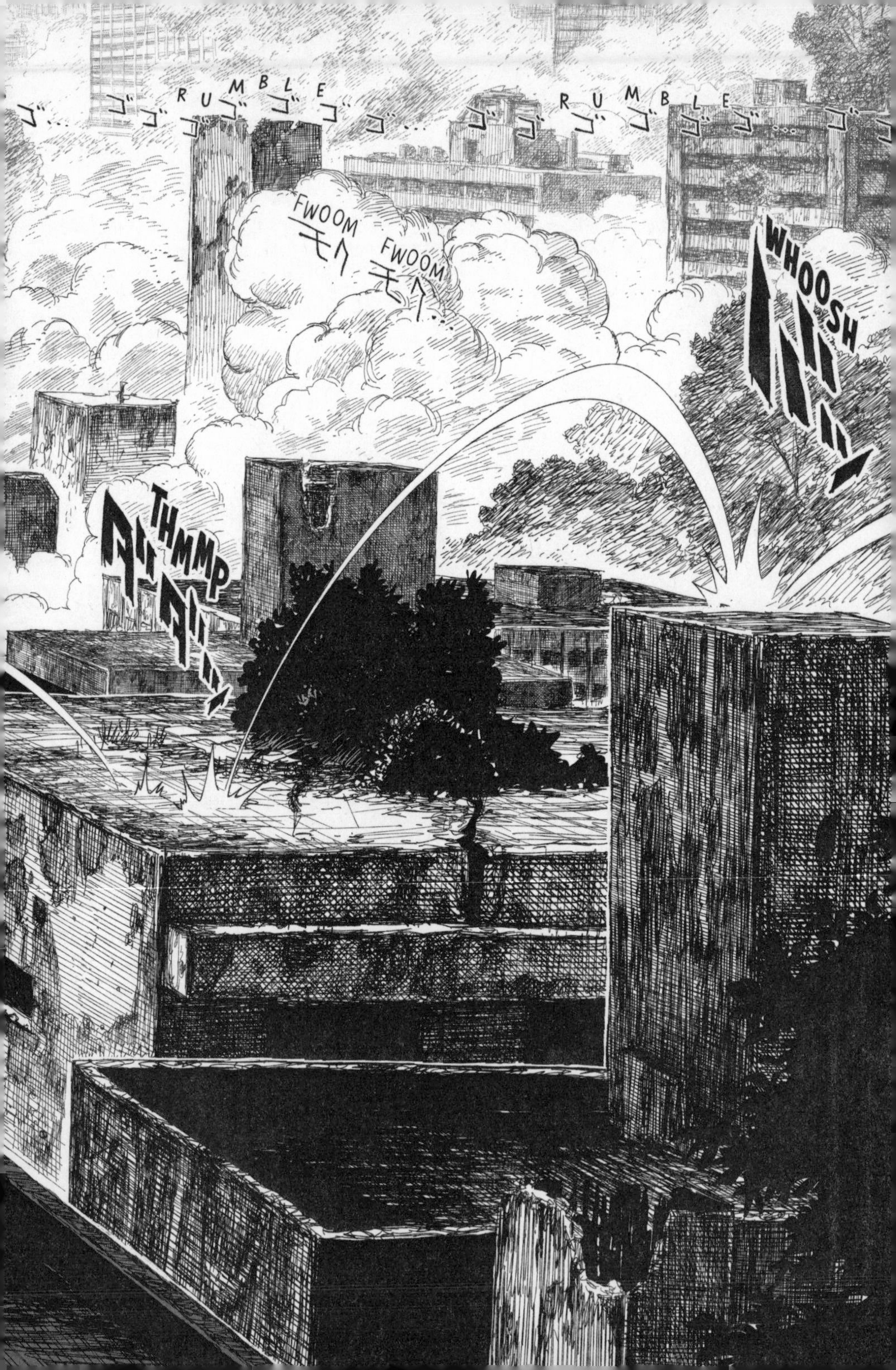

RUMBLE
RUMBLE
WHOOSH
FWOOM
FWOOM
THMMP

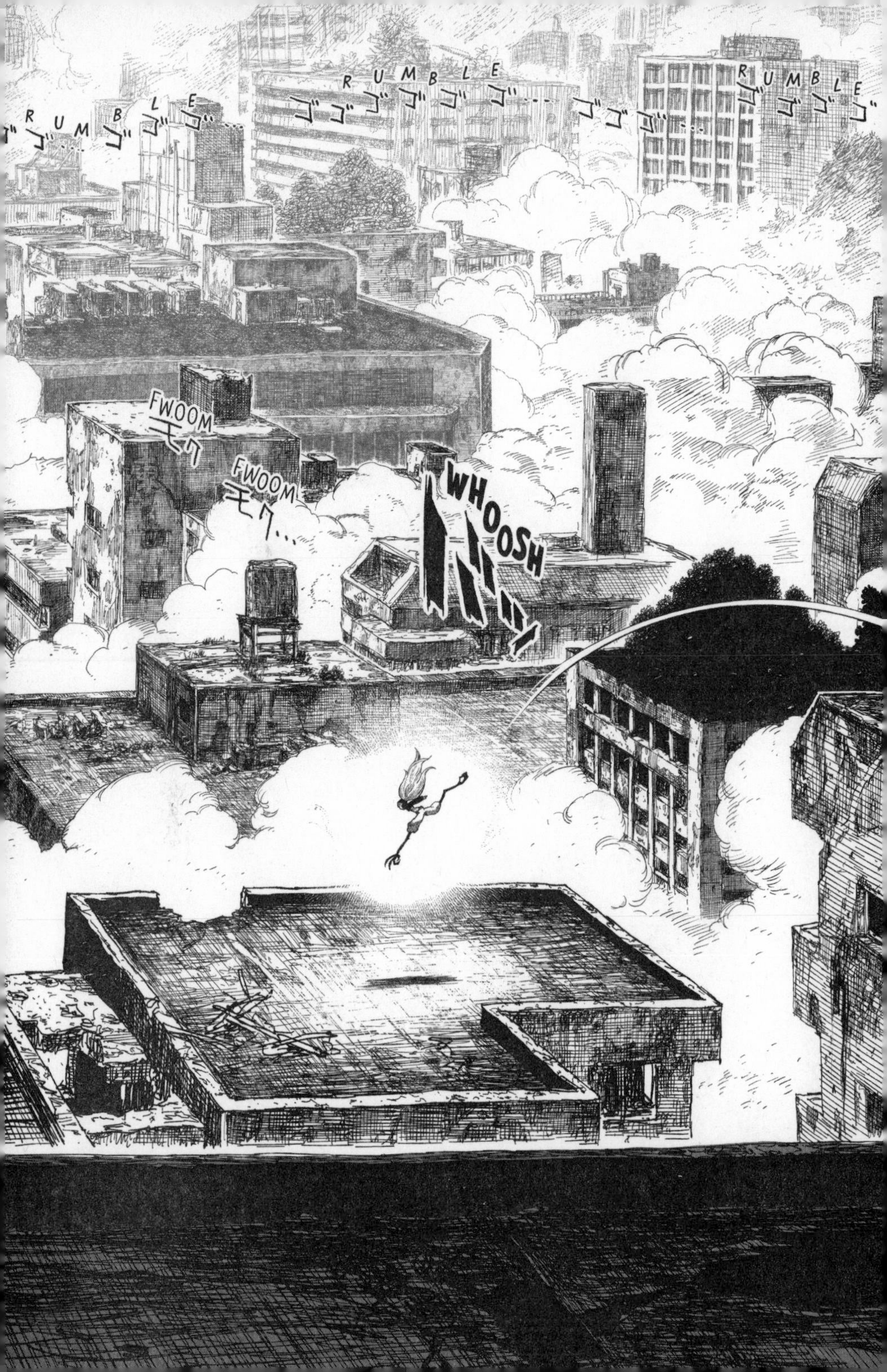
RUMBLE
ゴゴゴゴ
ゴゴゴ…
RUMBLE
ゴゴゴゴゴ…
RUMBLE
ゴ…ゴゴゴ…
FWOOM
モク
FWOOM
モク…
WHOOSH

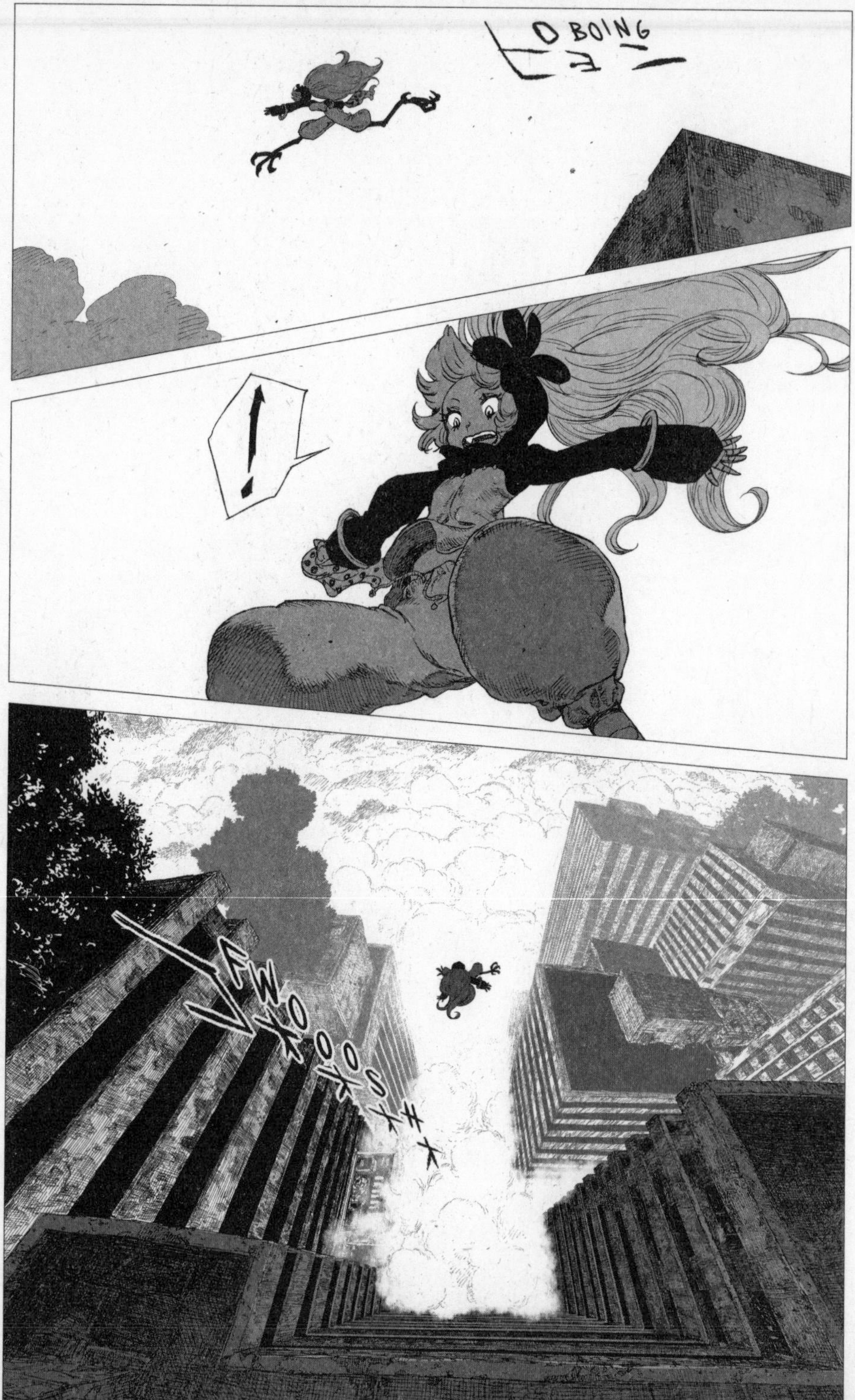
BOING
!
FWOOOS

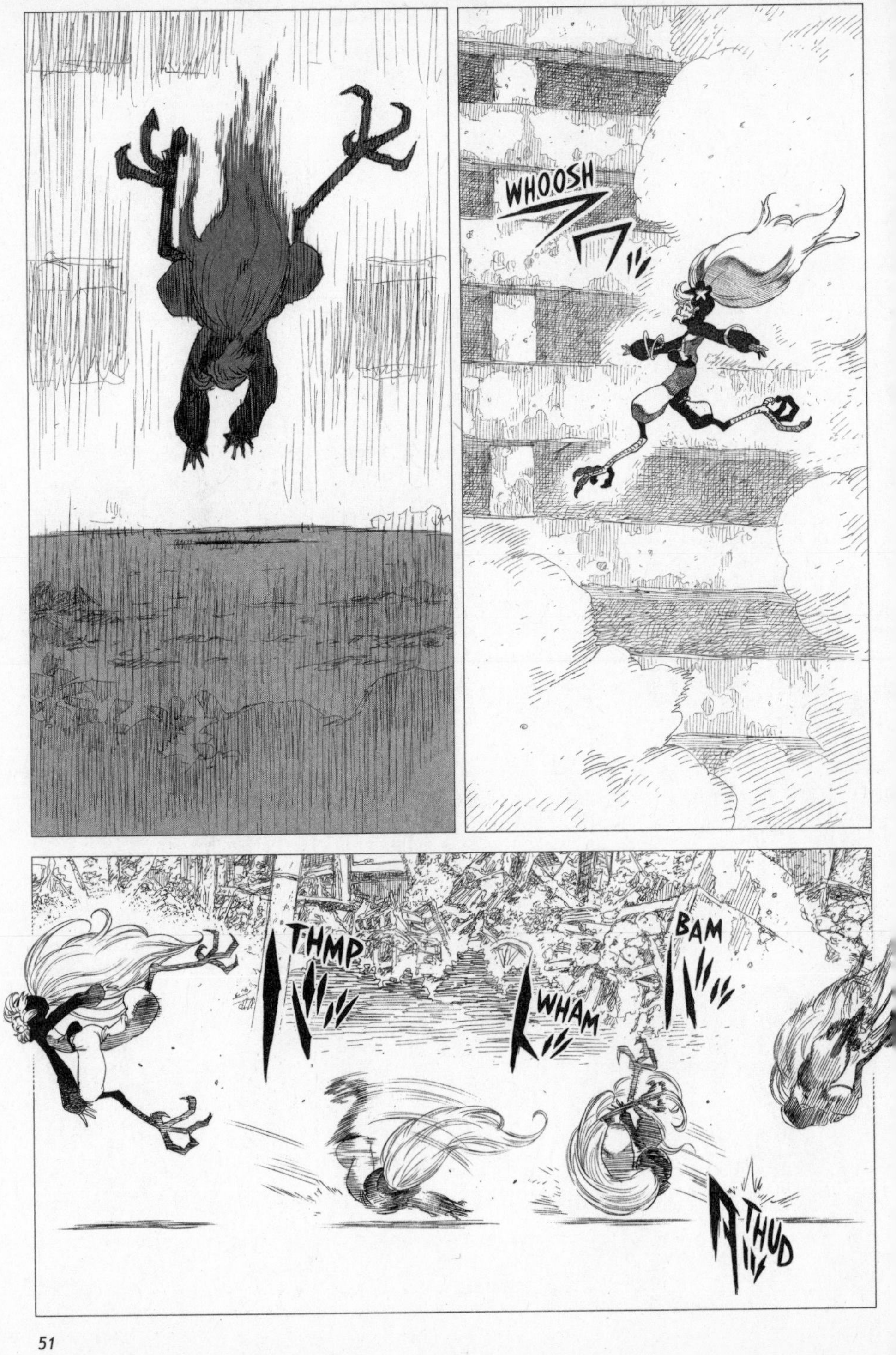
WHOOSH
BAM
WHAM
THMP
THUD

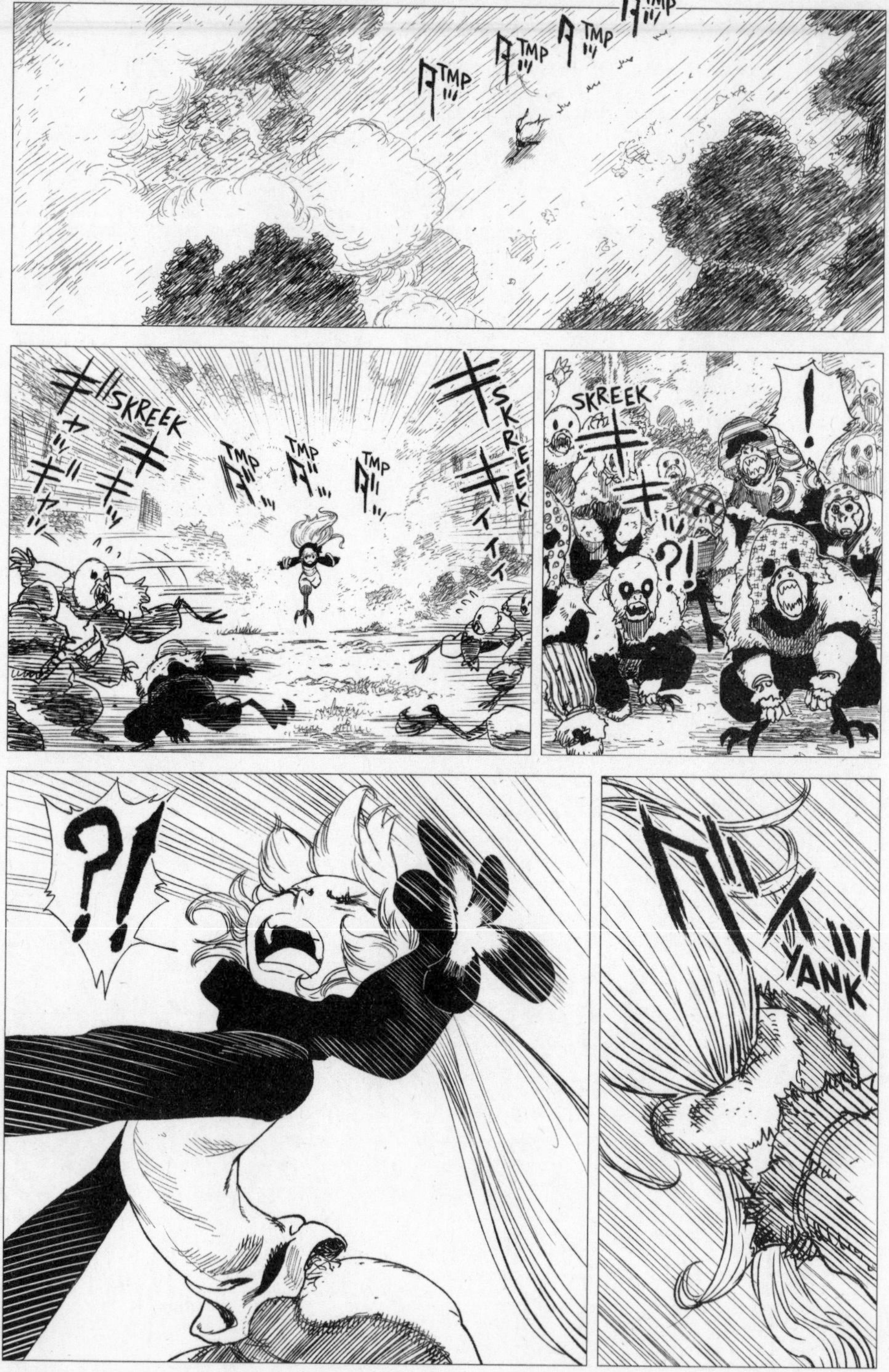
TMP
TMP
TMP
TMP
!
SKREEK
?!
SKREEK
TMP
TMP
TMP
SKREEK
YANK
?!

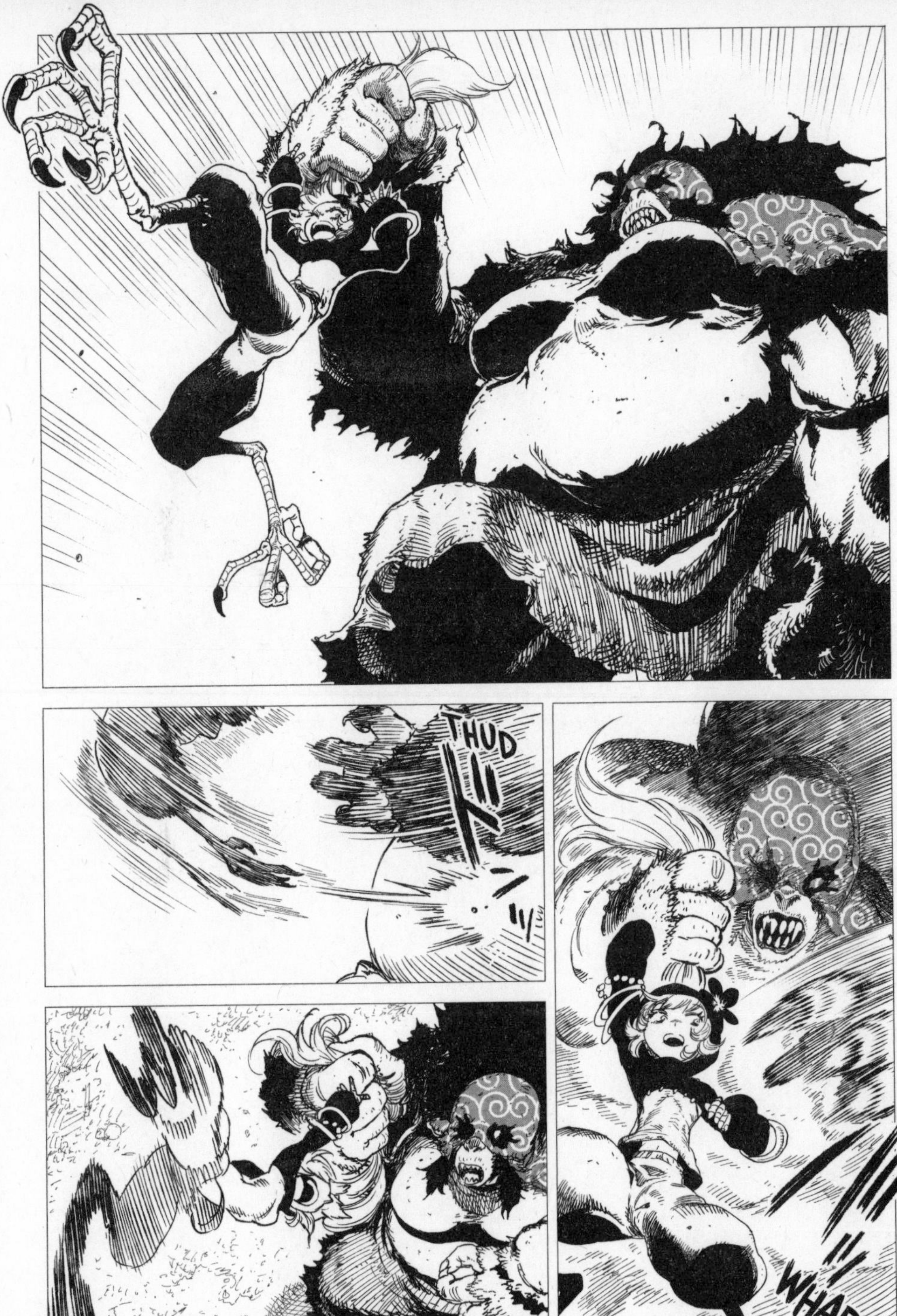
WHAP
THUD

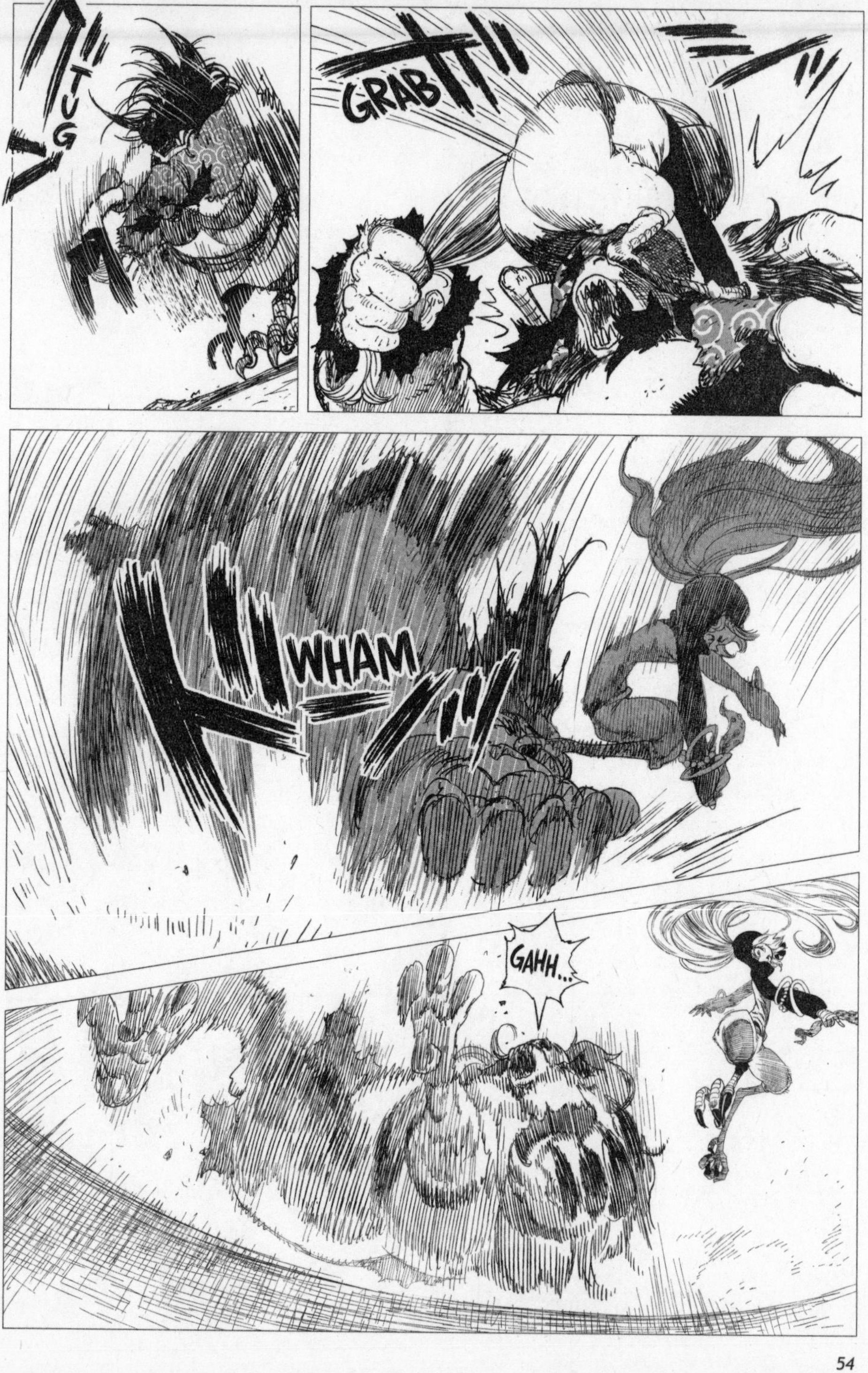
GRAB
TUG
WHAM
GAHH...

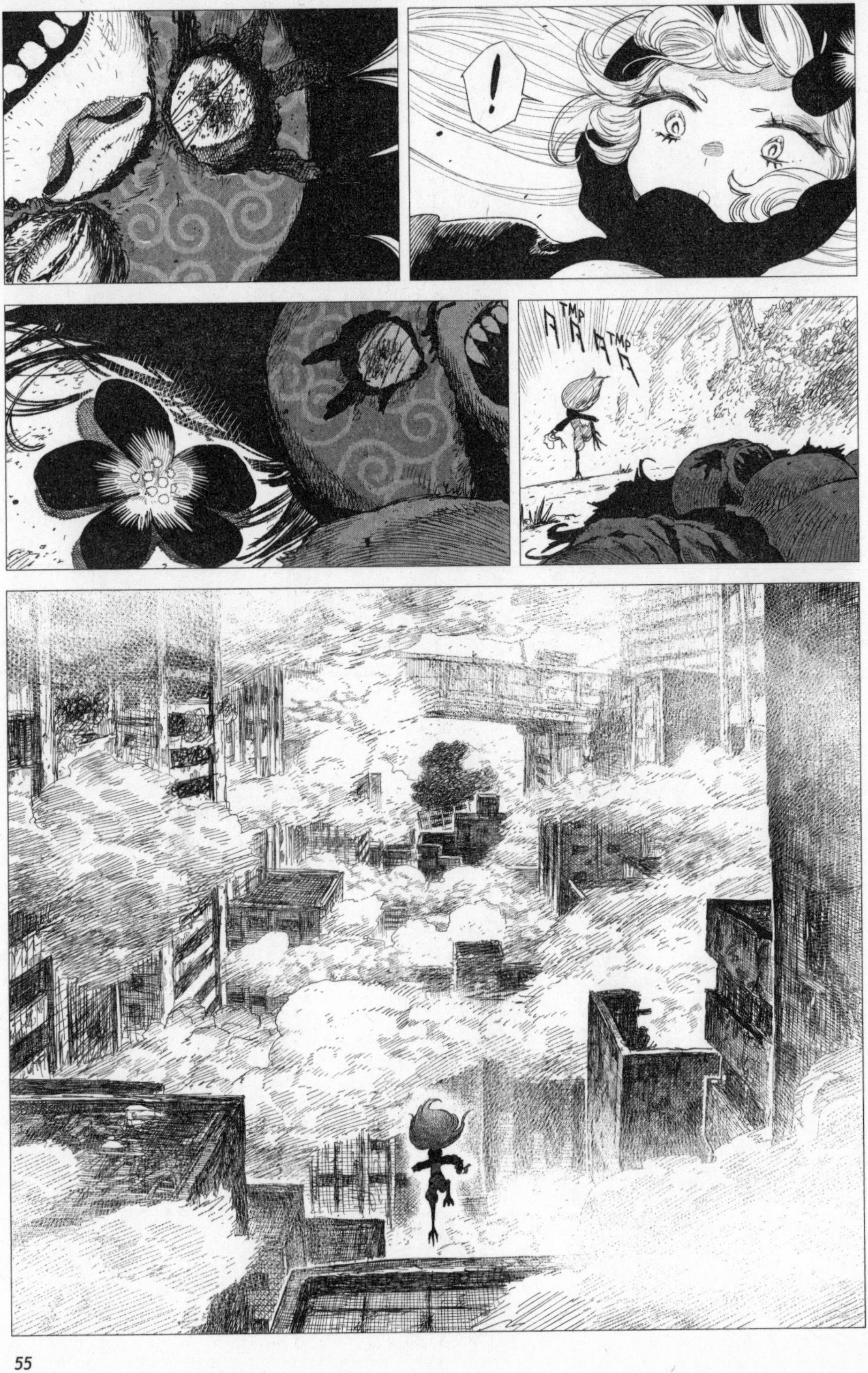
!
TMP TMP

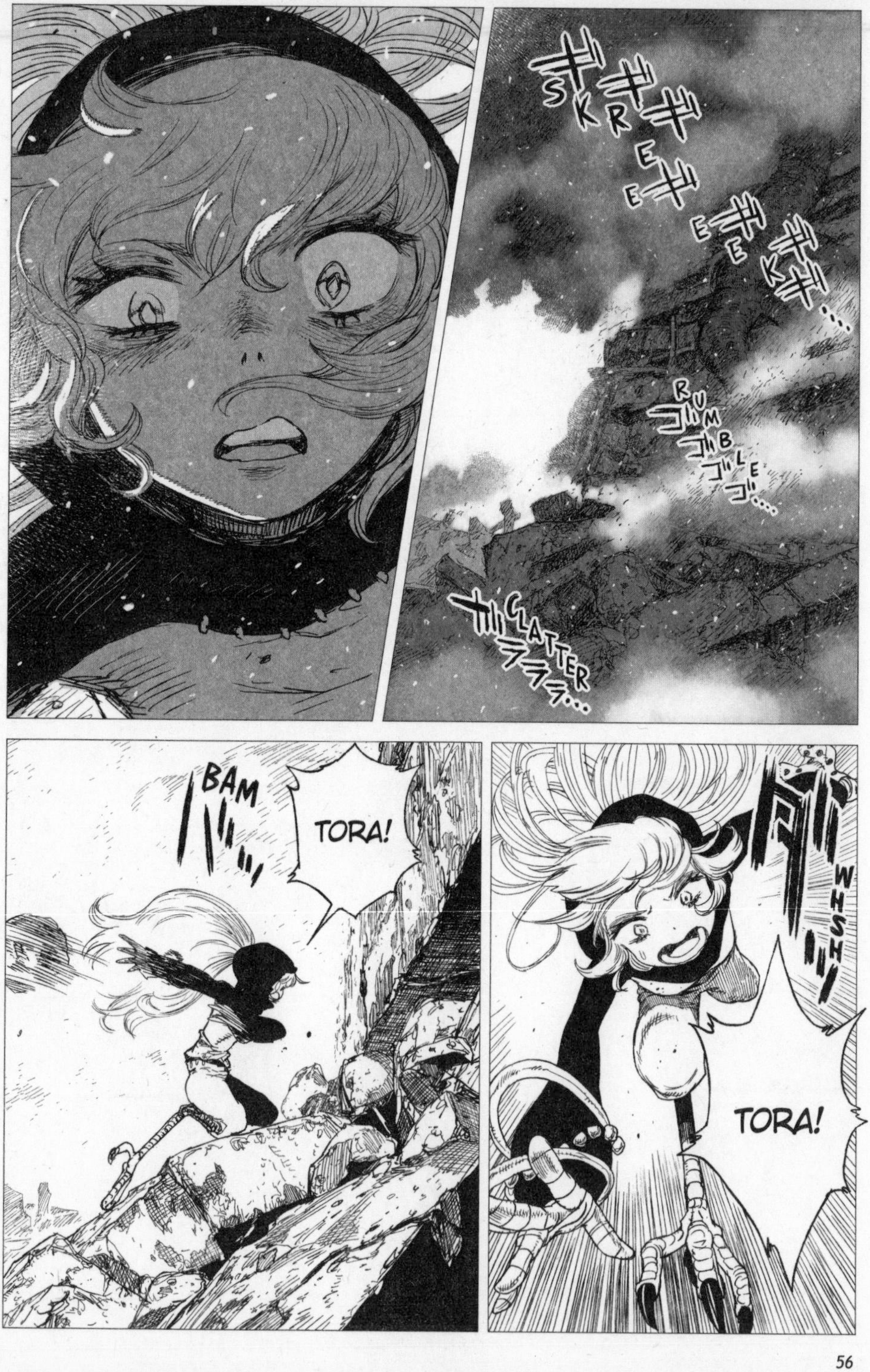
SKREEEK...
RUMBLE...
CLATTER...
WHSH!
TORA!
BAM
TORA!

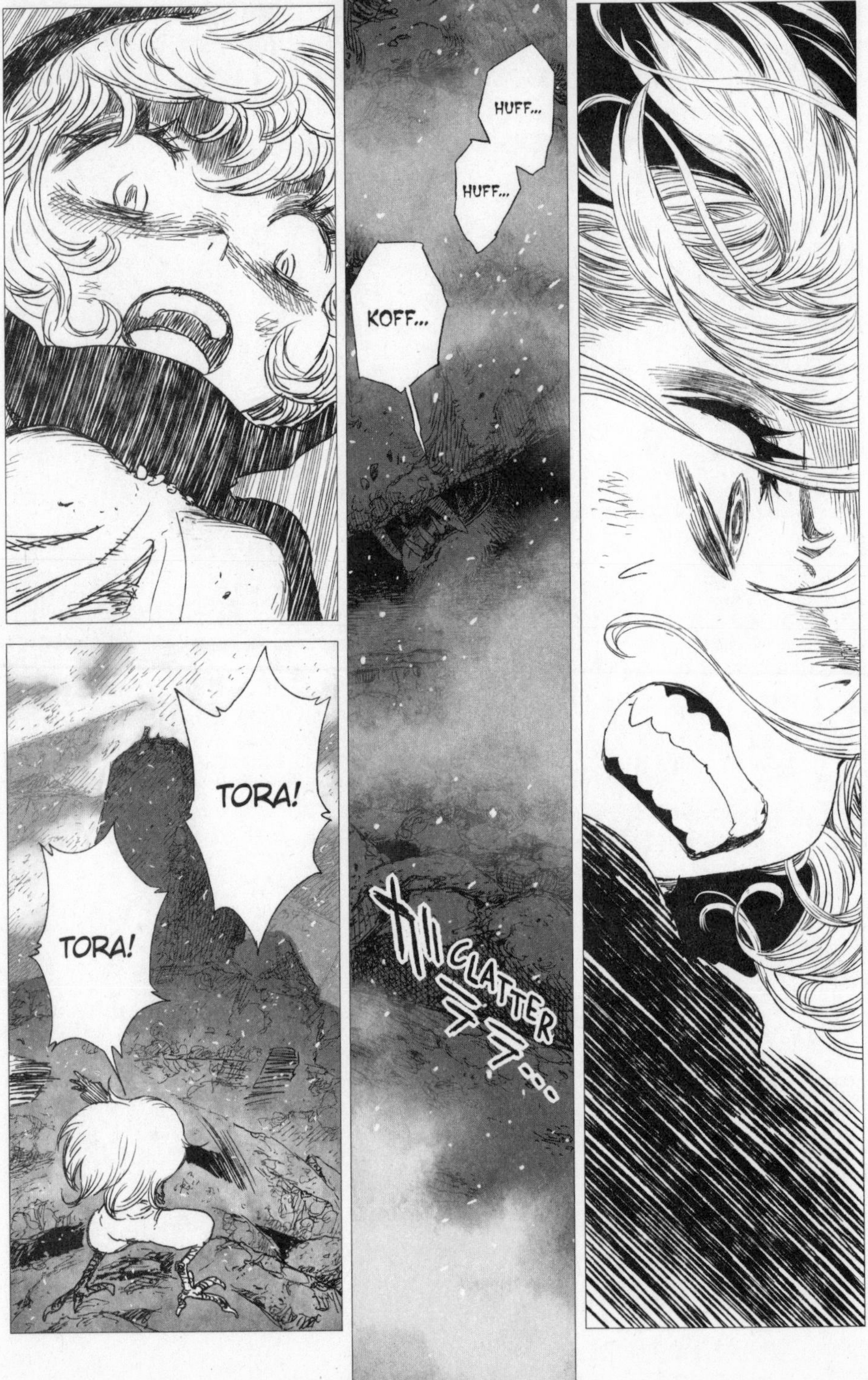
HUFF...
HUFF...
KOFF...
CLATTER
TORA!
TORA!

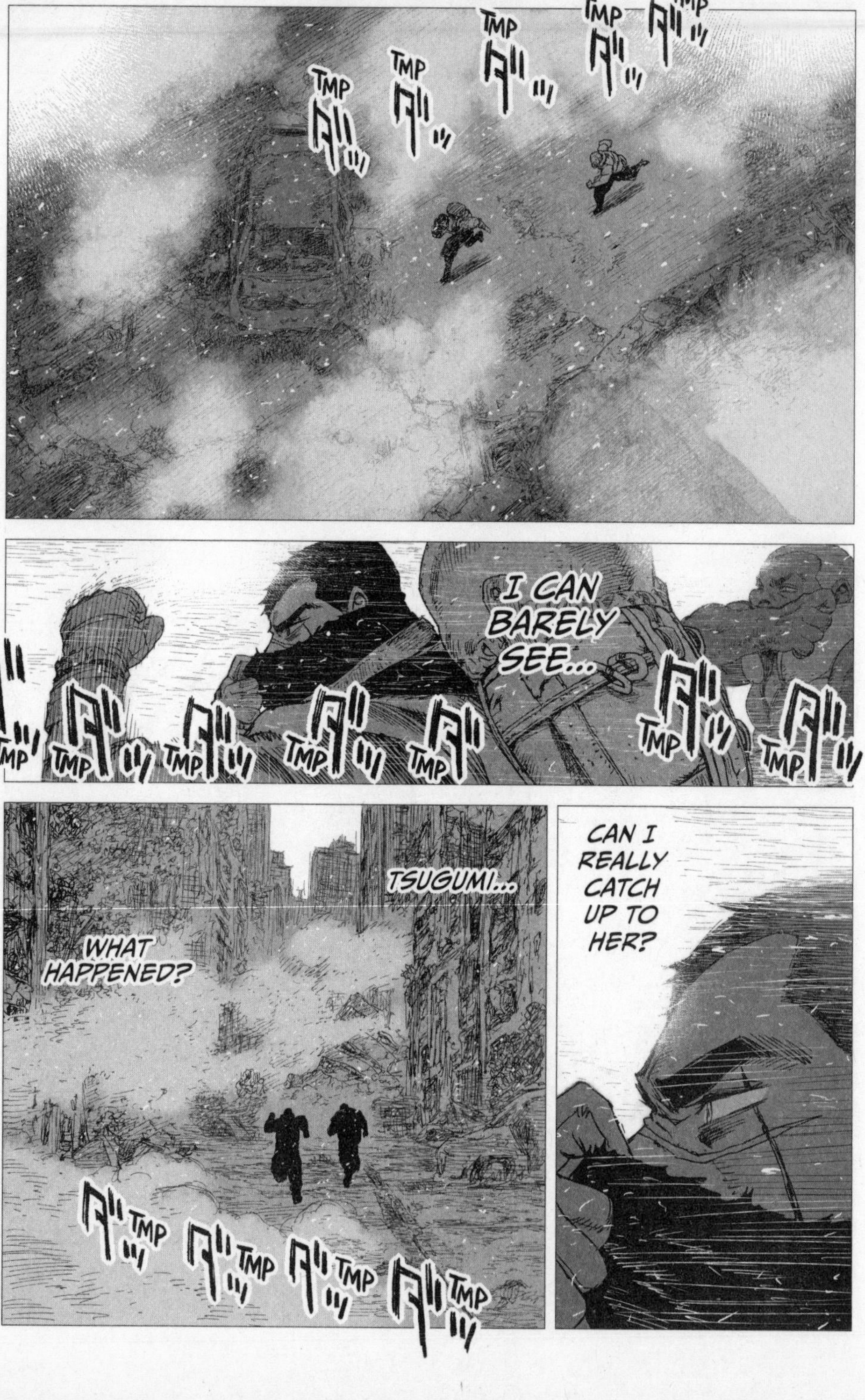
TMP
TMP
TMP
TMP
TMP
I CAN BARELY SEE...
TMP
TMP
TMP
TMP
TMP
TMP
TMP
CAN I REALLY CATCH UP TO HER?
TSUGUMI...
WHAT HAPPENED?
TMP
TMP
TMP
TMP

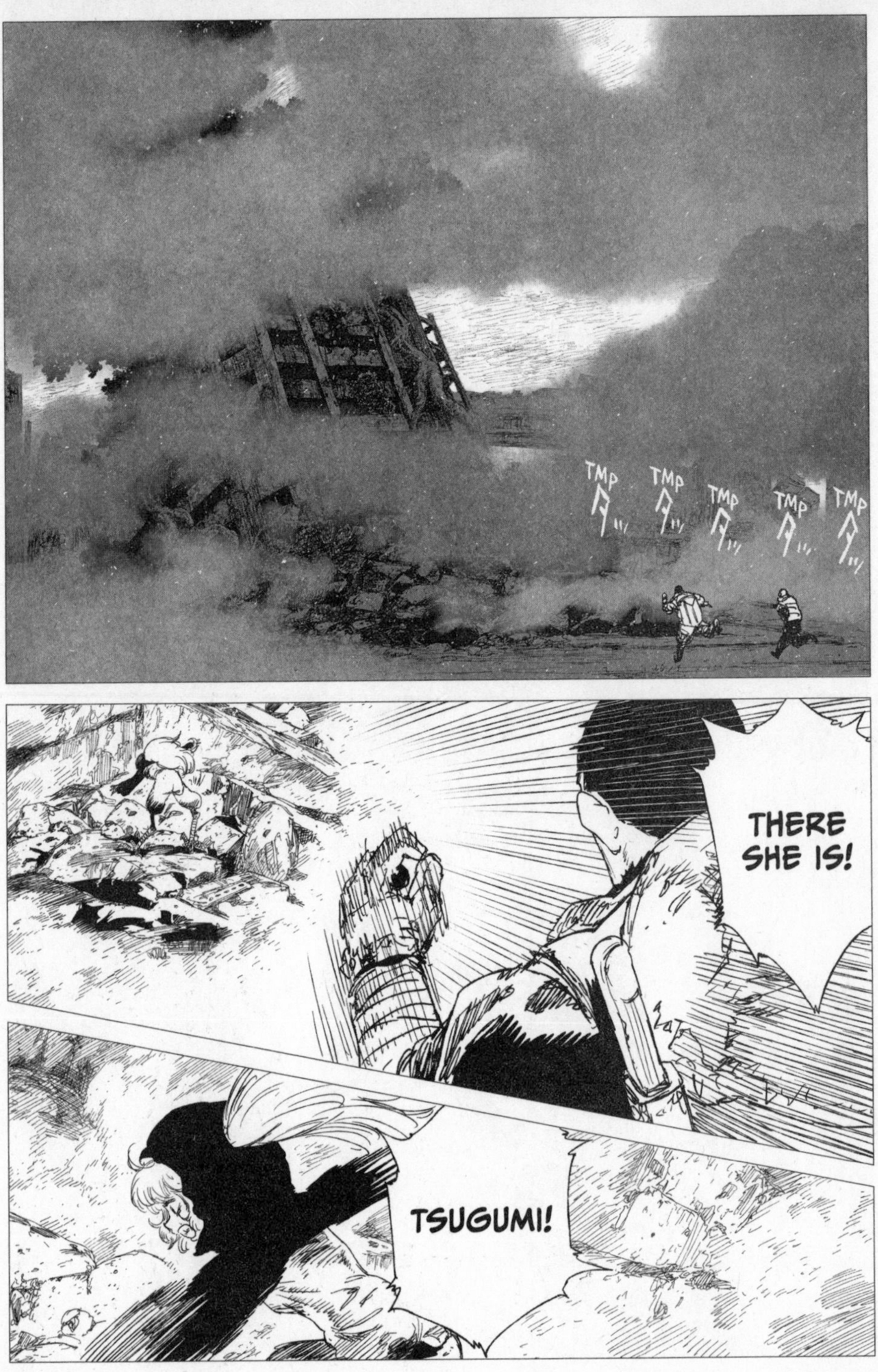
TMP
TMP
TMP
TMP
TMP
THERE SHE IS!
TSUGUMI!

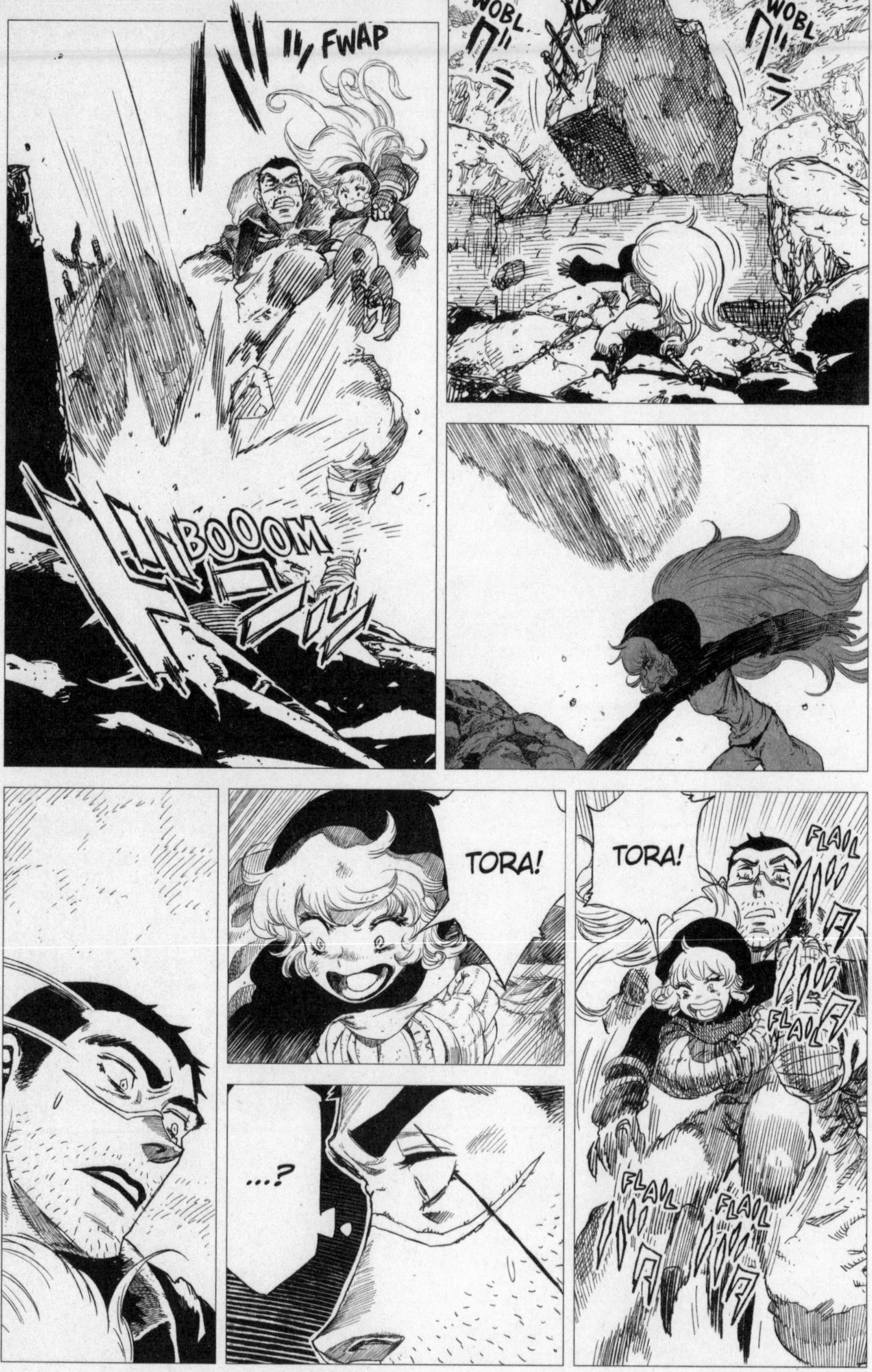
WOBL
WOBL
FWAP
BOOOM
FLAIL
FLAIL
FLAIL
FLAIL
TORA!
TORA!
...?

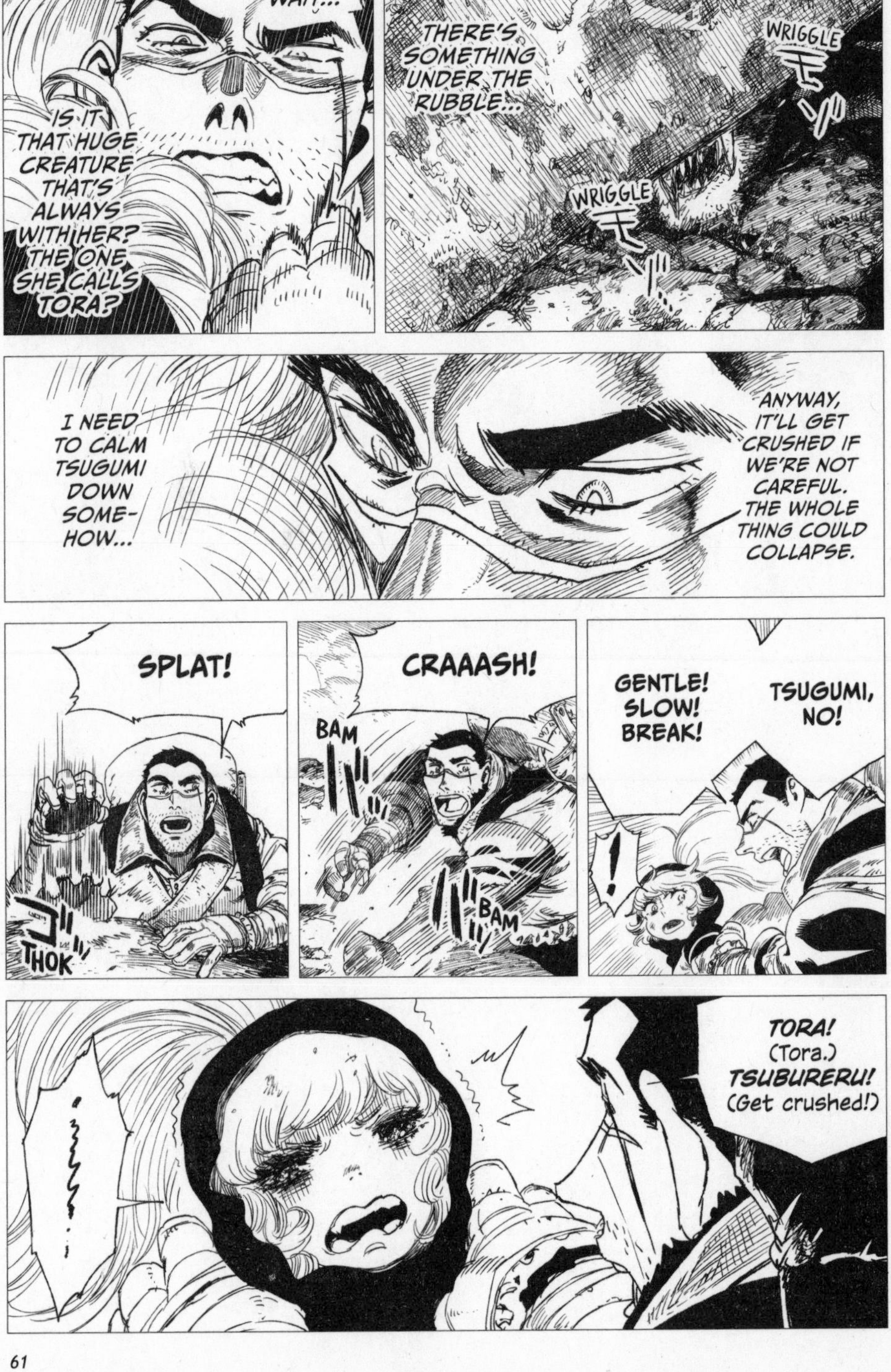
WRIGGLE
THERE'S SOMETHING UNDER THE RUBBLE...
WRIGGLE
WAIT...
IS IT THAT HUGE CREATURE THAT'S ALWAYS WITH HER? THE ONE SHE CALLS TORA?
ANYWAY, IT'LL GET CRUSHED IF WE'RE NOT CAREFUL. THE WHOLE THING COULD COLLAPSE.
I NEED TO CALM TSUGUMI DOWN SOME-HOW...
TSUGUMI, NO!
GENTLE! SLOW! BREAK!
!
CRAAASH!
BAM
BAM
SPLAT!
THOK
TORA! (Tora.) TSUBURERU! (Get crushed!)
....

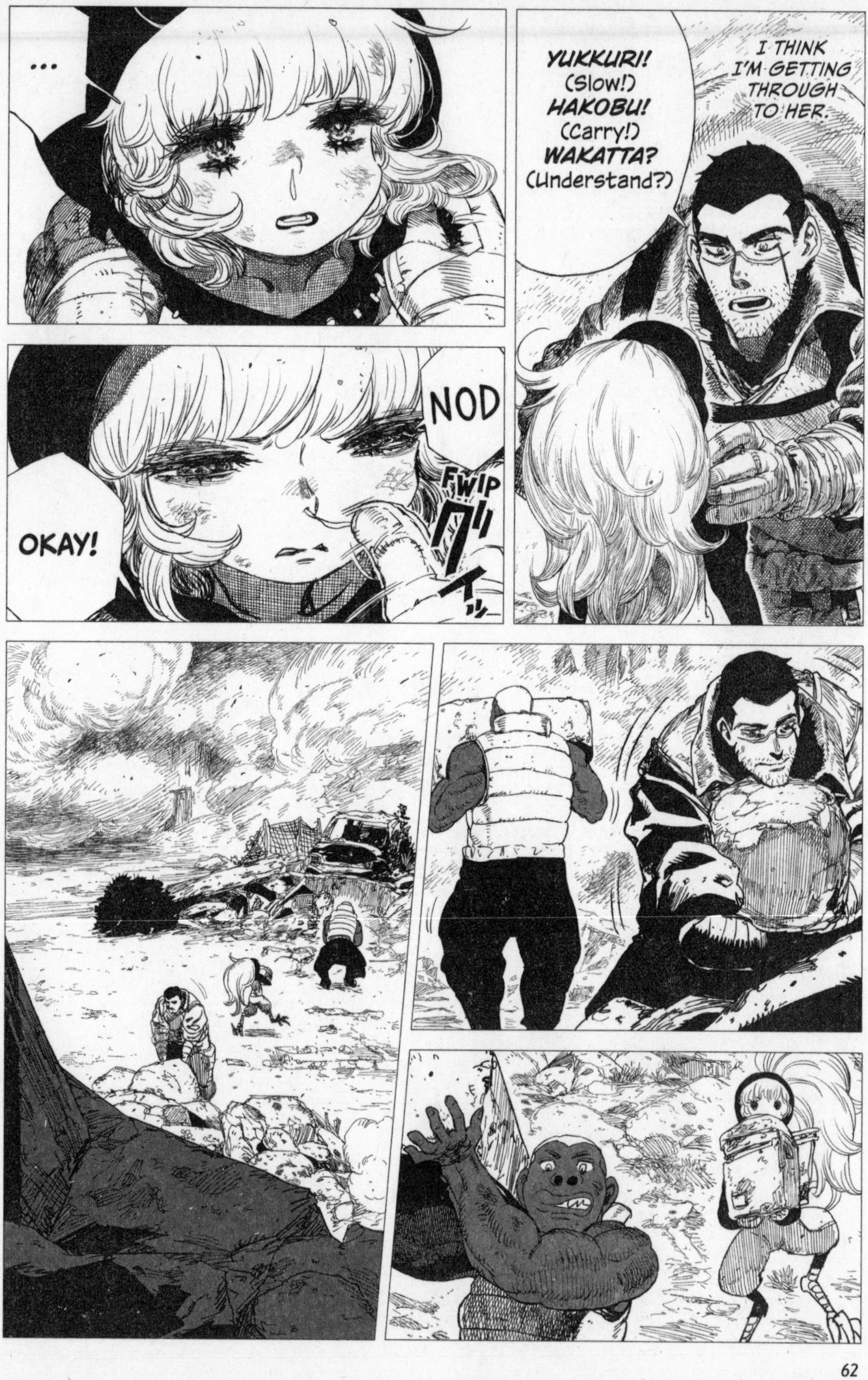
I THINK I'M GETTING THROUGH TO HER.
YUKKURI! (Slow!) HAKOBU! (Carry!) WAKATTA? (Understand?)
...
NOD
FWIP
OKAY!

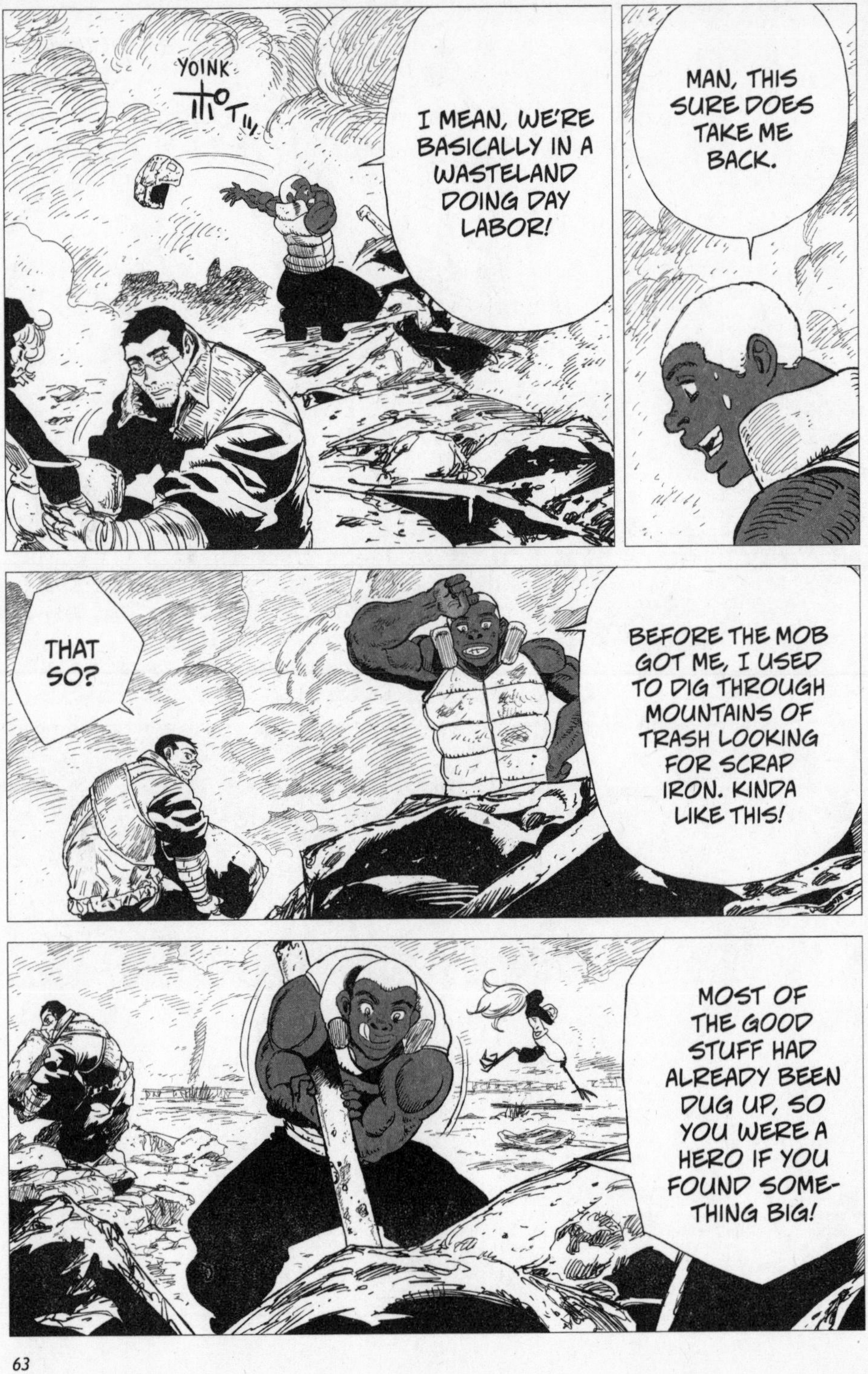
MAN, THIS SURE DOES TAKE ME BACK.
I MEAN, WE'RE BASICALLY IN A WASTELAND DOING DAY LABOR!
YOINK
BEFORE THE MOB GOT ME, I USED TO DIG THROUGH MOUNTAINS OF TRASH LOOKING FOR SCRAP IRON. KINDA LIKE THIS!
THAT SO?
MOST OF THE GOOD STUFF HAD ALREADY BEEN DUG UP, SO YOU WERE A HERO IF YOU FOUND SOME-THING BIG!

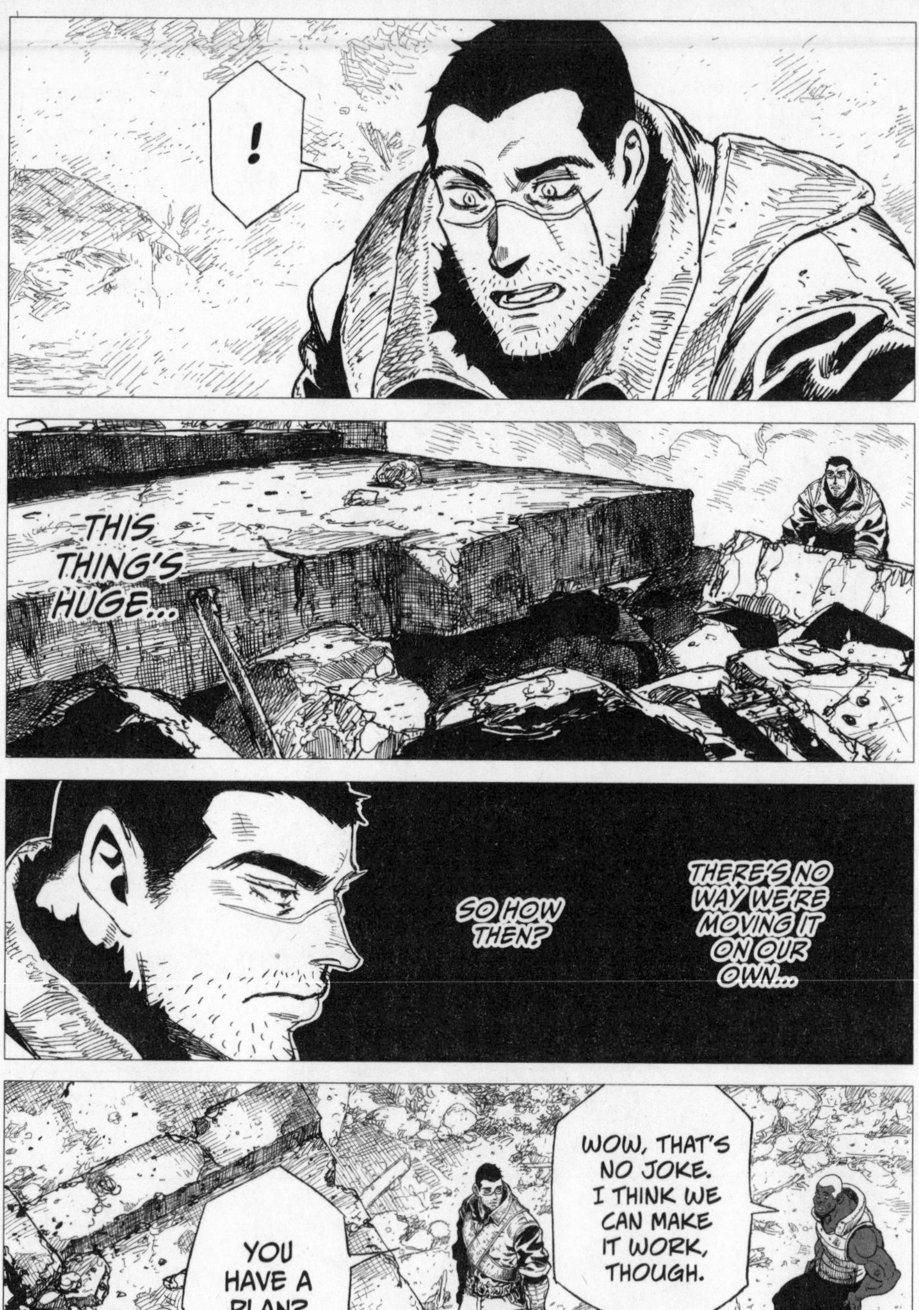
!
THIS THING'S HUGE...
THERE'S NO WAY WE'RE MOVING IT ON OUR OWN...
SO HOW THEN?
WOW, THAT'S NO JOKE. I THINK WE CAN MAKE IT WORK, THOUGH.
YOU HAVE A PLAN?

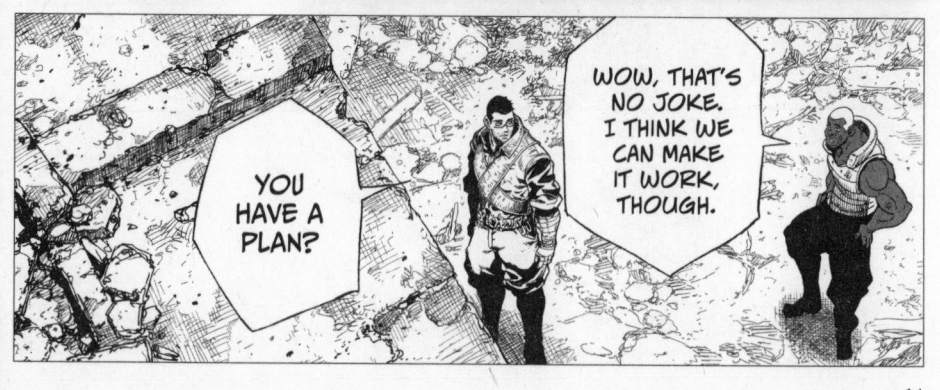

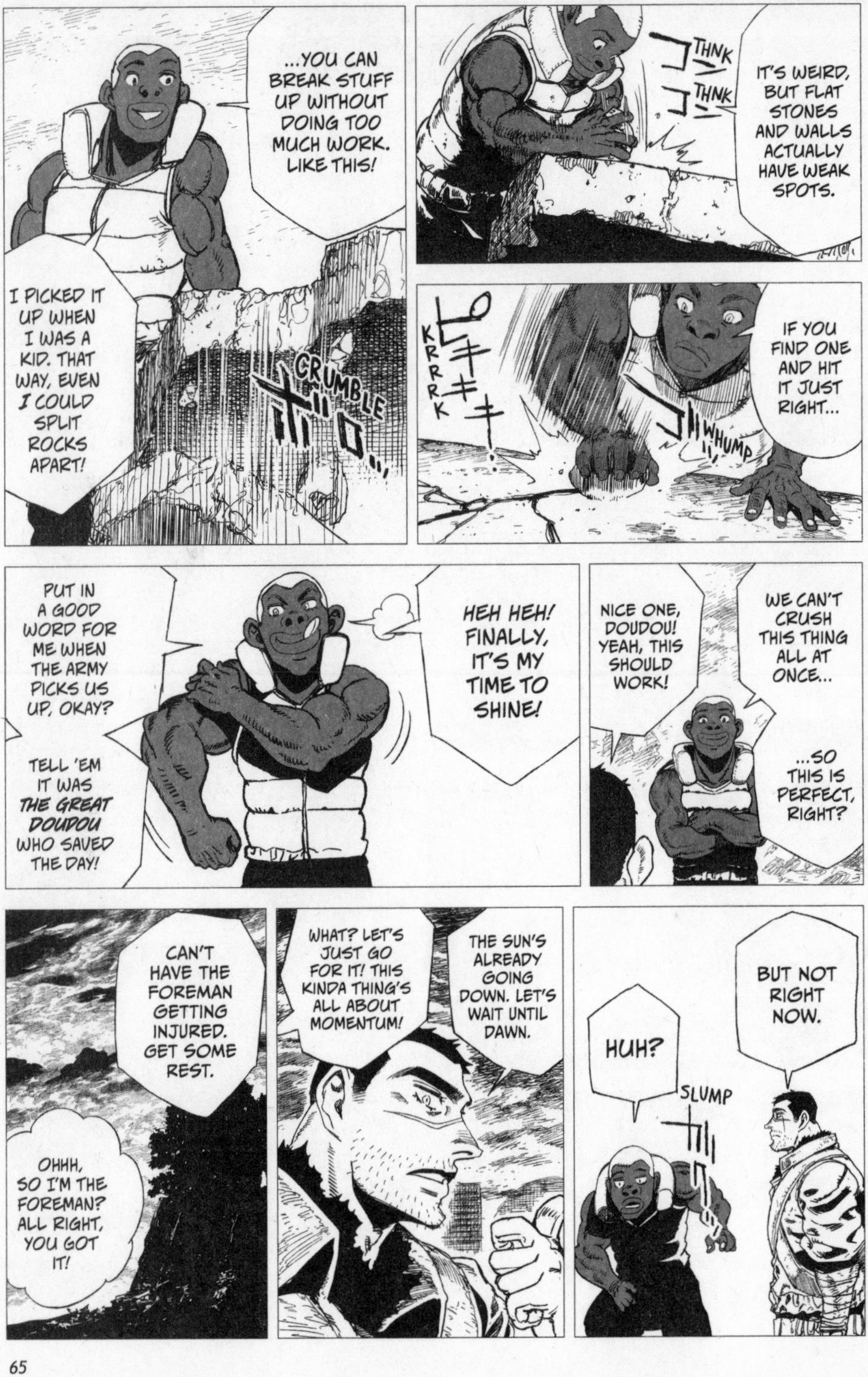
THNK
THNK
IT'S WEIRD, BUT FLAT STONES AND WALLS ACTUALLY HAVE WEAK SPOTS.
KRRRK
WHUMP
IF YOU FIND ONE AND HIT IT JUST RIGHT...
...YOU CAN BREAK STUFF UP WITHOUT DOING TOO MUCH WORK. LIKE THIS!
CRUMBLE
I PICKED IT UP WHEN I WAS A KID. THAT WAY, EVEN I COULD SPLIT ROCKS APART!
WE CAN'T CRUSH THIS THING ALL AT ONCE...
NICE ONE, DOUDOU! YEAH, THIS SHOULD WORK!
...SO THIS IS PERFECT, RIGHT?
HEH HEH! FINALLY, IT'S MY TIME TO SHINE!
PUT IN A GOOD WORD FOR ME WHEN THE ARMY PICKS US UP, OKAY?
TELL 'EM IT WAS THE GREAT DOUDOU WHO SAVED THE DAY!
BUT NOT RIGHT NOW.
SLUMP
HUH?
THE SUN'S ALREADY GOING DOWN. LET'S WAIT UNTIL DAWN.
WHAT? LET'S JUST GO FOR IT! THIS KINDA THING'S ALL ABOUT MOMENTUM!
CAN'T HAVE THE FOREMAN GETTING INJURED. GET SOME REST.
OHHH, SO I'M THE FOREMAN? ALL RIGHT, YOU GOT IT!

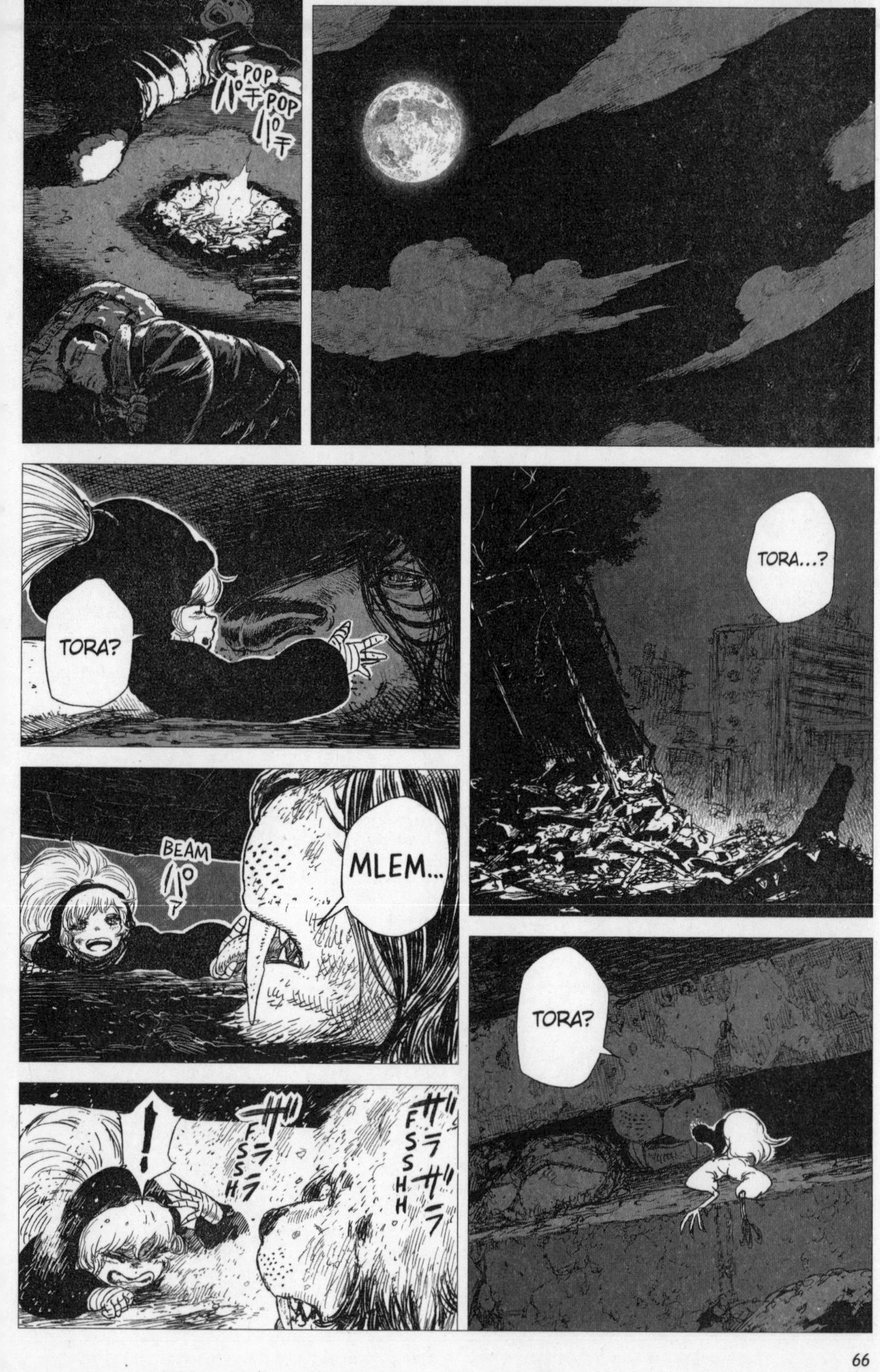

Z Z Z...
POP パチ POP パチ
TORA...?
TORA?
TORA?
MLEM...
BEAM パァ
!
FSSH ザラザラ
FSSH ザラザラ

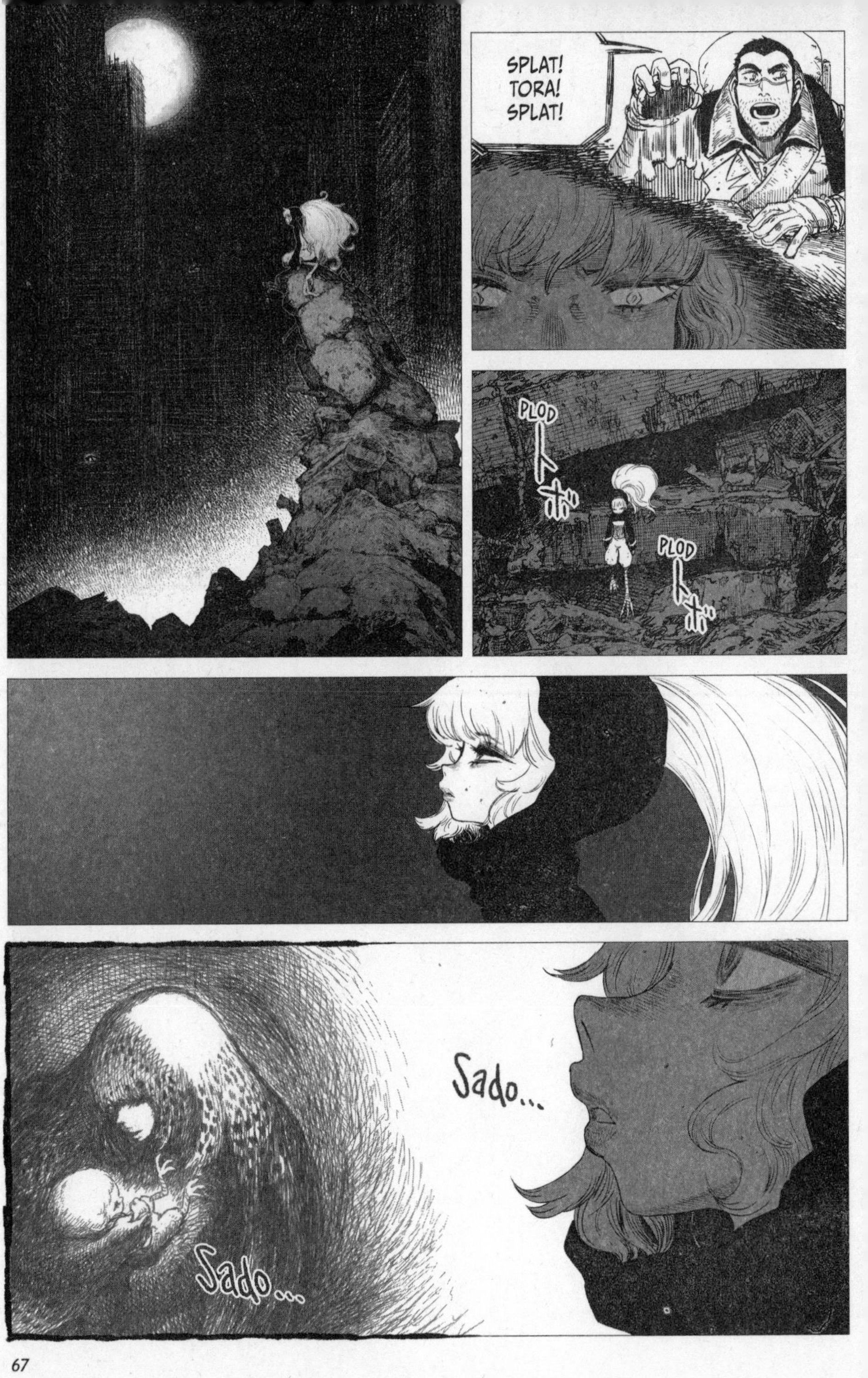
SPLAT! TORA! SPLAT!
PLOD トボ
PLOD トボ
Sado...
Sado...

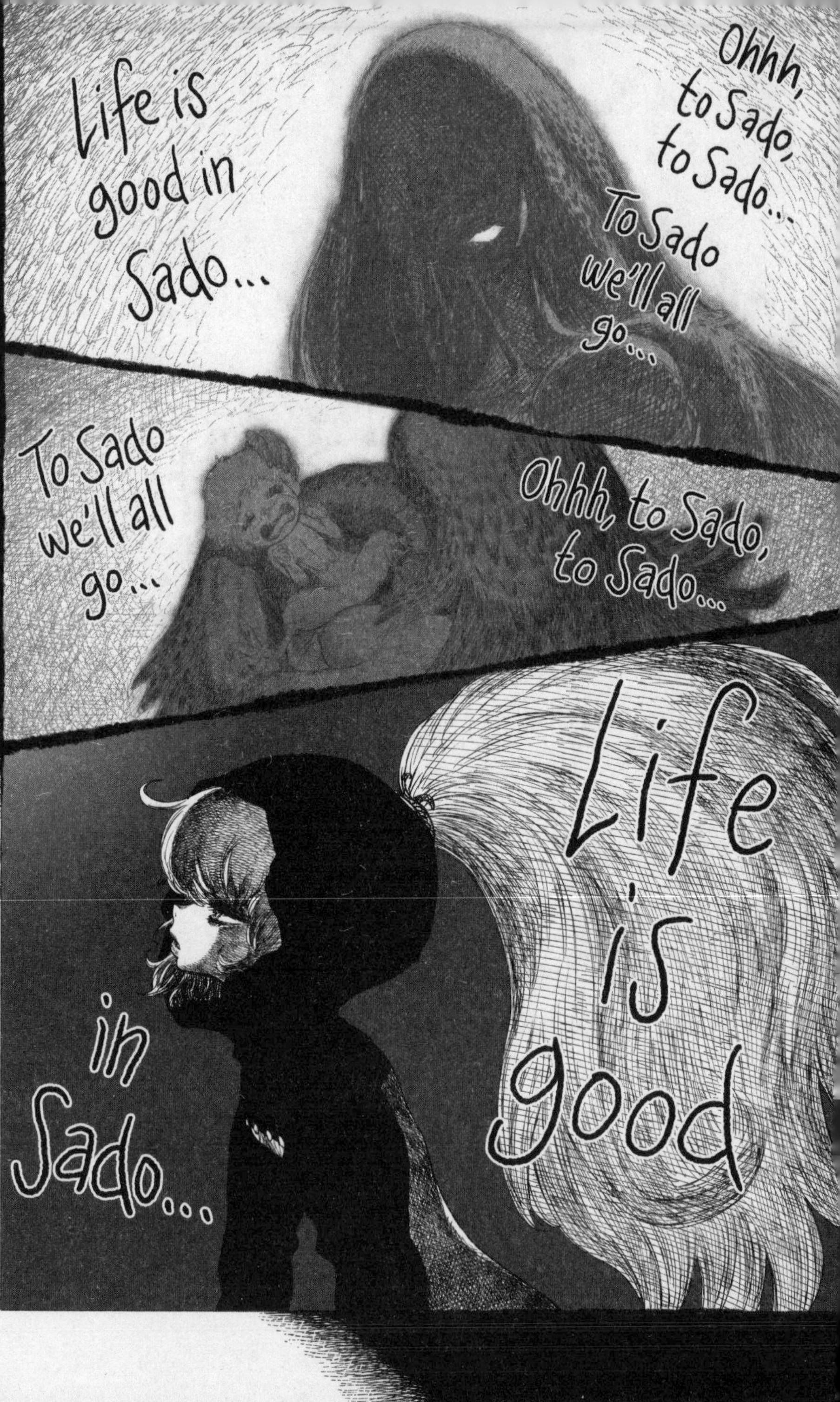
Ohhh, to Sado, to Sado...
To Sado we'll all go...
Life is good in Sado...
Ohhh, to Sado, to Sado...
To Sado we'll all go...
Life is good
in Sado...

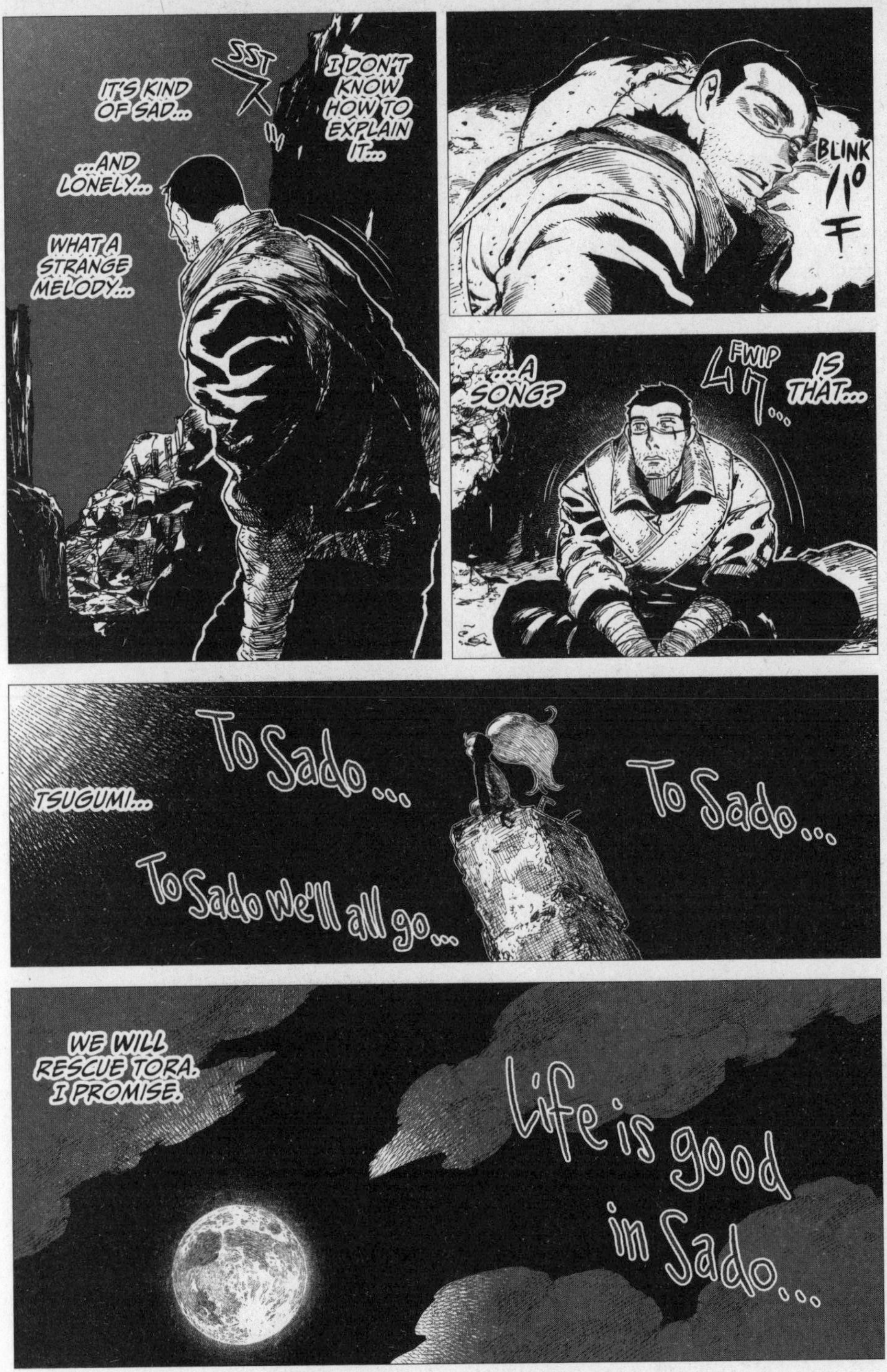
BLINK
FWIP
IS THAT...
...A SONG?
I DON'T KNOW HOW TO EXPLAIN IT...
SST
IT'S KIND OF SAD...
...AND LONELY...
WHAT A STRANGE MELODY...
To Sado...
To Sado...
TSUGUMI...
To Sado we'll all go...
Life is good in Sado...
WE WILL RESCUE TORA. I PROMISE.

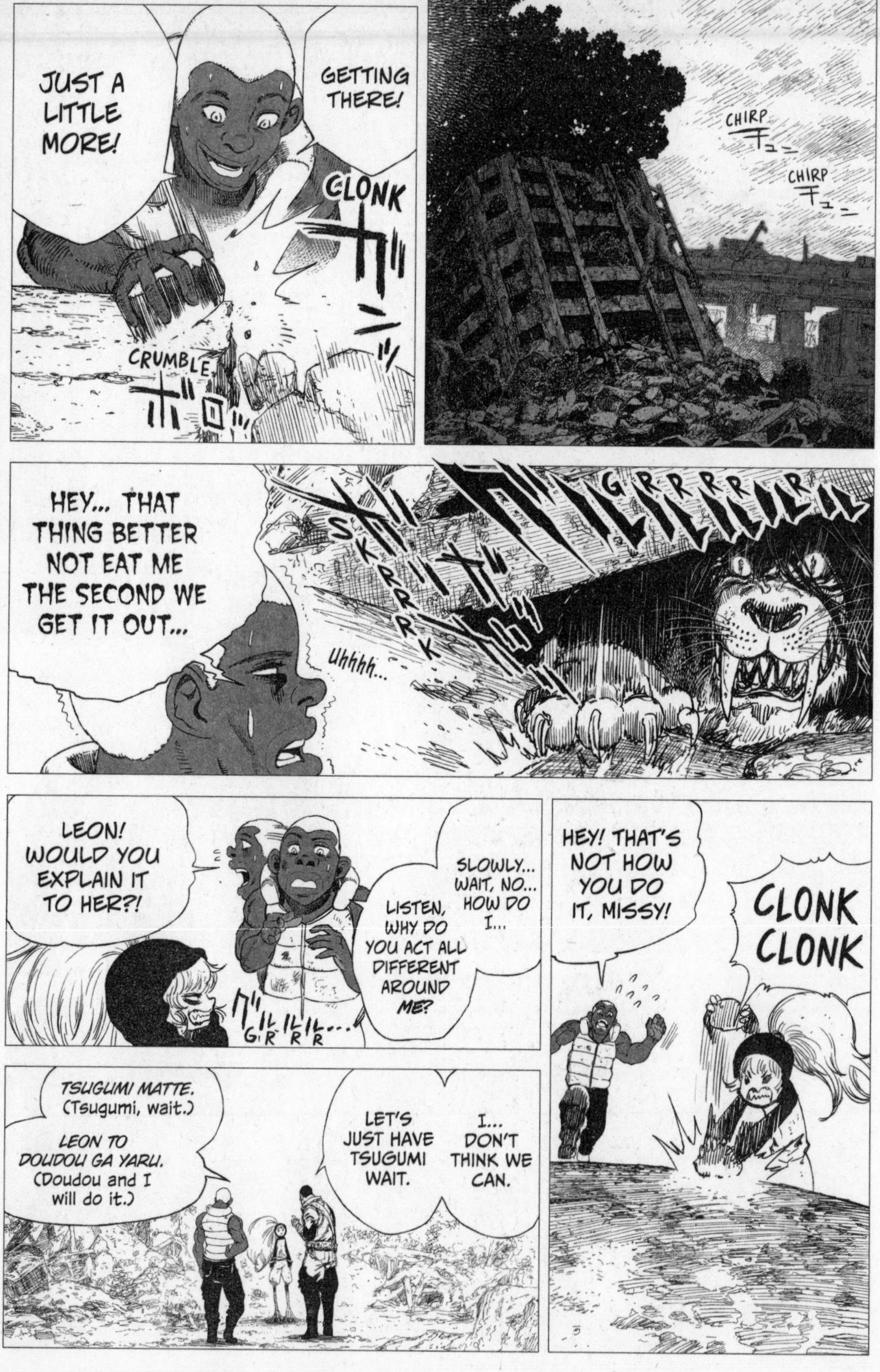
CHIRP
CHIRP
JUST A LITTLE MORE!
GETTING THERE!
CLONK
CRUMBLE
HEY... THAT THING BETTER NOT EAT ME THE SECOND WE GET IT OUT...
SKRRRRK
GRRRRRR
Uhhhh...
HEY! THAT'S NOT HOW YOU DO IT, MISSY!
CLONK CLONK
LEON! WOULD YOU EXPLAIN IT TO HER?!
SLOWLY... WAIT, NO... HOW DO I...
LISTEN, WHY DO YOU ACT ALL DIFFERENT AROUND ME?
GRRR
I... DON'T THINK WE CAN.
LET'S JUST HAVE TSUGUMI WAIT.
TSUGUMI MATTE. (Tsugumi, wait.)
LEON TO DOUDOU GA YARU. (Doudou and I will do it.)

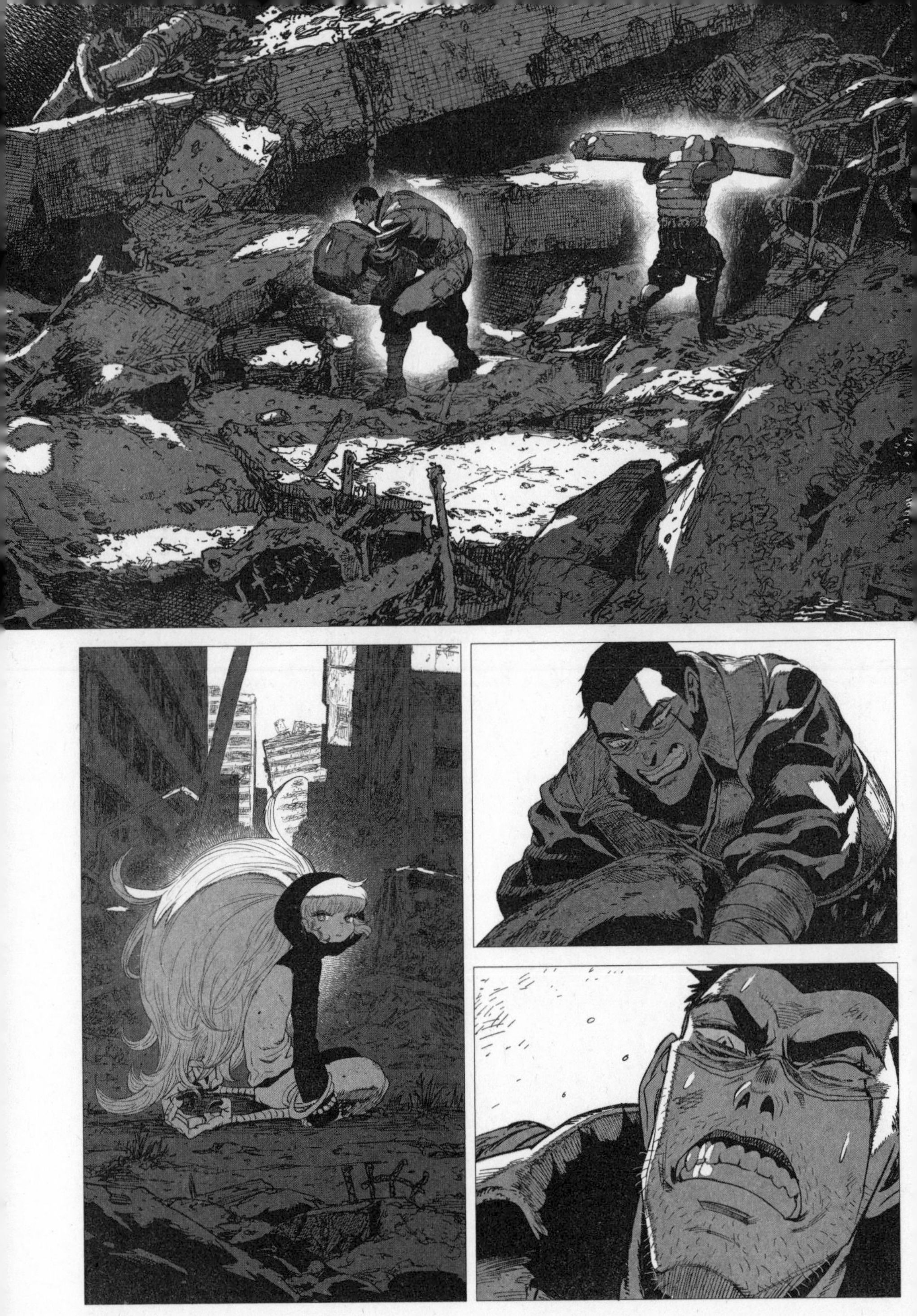

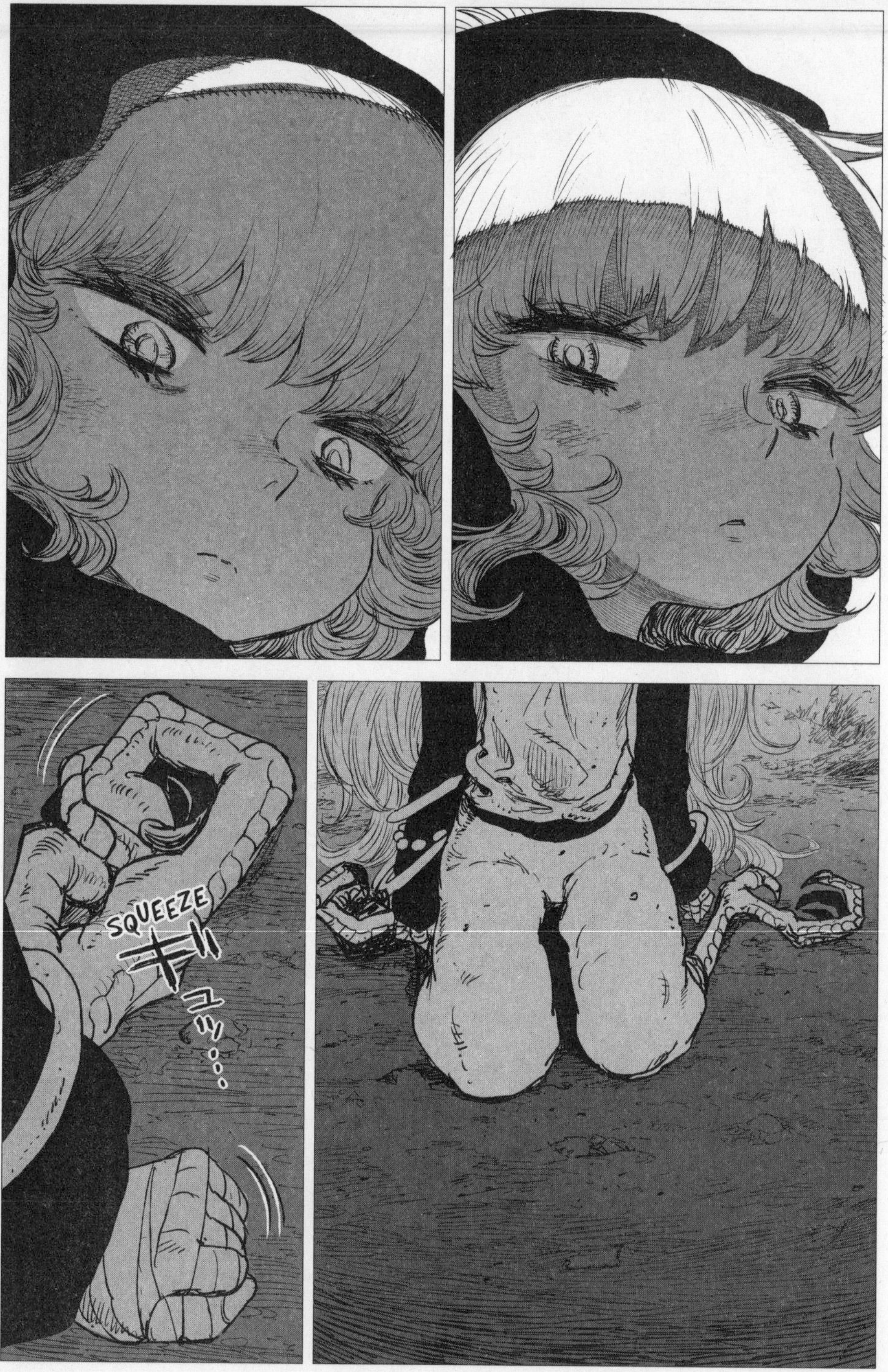
SQUEEZE
ギュッ…

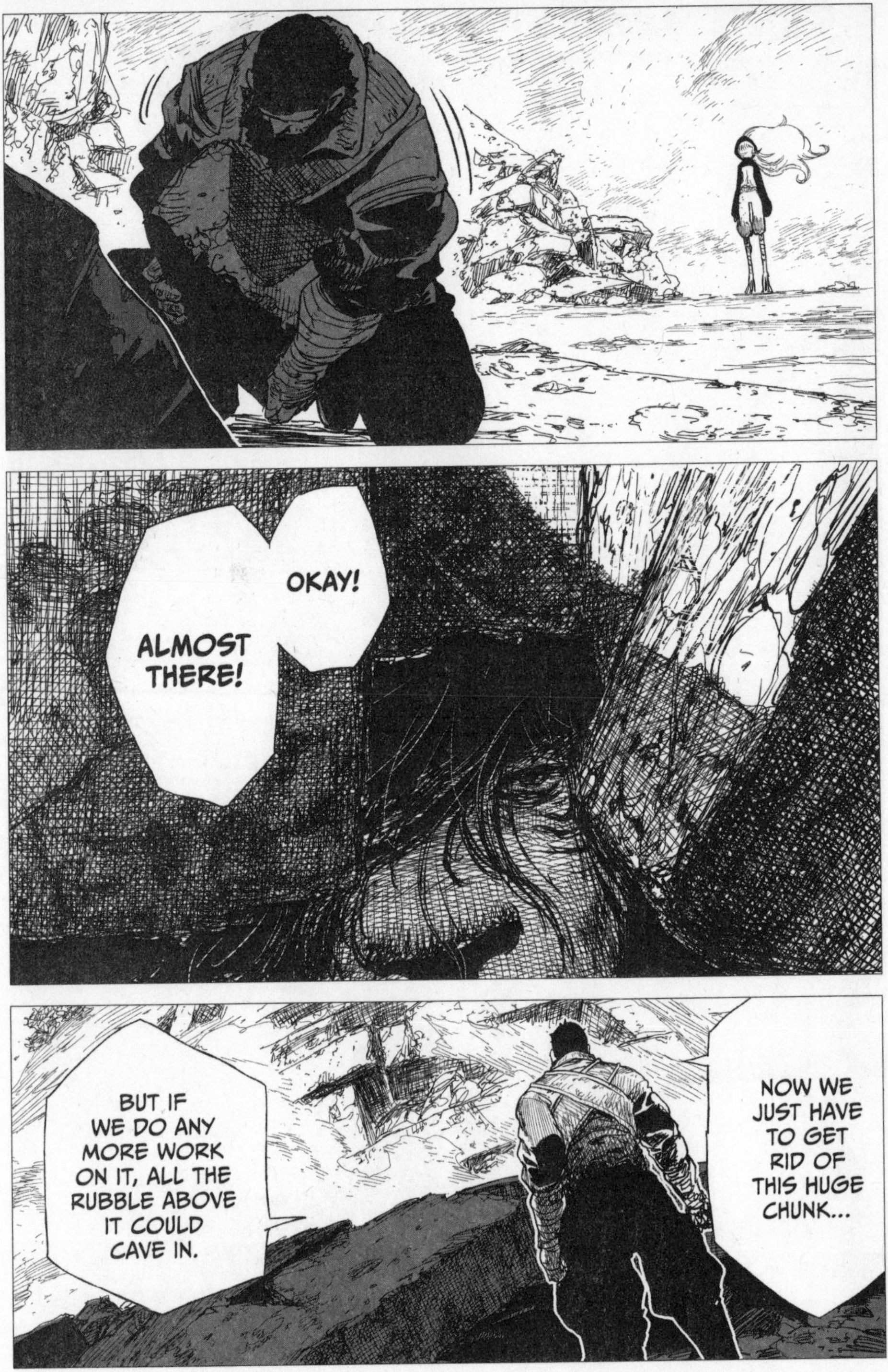
OKAY!
ALMOST THERE!
NOW WE JUST HAVE TO GET RID OF THIS HUGE CHUNK...
BUT IF WE DO ANY MORE WORK ON IT, ALL THE RUBBLE ABOVE IT COULD CAVE IN.

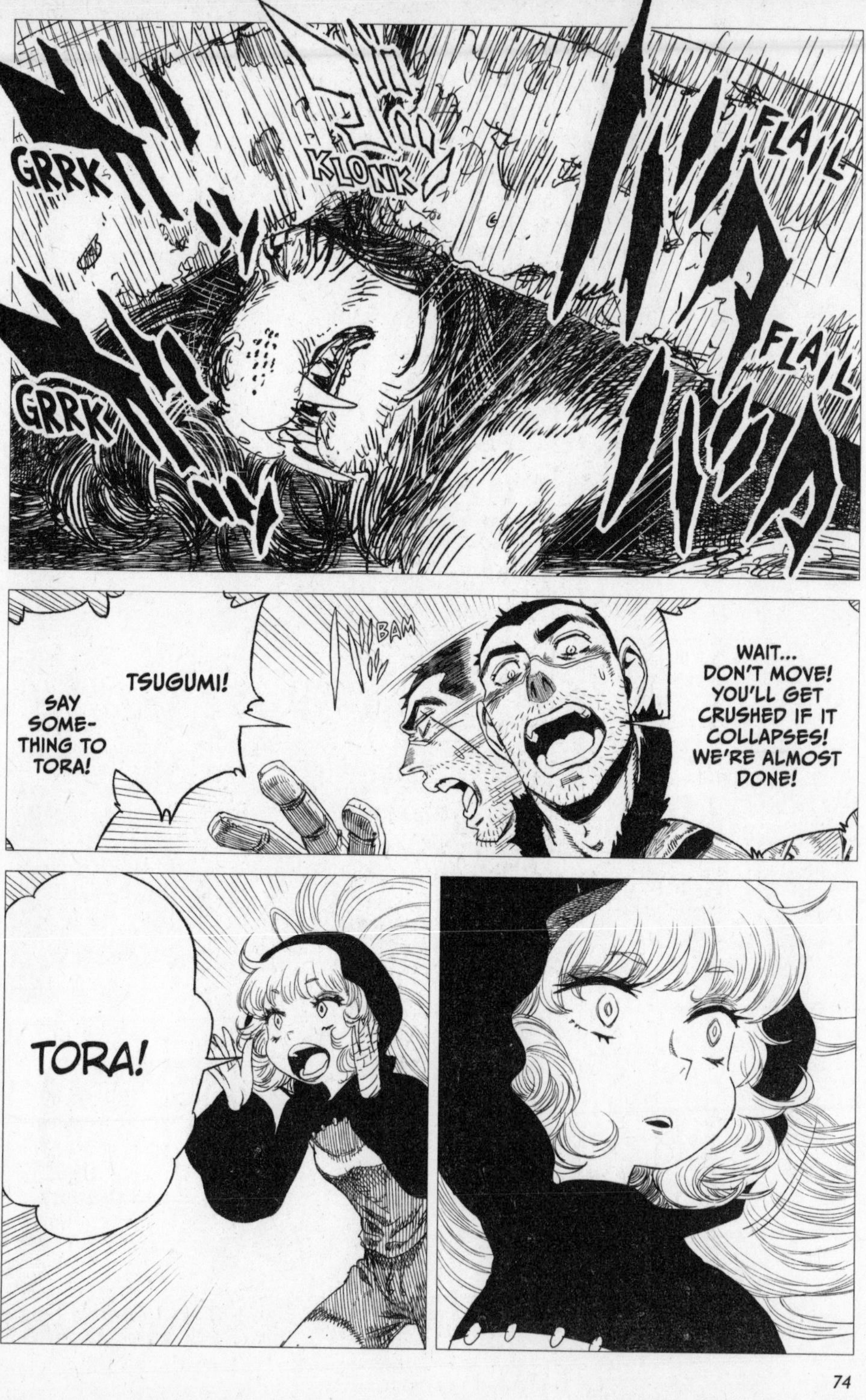
FLAIL
FLAIL
KLONK
GRRK
GRRK
WAIT... DON'T MOVE! YOU'LL GET CRUSHED IF IT COLLAPSES! WE'RE ALMOST DONE!
BAM
TSUGUMI!
SAY SOME-THING TO TORA!
TORA!

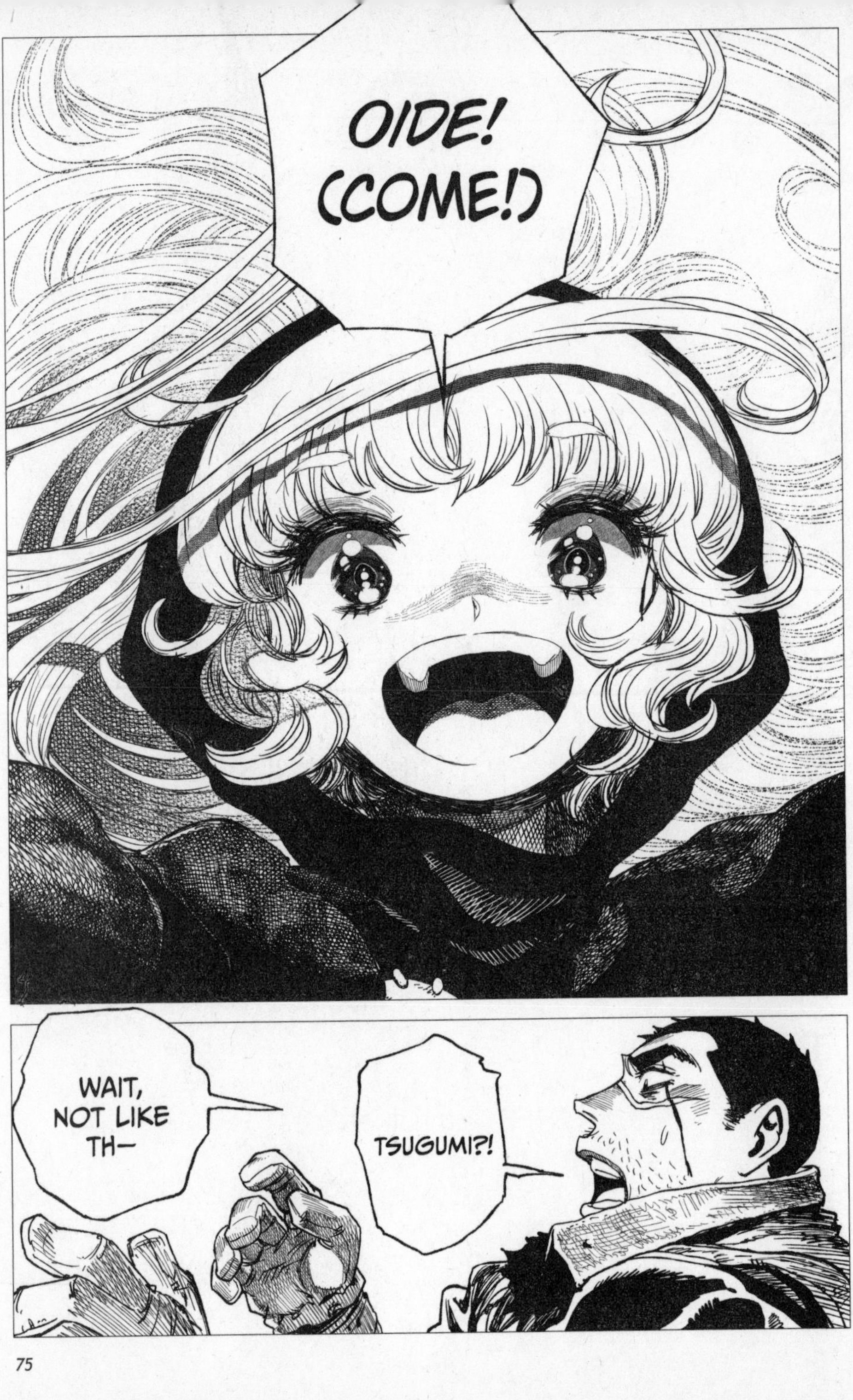
OIDE! (COME!)
TSUGUMI?!
WAIT, NOT LIKE TH—

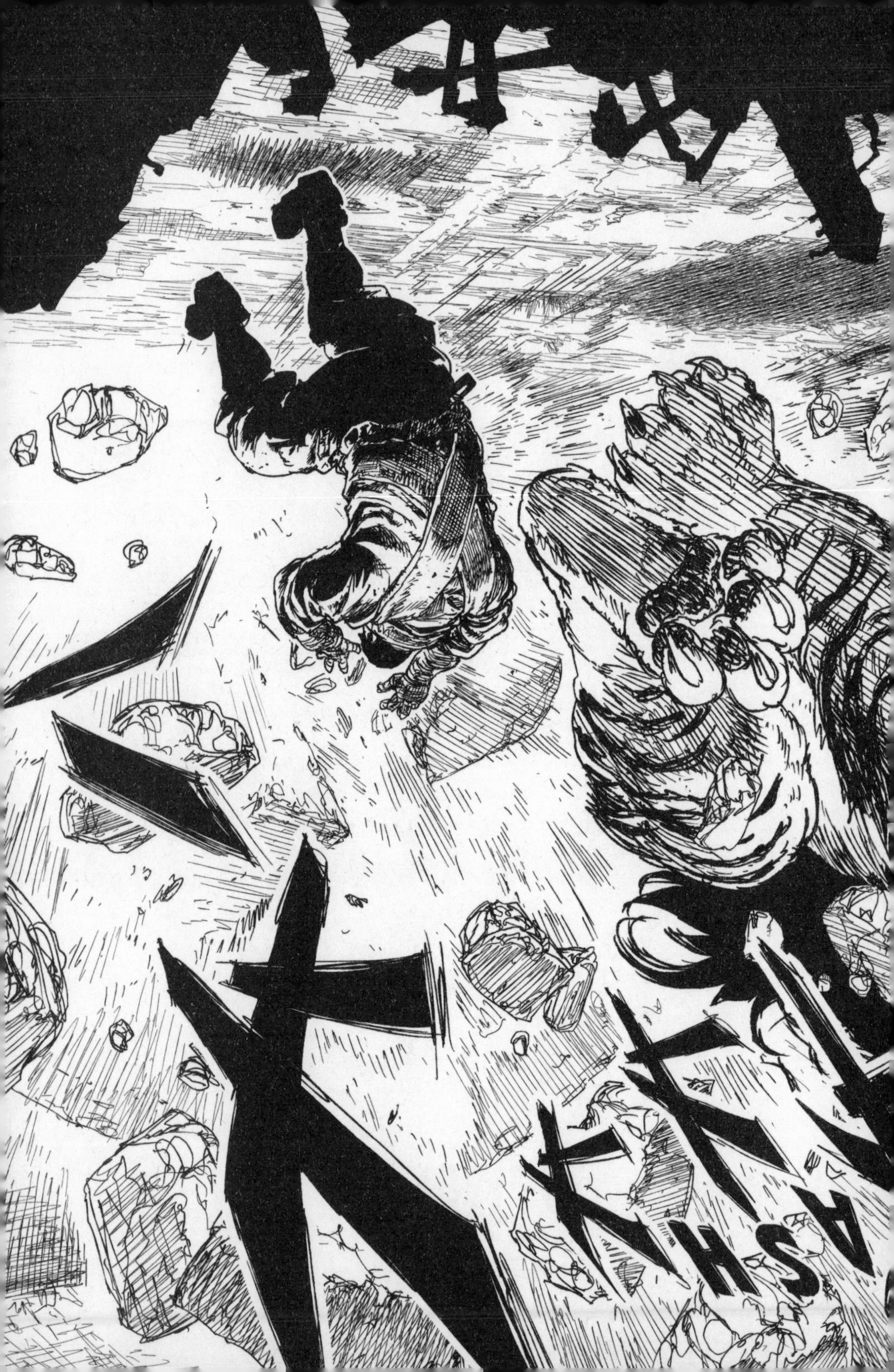

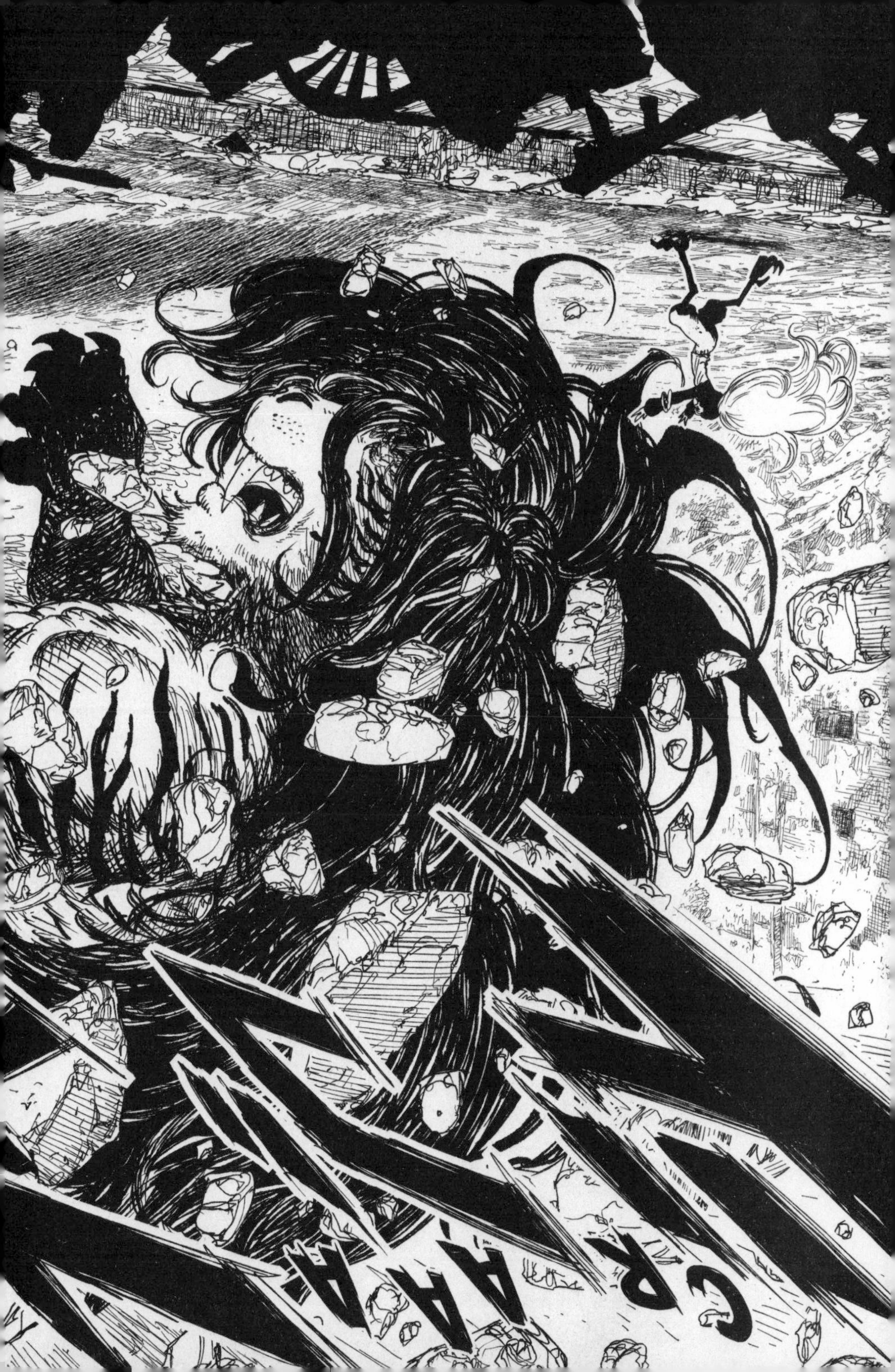
CRAAA

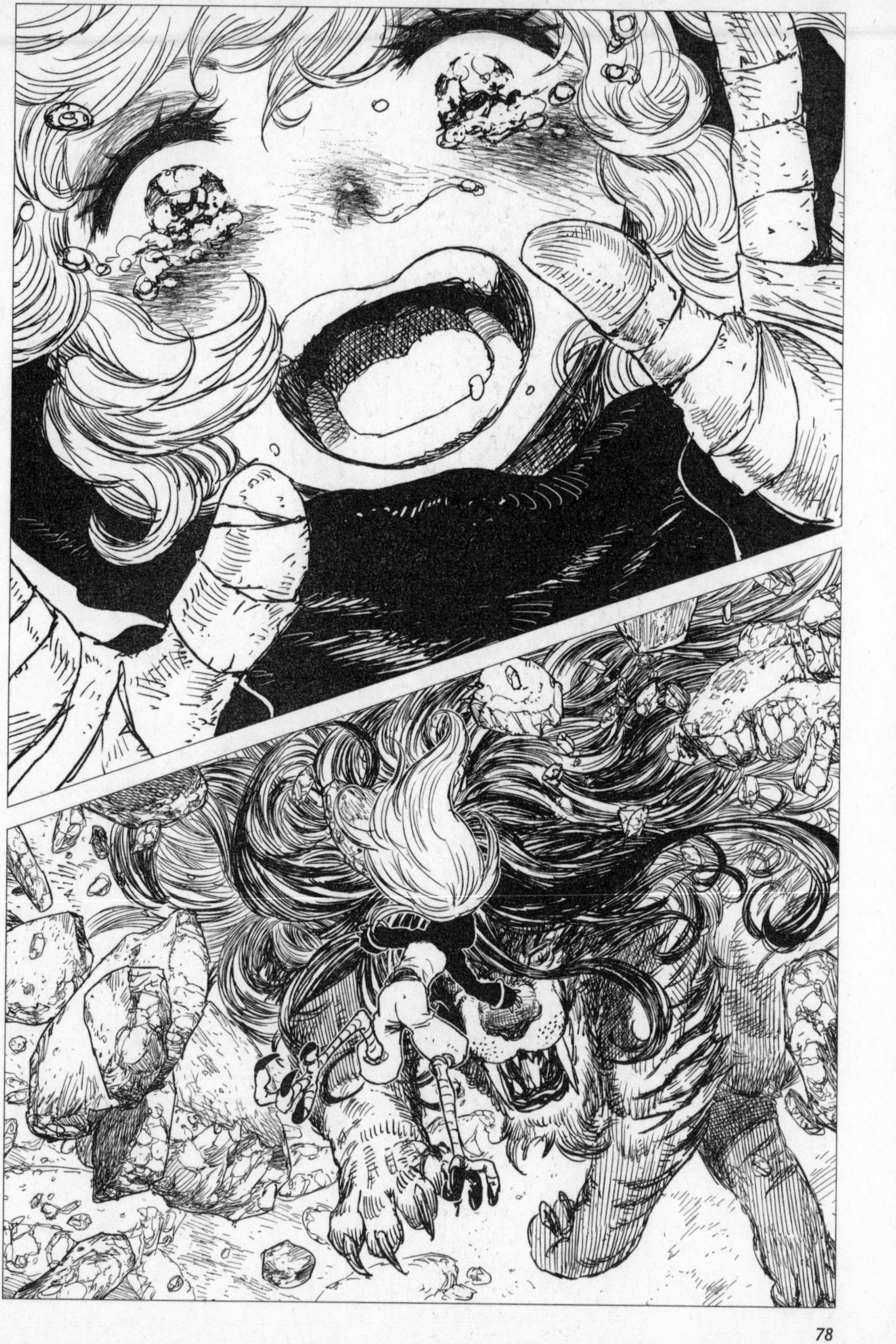

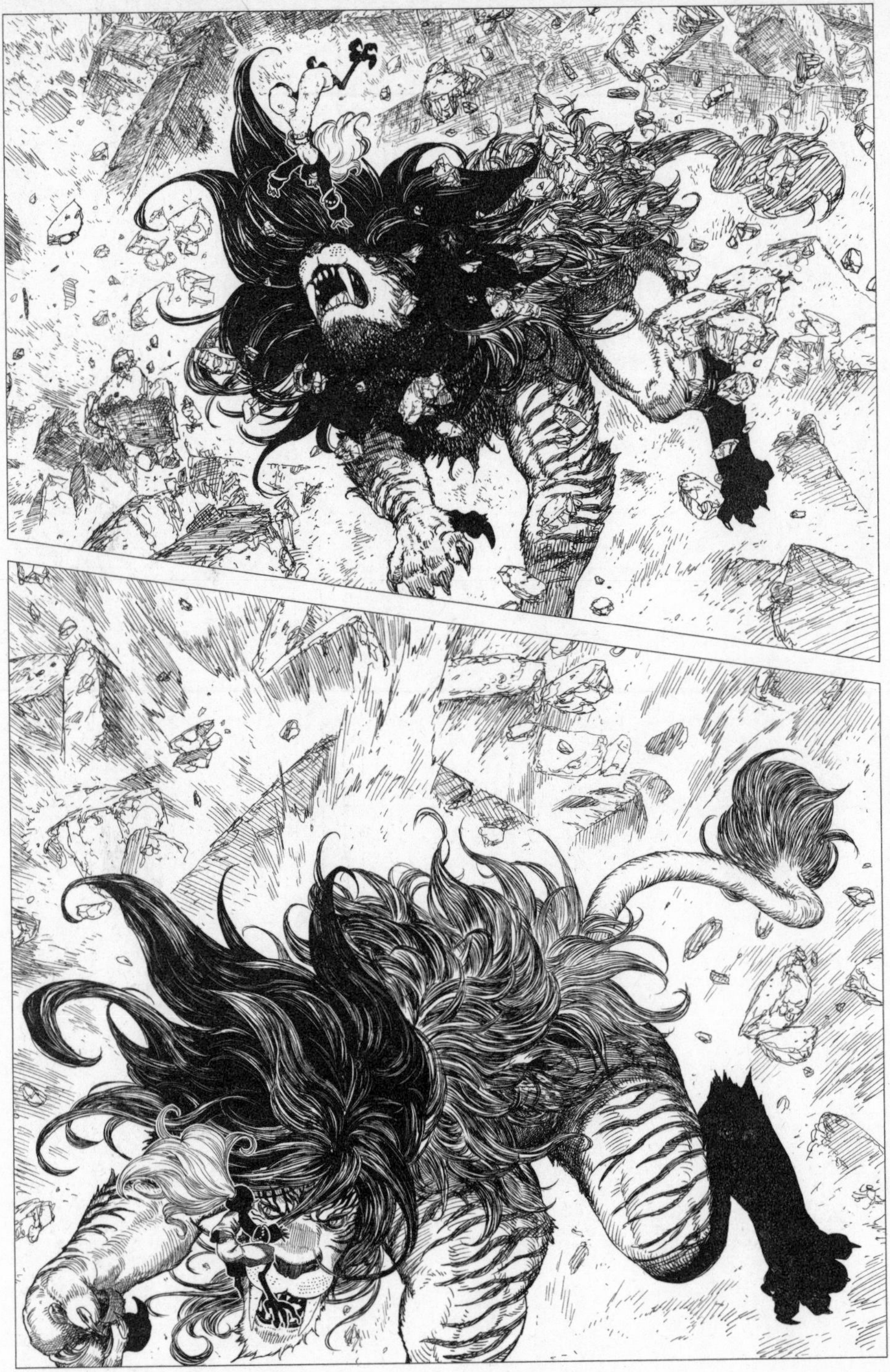

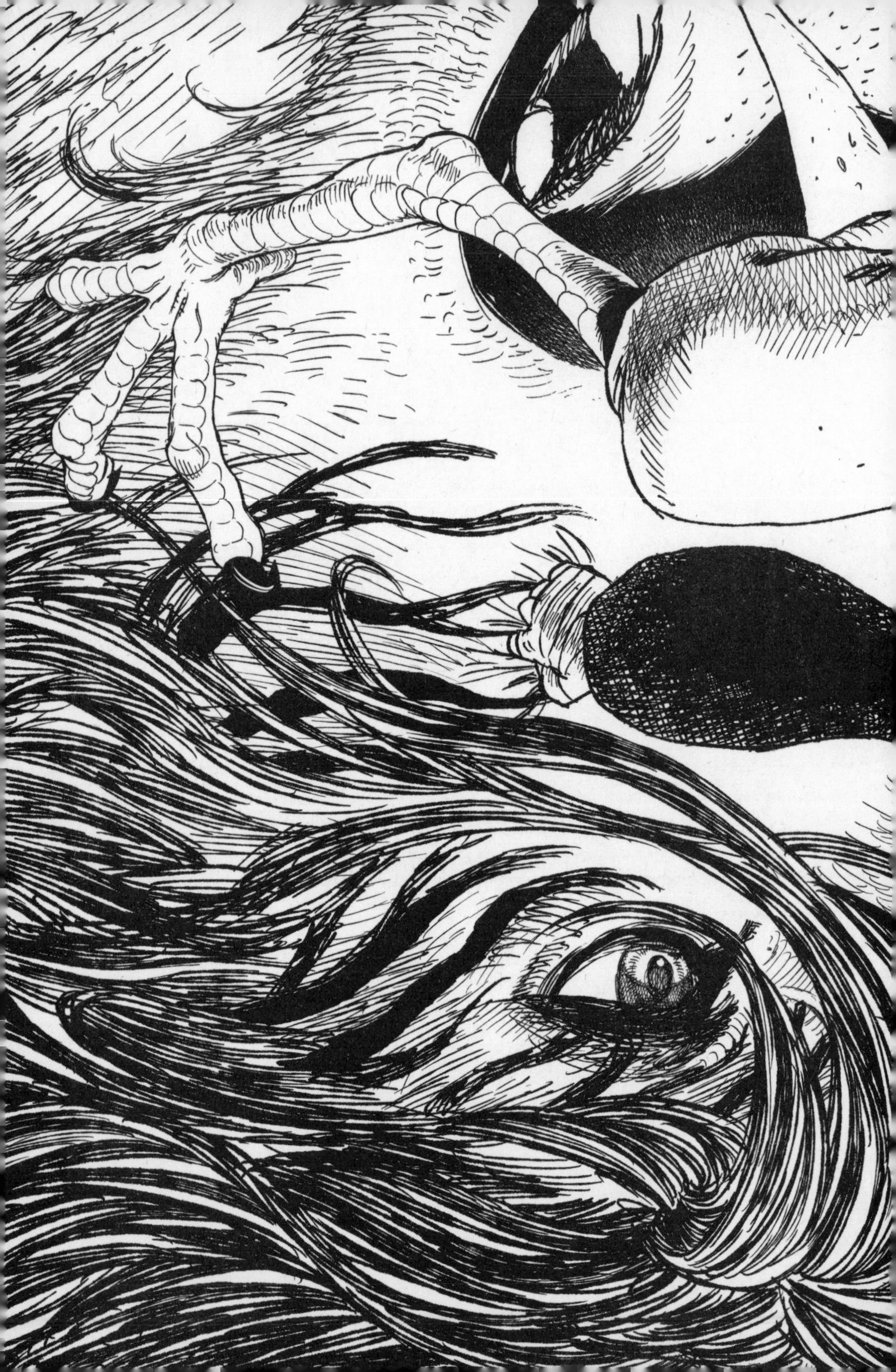

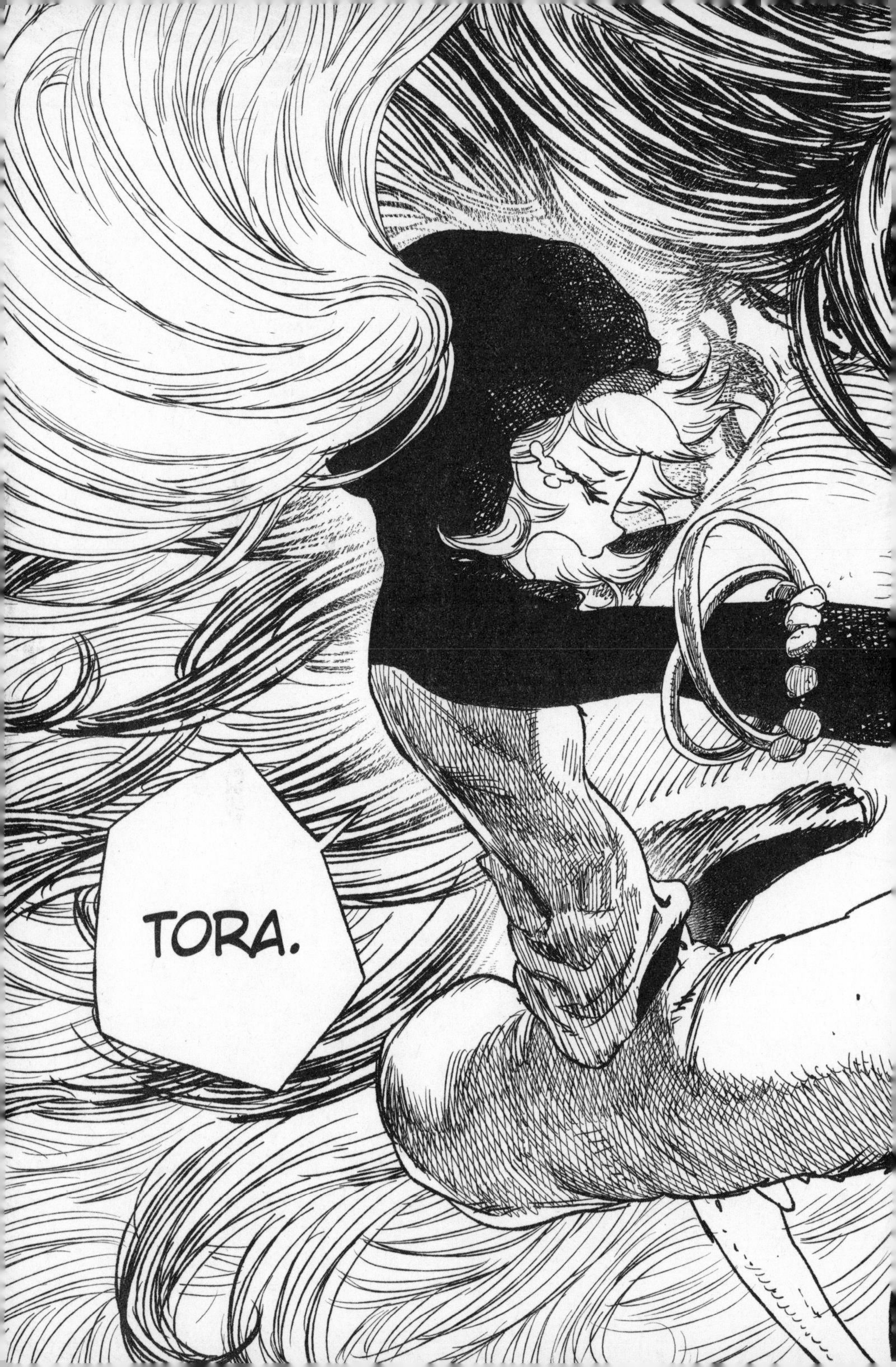
TORA.

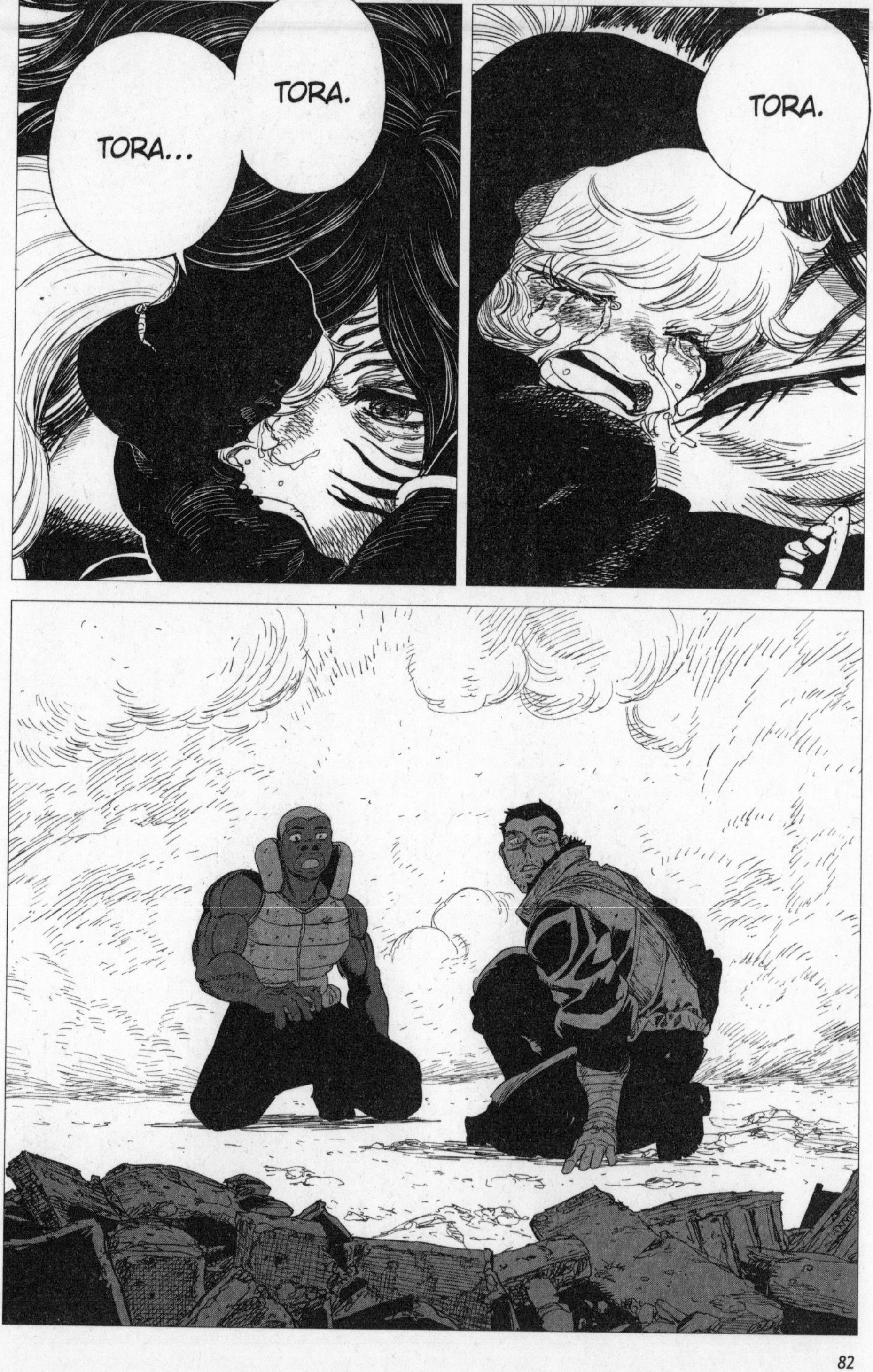
TORA.
TORA.
TORA...

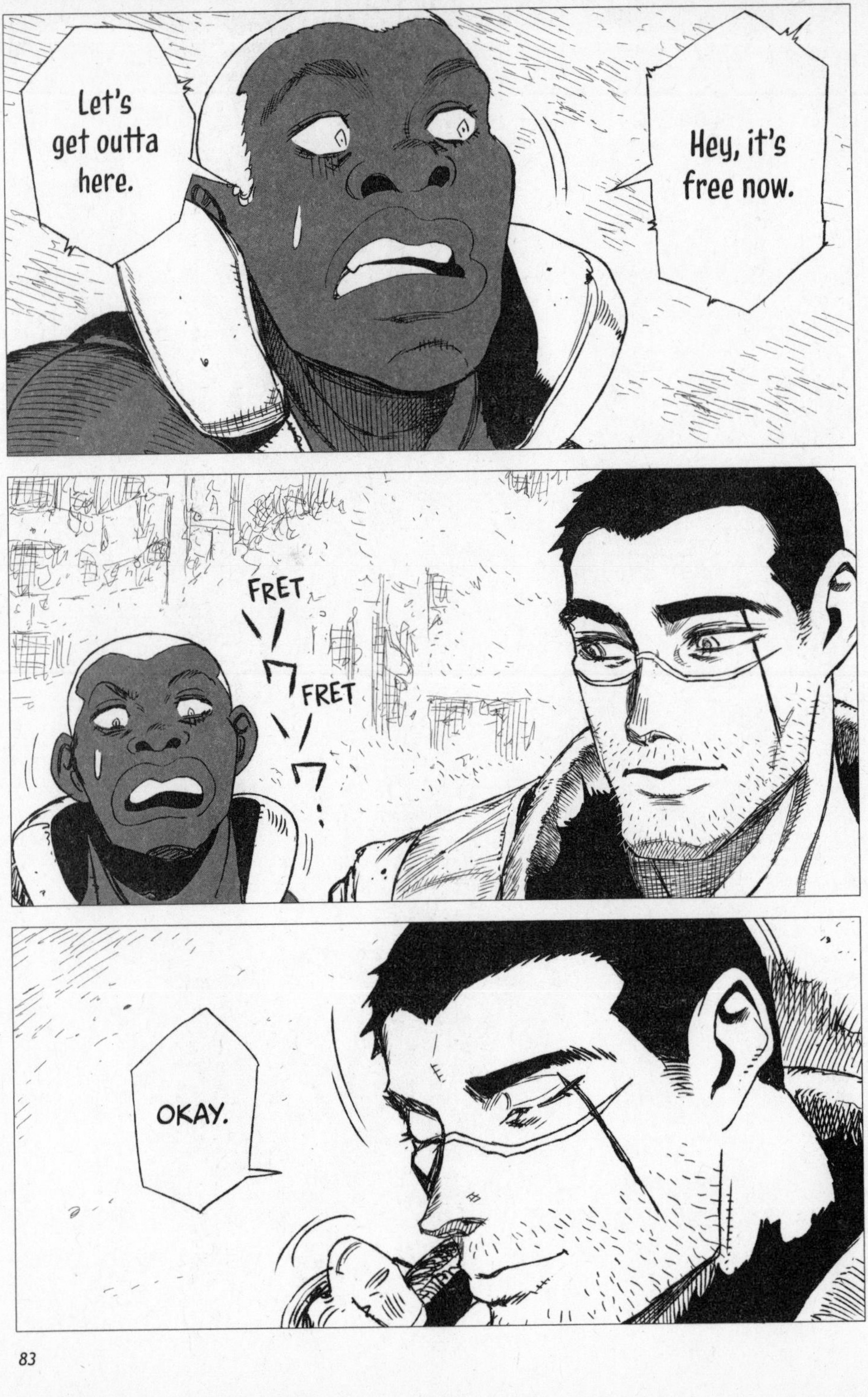
Hey, it's free now.
Let's get outta here.
FRET FRET
OKAY.

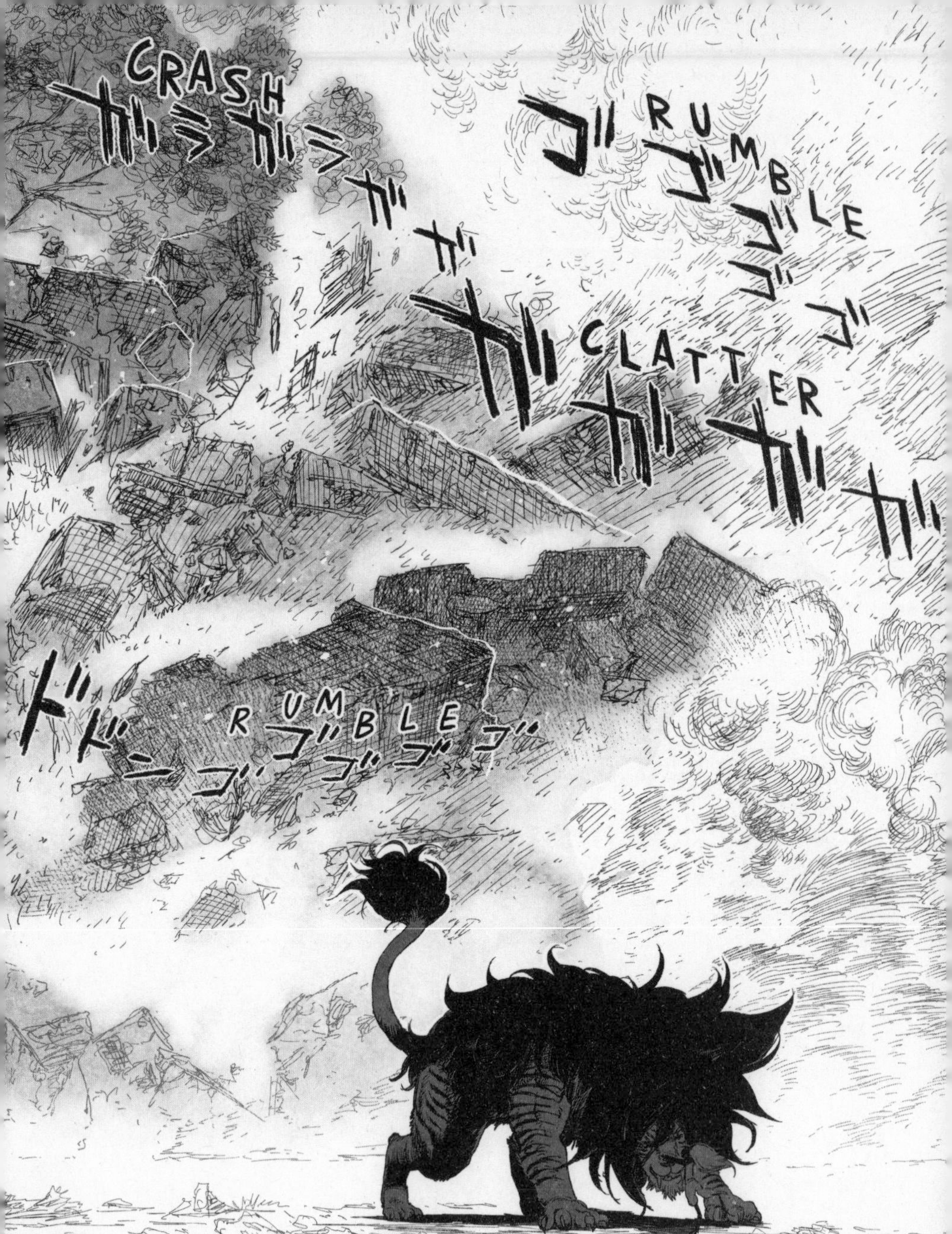
RUMBLE
ゴゴゴゴ
CLATTER
ガガガガ
CRASH
ガラガラ
RUMBLE
ドドーンゴゴゴゴ

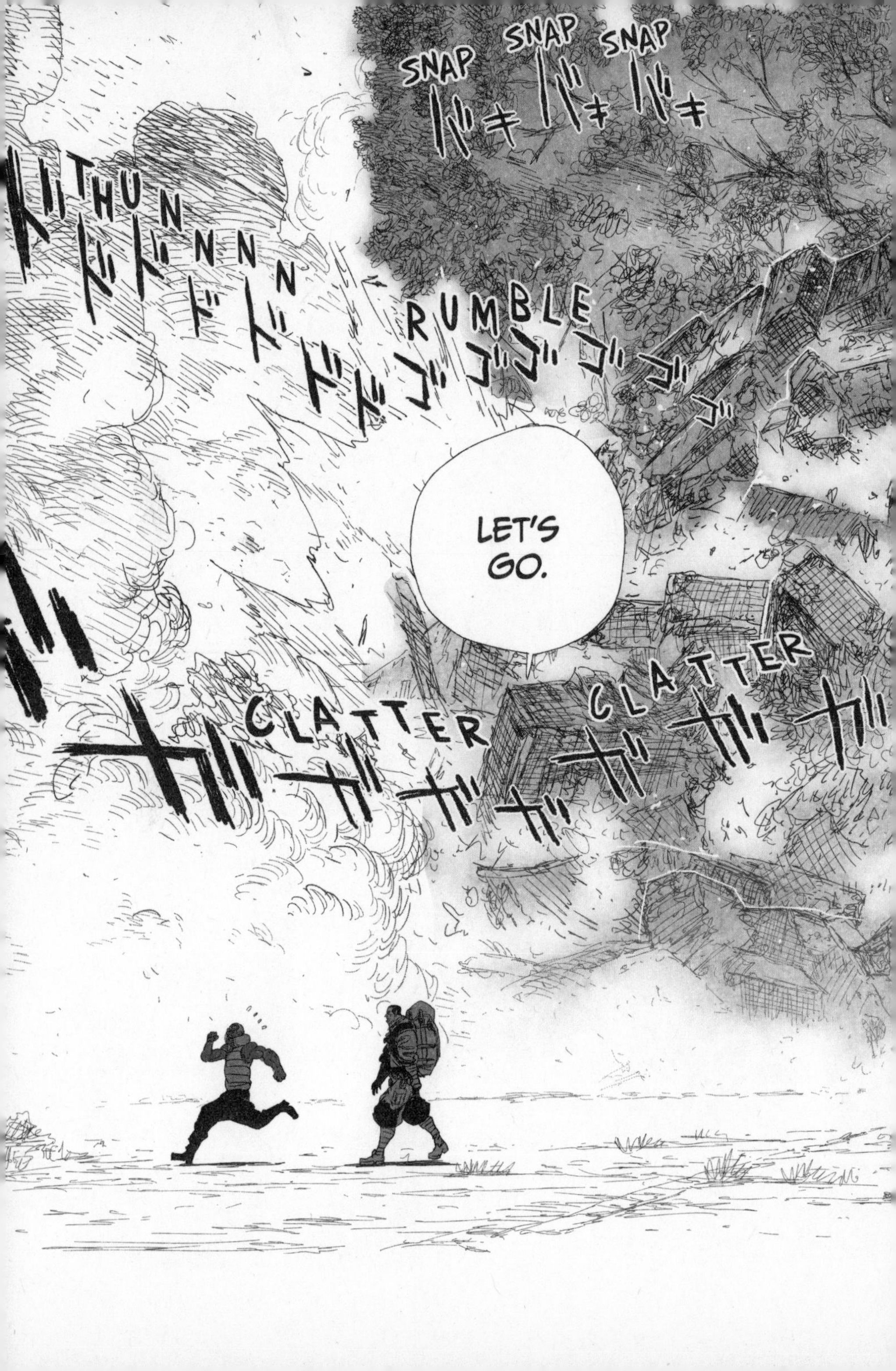
SNAP SNAP SNAP
バキバキバキ
THUNNNN
ドドドドド
RUMBLE
ドドゴゴゴゴ
LET'S GO.
CLATTER CLATTER
ガガガガガ

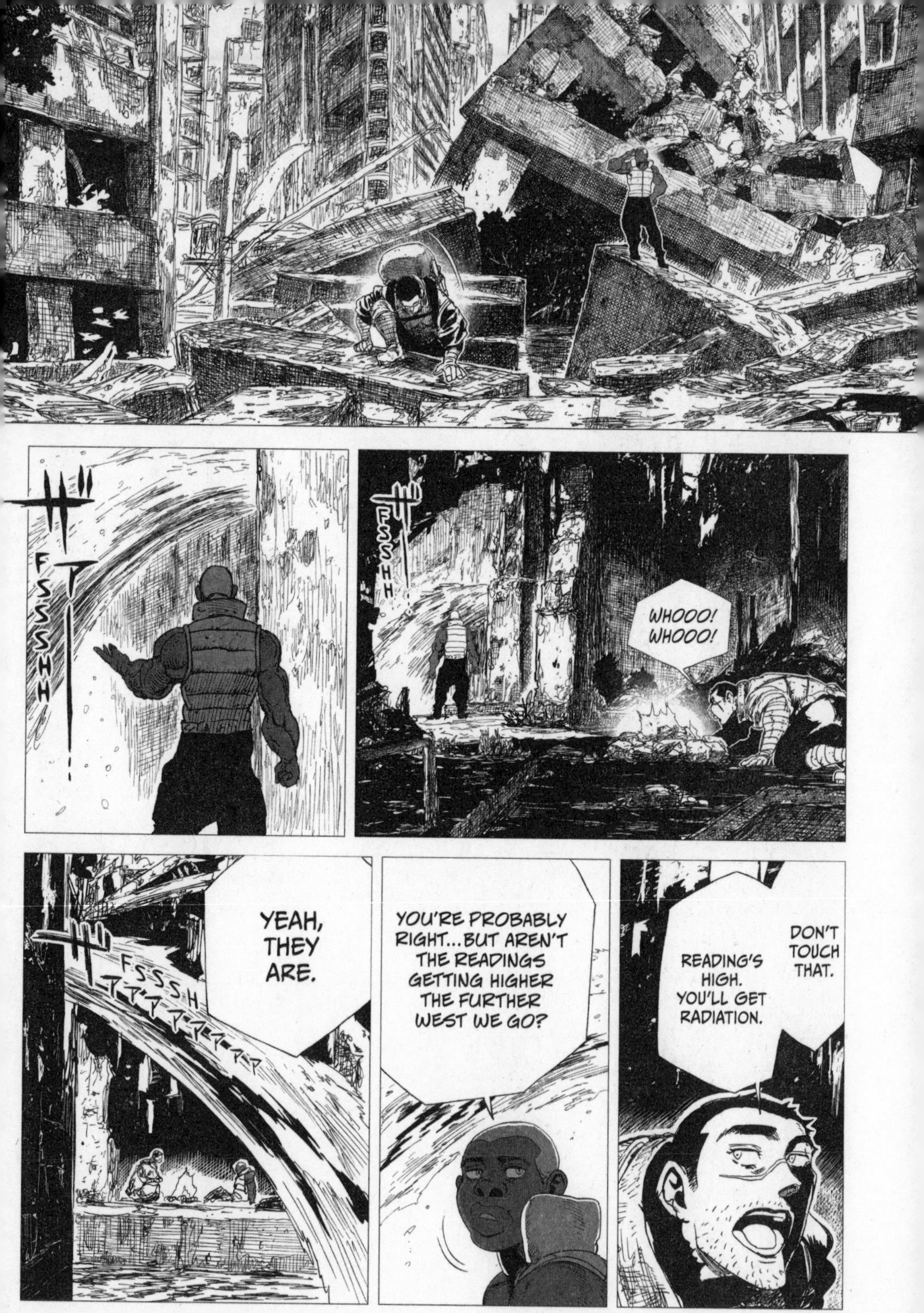
WHOOO! WHOOO!
FSSHH
FSSSHH
DON'T TOUCH THAT.
READING'S HIGH. YOU'LL GET RADIATION.
YOU'RE PROBABLY RIGHT...BUT AREN'T THE READINGS GETTING HIGHER THE FURTHER WEST WE GO?
YEAH, THEY ARE.
FSSSH

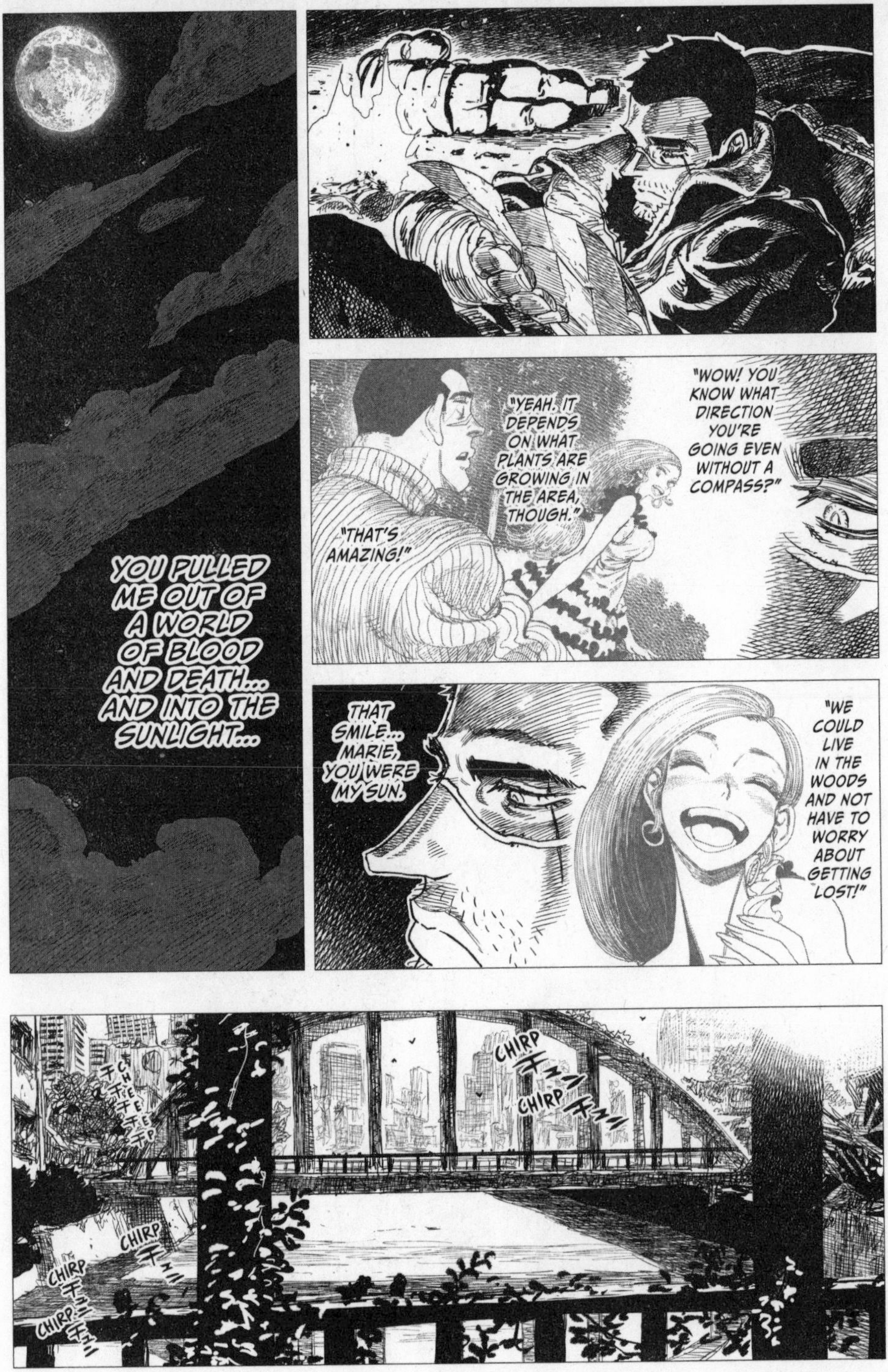
"WOW! YOU KNOW WHAT DIRECTION YOU'RE GOING EVEN WITHOUT A COMPASS?"
"YEAH. IT DEPENDS ON WHAT PLANTS ARE GROWING IN THE AREA, THOUGH."
"THAT'S AMAZING!"
"WE COULD LIVE IN THE WOODS AND NOT HAVE TO WORRY ABOUT GETTING LOST!"
THAT SMILE... MARIE, YOU WERE MY SUN.
YOU PULLED ME OUT OF A WORLD OF BLOOD AND DEATH... AND INTO THE SUNLIGHT...
CHIRP CHIRP
CHEEP
CHIRP
CHIRP
CHIRP

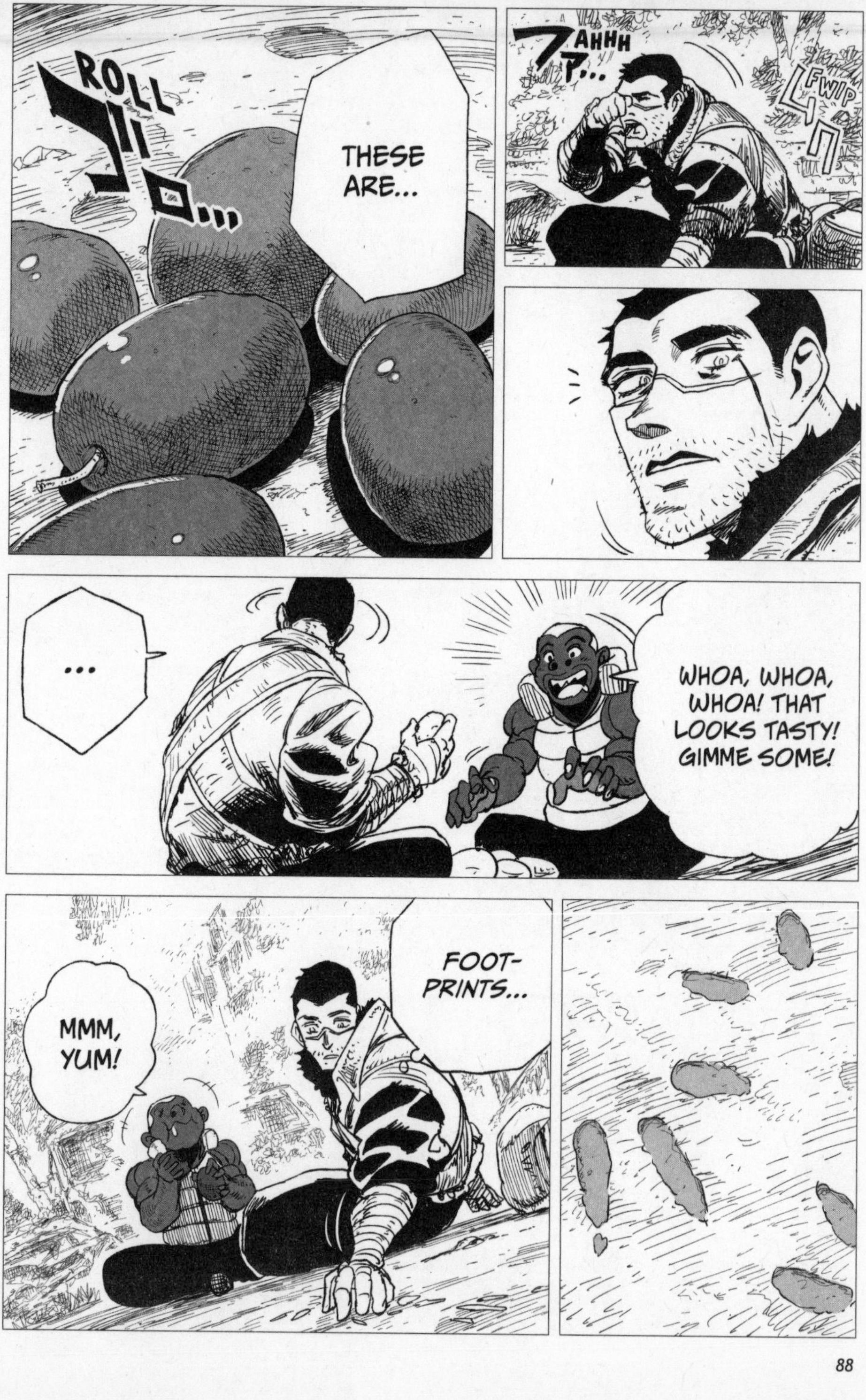
AHHH
FWIP
ROLL
THESE ARE...
...
WHOA, WHOA, WHOA! THAT LOOKS TASTY! GIMME SOME!
FOOT-PRINTS...
MMM, YUM!

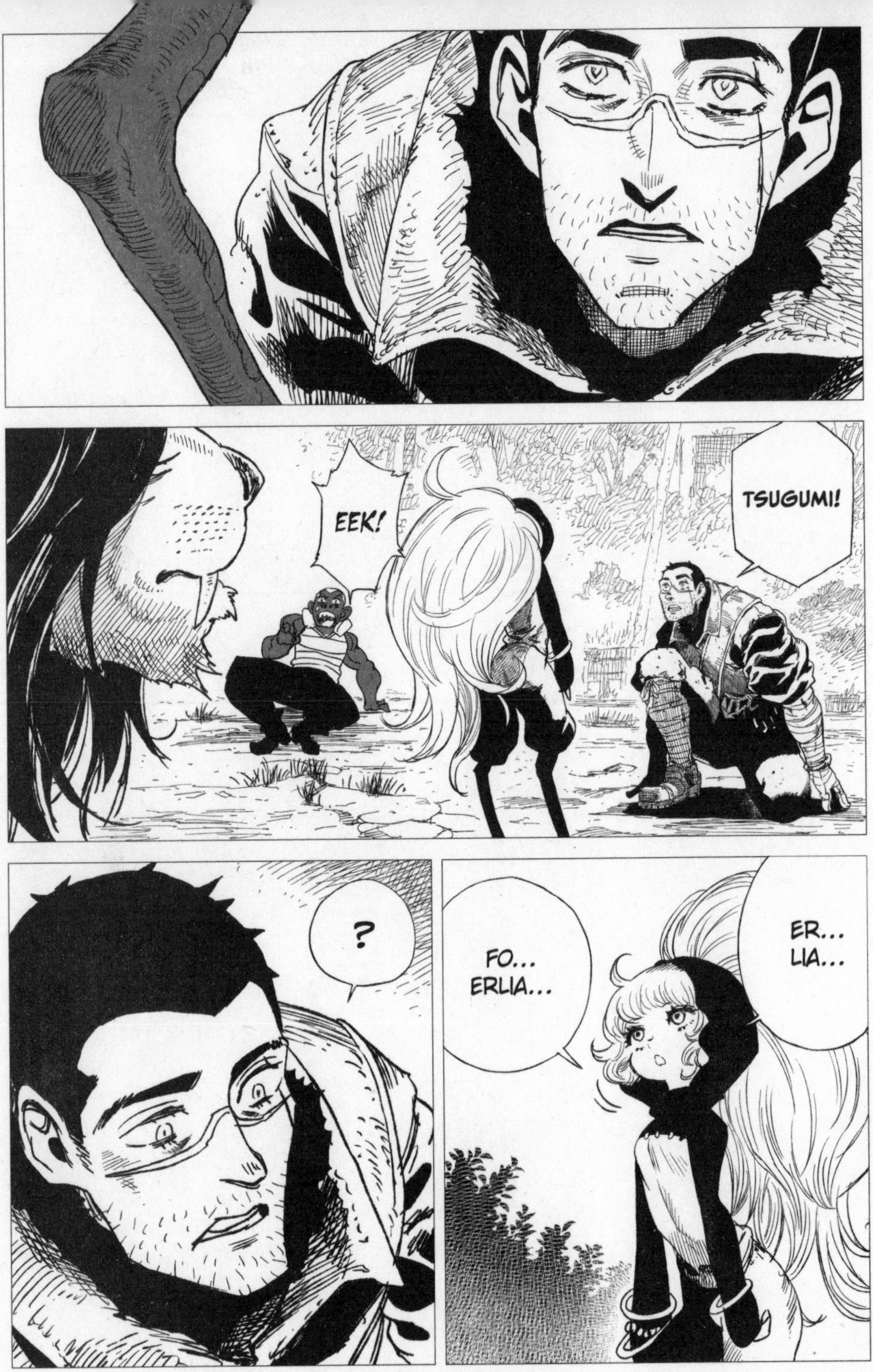
TSUGUMI!
EEK!
ER... LIA...
FO... ERLIA...
?

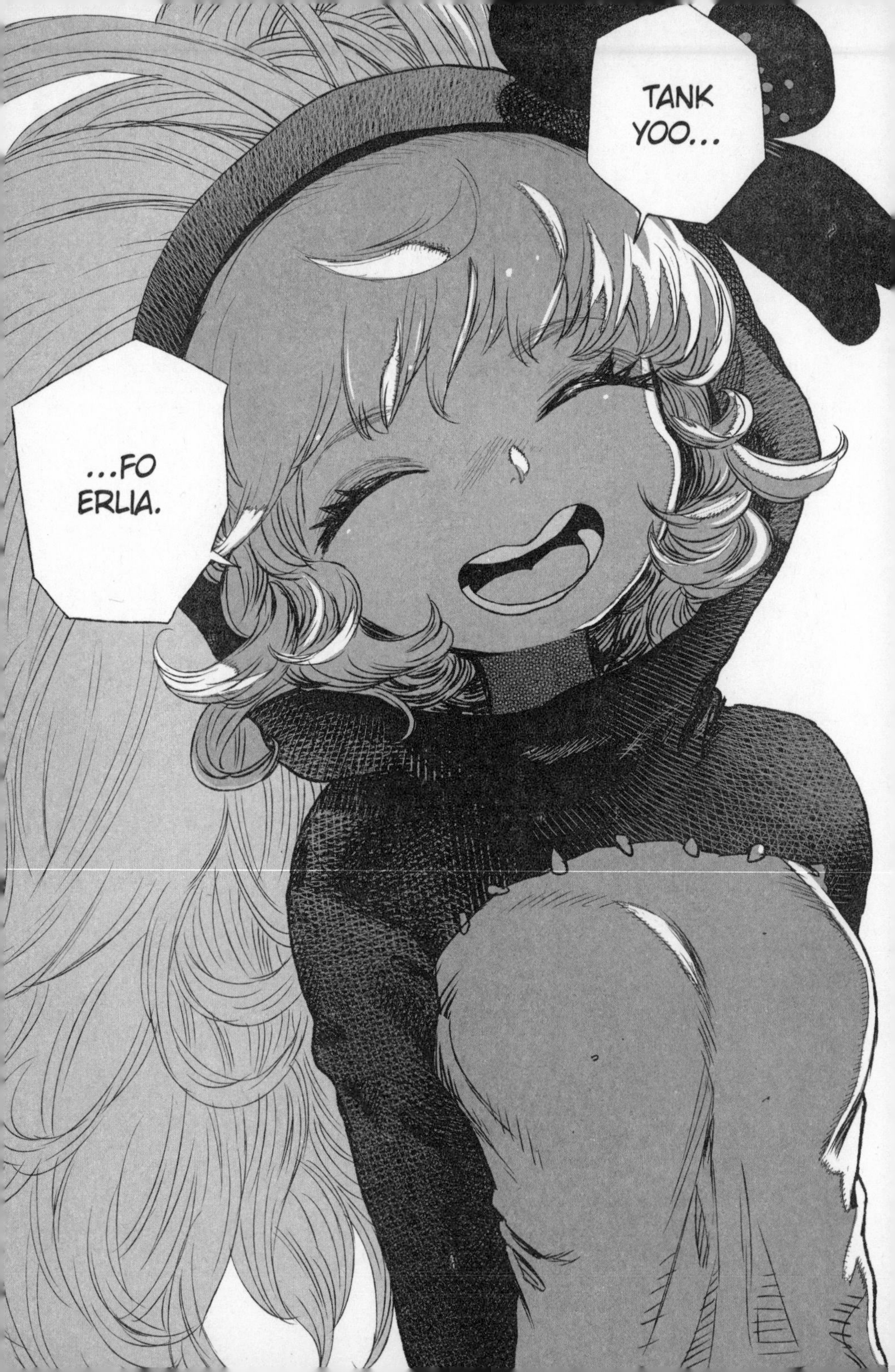
TANK YOO...
...FO ERLIA.

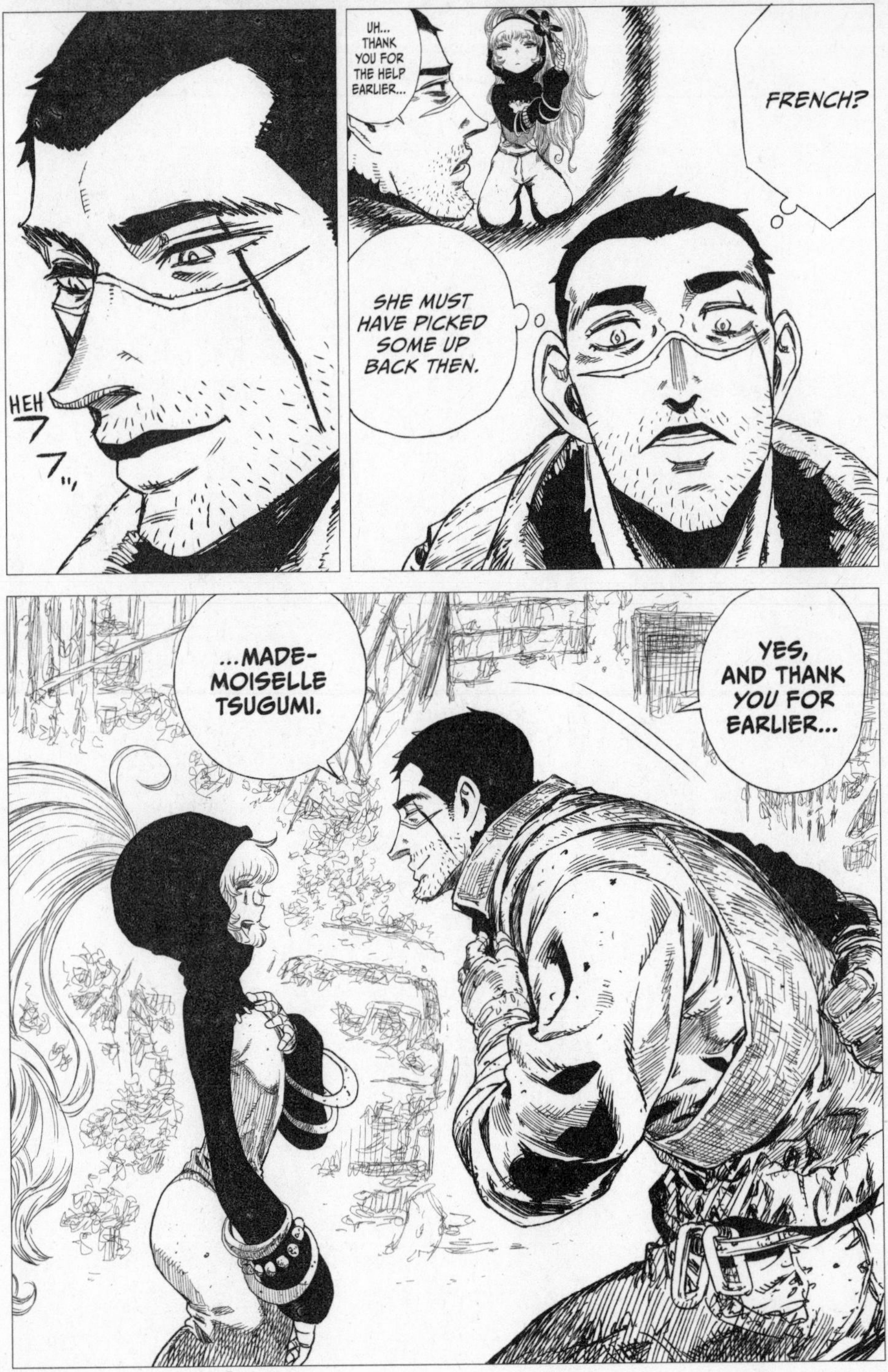
FRENCH?
UH... THANK YOU FOR THE HELP EARLIER...
SHE MUST HAVE PICKED SOME UP BACK THEN.
HEH
YES, AND THANK YOU FOR EARLIER...
...MADE-MOISELLE TSUGUMI.

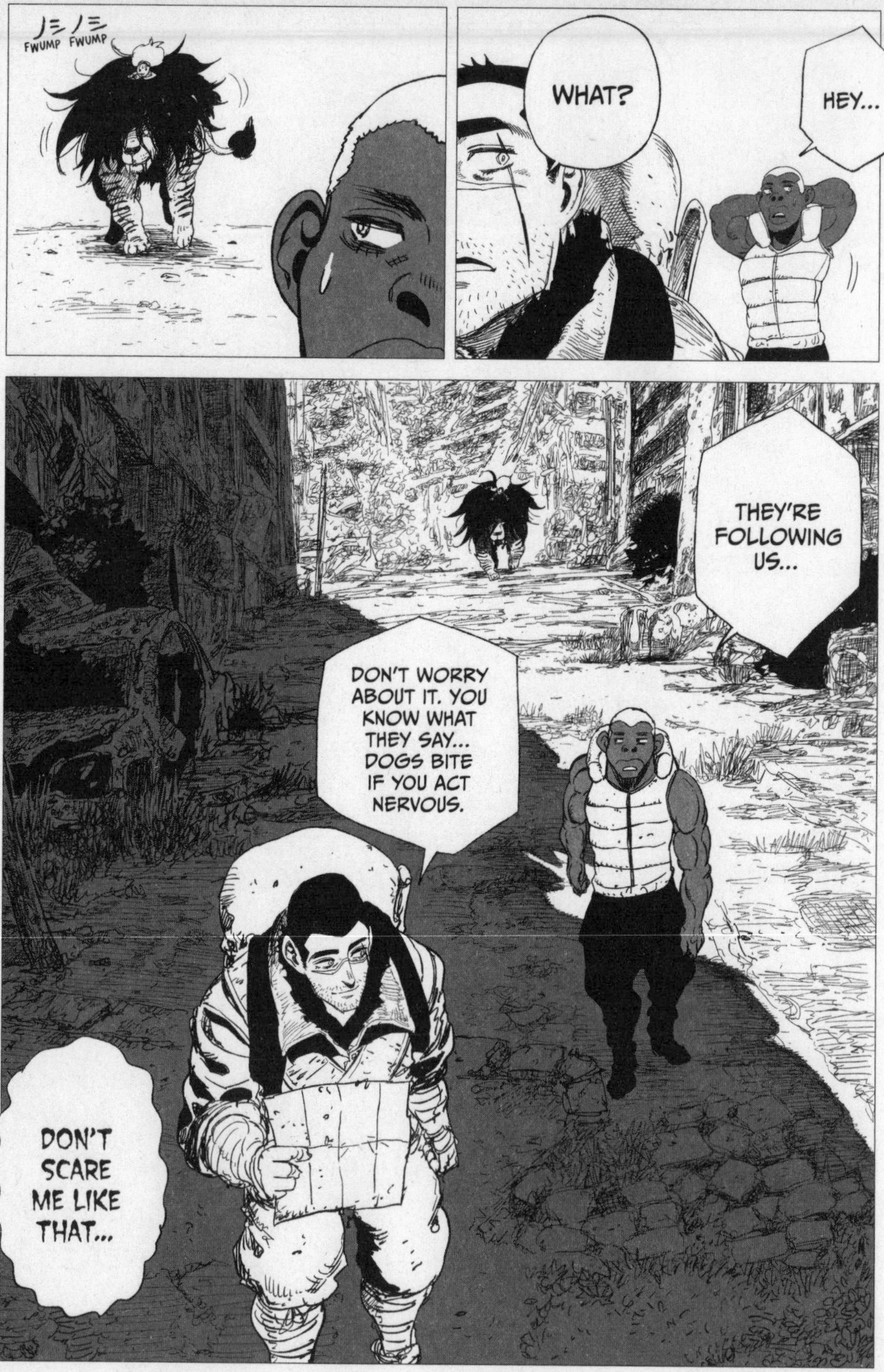
HEY...
WHAT?
ノミノミ
FWUMP FWUMP
THEY'RE FOLLOWING US...
DON'T WORRY ABOUT IT. YOU KNOW WHAT THEY SAY... DOGS BITE IF YOU ACT NERVOUS.
DON'T SCARE ME LIKE THAT...

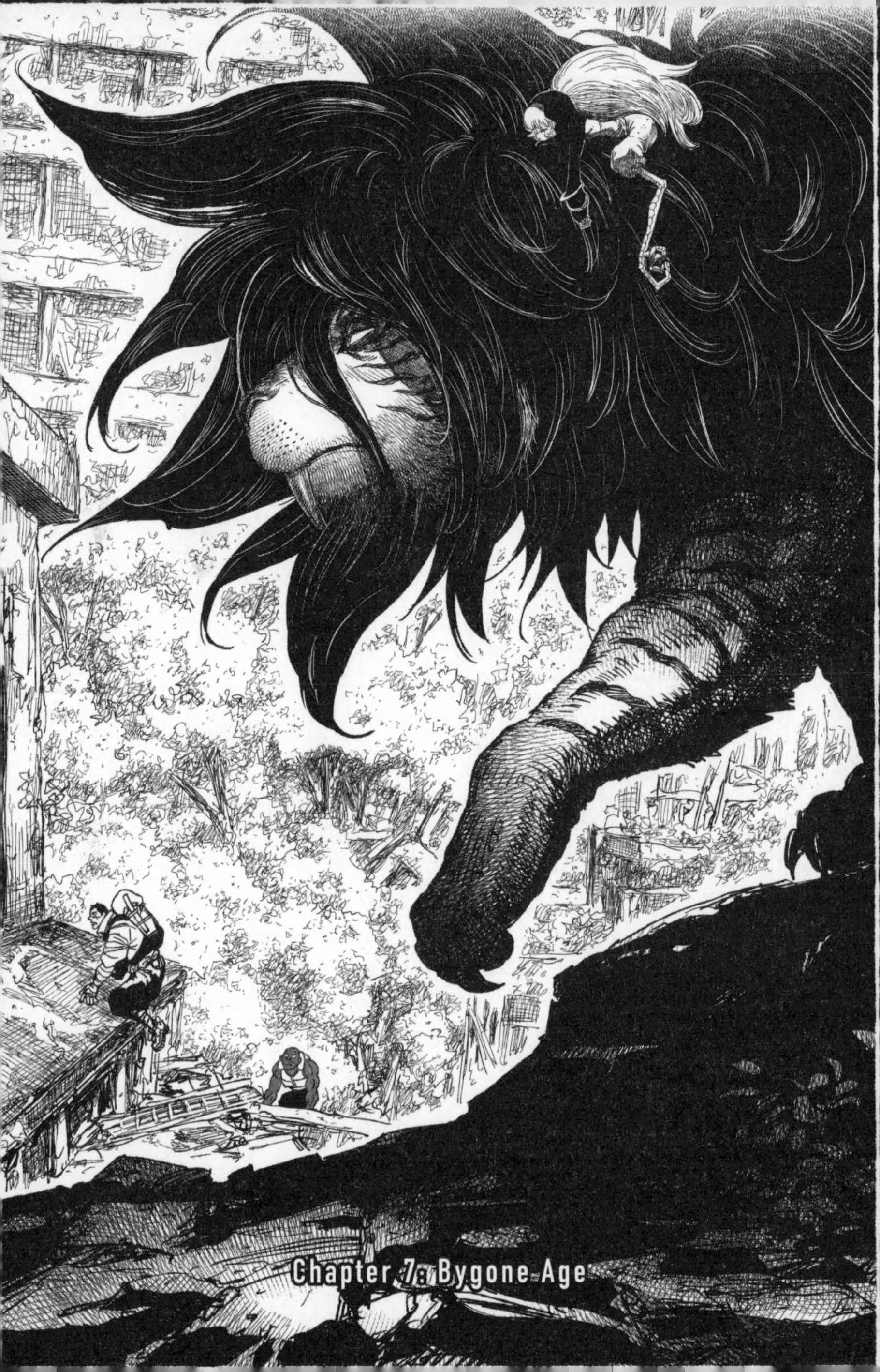
Chapter 7: Bygone Age

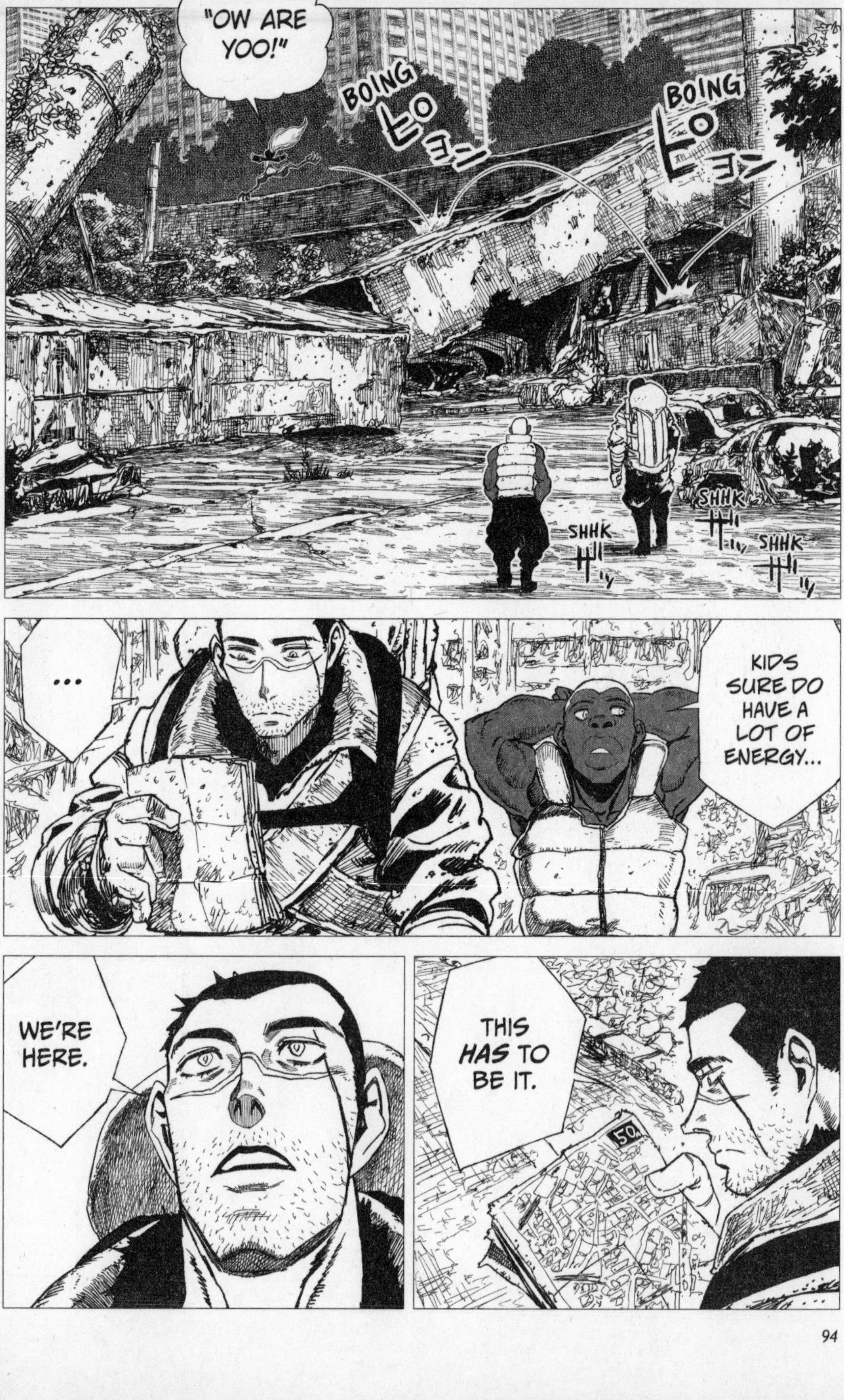
"OW ARE YOO!"
BOING
BOING
SHHK
SHHK
SHHK
KIDS SURE DO HAVE A LOT OF ENERGY...
...
THIS HAS TO BE IT.
WE'RE HERE.

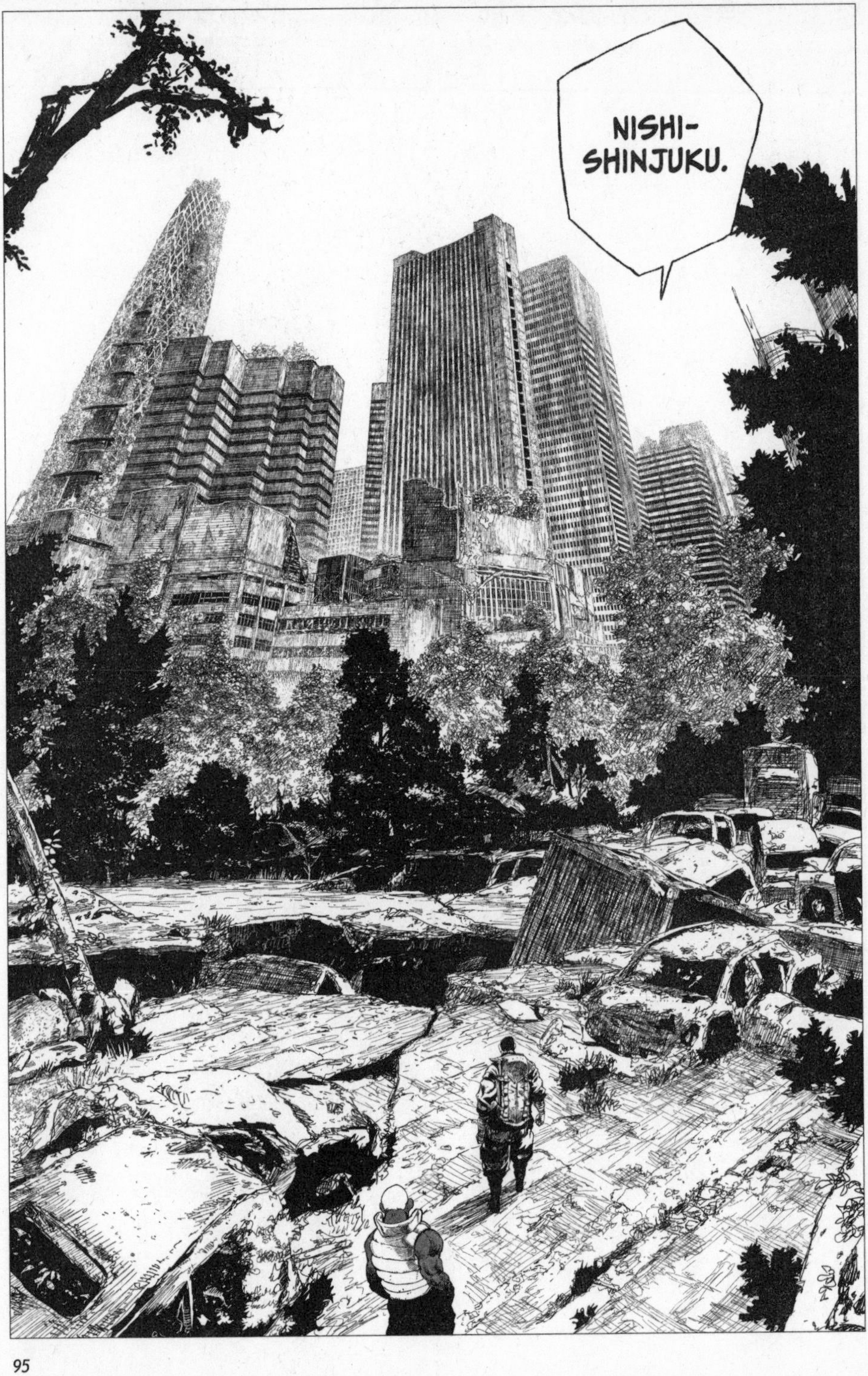
NISHI-SHINJUKU.

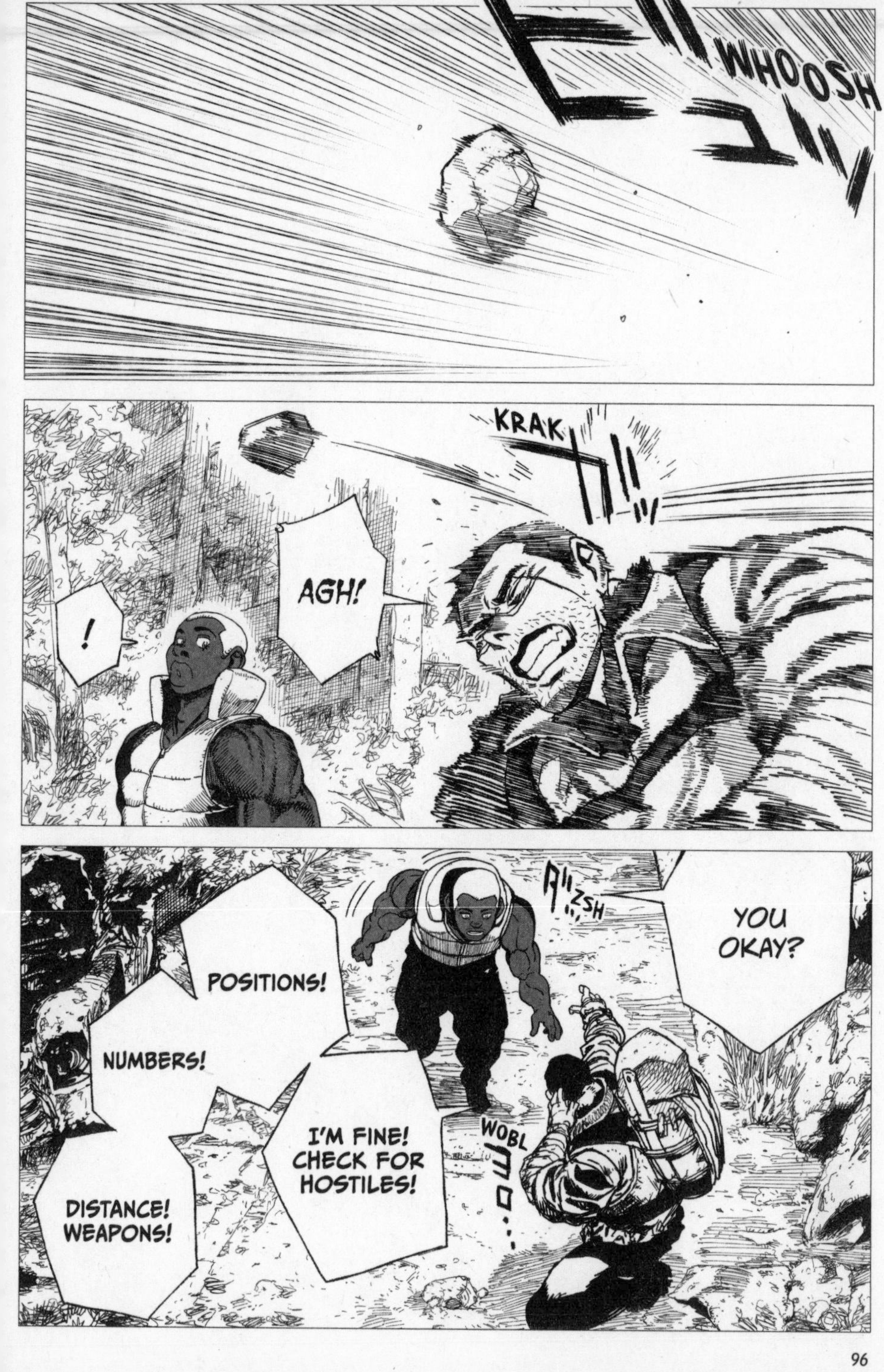
WHOOSH
KRAK
AGH!
!
YOU OKAY?
ZSH
WOBL
I'M FINE! CHECK FOR HOSTILES!
POSITIONS!
NUMBERS!
DISTANCE! WEAPONS!

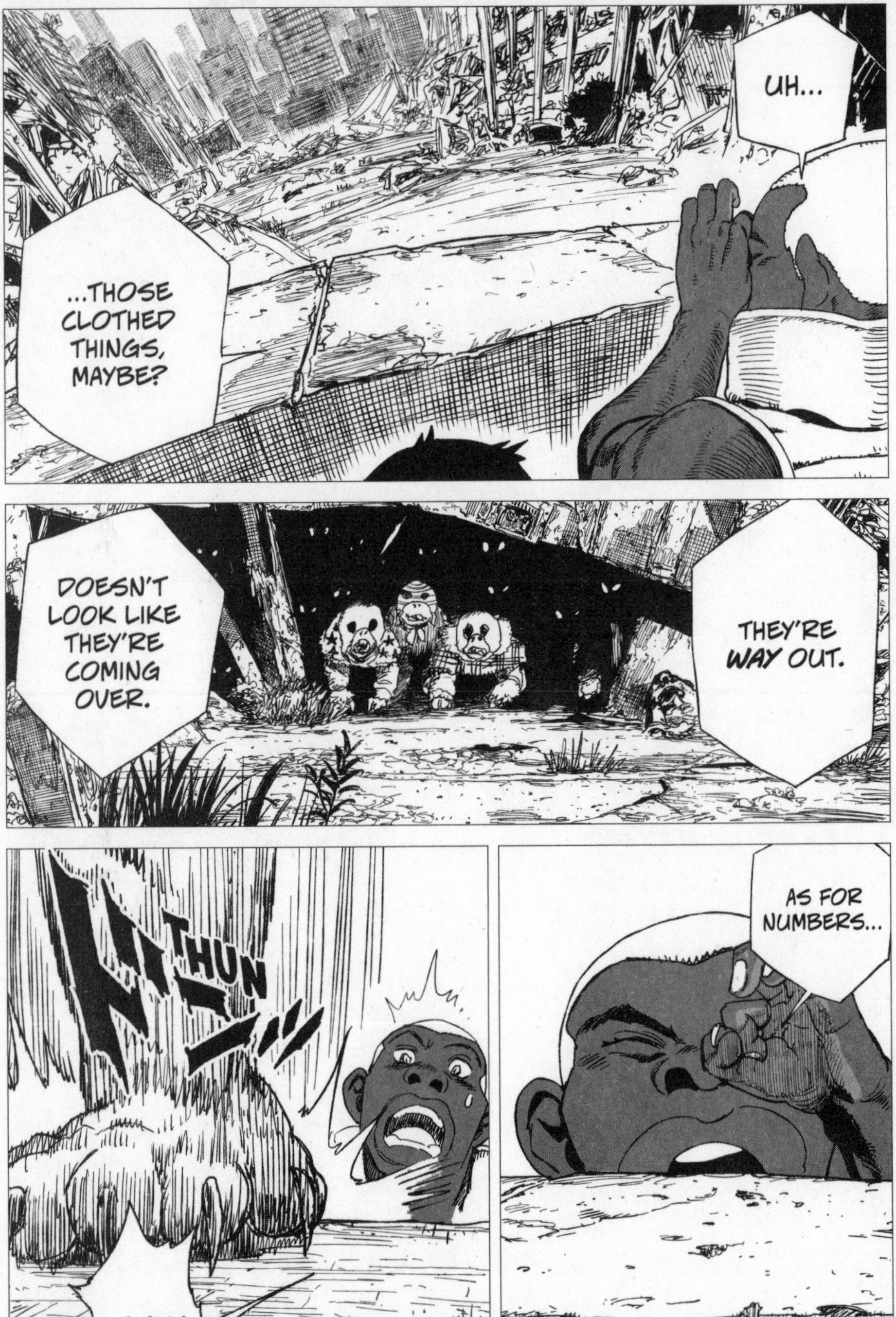
UH...
...THOSE CLOTHED THINGS, MAYBE?
THEY'RE WAY OUT.
DOESN'T LOOK LIKE THEY'RE COMING OVER.
AS FOR NUMBERS...
THUN
ACK!

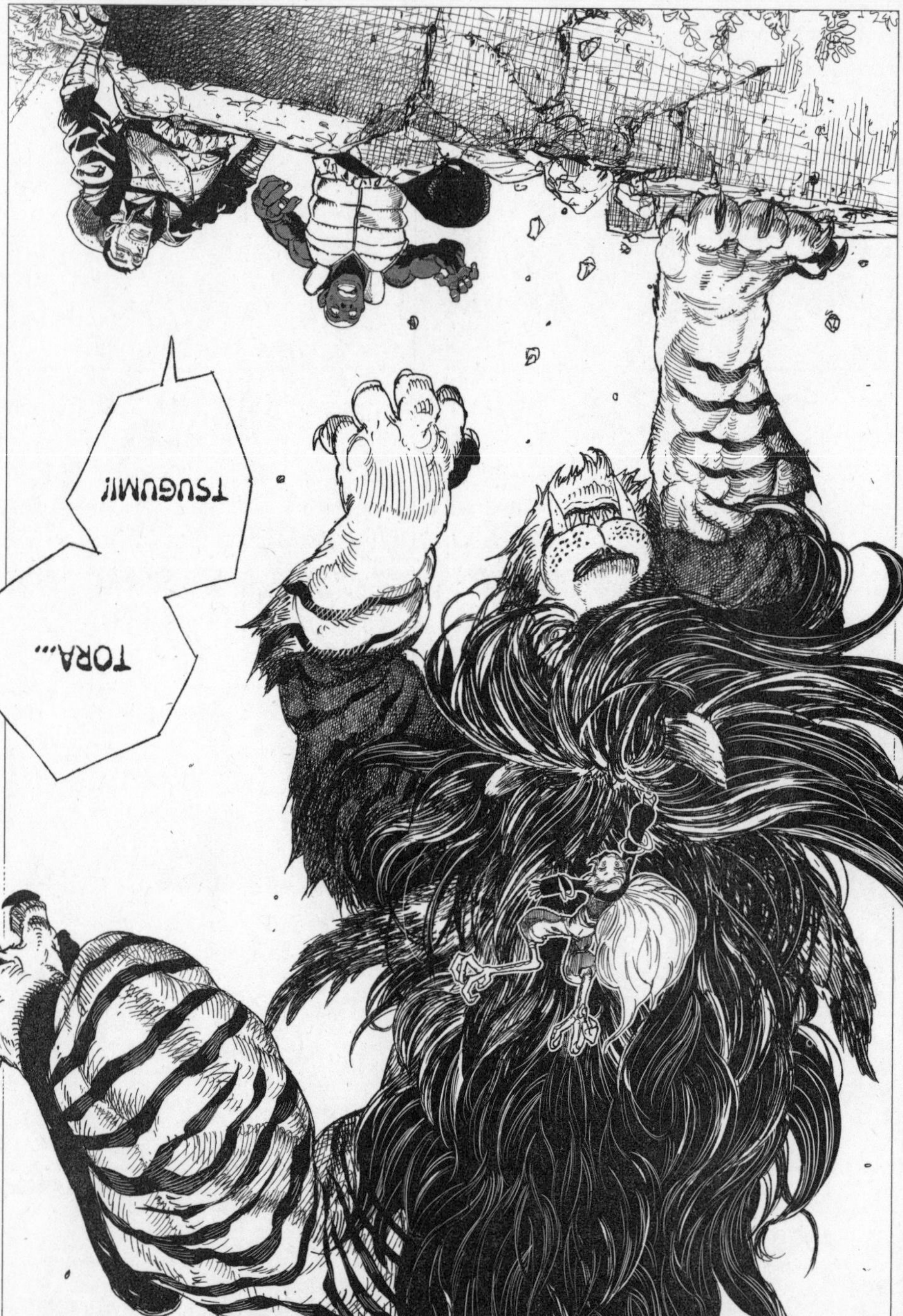
TORA...
TSUGUMI!!

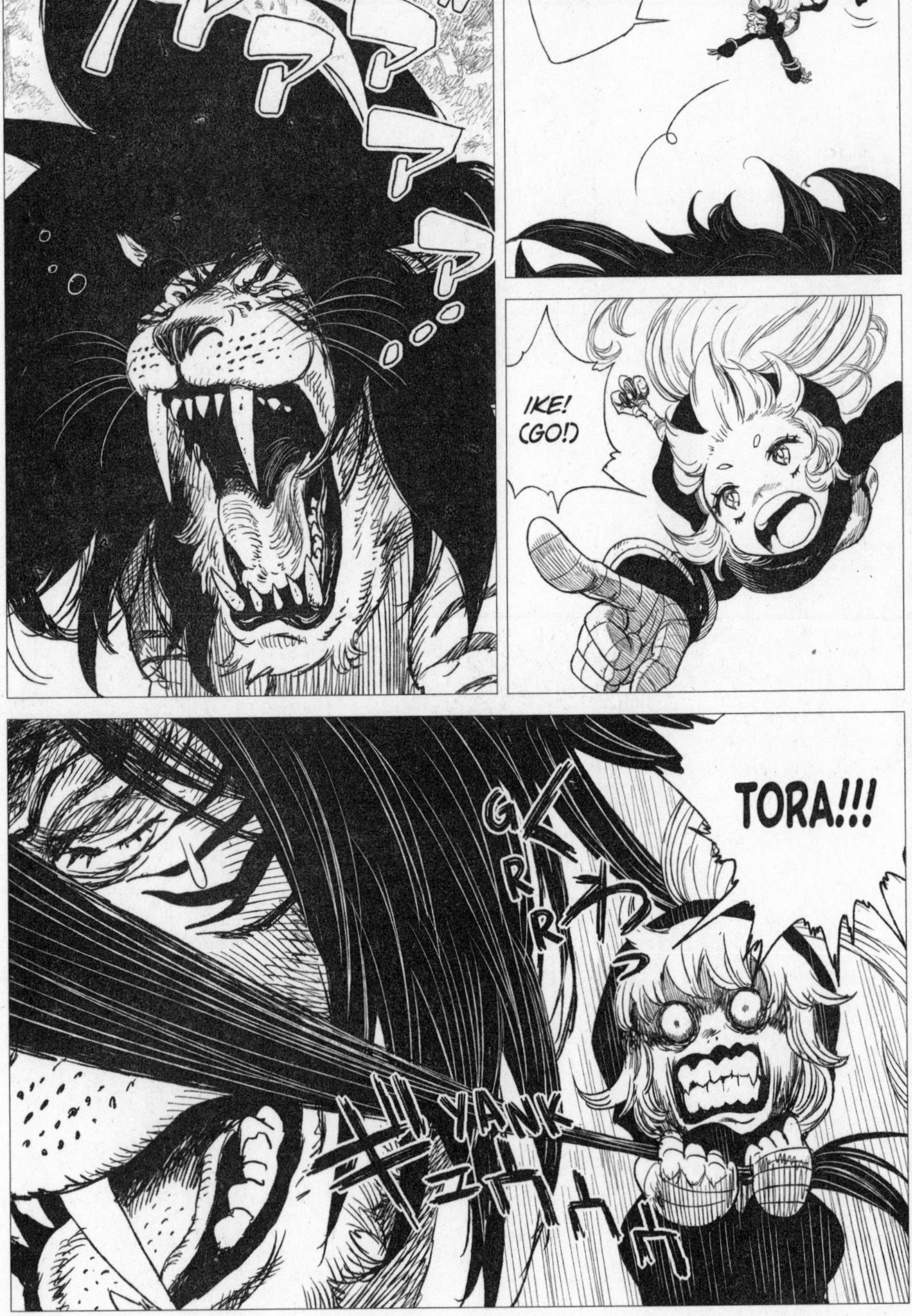
くるん
TWIRL
TORA!
IKE! (GO!)
YAAAWN
TORA!!!
GRRR
YANK

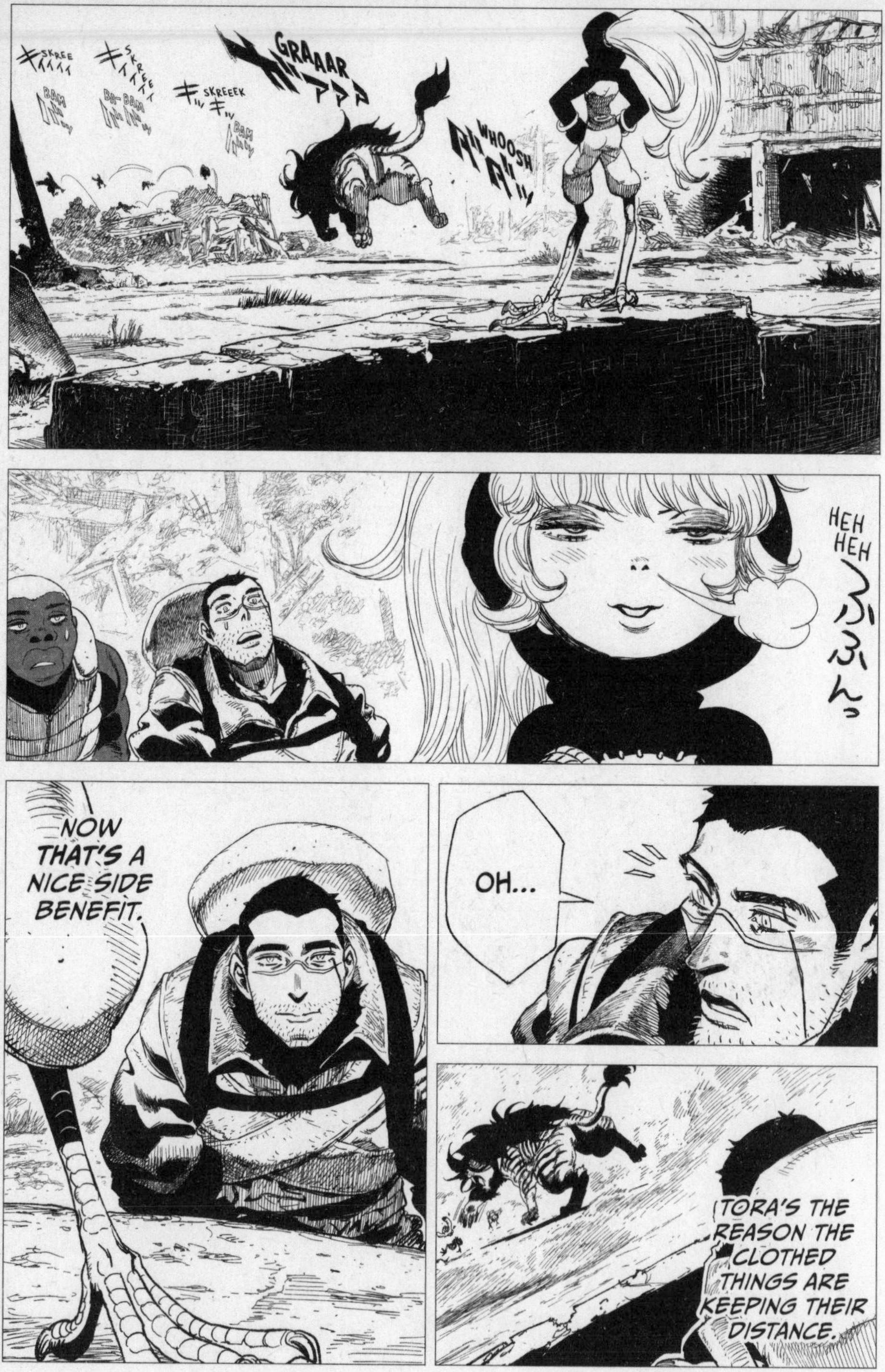

WHOOSH
GRAAAR
SKREEEK
BAM
SKREEE
BA-BAM
SKREE
BAM
HEH HEH
ふふんっ
OH...
TORA'S THE REASON THE CLOTHED THINGS ARE KEEPING THEIR DISTANCE.
NOW THAT'S A NICE SIDE BENEFIT.

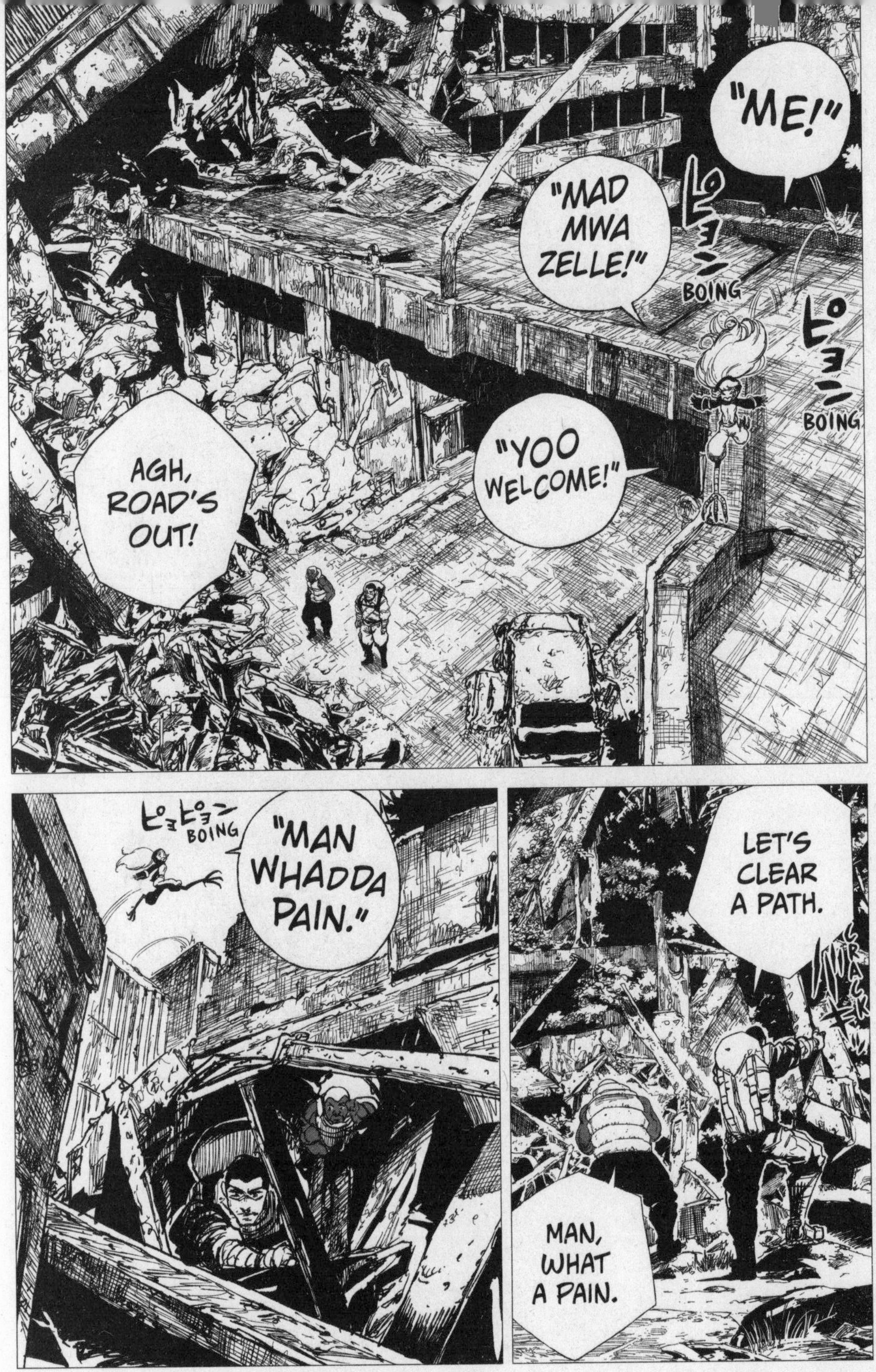
"ME!"
ピョン
BOING
"MAD MWA ZELLE!"
ピョン
BOING
"YOO WELCOME!"
AGH, ROAD'S OUT!
LET'S CLEAR A PATH.
CRACK
MAN, WHAT A PAIN.
ピョピョン
BOING
"MAN WHADDA PAIN."

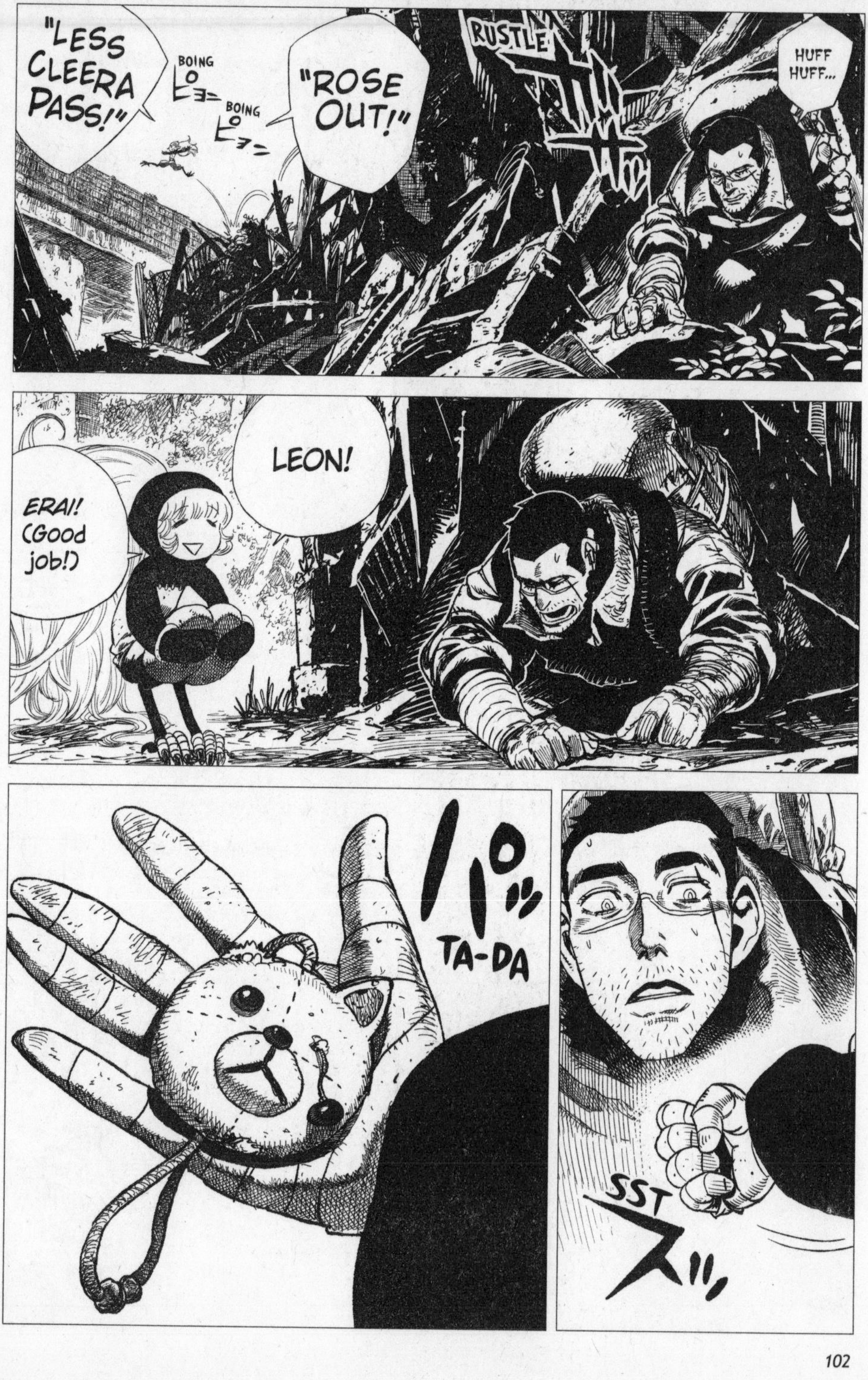
HUFF HUFF...
RUSTLE
"ROSE OUT!"
BOING
BOING
"LESS CLEERA PASS!"
LEON!
ERAI! (Good job!)
SST
TA-DA

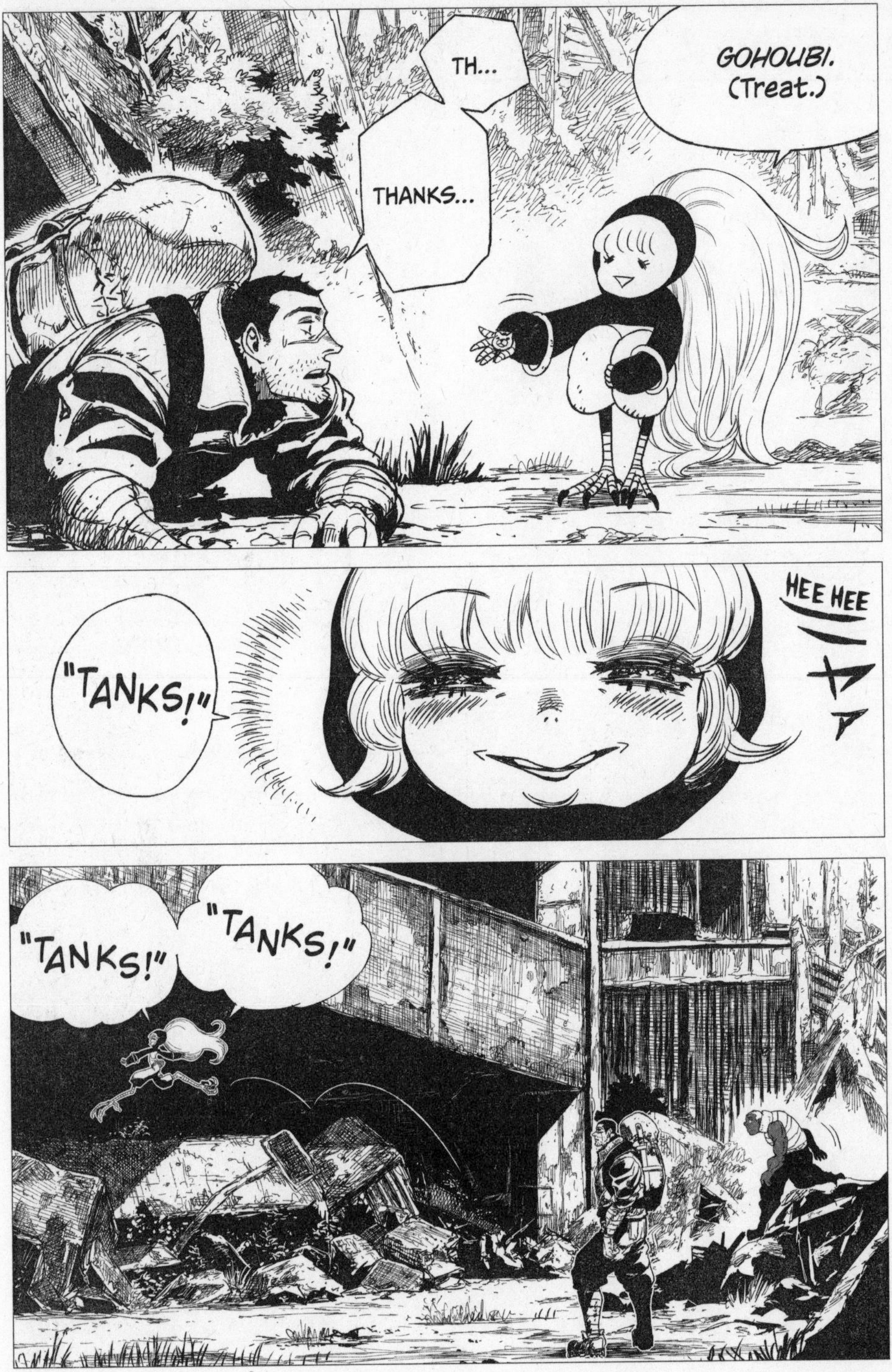
GOHOUBI. (Treat.)
TH...
THANKS...
HEE HEE
"TANKS!"
"TANKS!"
"TANKS!"

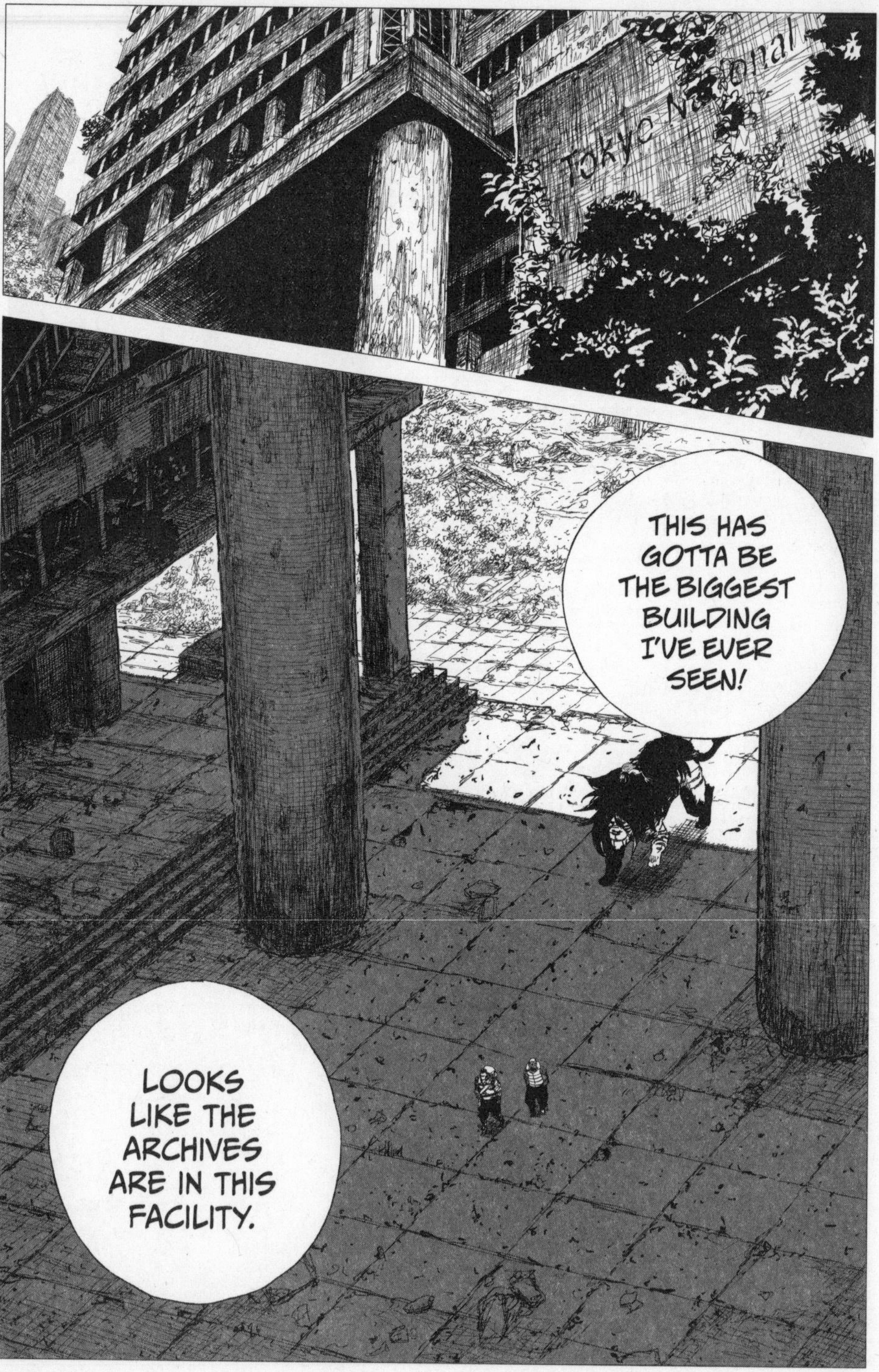
THIS HAS GOTTA BE THE BIGGEST BUILDING I'VE EVER SEEN!
LOOKS LIKE THE ARCHIVES ARE IN THIS FACILITY.

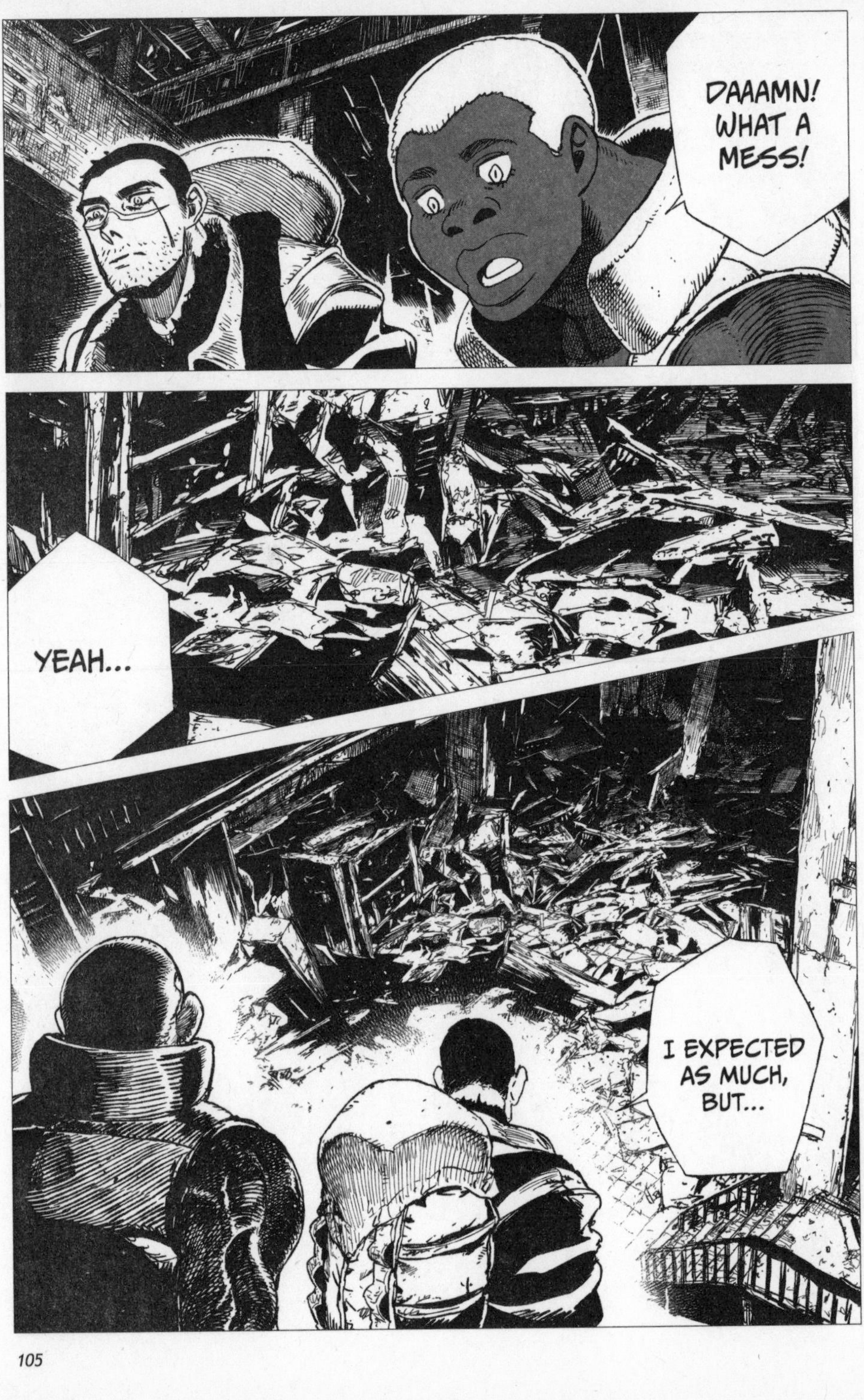
DAAAMN! WHAT A MESS!
YEAH...
I EXPECTED AS MUCH, BUT...

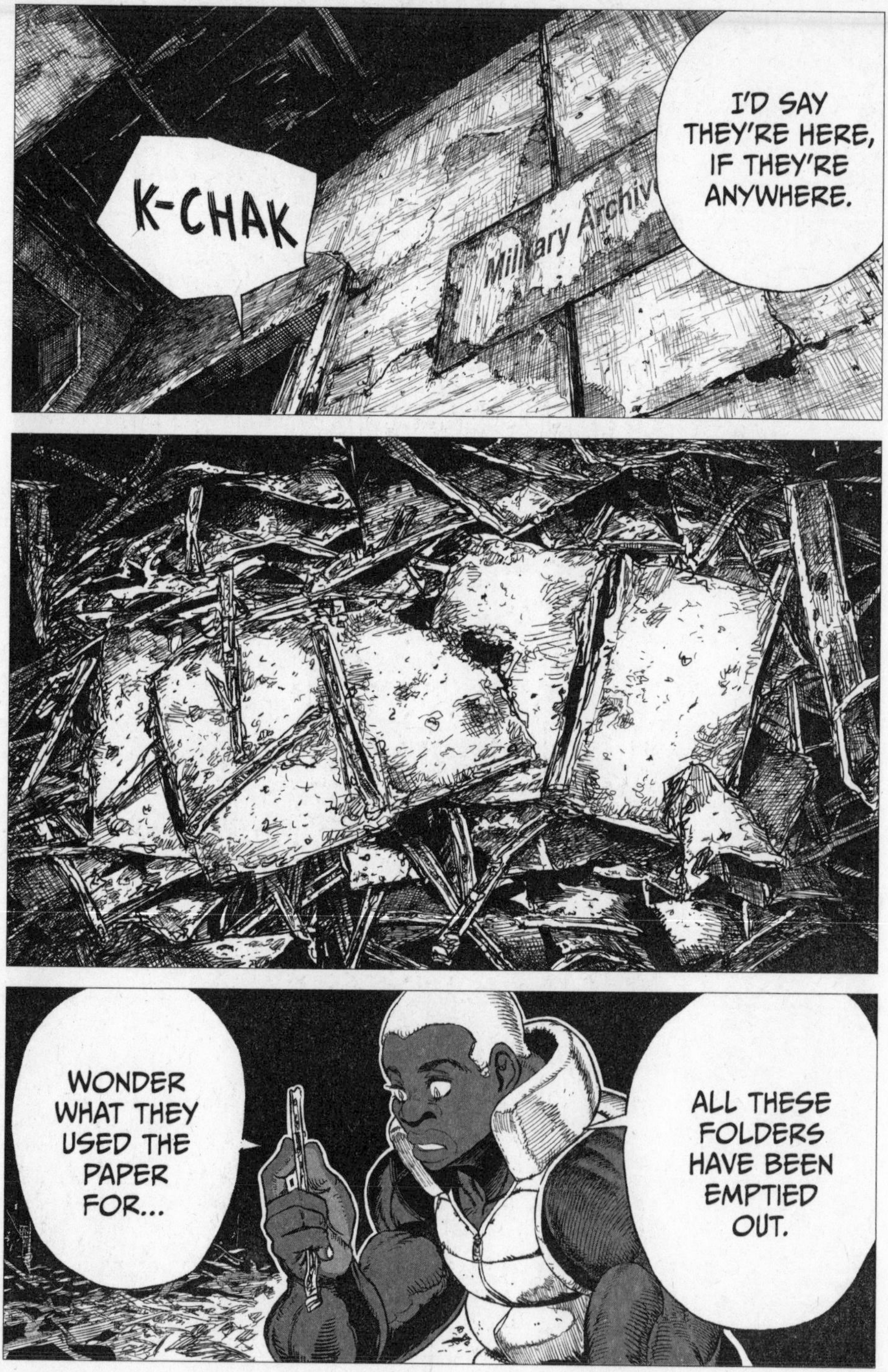
I'D SAY THEY'RE HERE, IF THEY'RE ANYWHERE.
Military Archiv
K-CHAK
ALL THESE FOLDERS HAVE BEEN EMPTIED OUT.
WONDER WHAT THEY USED THE PAPER FOR...

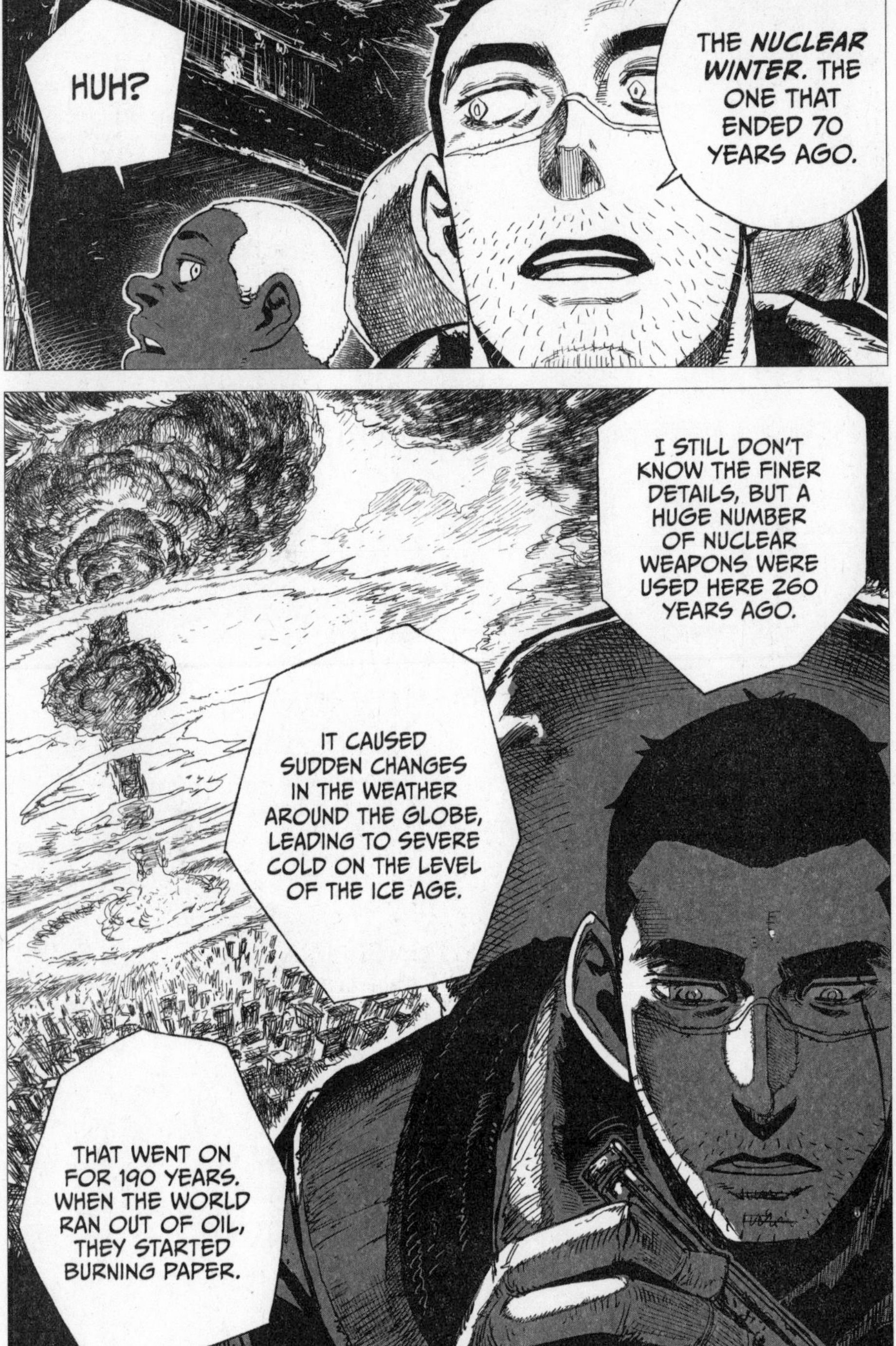
THE *NUCLEAR WINTER*. THE ONE THAT ENDED 70 YEARS AGO.
HUH?
I STILL DON'T KNOW THE FINER DETAILS, BUT A HUGE NUMBER OF NUCLEAR WEAPONS WERE USED HERE 260 YEARS AGO.
IT CAUSED SUDDEN CHANGES IN THE WEATHER AROUND THE GLOBE, LEADING TO SEVERE COLD ON THE LEVEL OF THE ICE AGE.
THAT WENT ON FOR 190 YEARS. WHEN THE WORLD RAN OUT OF OIL, THEY STARTED BURNING PAPER.

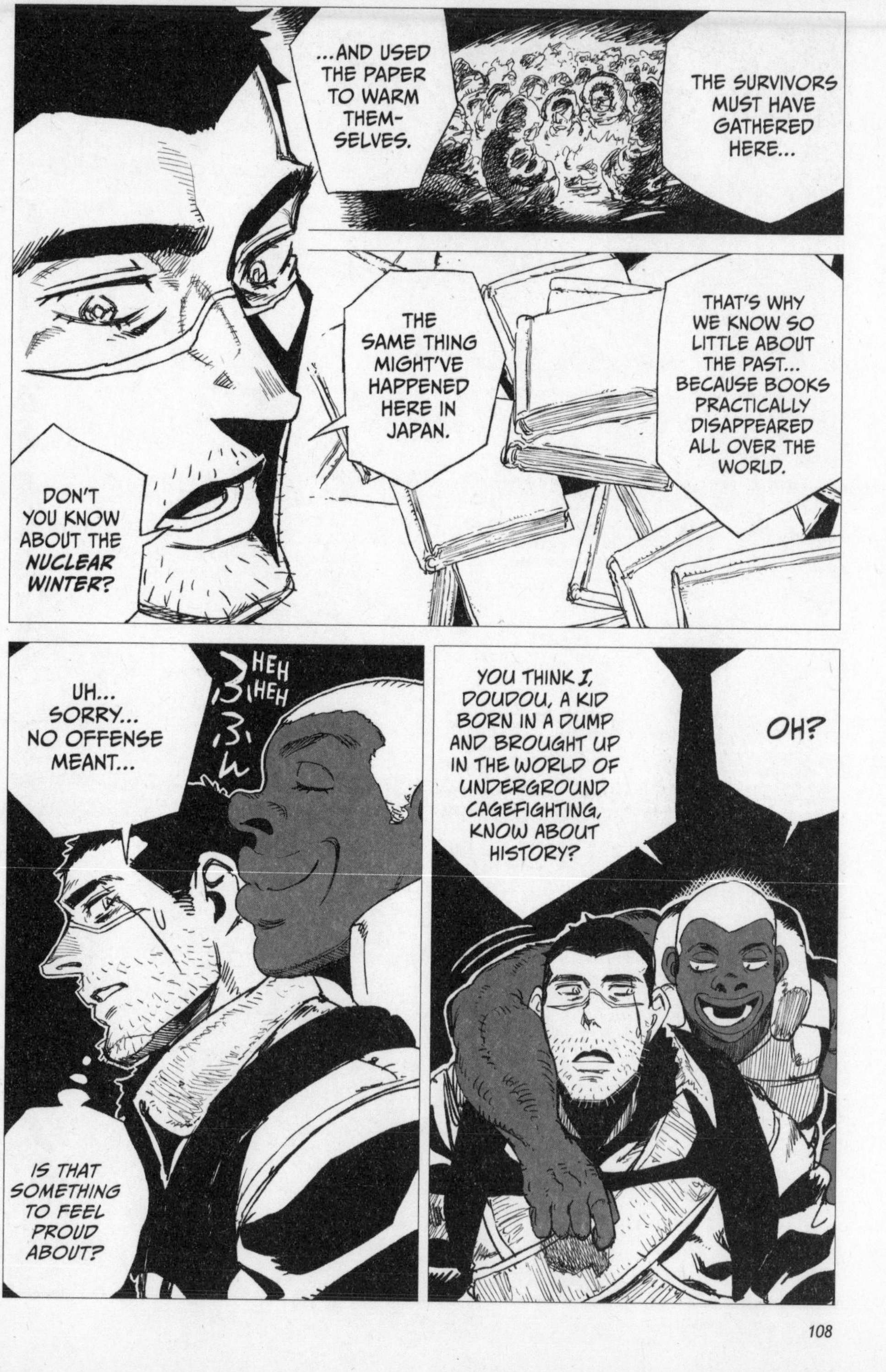
THE SURVIVORS MUST HAVE GATHERED HERE...
...AND USED THE PAPER TO WARM THEM-SELVES.
DON'T YOU KNOW ABOUT THE NUCLEAR WINTER?
THE SAME THING MIGHT'VE HAPPENED HERE IN JAPAN.
THAT'S WHY WE KNOW SO LITTLE ABOUT THE PAST... BECAUSE BOOKS PRACTICALLY DISAPPEARED ALL OVER THE WORLD.
OH?
YOU THINK I, DOUDOU, A KID BORN IN A DUMP AND BROUGHT UP IN THE WORLD OF UNDERGROUND CAGEFIGHTING, KNOW ABOUT HISTORY?
HEH HEH
UH... SORRY... NO OFFENSE MEANT...
IS THAT SOMETHING TO FEEL PROUD ABOUT?

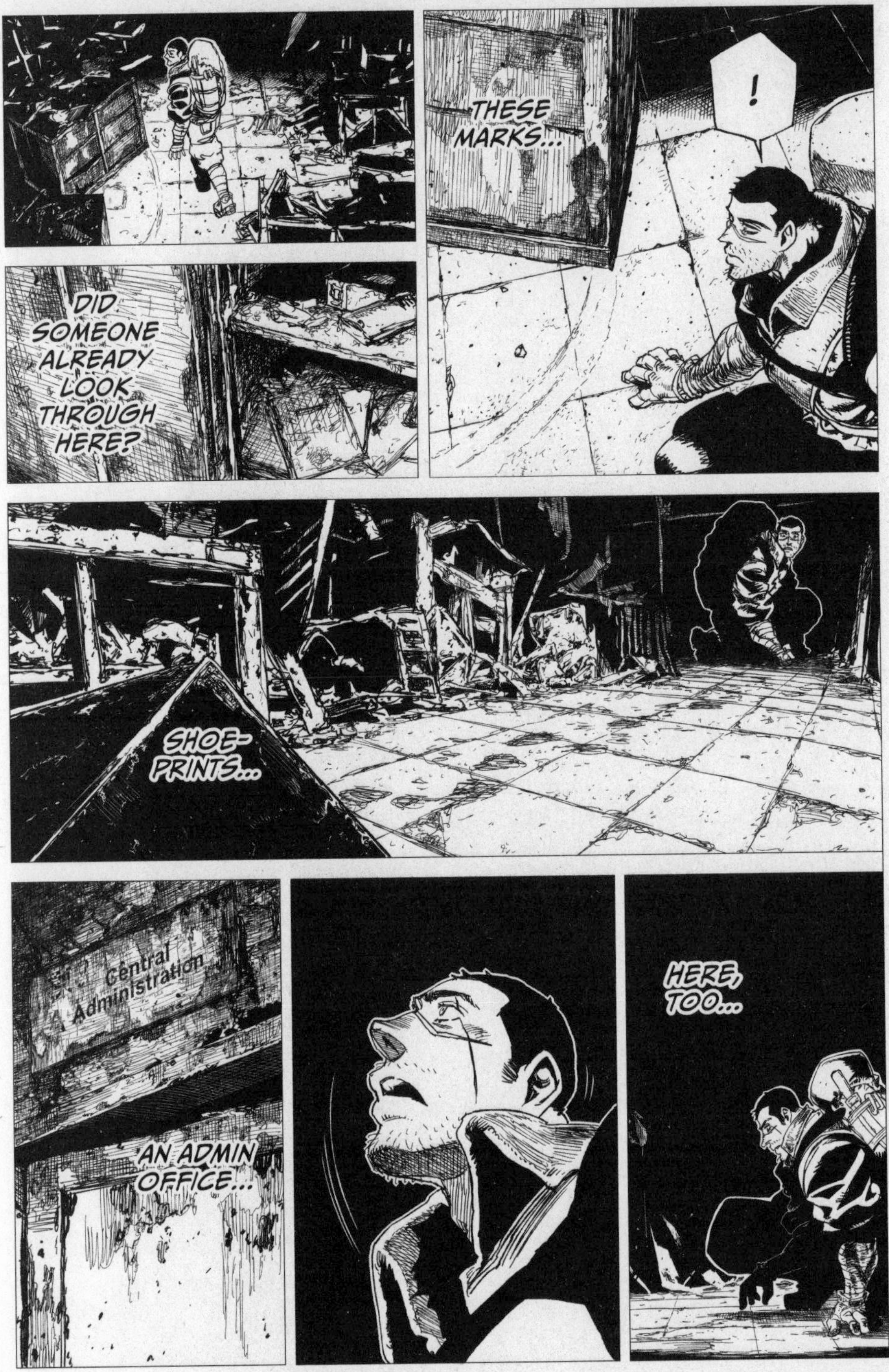
!
THESE MARKS...
DID SOMEONE ALREADY LOOK THROUGH HERE?
SHOE-PRINTS...
HERE, TOO...
AN ADMIN OFFICE...
Central Administration

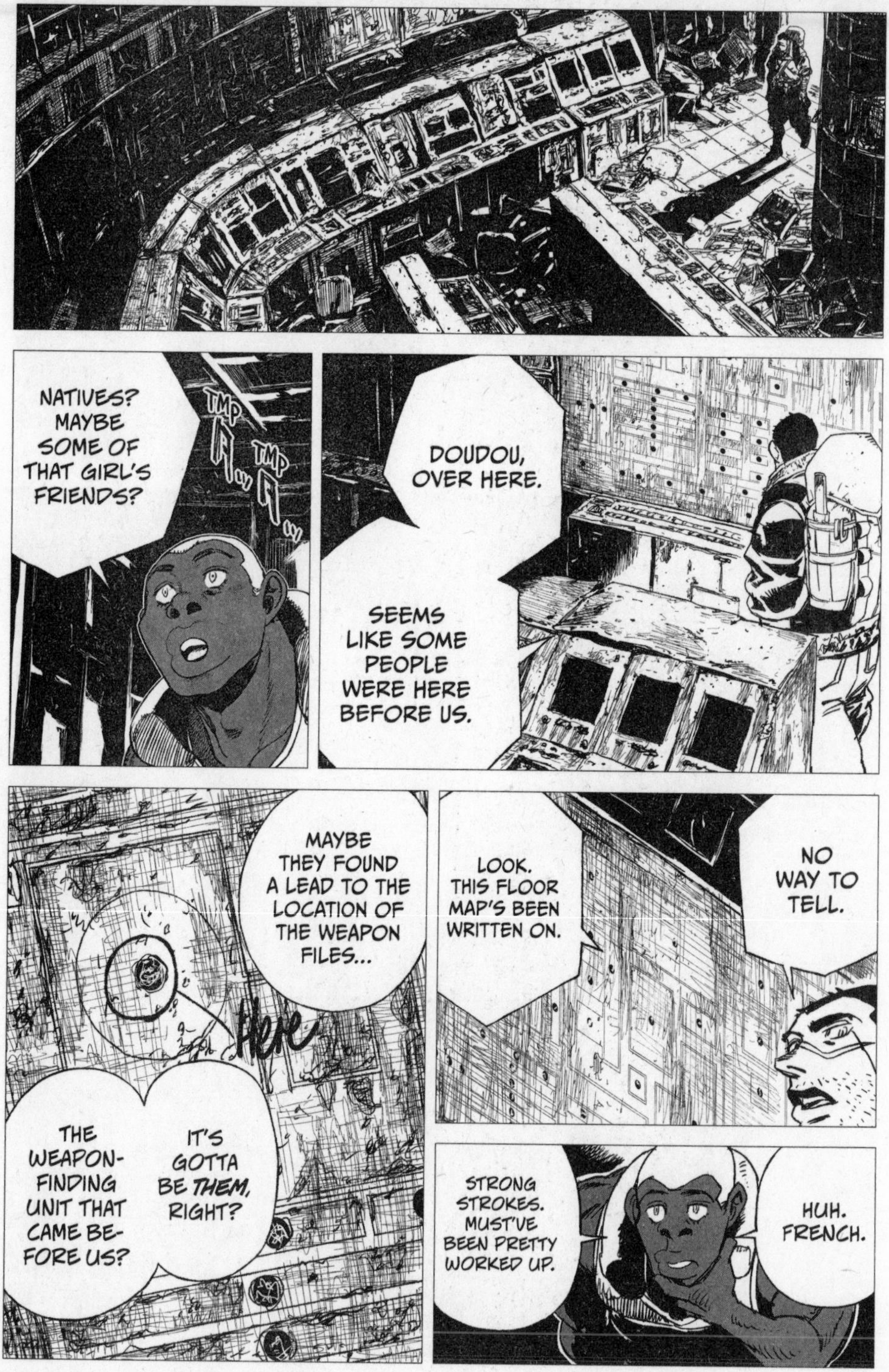
DOUDOU, OVER HERE.
SEEMS LIKE SOME PEOPLE WERE HERE BEFORE US.
NATIVES? MAYBE SOME OF THAT GIRL'S FRIENDS?
TMP TMP
NO WAY TO TELL.
LOOK. THIS FLOOR MAP'S BEEN WRITTEN ON.
HUH. FRENCH.
STRONG STROKES. MUST'VE BEEN PRETTY WORKED UP.
MAYBE THEY FOUND A LEAD TO THE LOCATION OF THE WEAPON FILES...
Here
IT'S GOTTA BE *THEM*, RIGHT?
THE WEAPON-FINDING UNIT THAT CAME BE-FORE US?

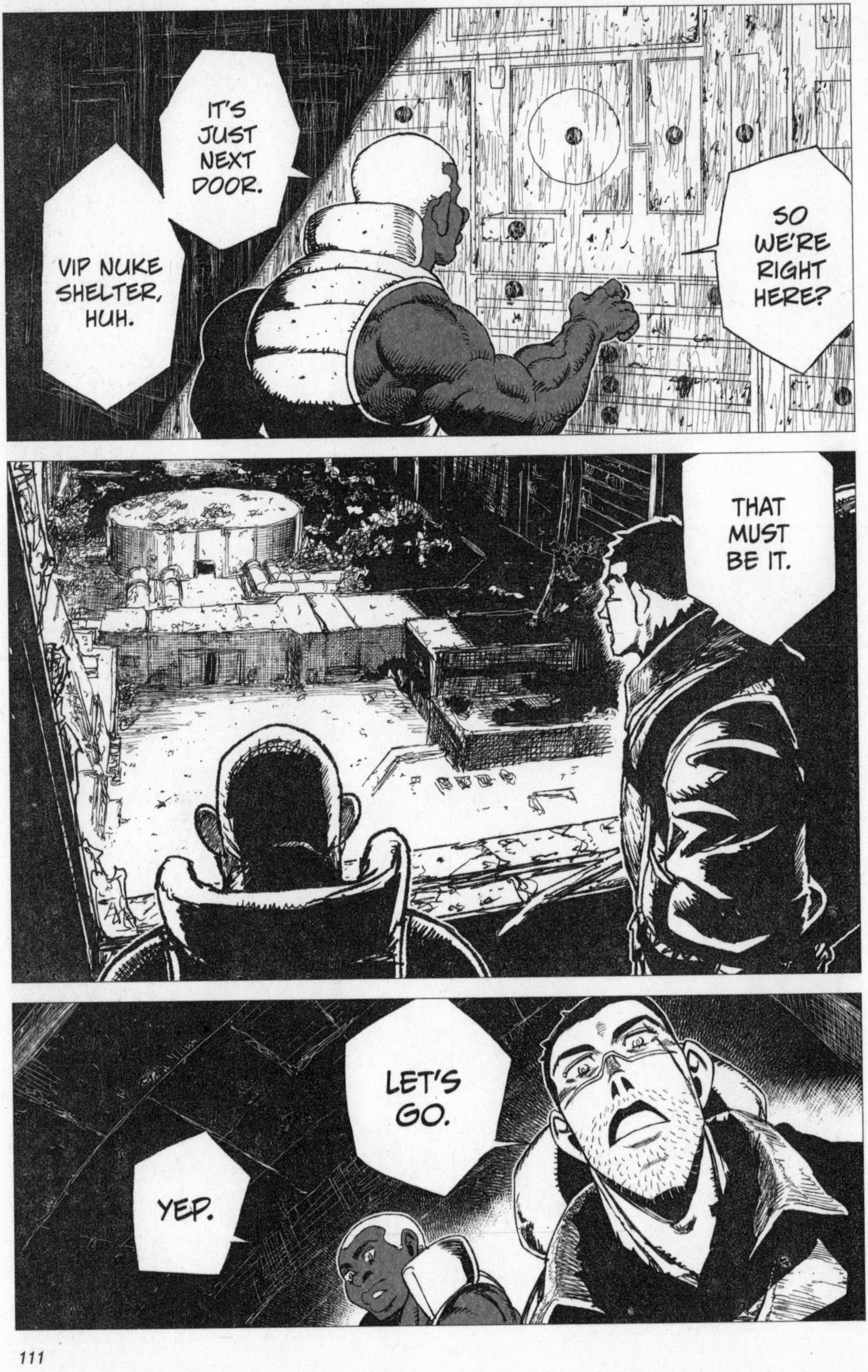
SO WE'RE RIGHT HERE?
IT'S JUST NEXT DOOR.
VIP NUKE SHELTER, HUH.
THAT MUST BE IT.
LET'S GO.
YEP.

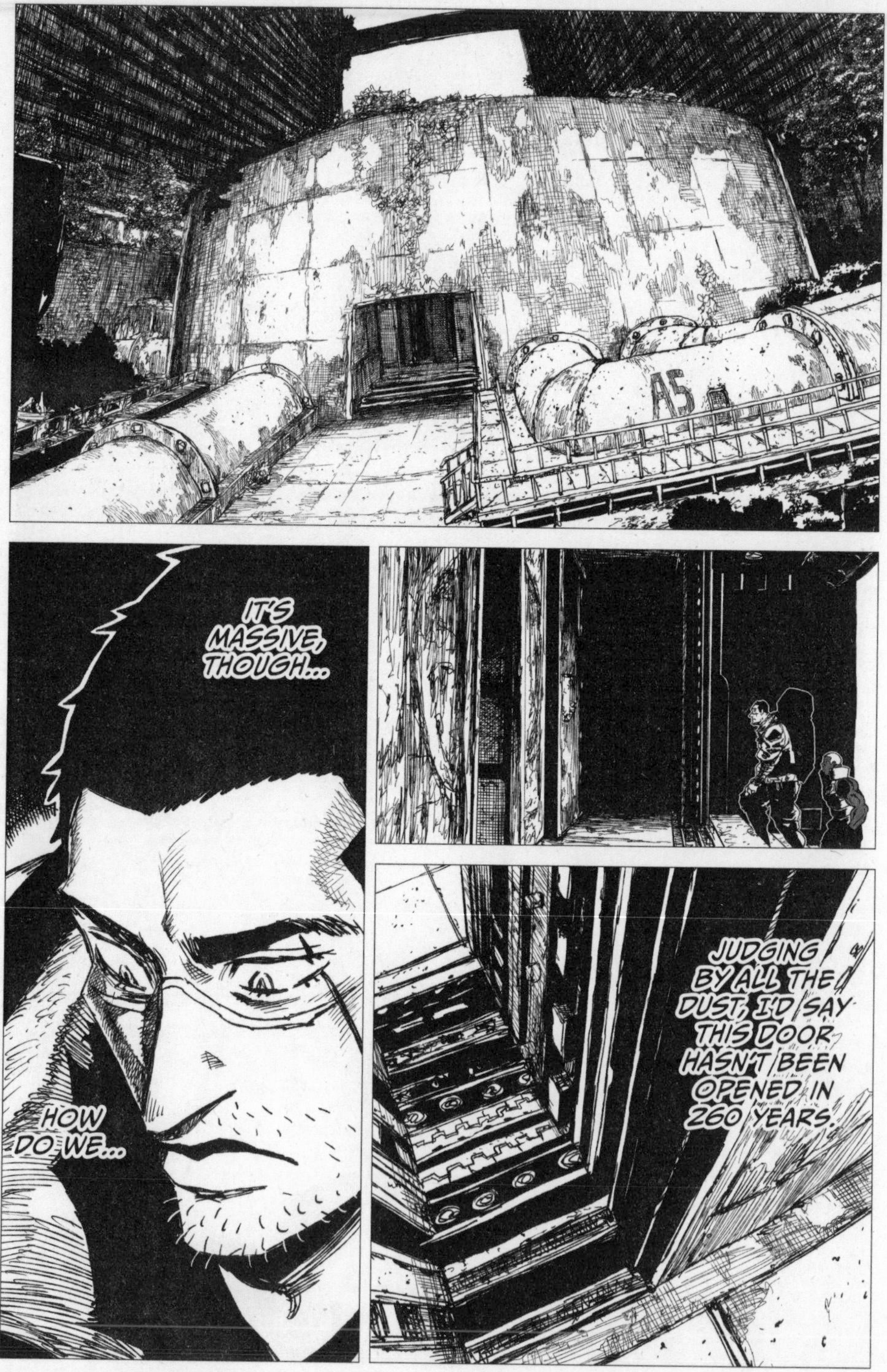
A5
JUDGING BY ALL THE DUST, I'D SAY THIS DOOR HASN'T BEEN OPENED IN 260 YEARS.
IT'S MASSIVE, THOUGH...
HOW DO WE...

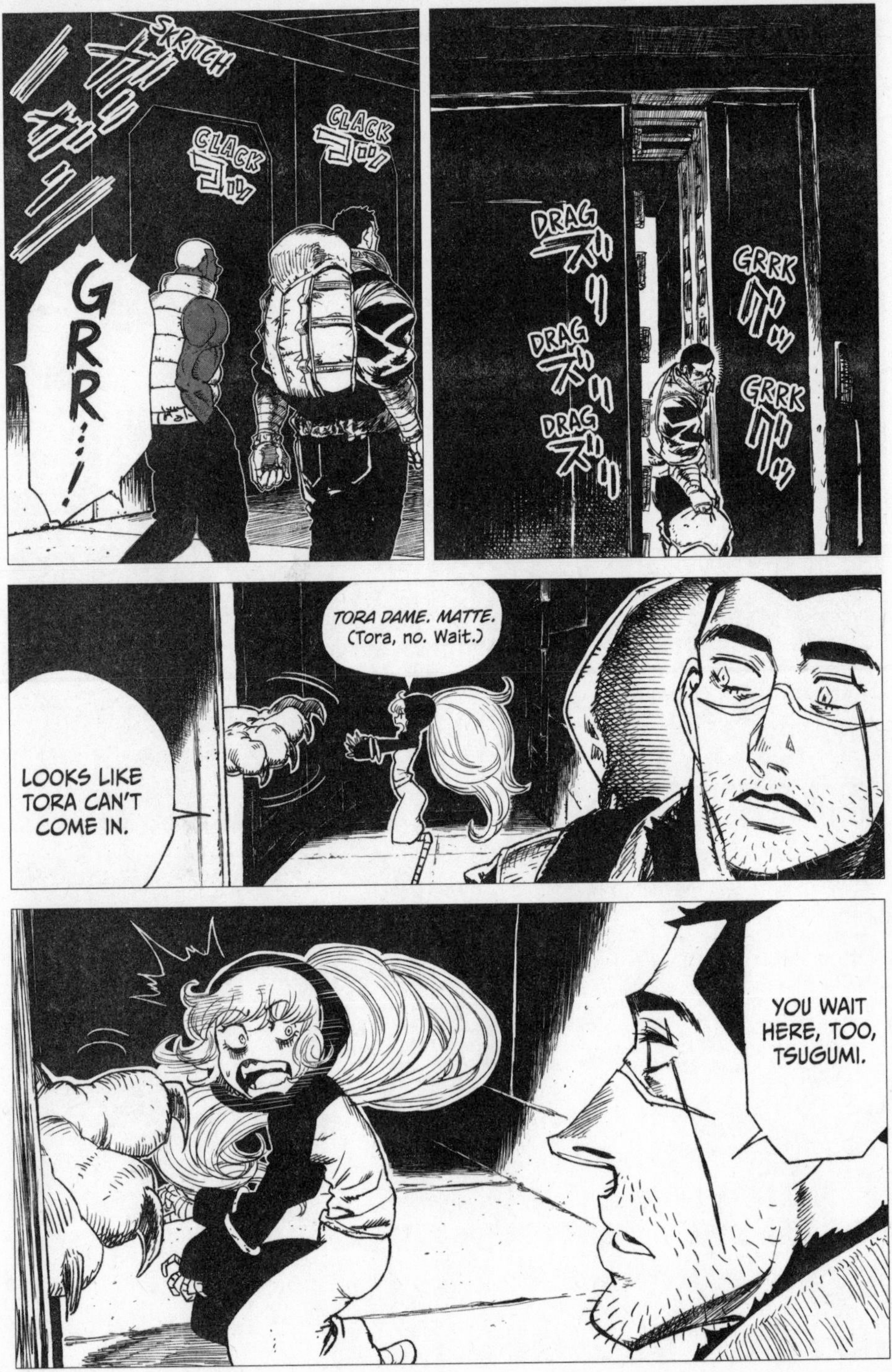
GRRK
GRRK
DRAG
DRAG
DRAG
SKRITCH
CLACK
CLACK
GRR...!
TORA DAME. MATTE.
(Tora, no. Wait.)
LOOKS LIKE TORA CAN'T COME IN.
YOU WAIT HERE, TOO, TSUGUMI.

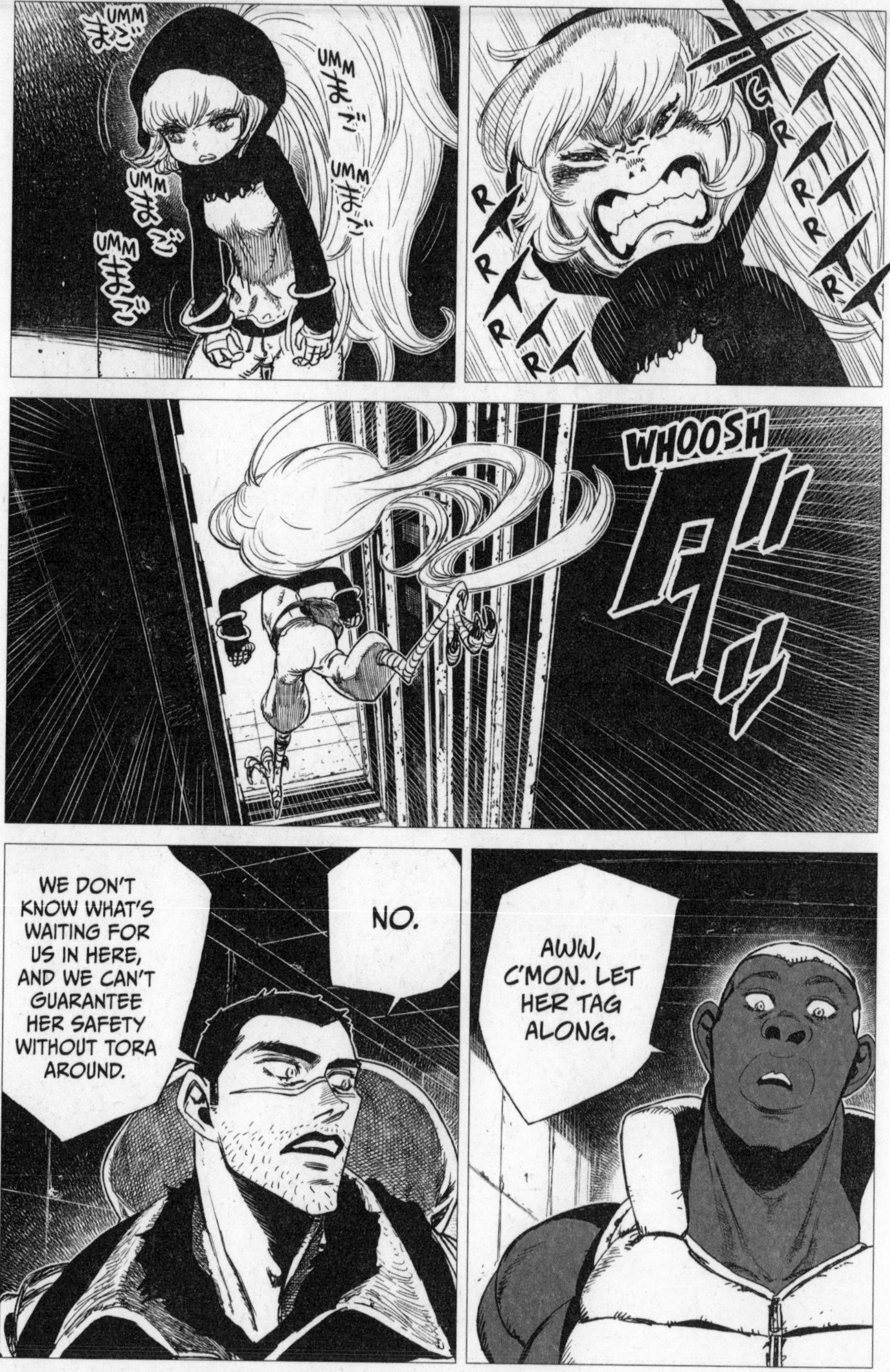
GRRRR
RRRRR
UMM まご
UMM まご
UMM まご
UMM まご
UMM まご
WHOOSH
AWW, C'MON. LET HER TAG ALONG.
NO.
WE DON'T KNOW WHAT'S WAITING FOR US IN HERE, AND WE CAN'T GUARANTEE HER SAFETY WITHOUT TORA AROUND.

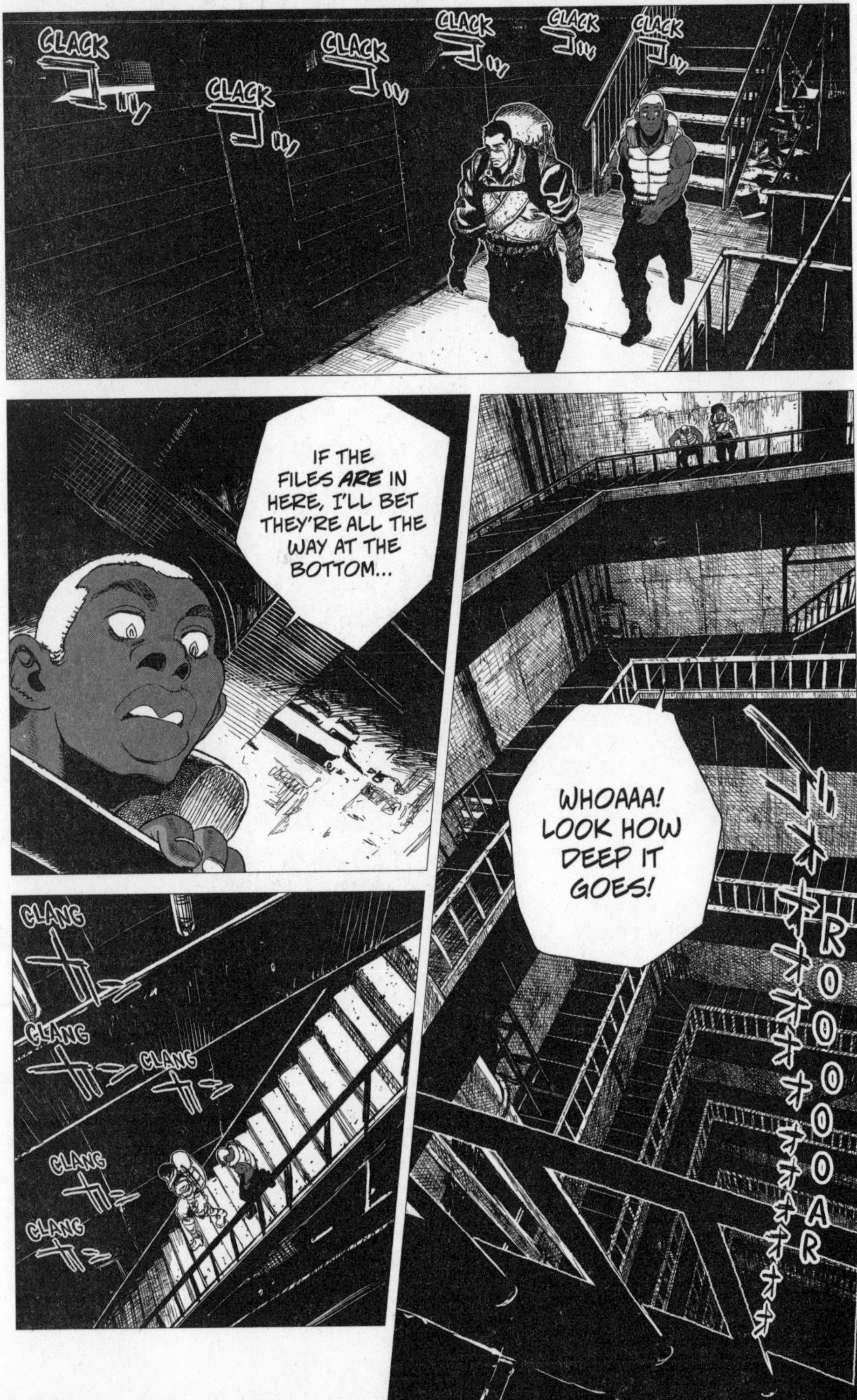

CLACK
CLACK
CLACK
CLACK
CLACK
CLACK
WHOAAA! LOOK HOW DEEP IT GOES!
ROOOOOOAR
IF THE FILES ARE IN HERE, I'LL BET THEY'RE ALL THE WAY AT THE BOTTOM...
CLANG
CLANG
CLANG
CLANG
CLANG

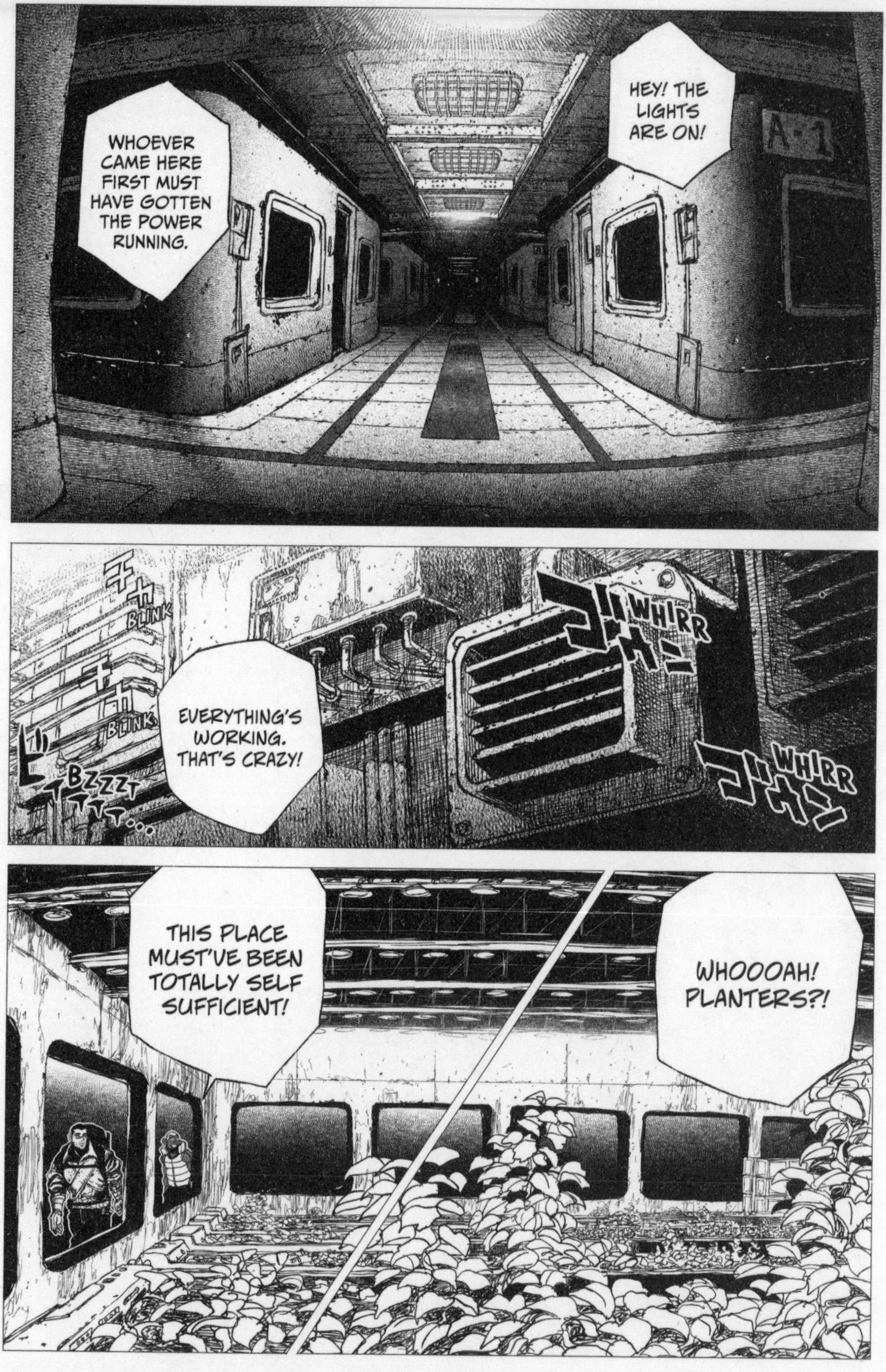
HEY! THE LIGHTS ARE ON!
A-1
WHOEVER CAME HERE FIRST MUST HAVE GOTTEN THE POWER RUNNING.
WHIRR
WHIRR
EVERYTHING'S WORKING. THAT'S CRAZY!
BLINK
BLINK
BZZZT...
WHOOOAH! PLANTERS?!
THIS PLACE MUST'VE BEEN TOTALLY SELF SUFFICIENT!

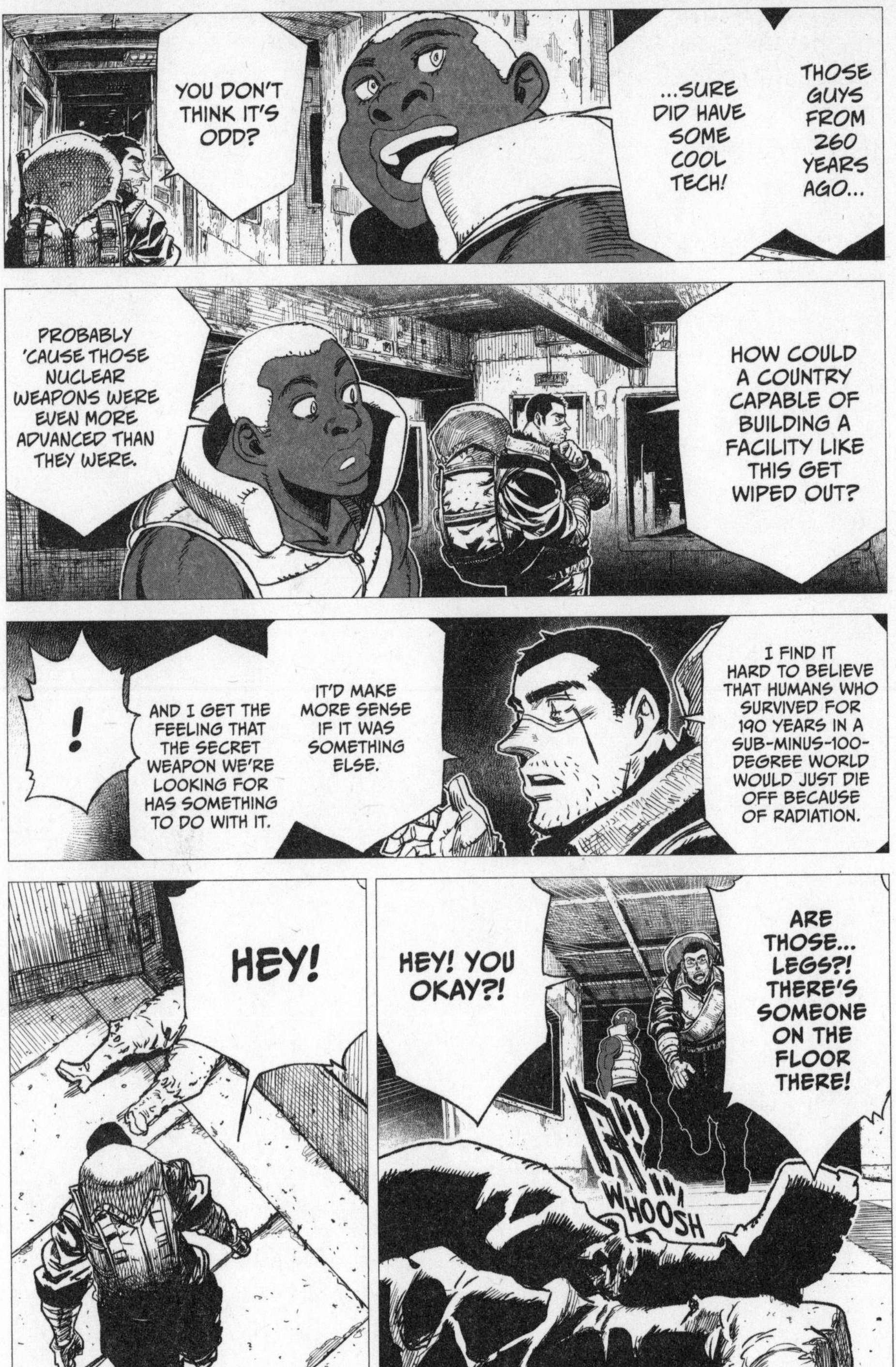
THOSE GUYS FROM 260 YEARS AGO...
...SURE DID HAVE SOME COOL TECH!
YOU DON'T THINK IT'S ODD?
HOW COULD A COUNTRY CAPABLE OF BUILDING A FACILITY LIKE THIS GET WIPED OUT?
PROBABLY 'CAUSE THOSE NUCLEAR WEAPONS WERE EVEN MORE ADVANCED THAN THEY WERE.
I FIND IT HARD TO BELIEVE THAT HUMANS WHO SURVIVED FOR 190 YEARS IN A SUB-MINUS-100-DEGREE WORLD WOULD JUST DIE OFF BECAUSE OF RADIATION.
IT'D MAKE MORE SENSE IF IT WAS SOMETHING ELSE.
AND I GET THE FEELING THAT THE SECRET WEAPON WE'RE LOOKING FOR HAS SOMETHING TO DO WITH IT.
!
ARE THOSE... LEGS?! THERE'S SOMEONE ON THE FLOOR THERE!
WHOOSH
HEY! YOU OKAY?!
HEY!

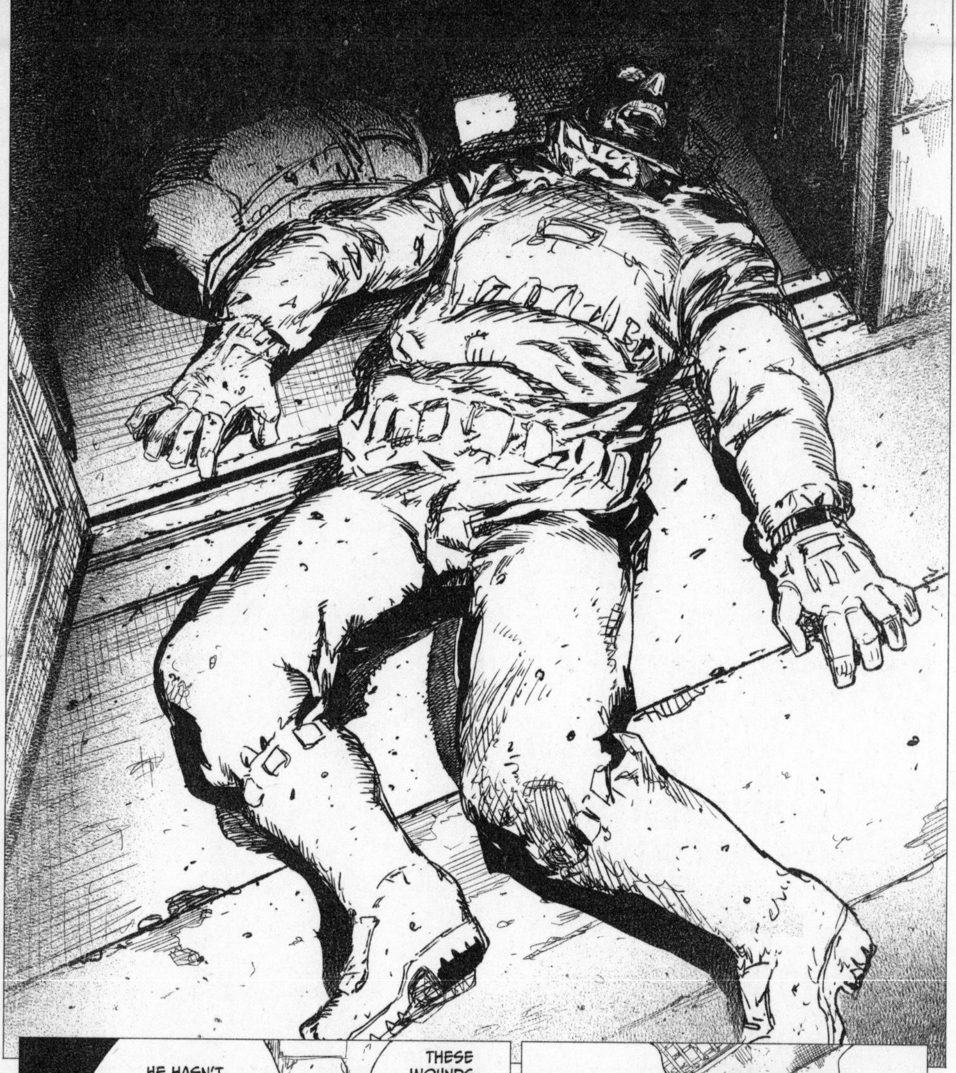

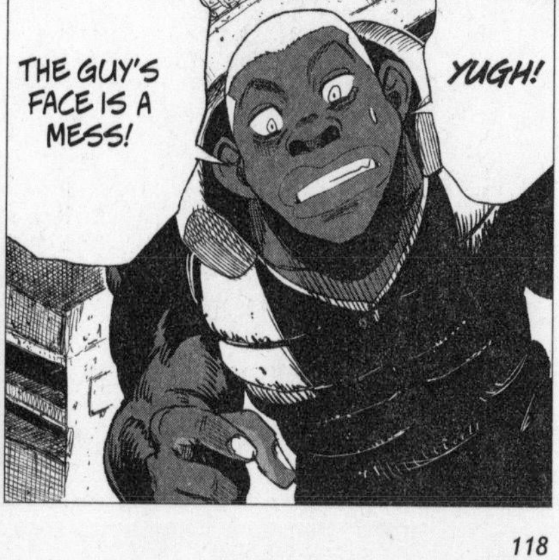
YUGH!
THE GUY'S FACE IS A MESS!

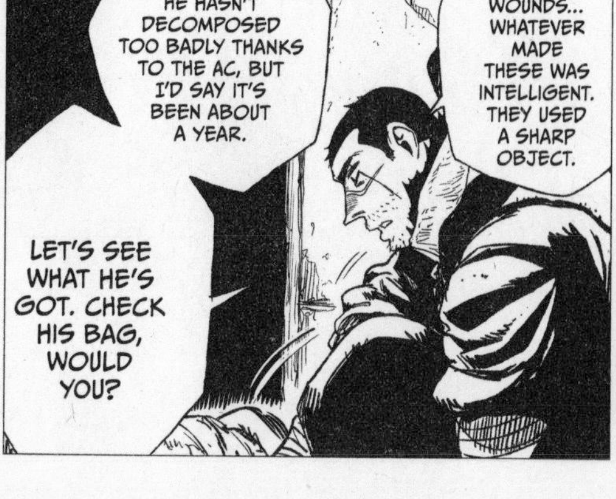
THESE WOUNDS... WHATEVER MADE THESE WAS INTELLIGENT. THEY USED A SHARP OBJECT.
HE HASN'T DECOMPOSED TOO BADLY THANKS TO THE AC, BUT I'D SAY IT'S BEEN ABOUT A YEAR.
LET'S SEE WHAT HE'S GOT. CHECK HIS BAG, WOULD YOU?

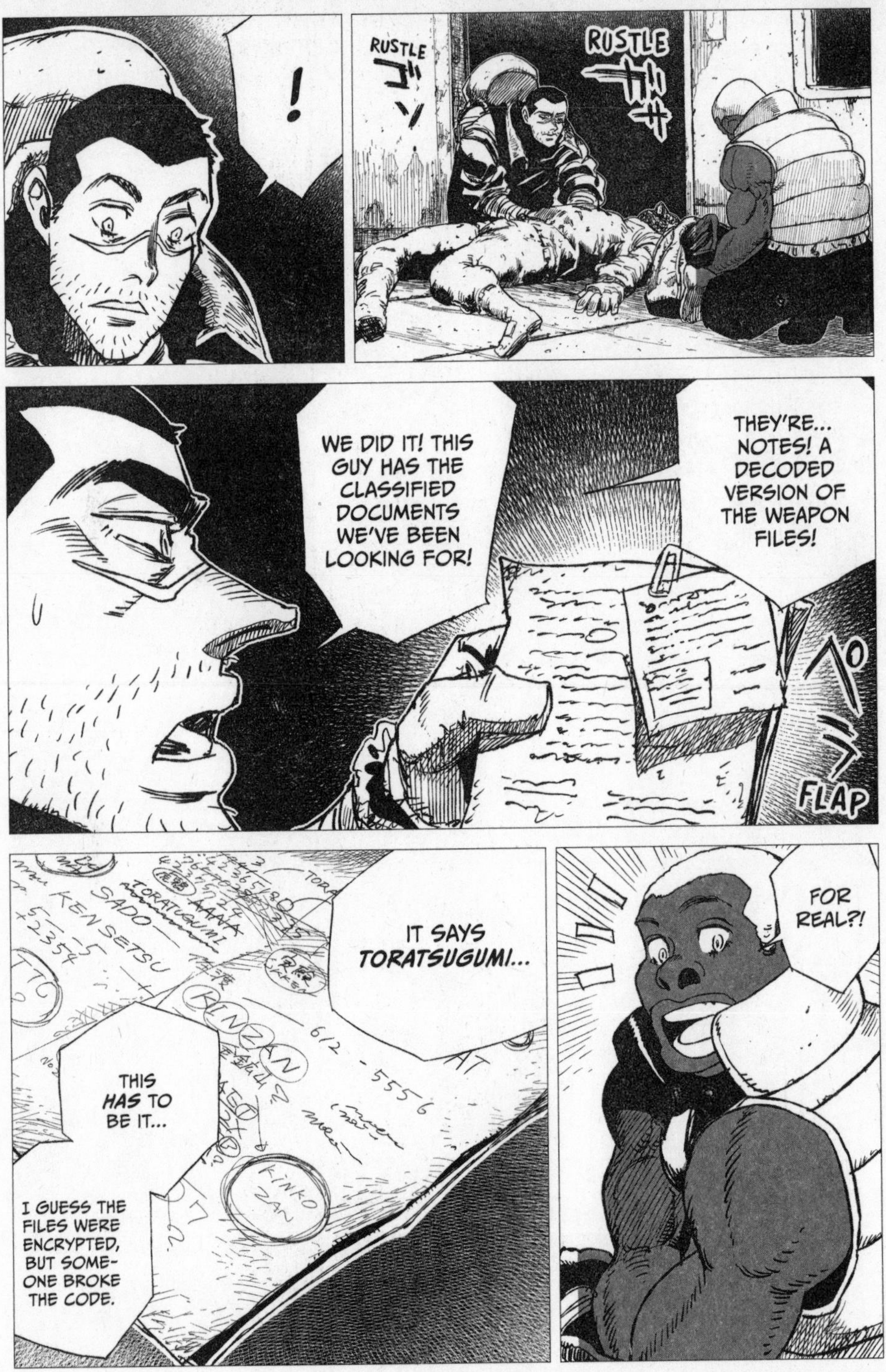
RUSTLE
RUSTLE
!
THEY'RE... NOTES! A DECODED VERSION OF THE WEAPON FILES!
WE DID IT! THIS GUY HAS THE CLASSIFIED DOCUMENTS WE'VE BEEN LOOKING FOR!
FLAP
FOR REAL?!
IT SAYS *TORATSUGUMI*...
THIS *HAS* TO BE IT...
I GUESS THE FILES WERE ENCRYPTED, BUT SOME-ONE BROKE THE CODE.

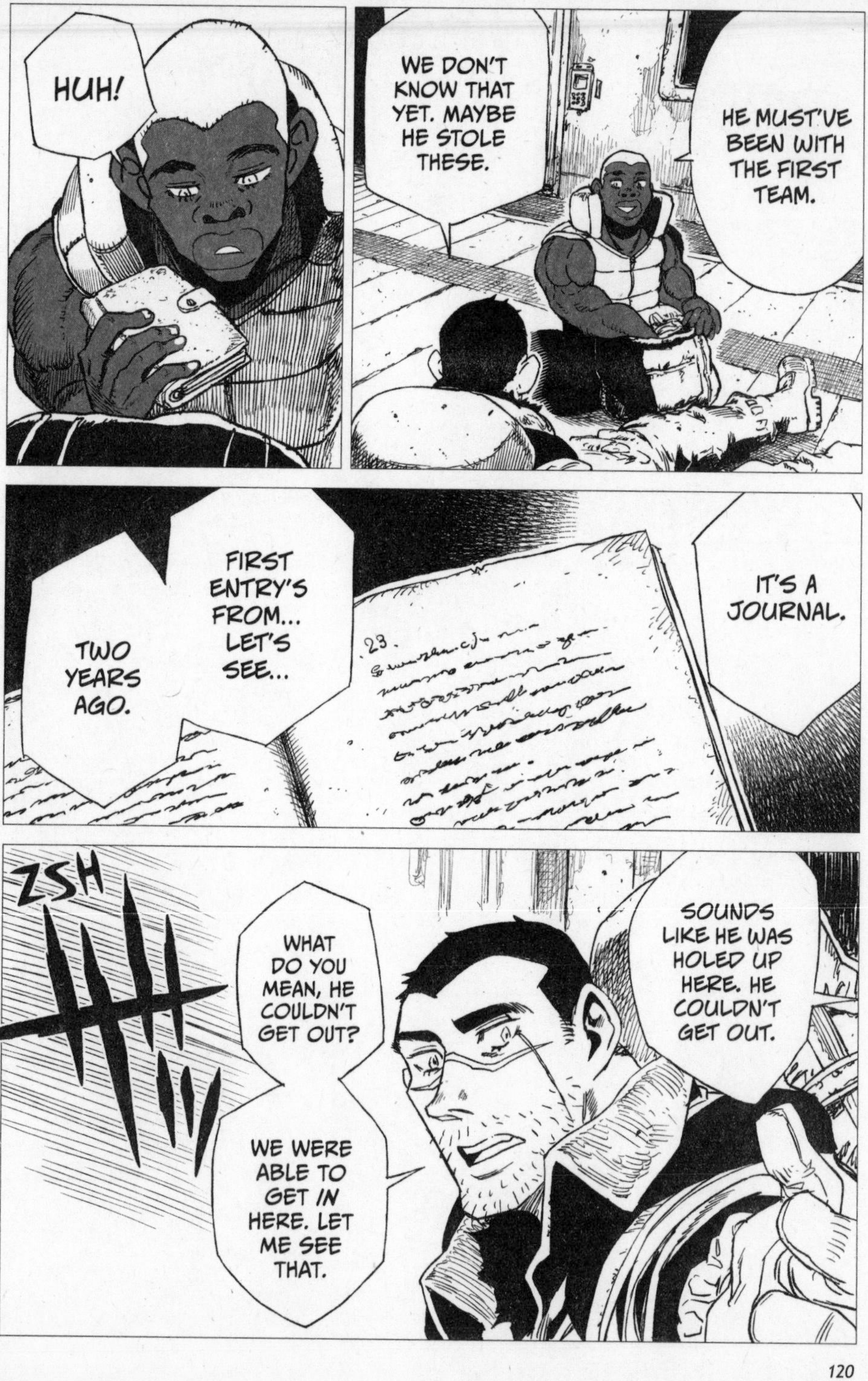
HE MUST'VE BEEN WITH THE FIRST TEAM.
WE DON'T KNOW THAT YET. MAYBE HE STOLE THESE.
HUH!
IT'S A JOURNAL.
FIRST ENTRY'S FROM... LET'S SEE...
TWO YEARS AGO.
SOUNDS LIKE HE WAS HOLED UP HERE. HE COULDN'T GET OUT.
WHAT DO YOU MEAN, HE COULDN'T GET OUT?
WE WERE ABLE TO GET IN HERE. LET ME SEE THAT.
ZSH

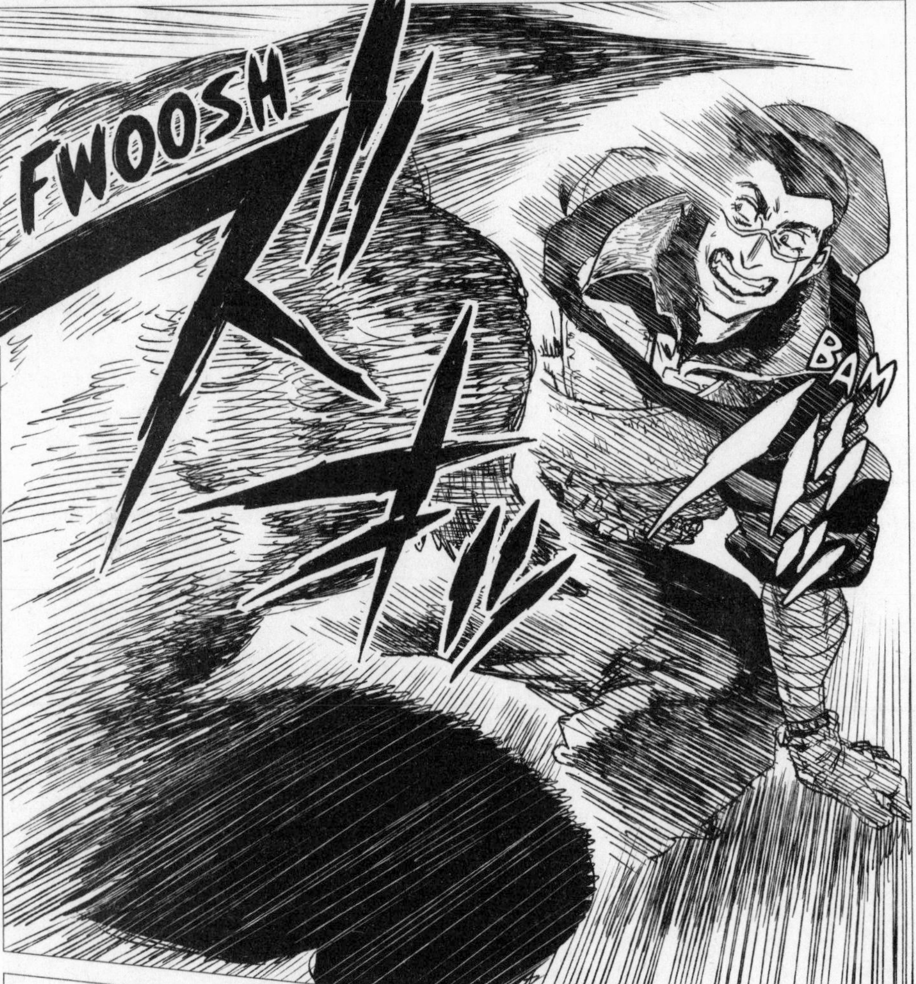
FWOOSH
BAM

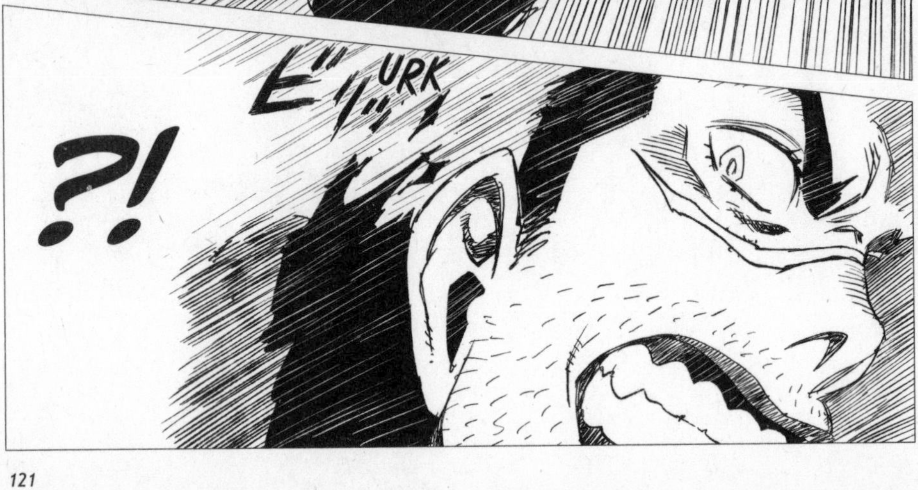
URK
?!

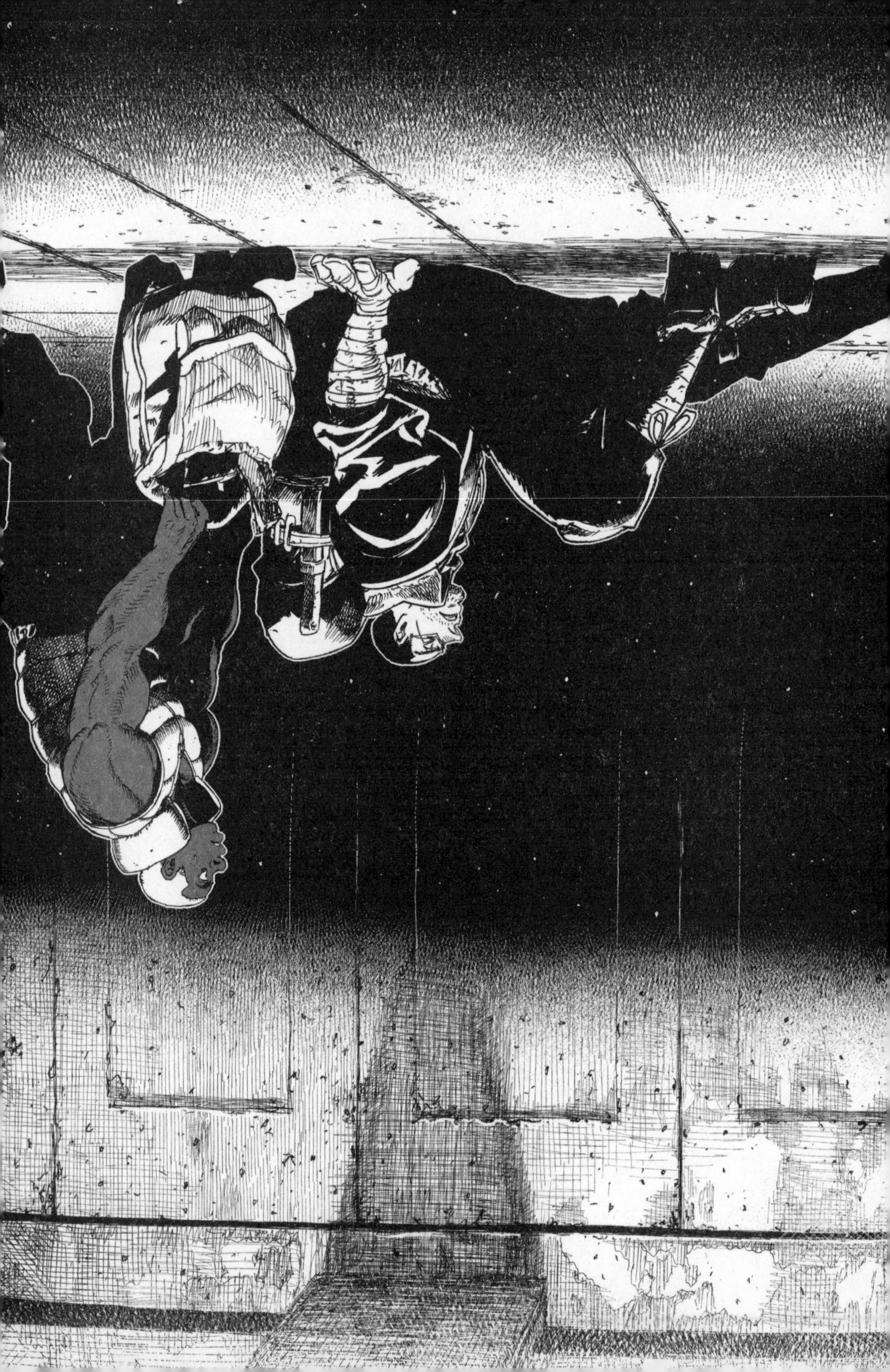

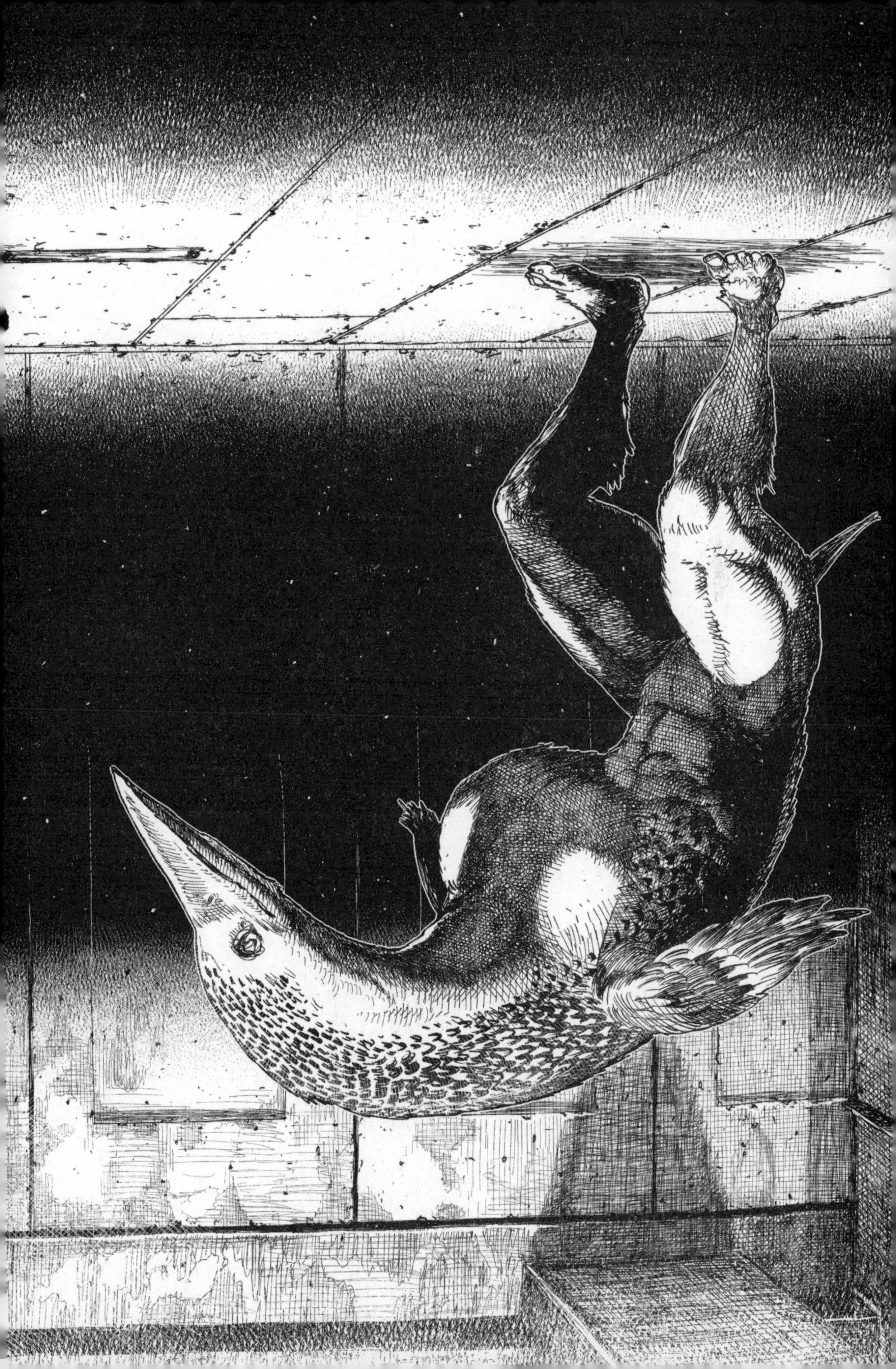

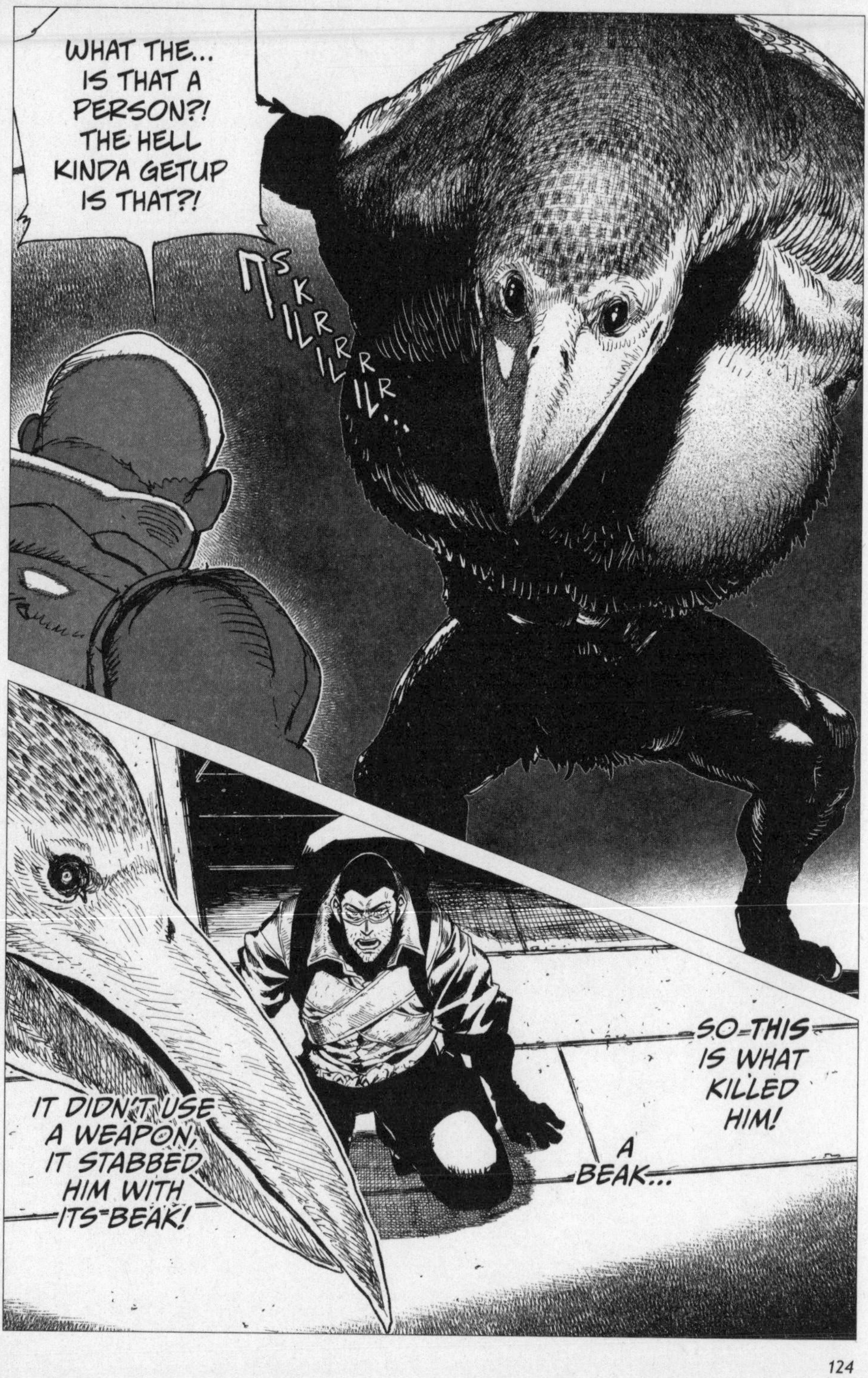
WHAT THE... IS THAT A PERSON?! THE HELL KINDA GETUP IS THAT?!
SKRRRR...
SO THIS IS WHAT KILLED HIM!
A BEAK...
IT DIDN'T USE A WEAPON, IT STABBED HIM WITH ITS BEAK!

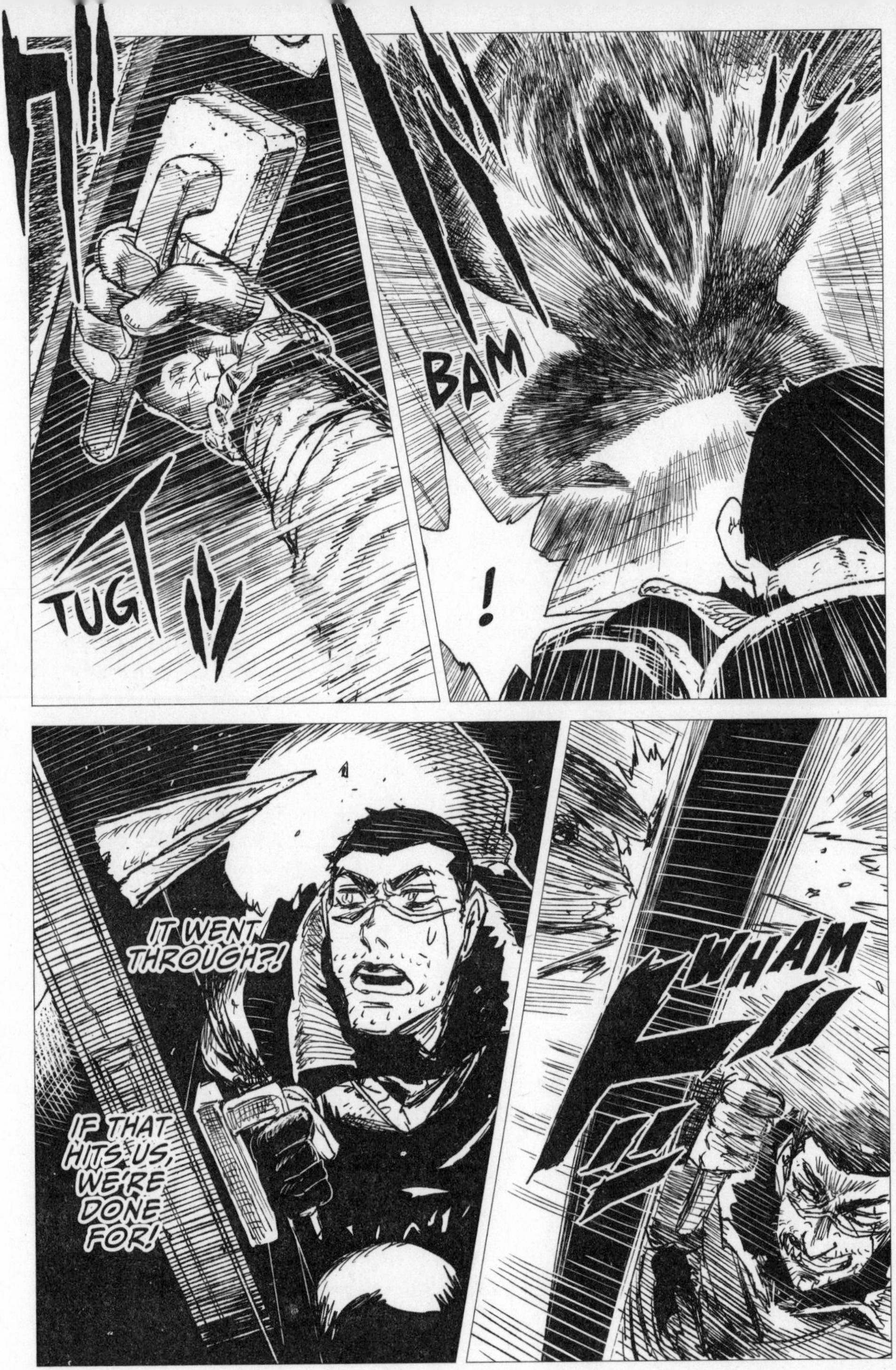
BAM
!
TUG
WHAM
IT WENT THROUGH?!
IF THAT HITS US, WE'RE DONE FOR!

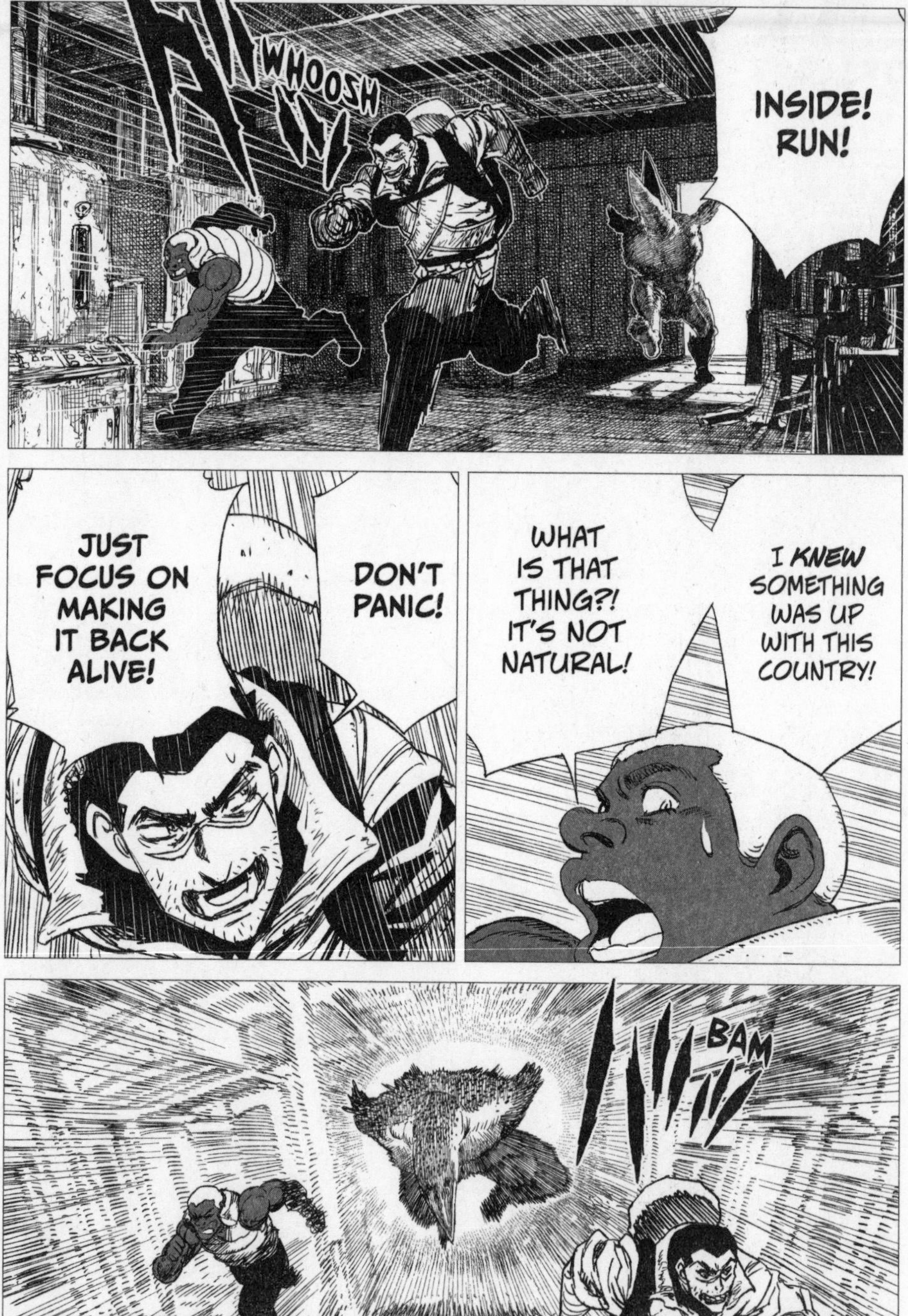
INSIDE! RUN!
WHOOSH
I KNEW SOMETHING WAS UP WITH THIS COUNTRY!
WHAT IS THAT THING?! IT'S NOT NATURAL!
DON'T PANIC!
JUST FOCUS ON MAKING IT BACK ALIVE!
BAM

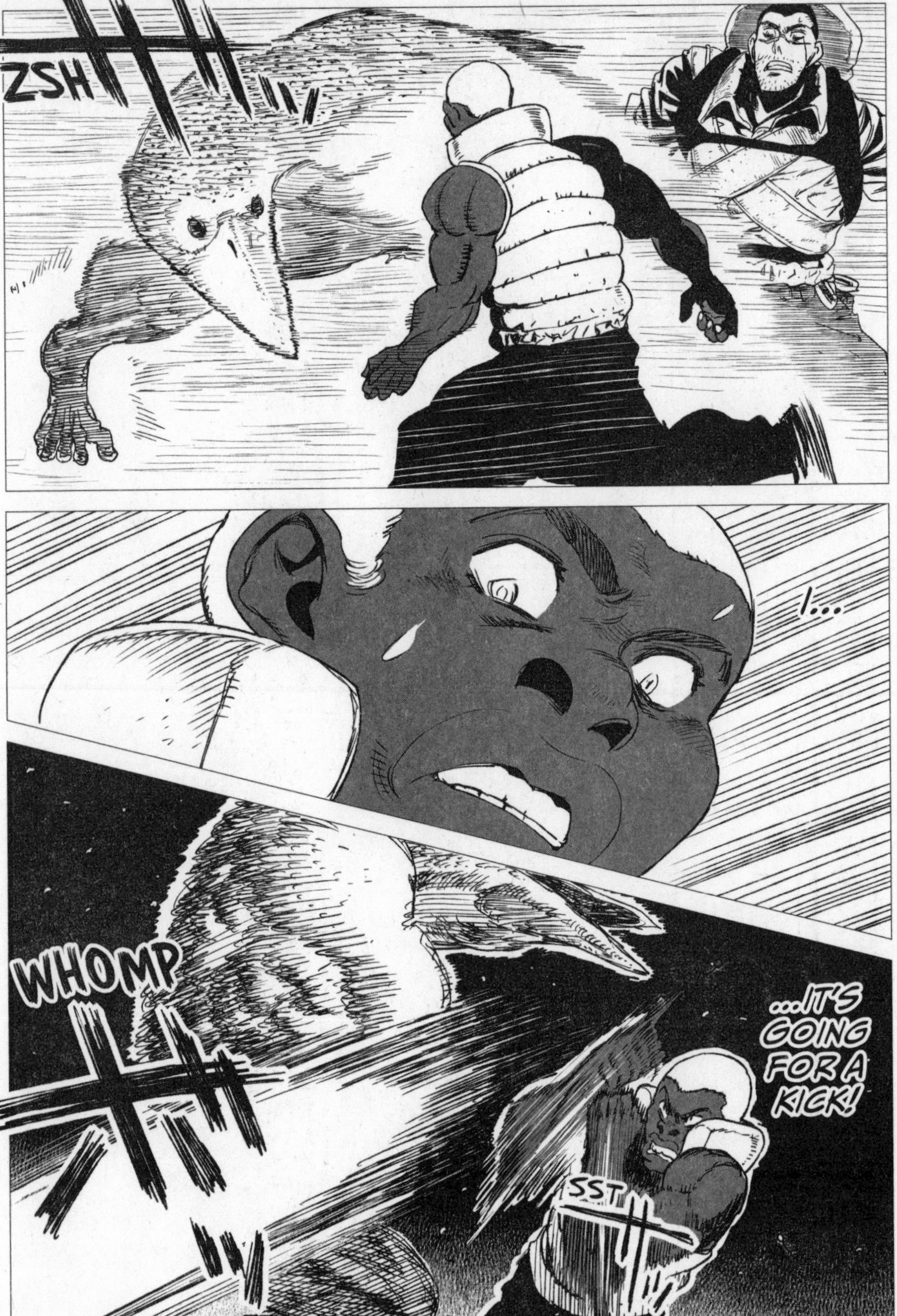
ZSH
I...
...IT'S GOING FOR A KICK!
WHOMP
SST

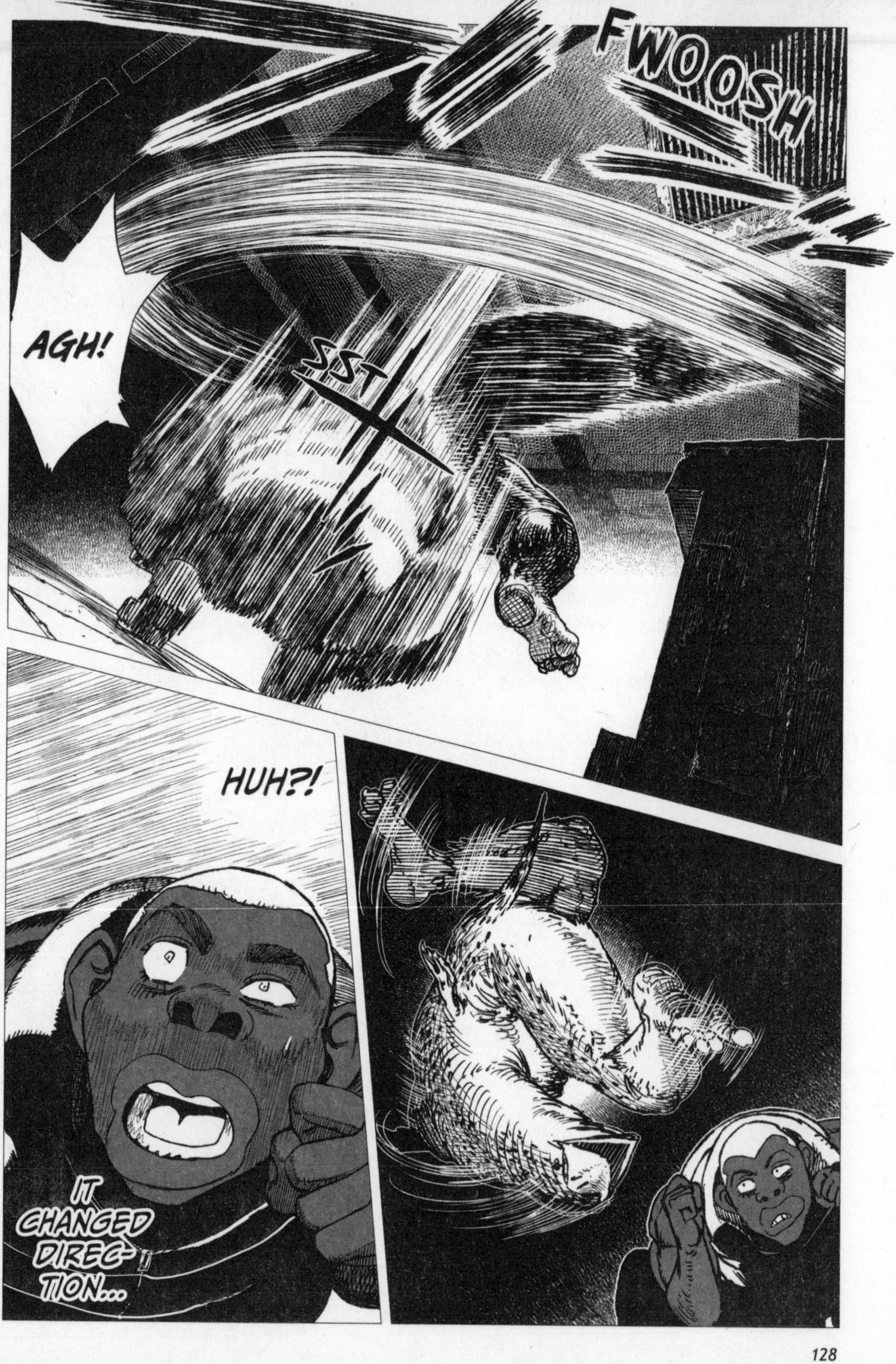
FWOOSH
SST
AGH!
HUH?!
IT CHANGED DIREC-TION...

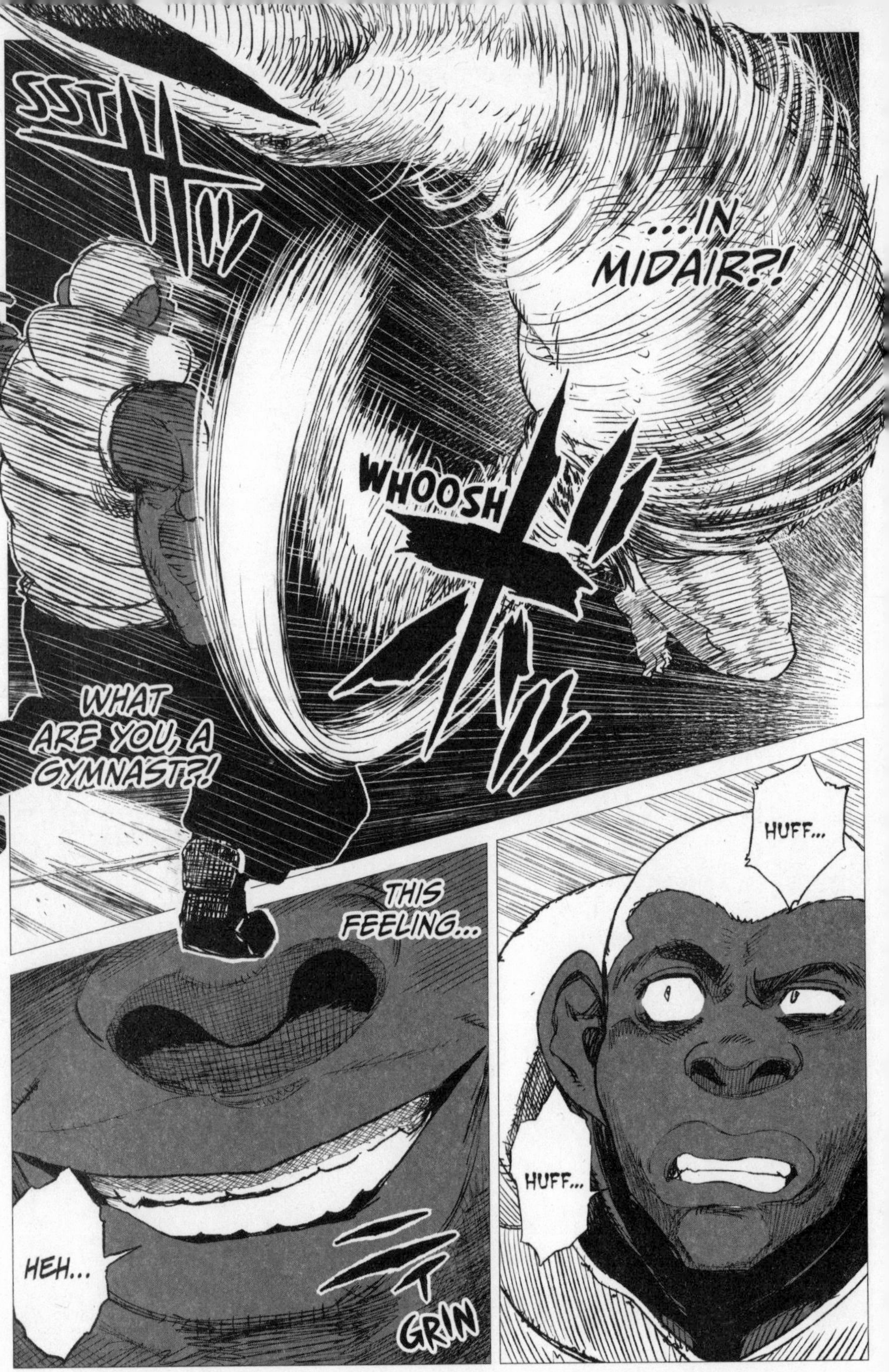
...IN MIDAIR?!
SST
WHOOSH
WHAT ARE YOU, A GYMNAST?!
HUFF...
HUFF...
THIS FEELING...
HEH...
GRIN

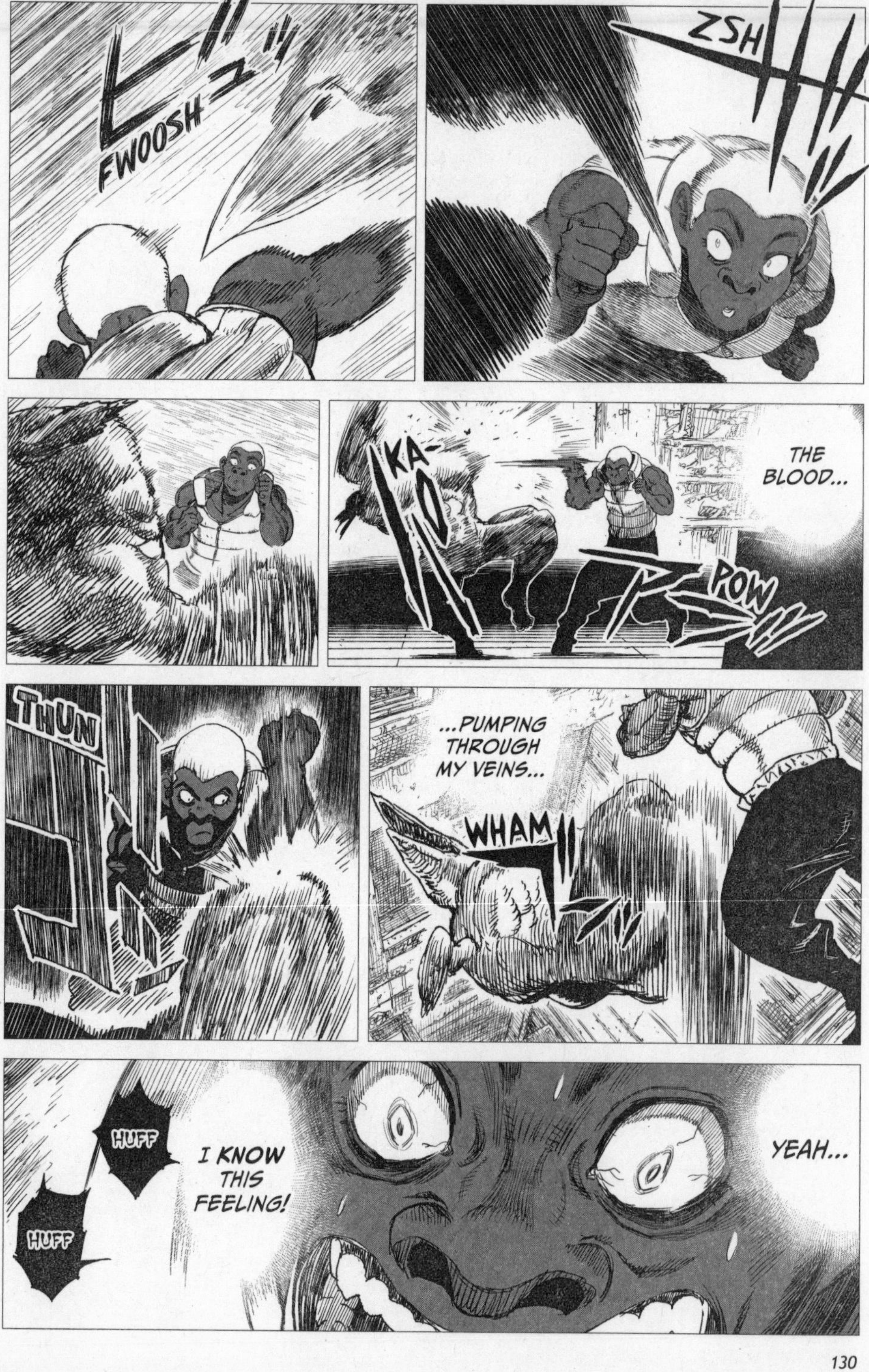
ZSH
FWOOSH
THE BLOOD...
KA-
POW
...PUMPING THROUGH MY VEINS...
WHAM!!
THUN
YEAH...
I KNOW THIS FEELING!
HUFF
HUFF

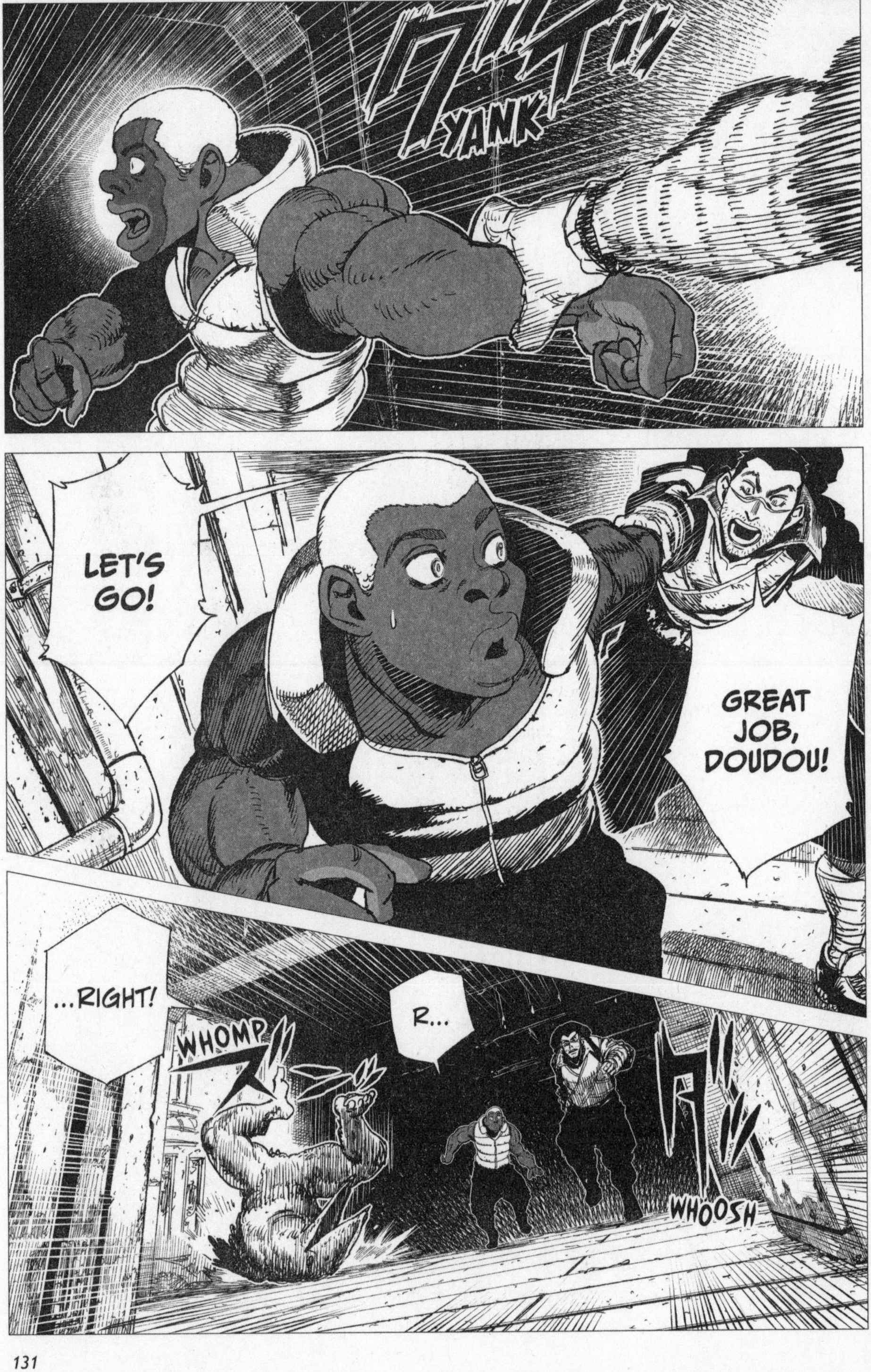
YANK
GREAT JOB, DOUDOU!
LET'S GO!
WHOOSH
R...
...RIGHT!
WHOMP

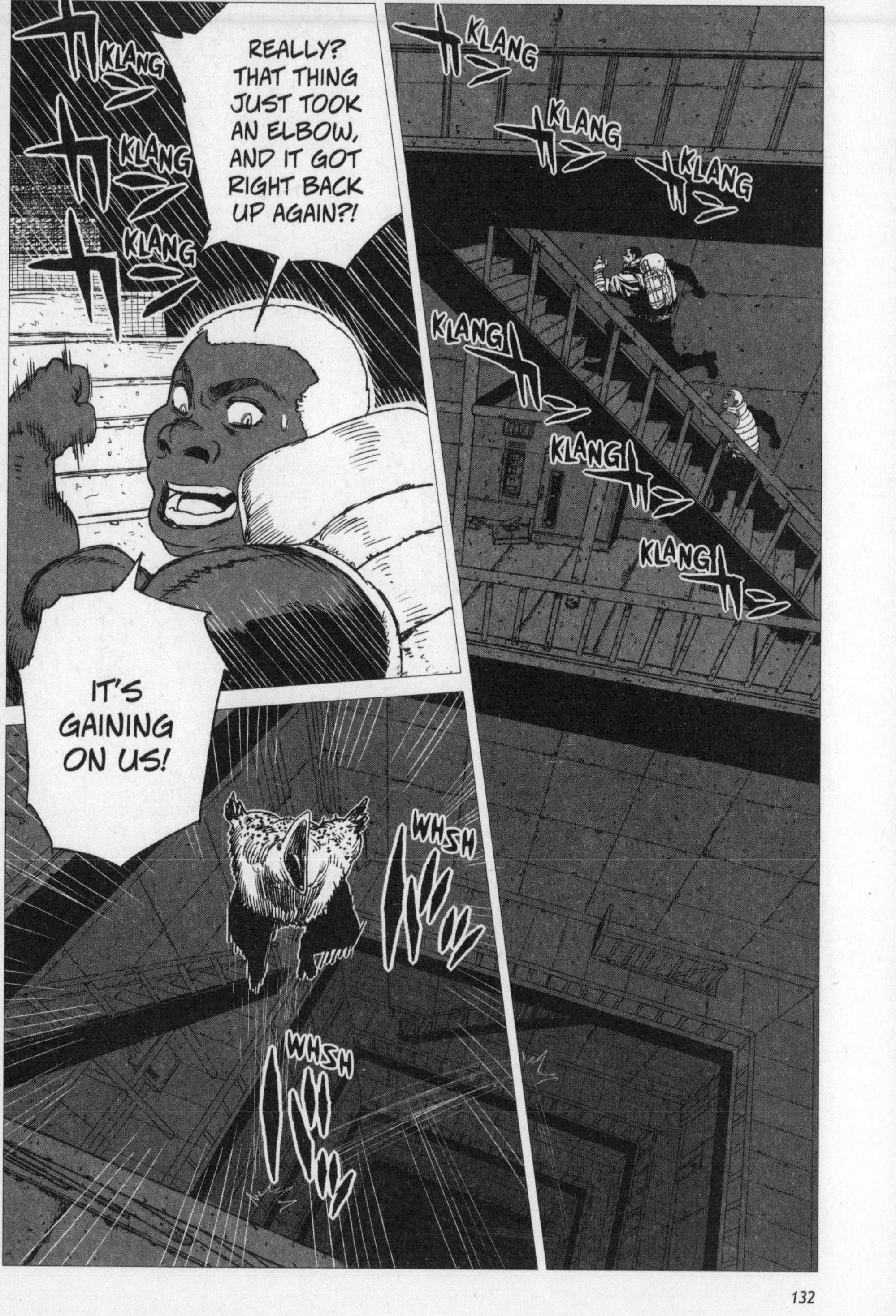
KLANG
KLANG
KLANG
KLANG
KLANG
KLANG
KLANG
KLANG
REALLY? THAT THING JUST TOOK AN ELBOW, AND IT GOT RIGHT BACK UP AGAIN?!
IT'S GAINING ON US!
WHSH
WHSH

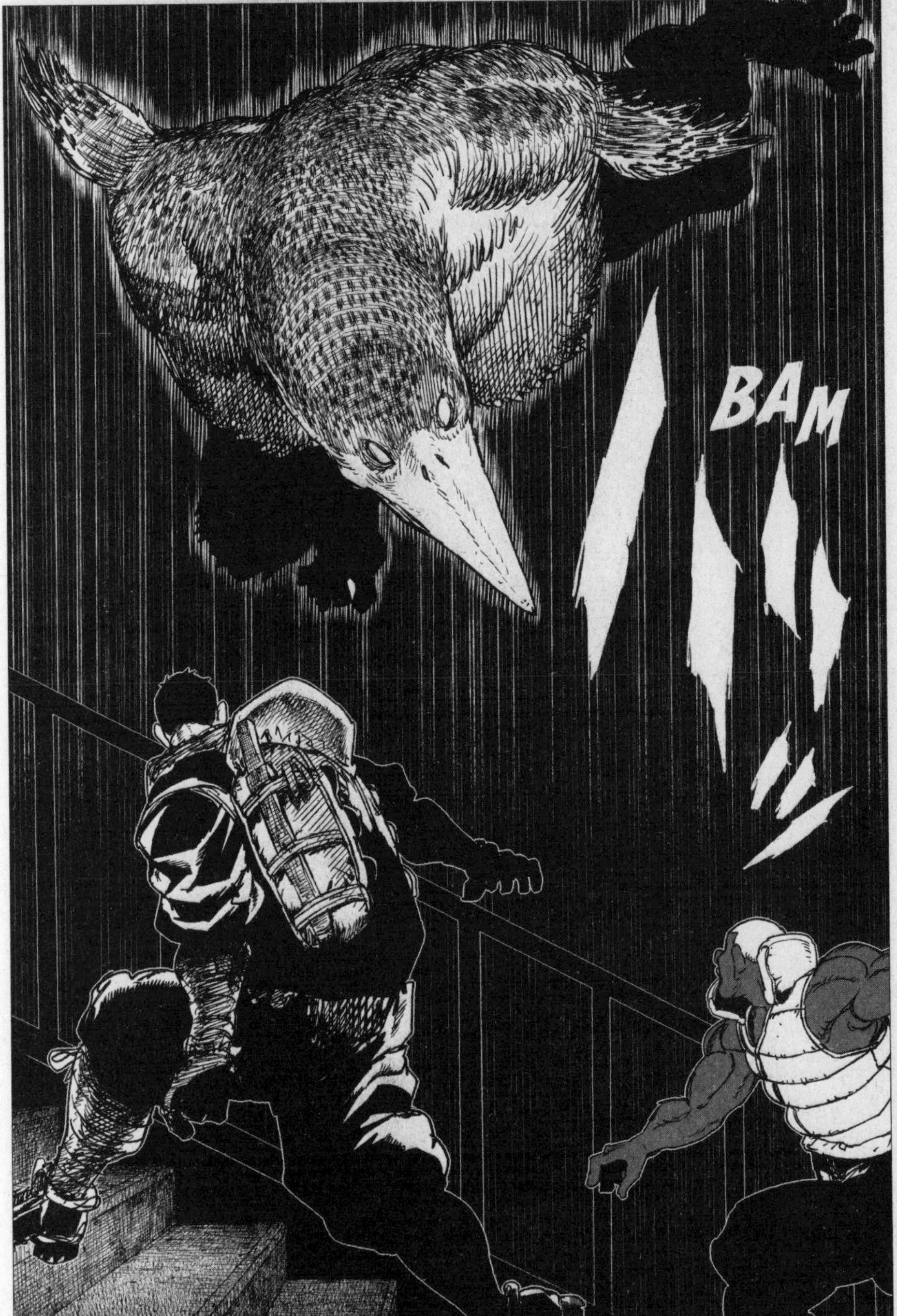
BAM

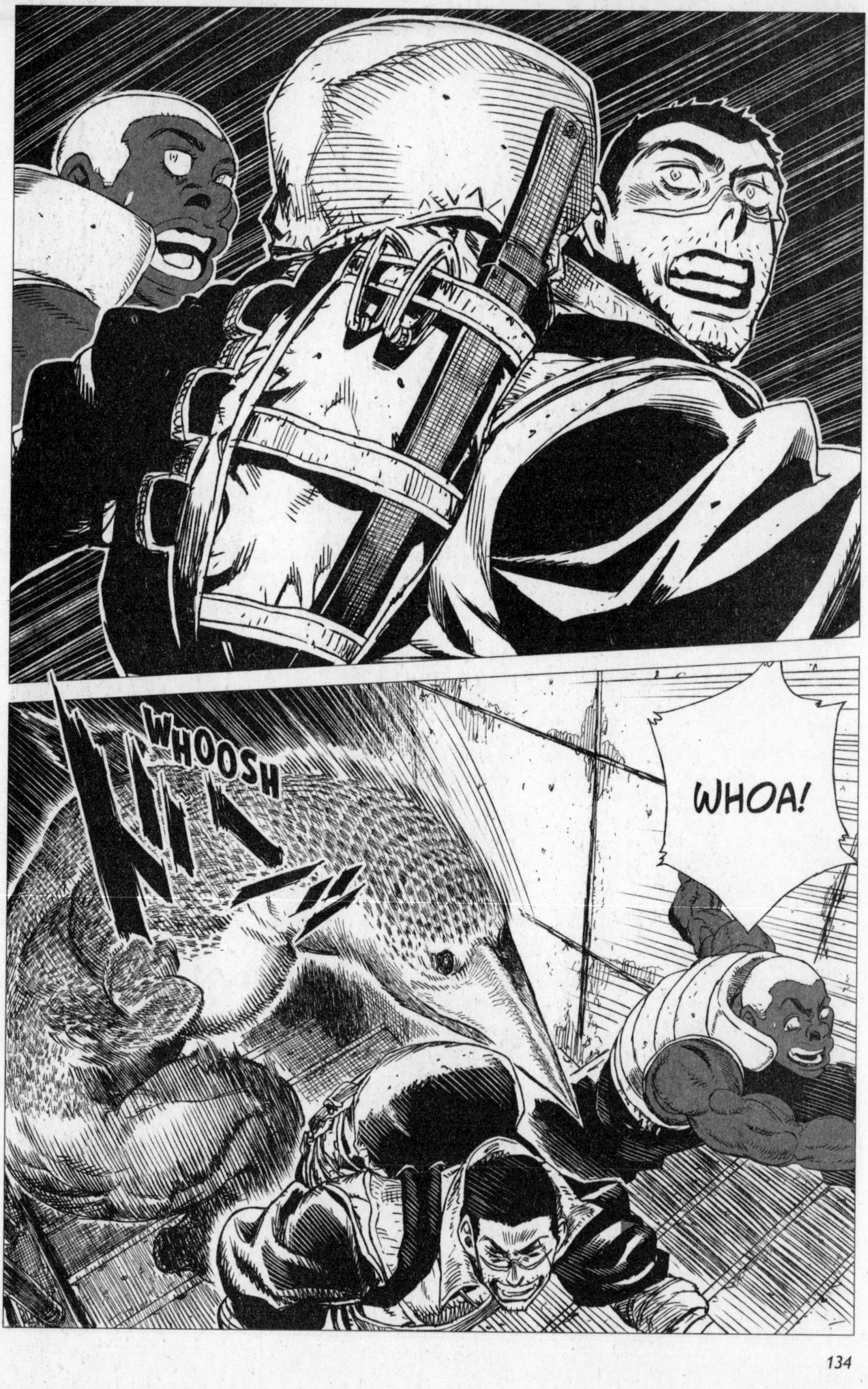
WHOA!
WHOOSH

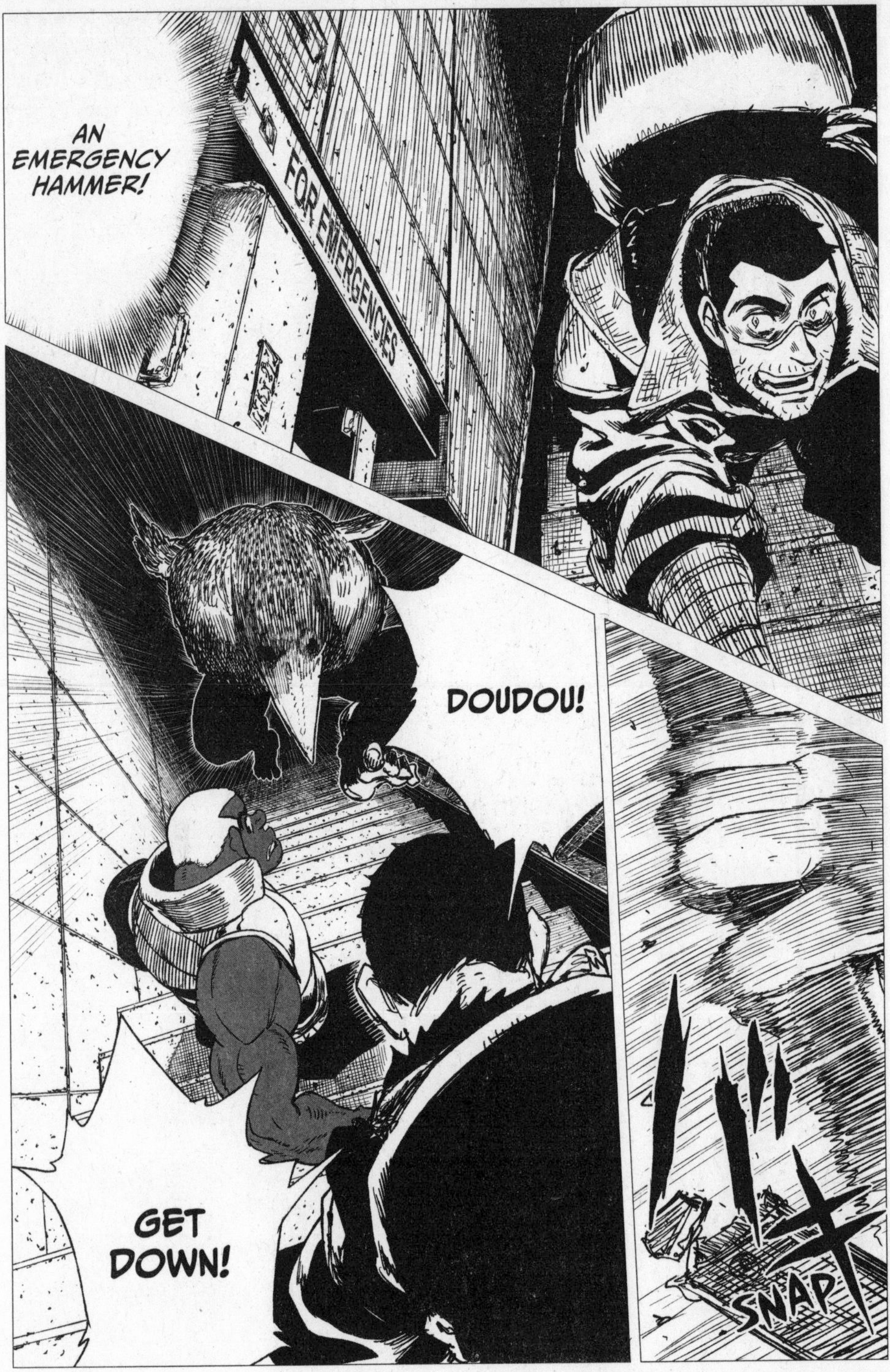
AN EMERGENCY HAMMER!
FOR EMERGENCIES
SNAP
DOUDOU!
GET DOWN!

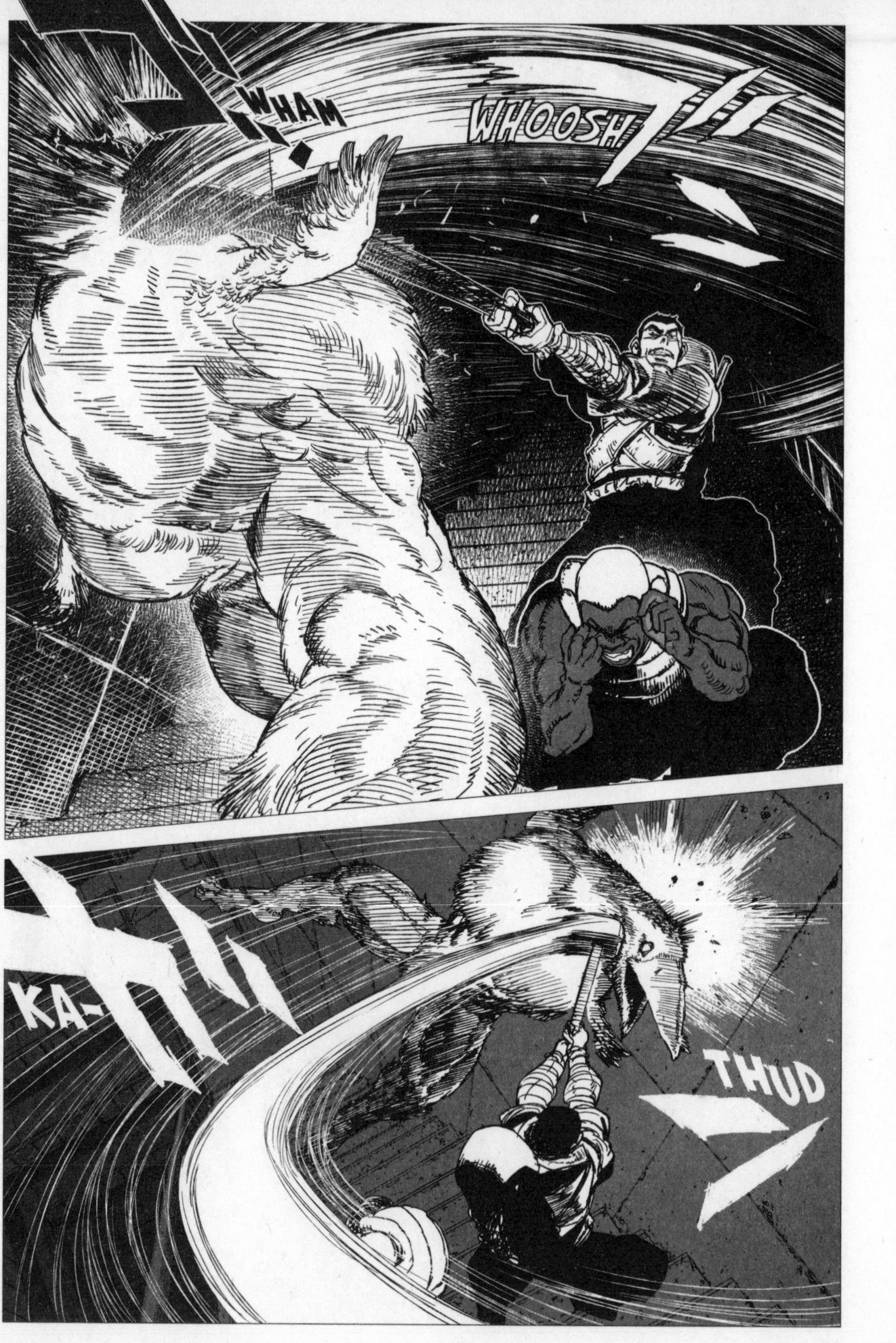
WHOOSH
WHAM
KA-
THUD

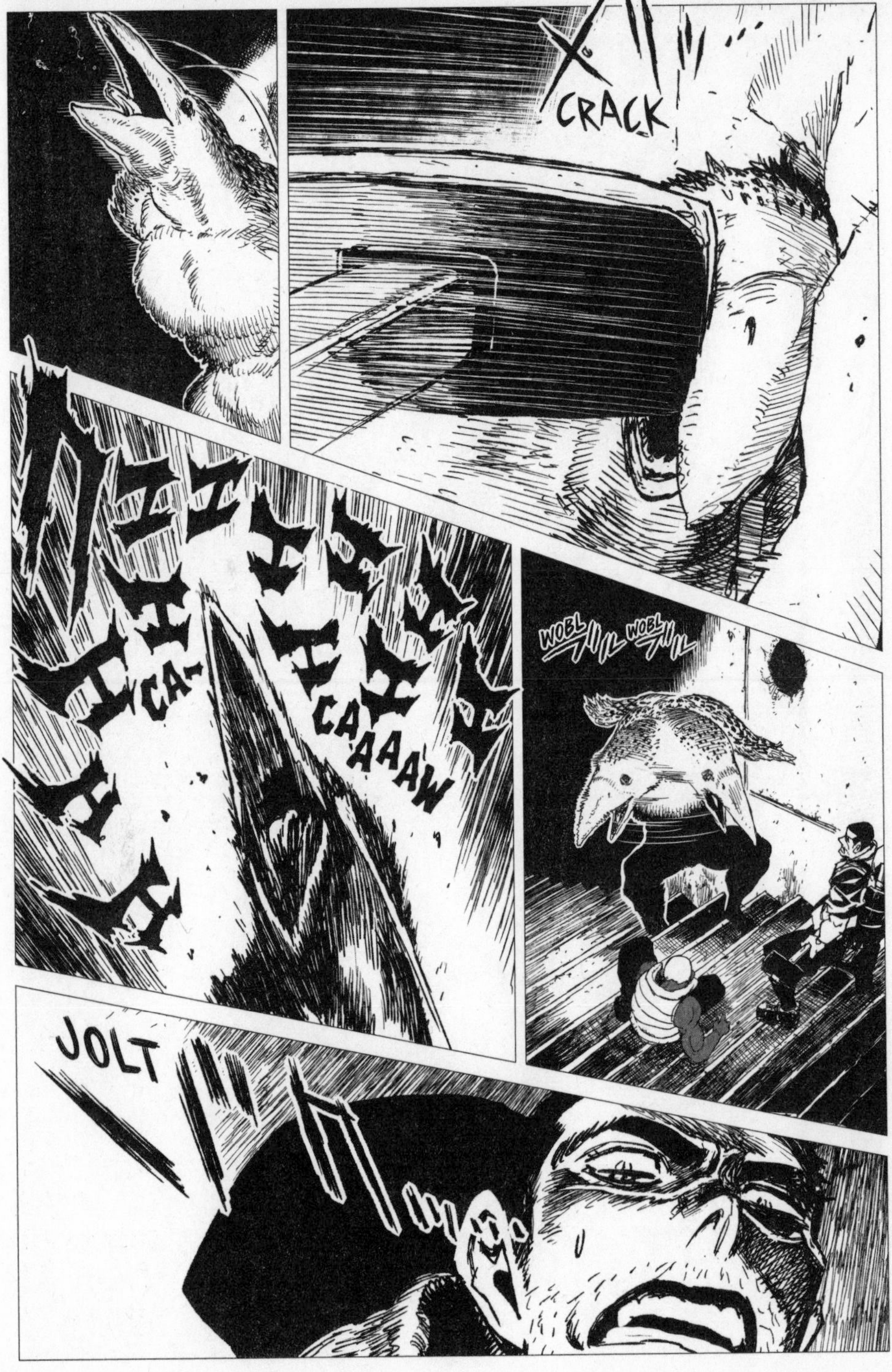
CRACK
WOBL WOBL
CA-
CAAAAW
JOLT

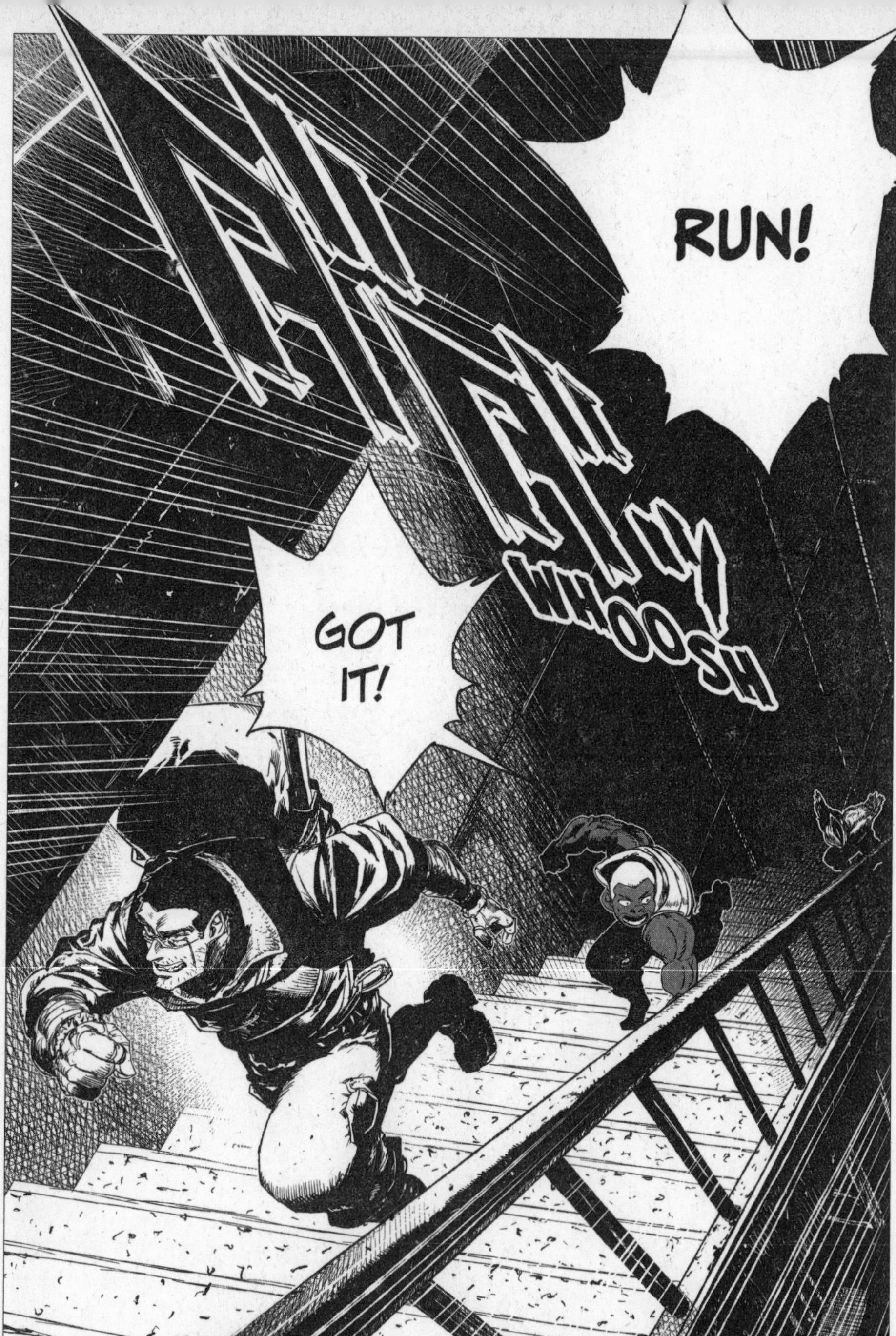
RUN!
WHOOSH
GOT IT!

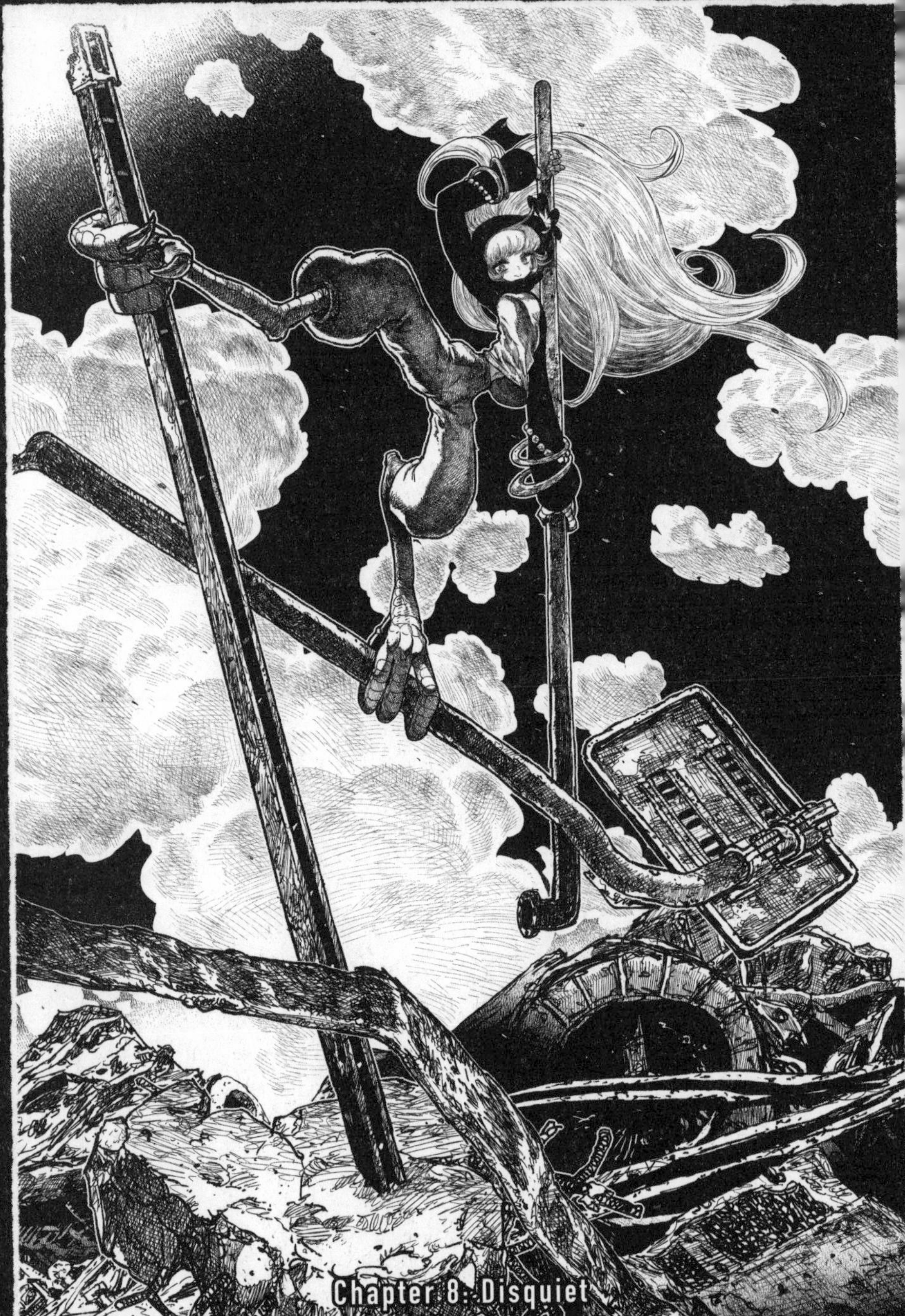
Chapter 8: Disquiet

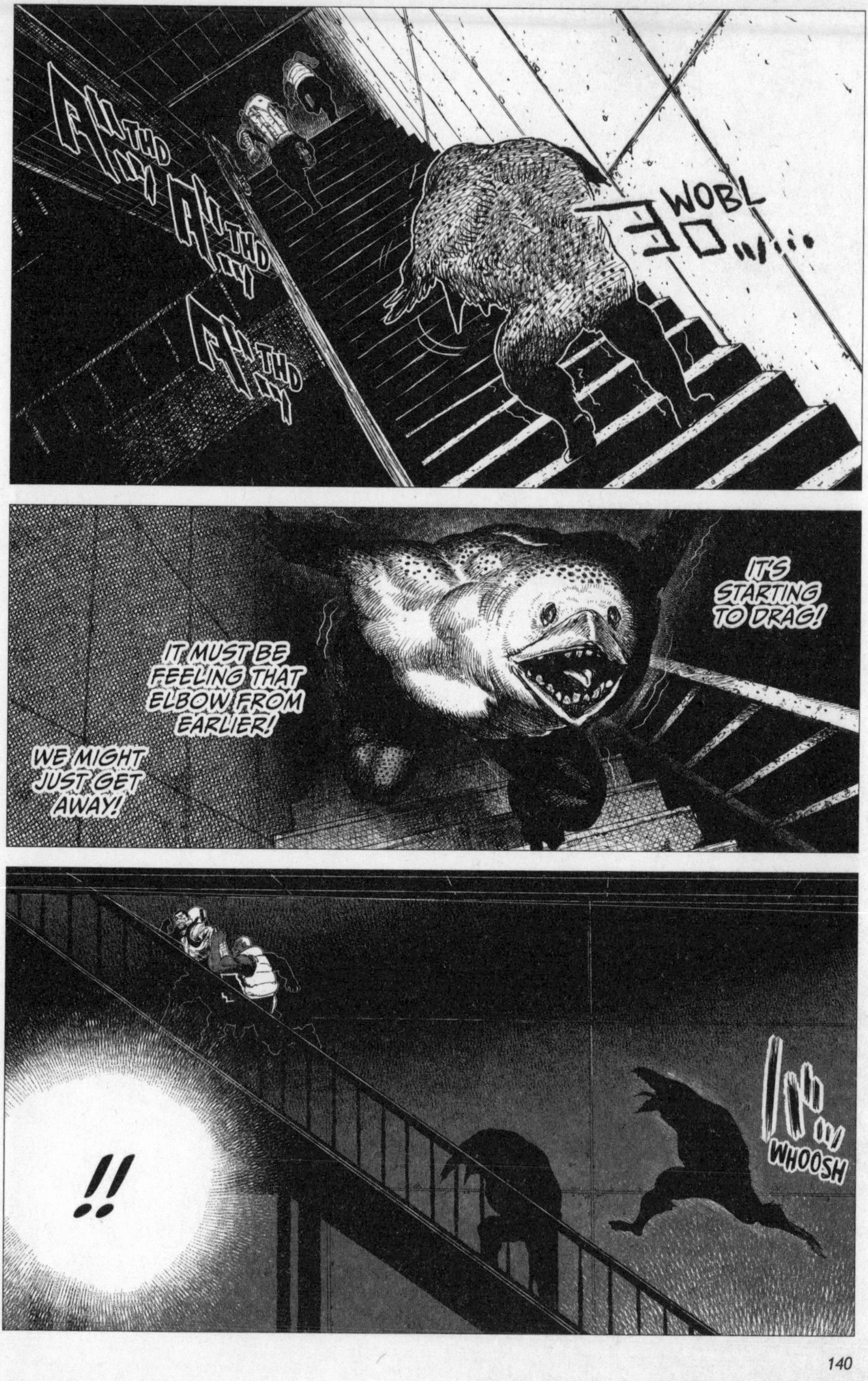
WOBL
THD
THD
THD
IT'S STARTING TO DRAG!
IT MUST BE FEELING THAT ELBOW FROM EARLIER!
WE MIGHT JUST GET AWAY!
WHOOSH
!!

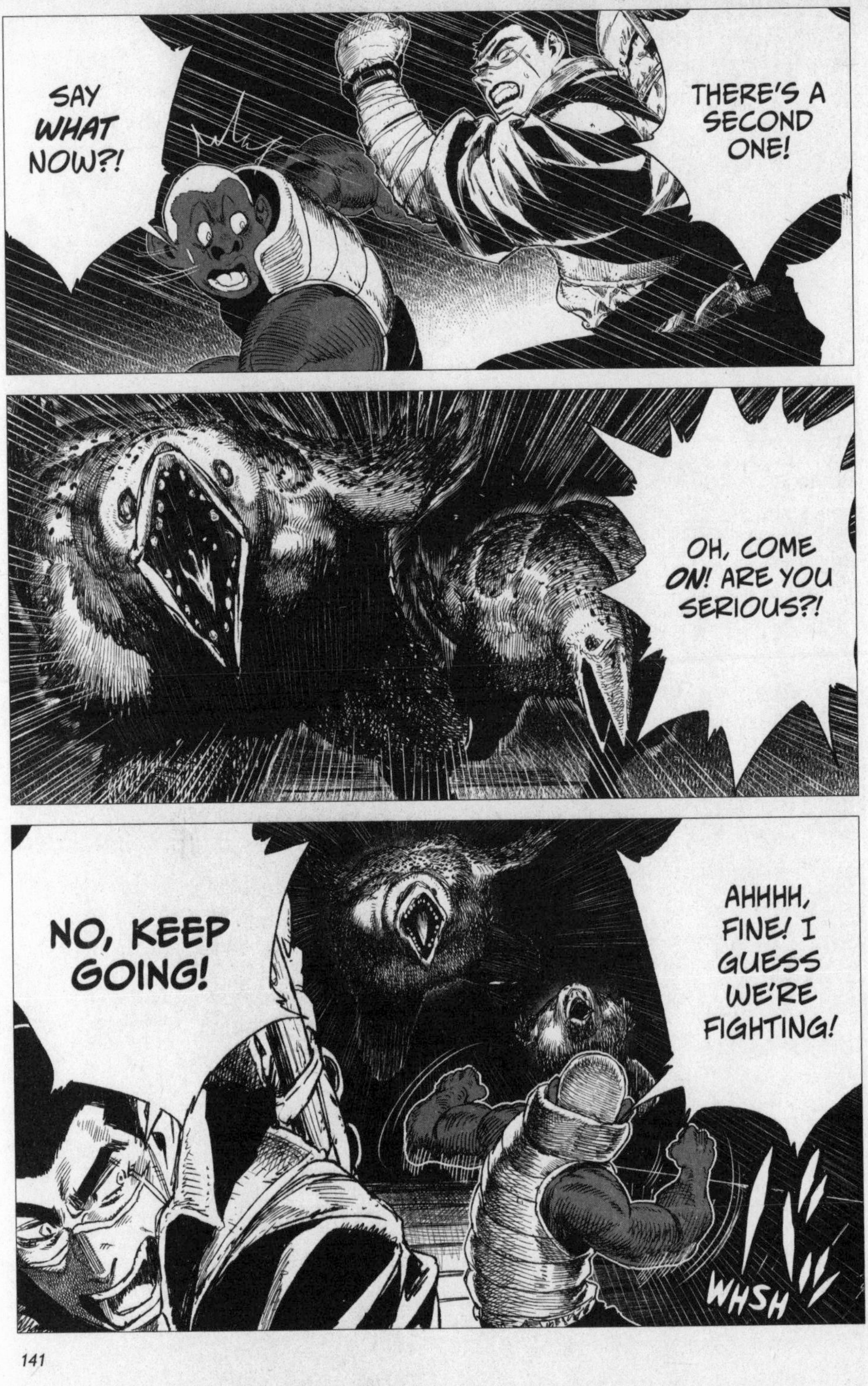
THERE'S A SECOND ONE!
SAY WHAT NOW?!
OH, COME ON! ARE YOU SERIOUS?!
AHHHH, FINE! I GUESS WE'RE FIGHTING!
WHSH
NO, KEEP GOING!

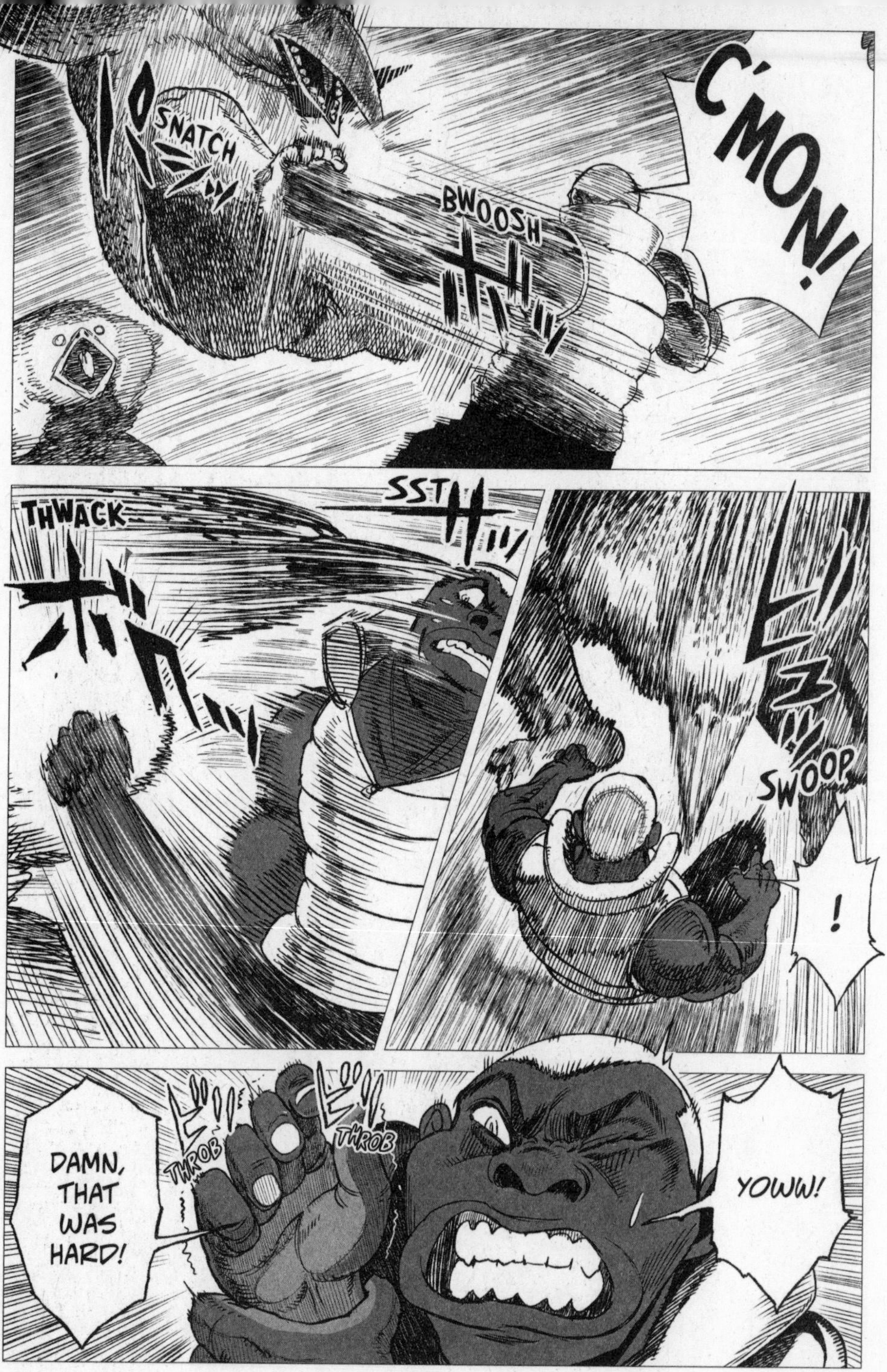
C'MON!
BWOOSH
SNATCH
SWOOP
!
SST
THWACK
YOWW!
THROB
THROB
DAMN, THAT WAS HARD!

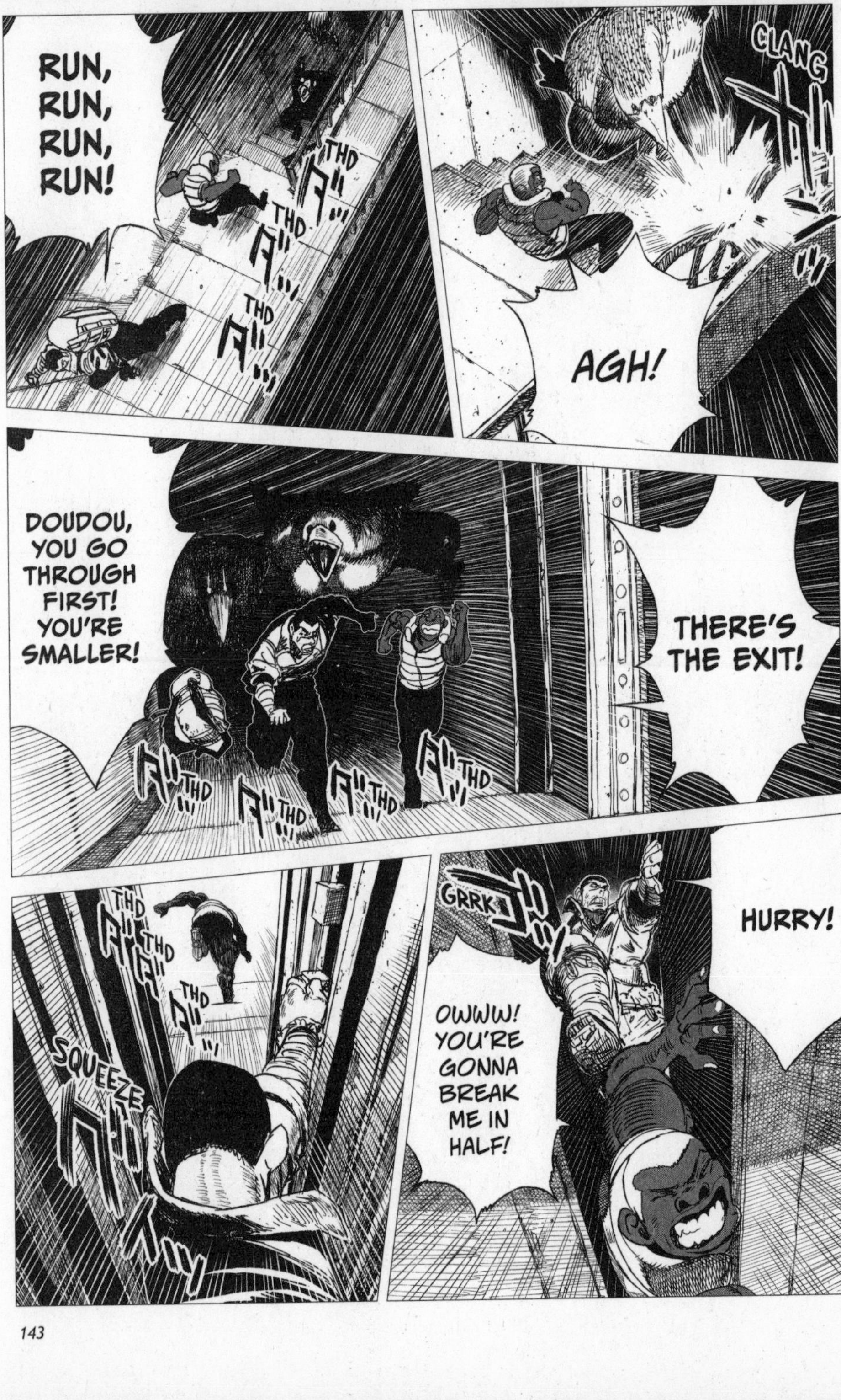
CLANG
AGH!
RUN, RUN, RUN, RUN!
THD
THD
THD
THERE'S THE EXIT!
DOUDOU, YOU GO THROUGH FIRST! YOU'RE SMALLER!
THD
THD
THD
THD
HURRY!
GRRK
OWWW! YOU'RE GONNA BREAK ME IN HALF!
THD
THD
THD
SQUEEZE

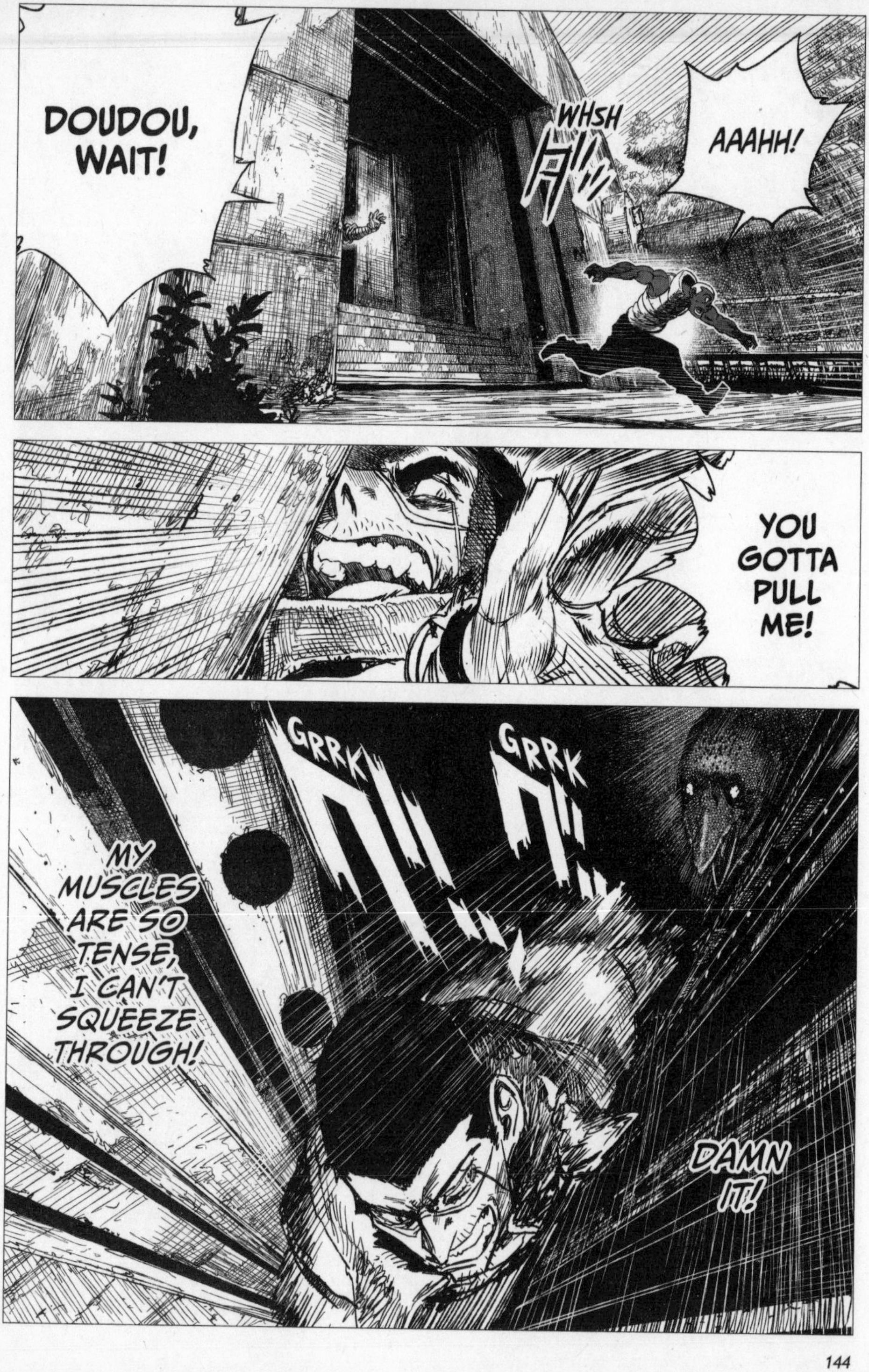
AAAHH!
WHSH
DOUDOU, WAIT!
YOU GOTTA PULL ME!
GRRK
GRRK
MY MUSCLES ARE SO TENSE, I CAN'T SQUEEZE THROUGH!
DAMN IT!

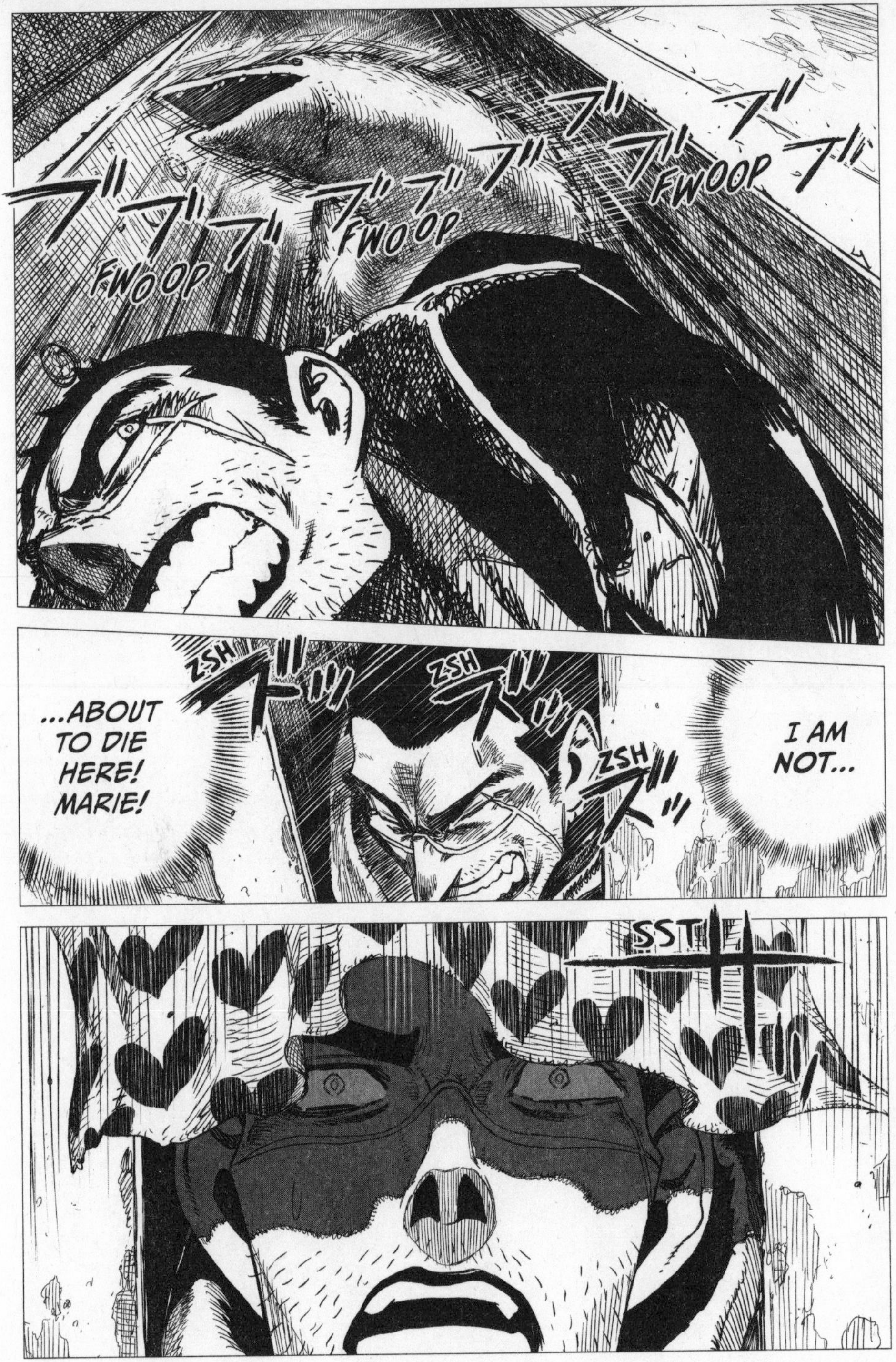
FWOOP
FWOOP
FWOOP
I AM NOT...
ZSH
ZSH
ZSH
...ABOUT TO DIE HERE! MARIE!
SST

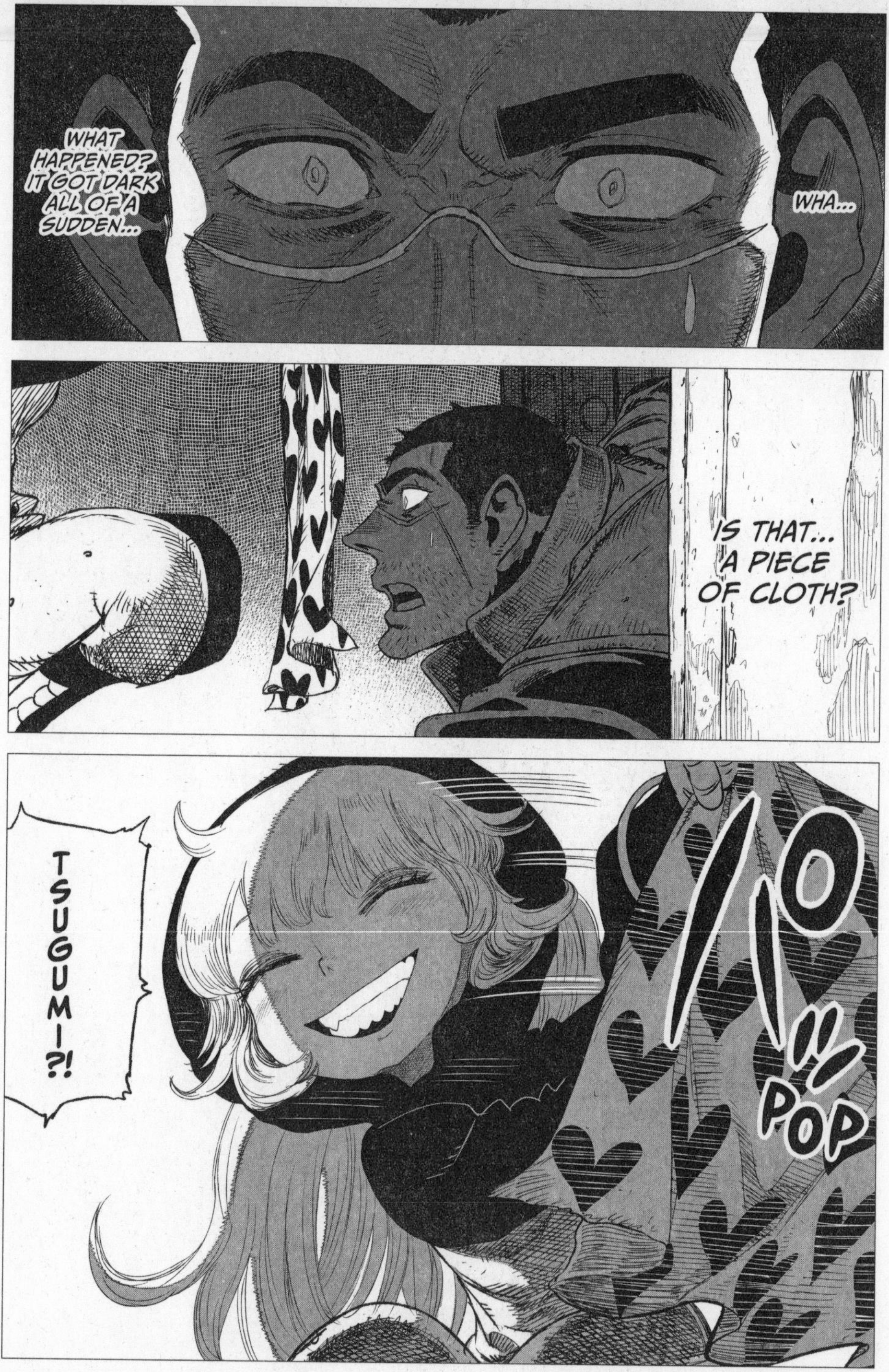
WHA...
WHAT HAPPENED? IT GOT DARK ALL OF A SUDDEN...
IS THAT... A PIECE OF CLOTH?
POP
TSUGUMI?!

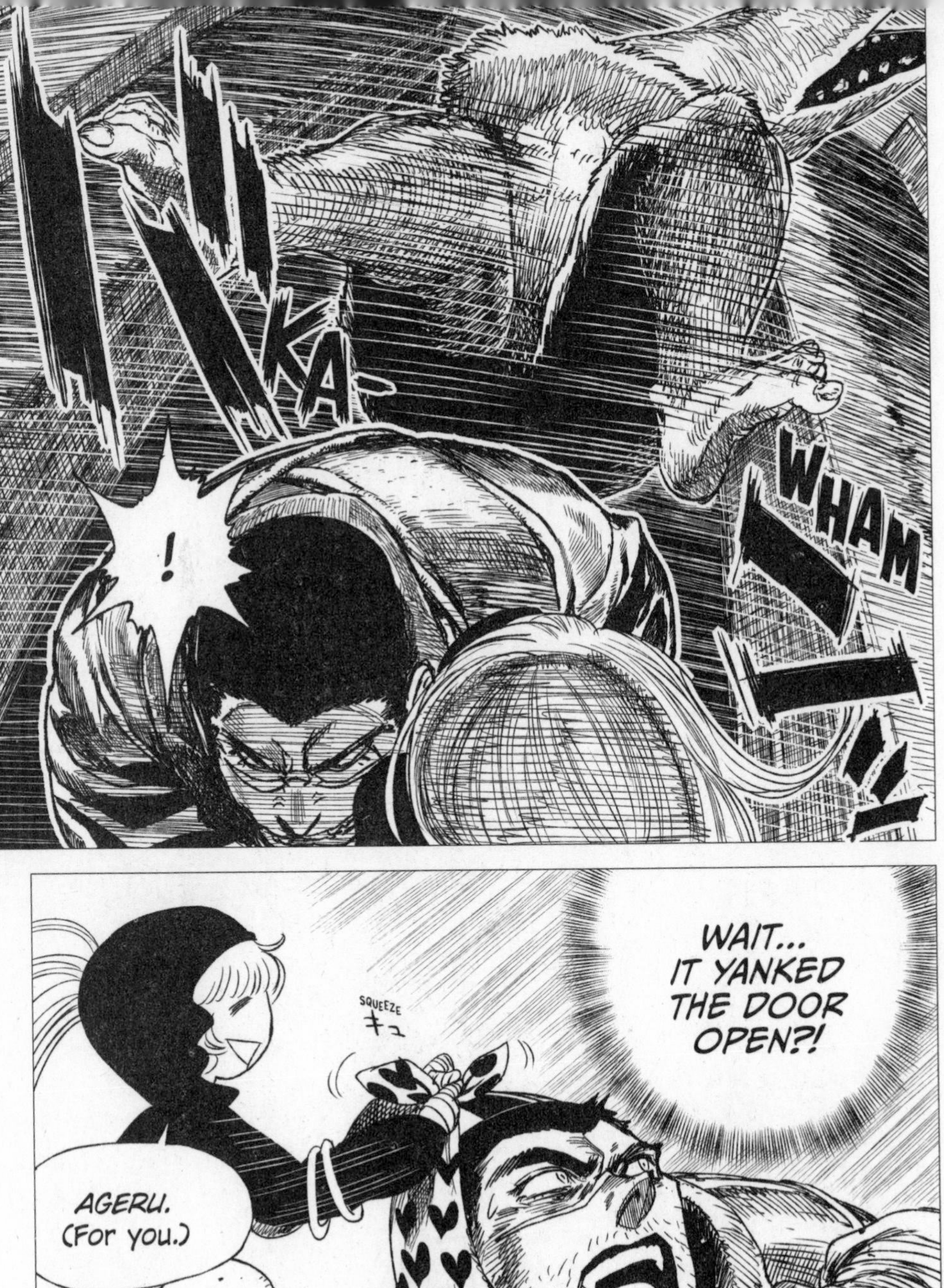
KA-
WHAM
!
WAIT... IT YANKED THE DOOR OPEN?!
SQUEEZE
キュ
AGERU. (For you.)

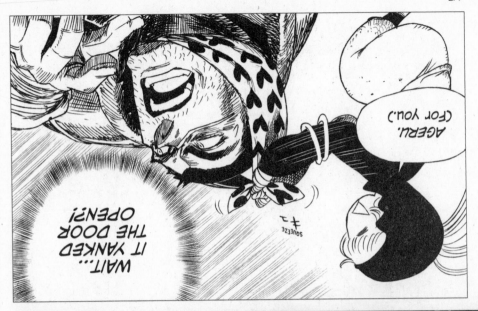

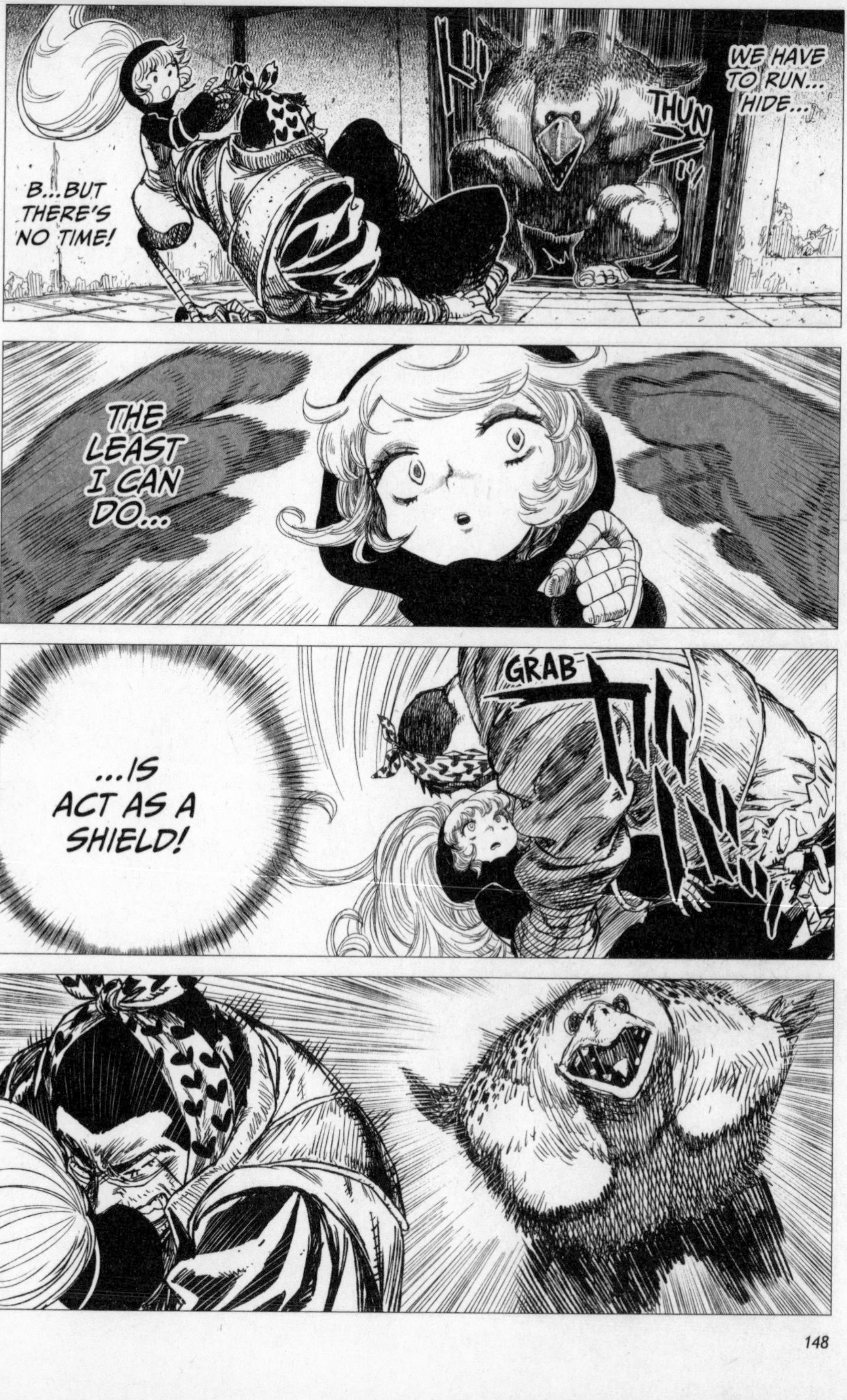
WE HAVE TO RUN... HIDE...
THUN
B...BUT THERE'S NO TIME!
THE LEAST I CAN DO...
GRAB
...IS ACT AS A SHIELD!

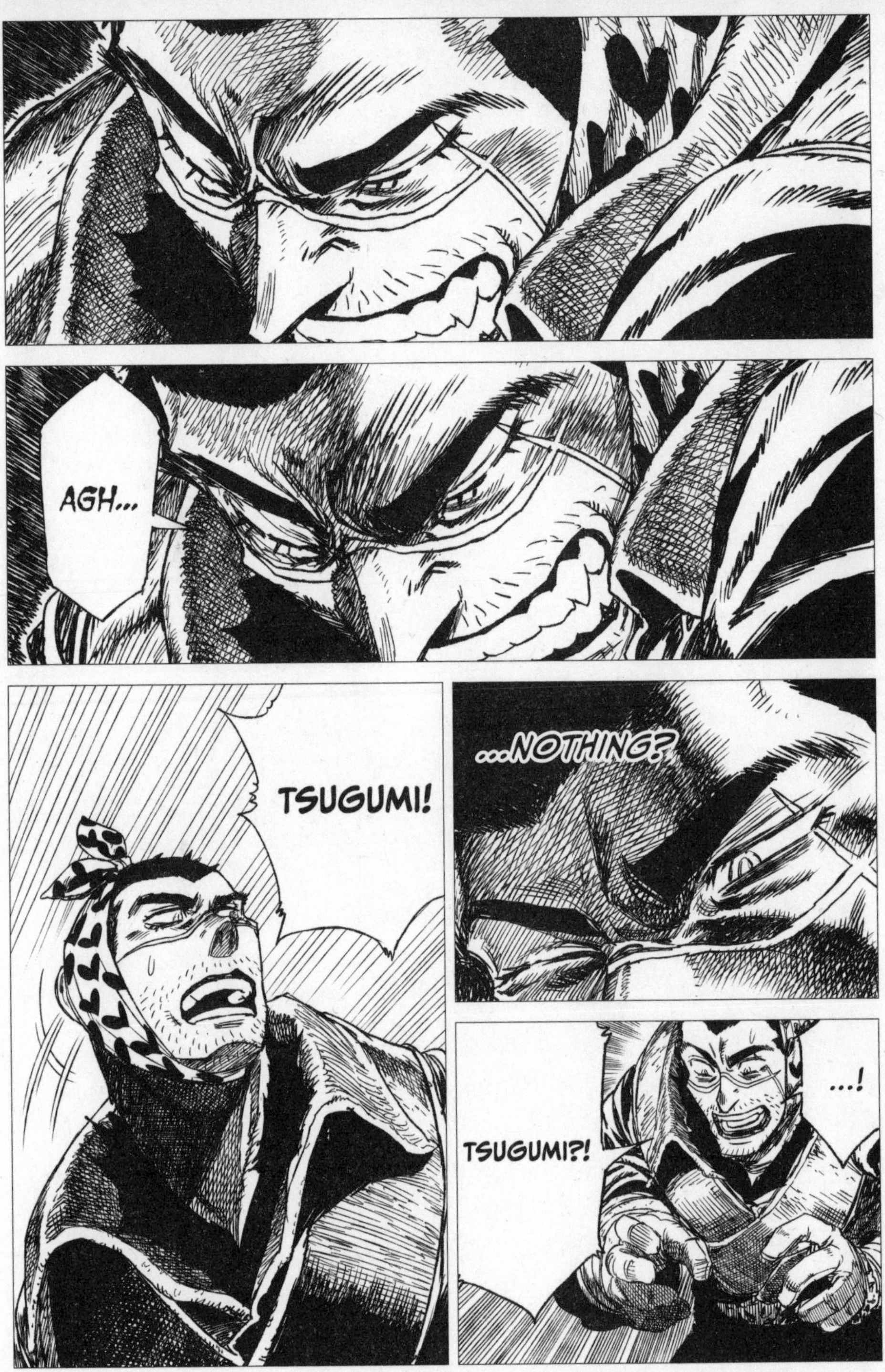
AGH...
...NOTHING?
...!
TSUGUMI?!
TSUGUMI!

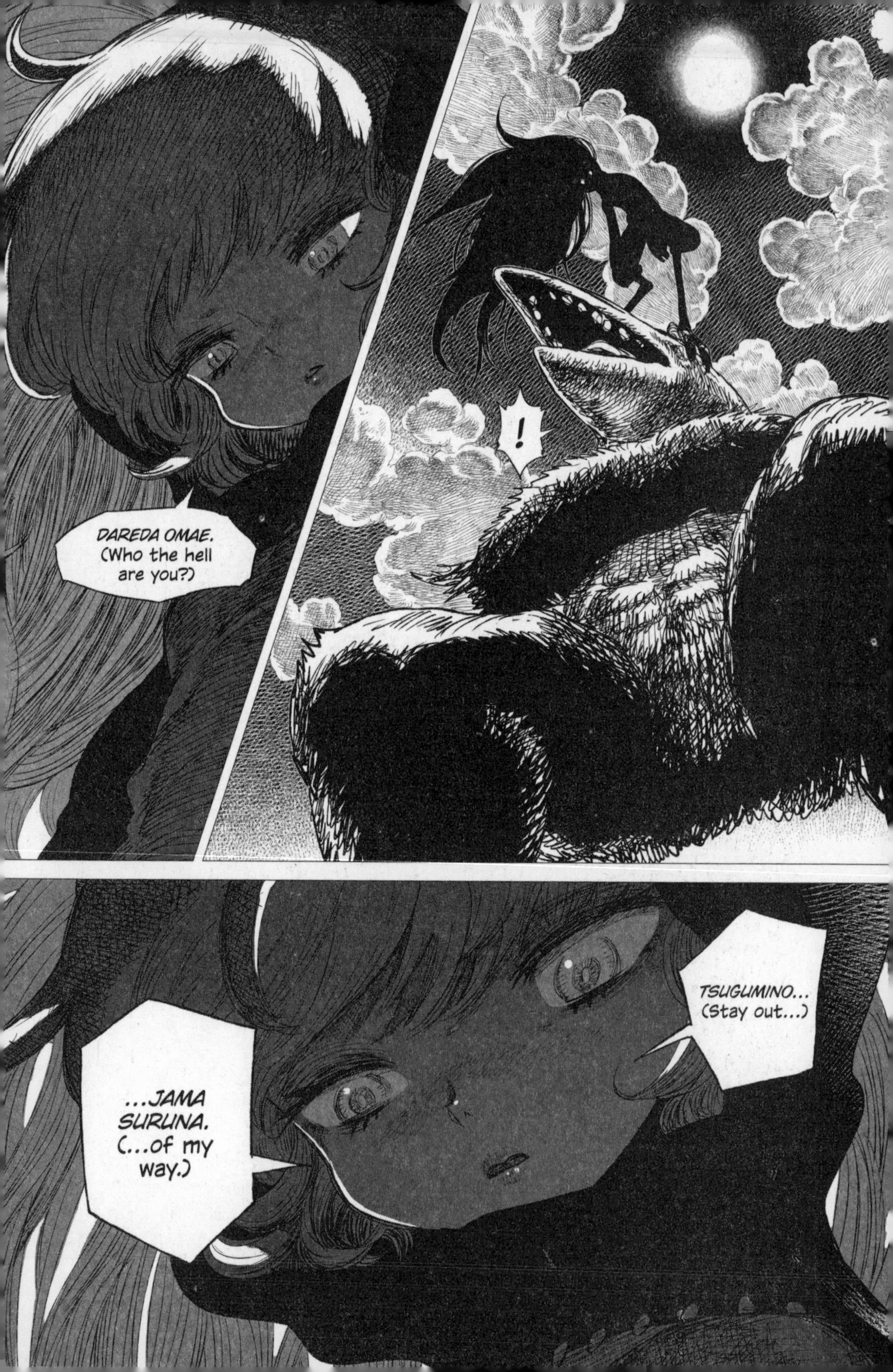
!
DAREDA OMAE.
(Who the hell are you?)
TSUGUMINO...
(Stay out...)
...JAMA SURUNA.
(...of my way.)

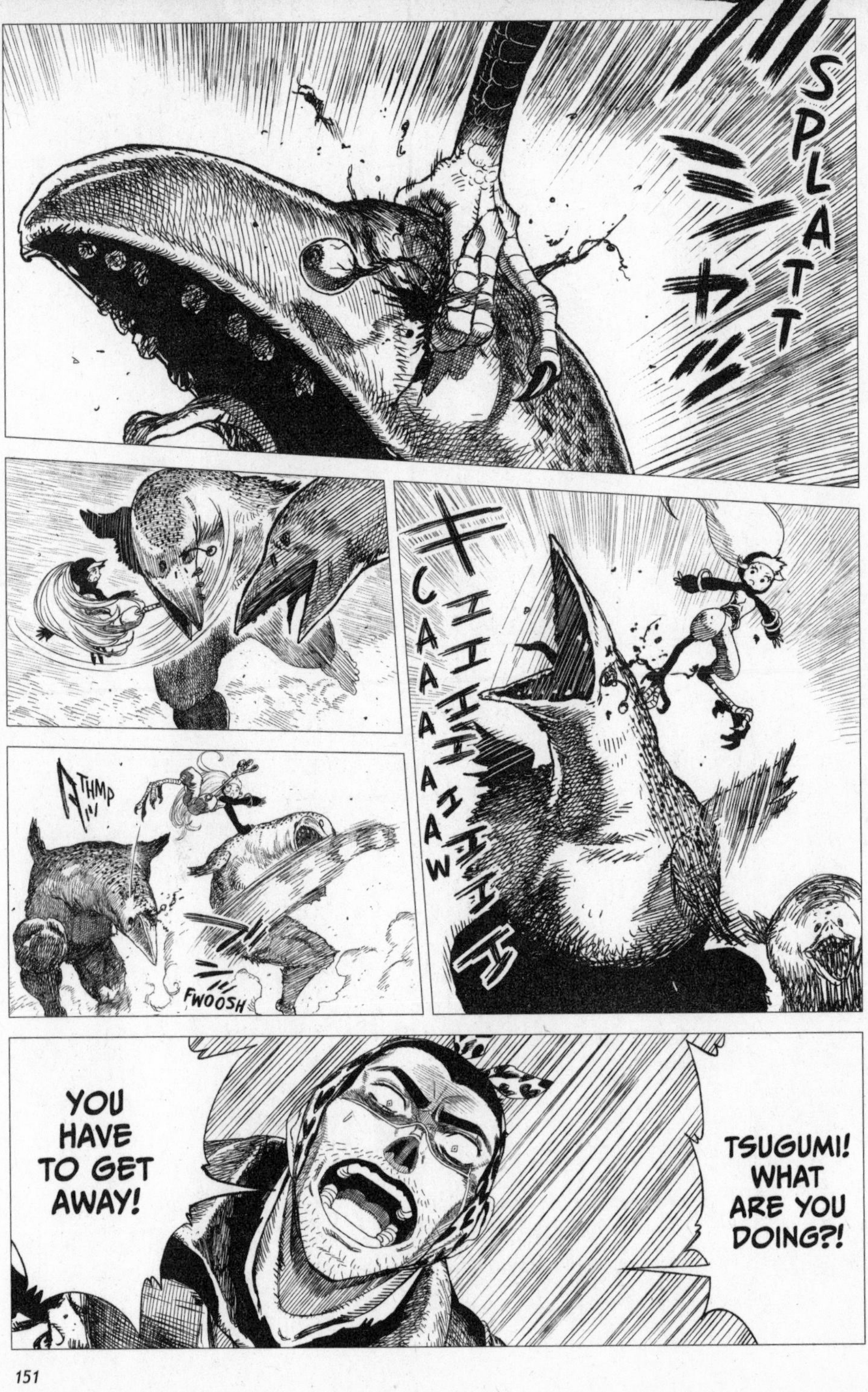
SPLATT
KIIIIIIIH
CAAAAAW
THMP
FWOOSH
TSUGUMI! WHAT ARE YOU DOING?!
YOU HAVE TO GET AWAY!

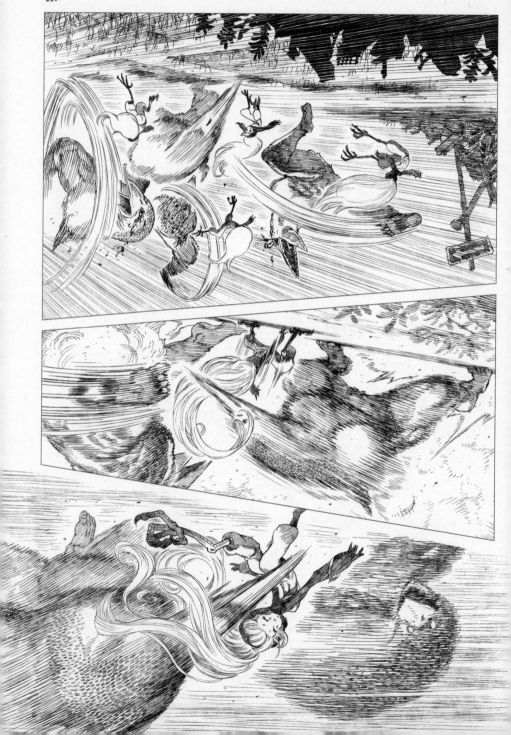

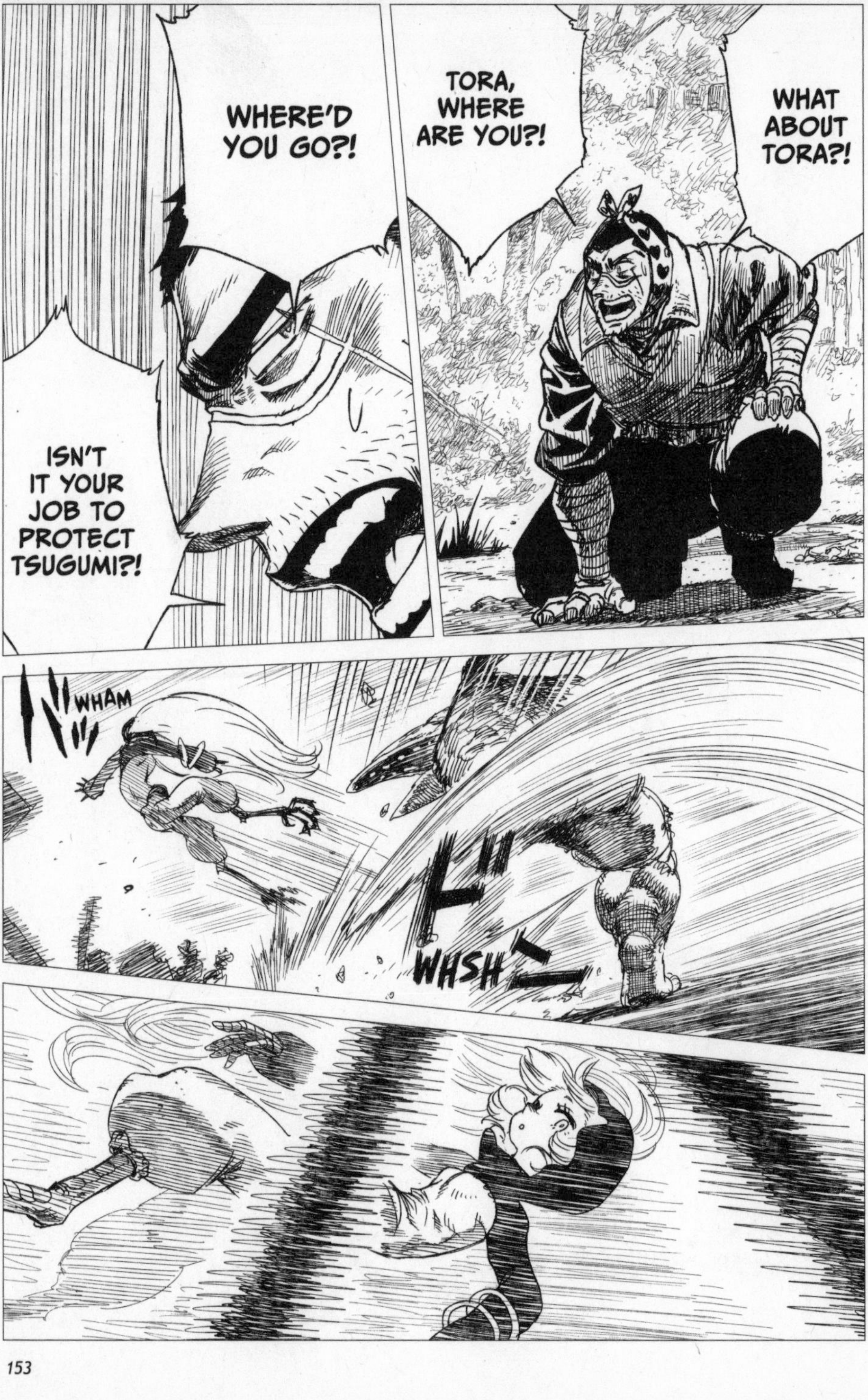
WHAT ABOUT TORA?!
TORA, WHERE ARE YOU?!
WHERE'D YOU GO?!
ISN'T IT YOUR JOB TO PROTECT TSUGUMI?!
WHSH
WHAM

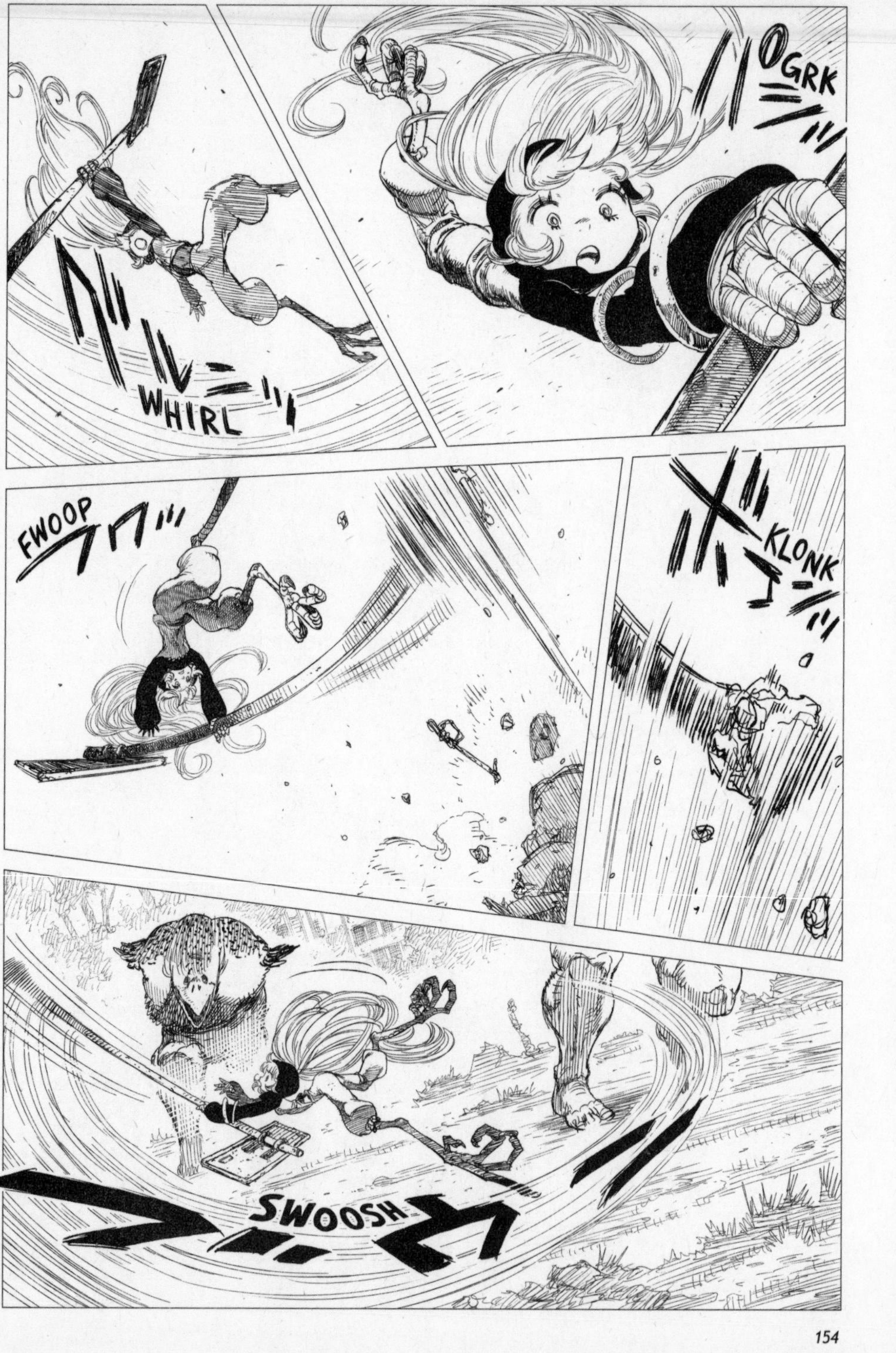
GRK
WHIRL
KLONK
FWOOP
SWOOSH

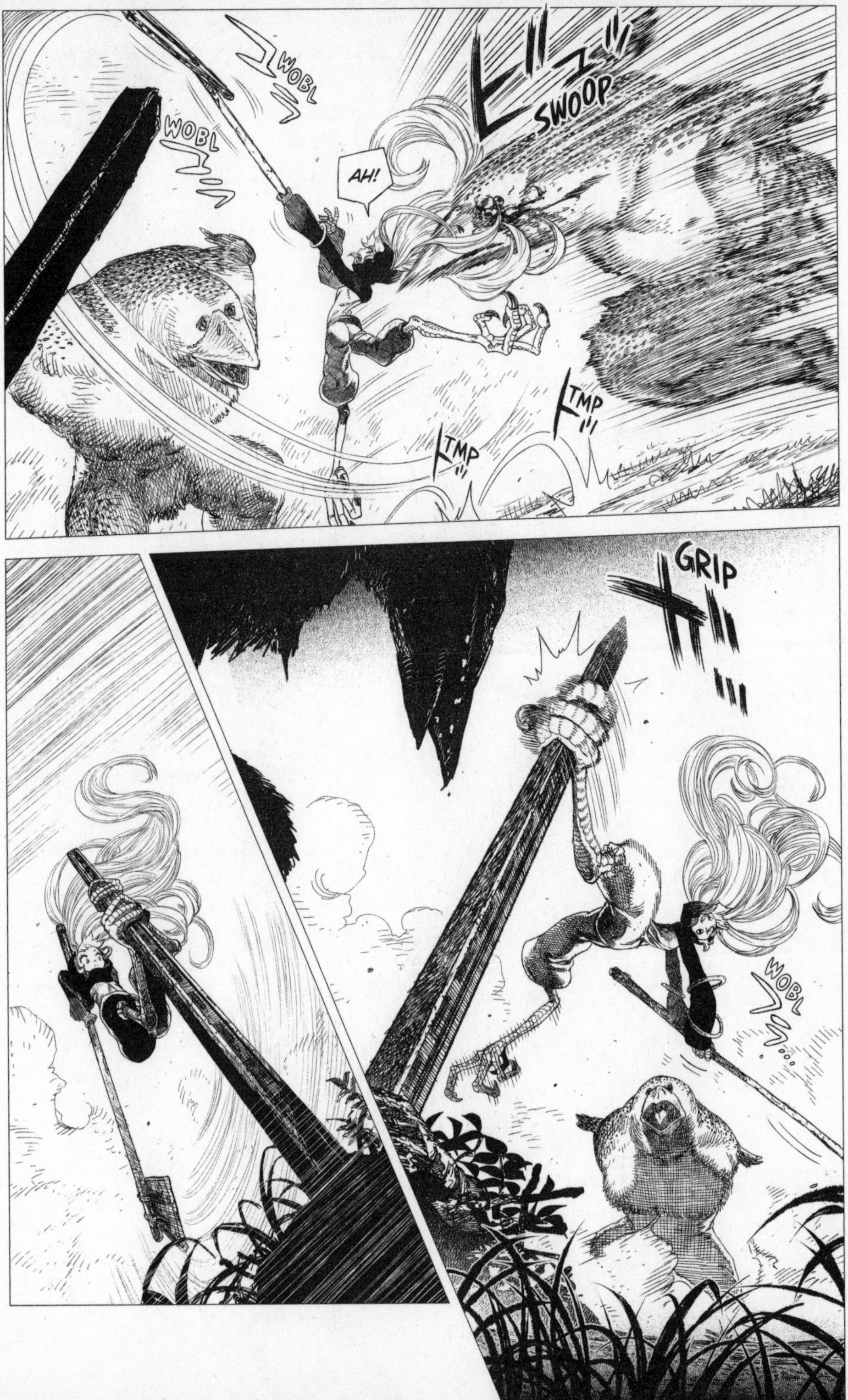
SWOOP
AH!
WOBL
WOBL
TMP
TMP
GRIP
WOBL

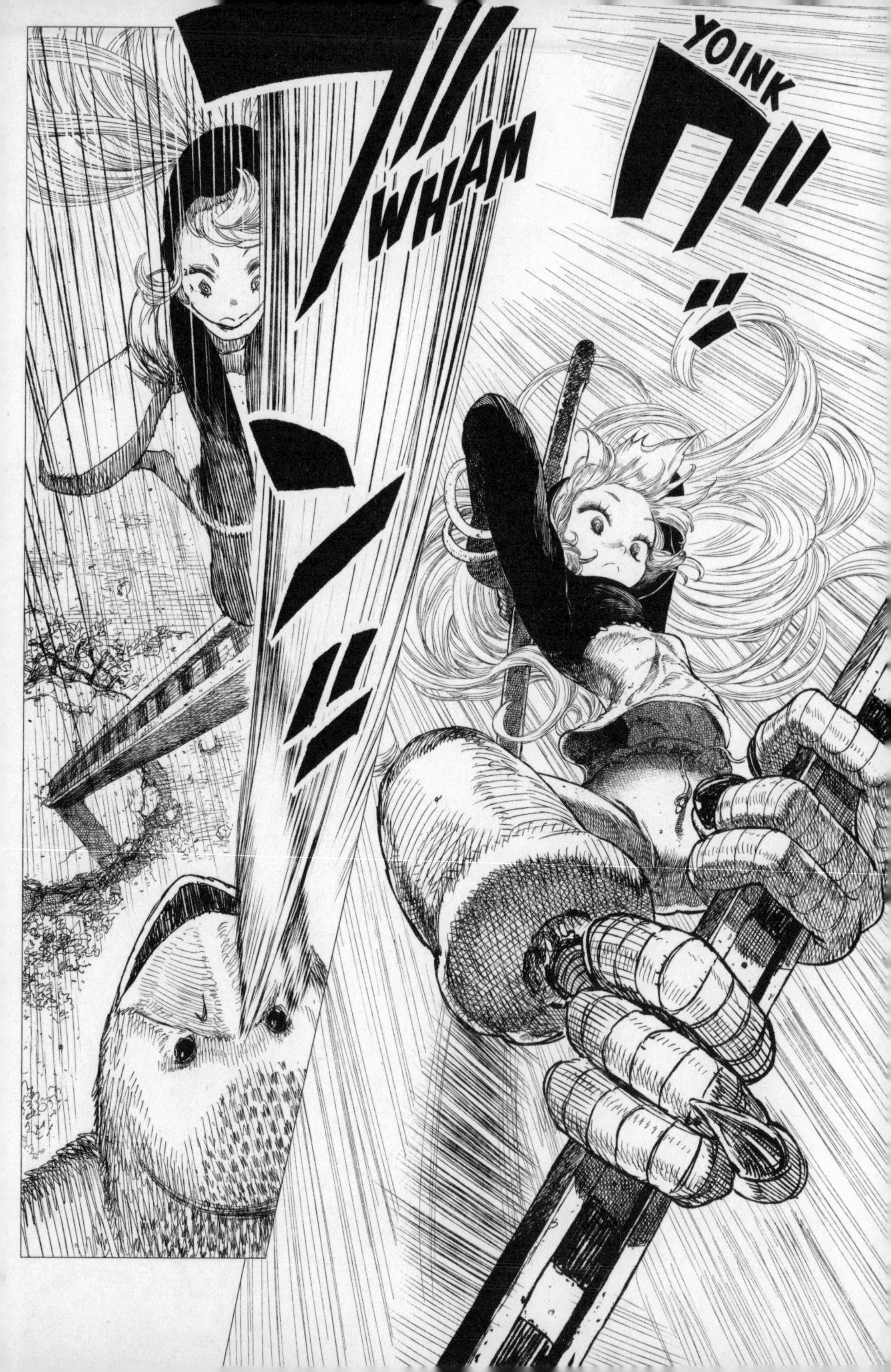
YOINK
WHAM

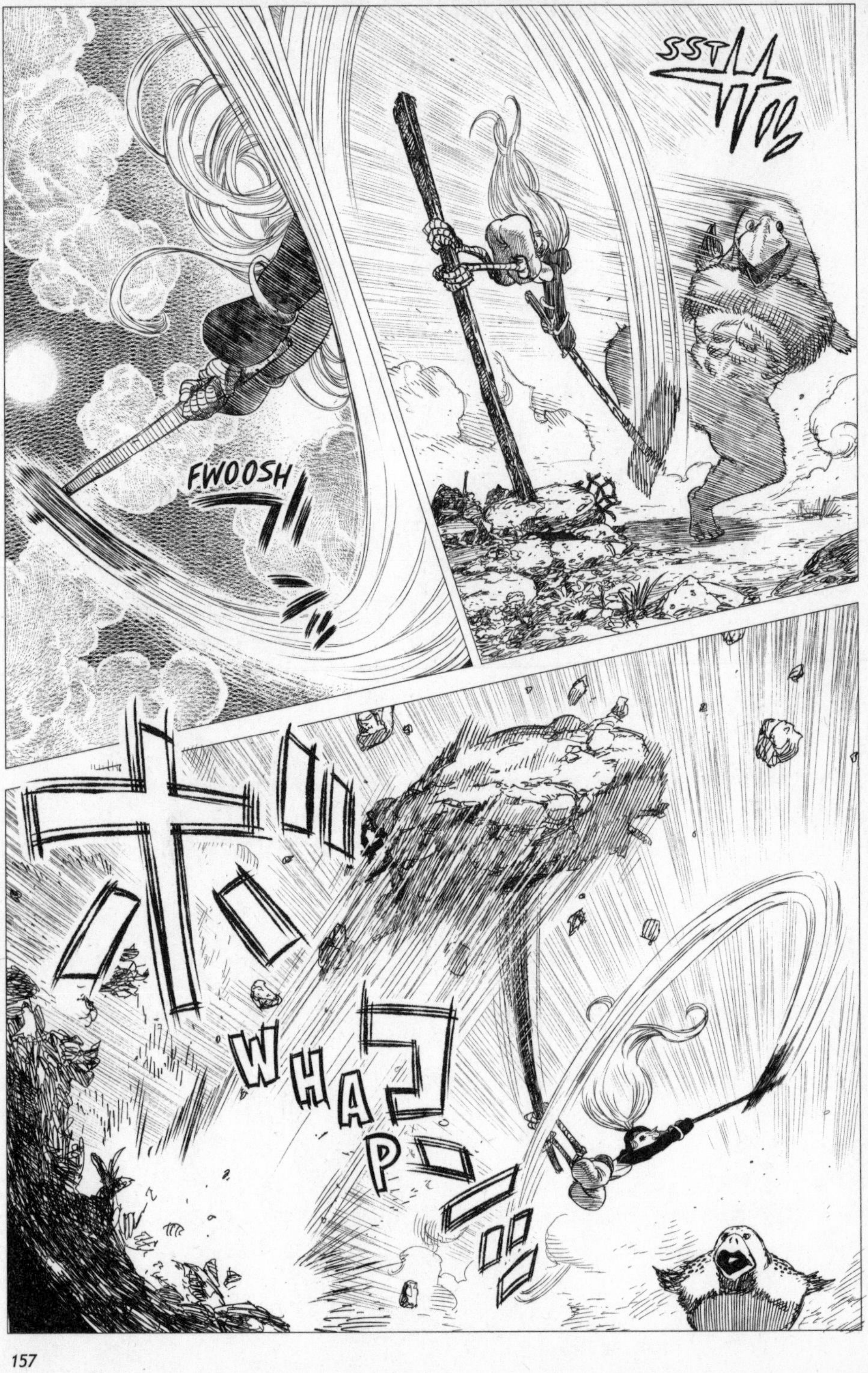
SSST
FWOOSH
WHAP

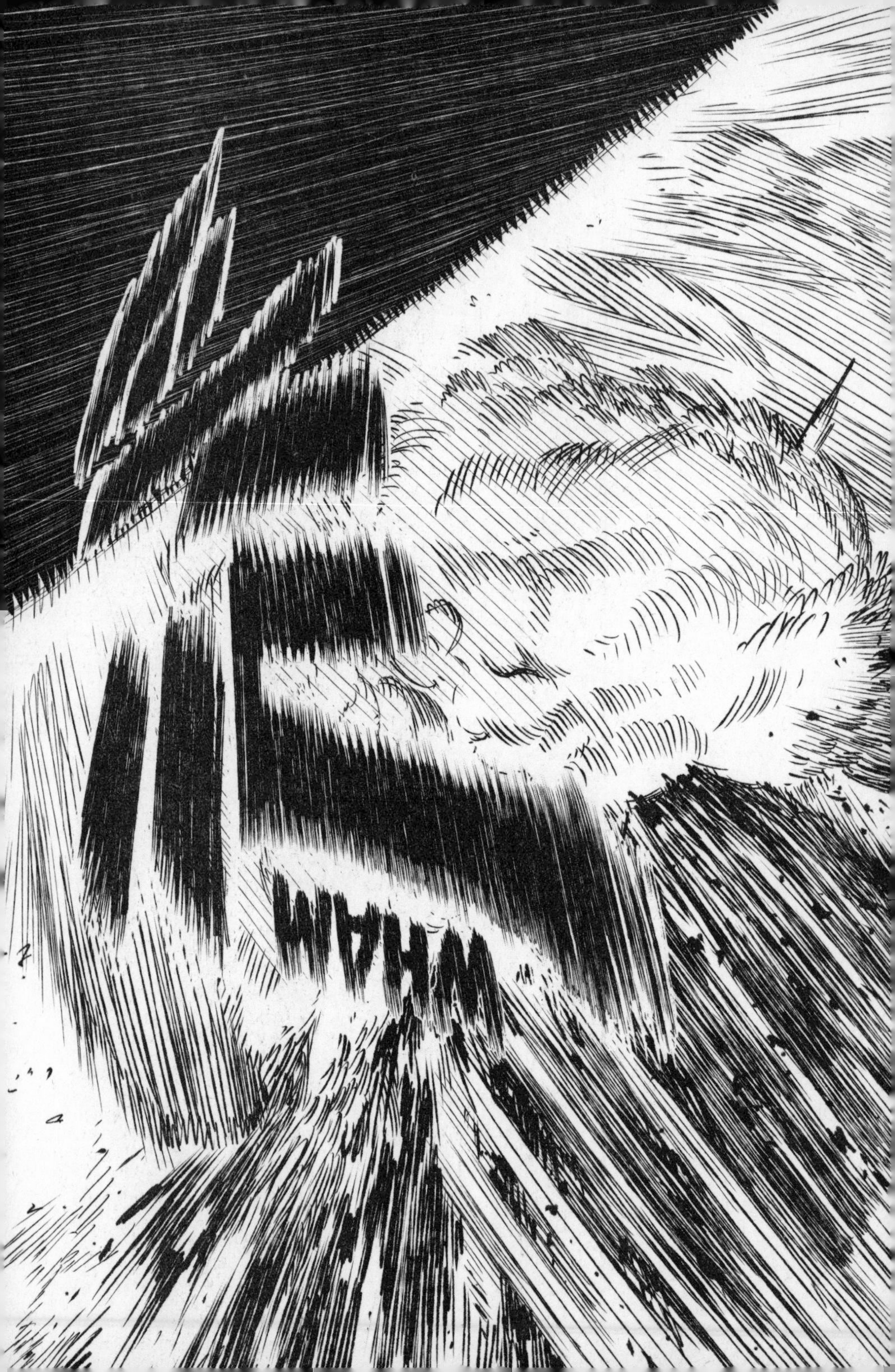
WHAM

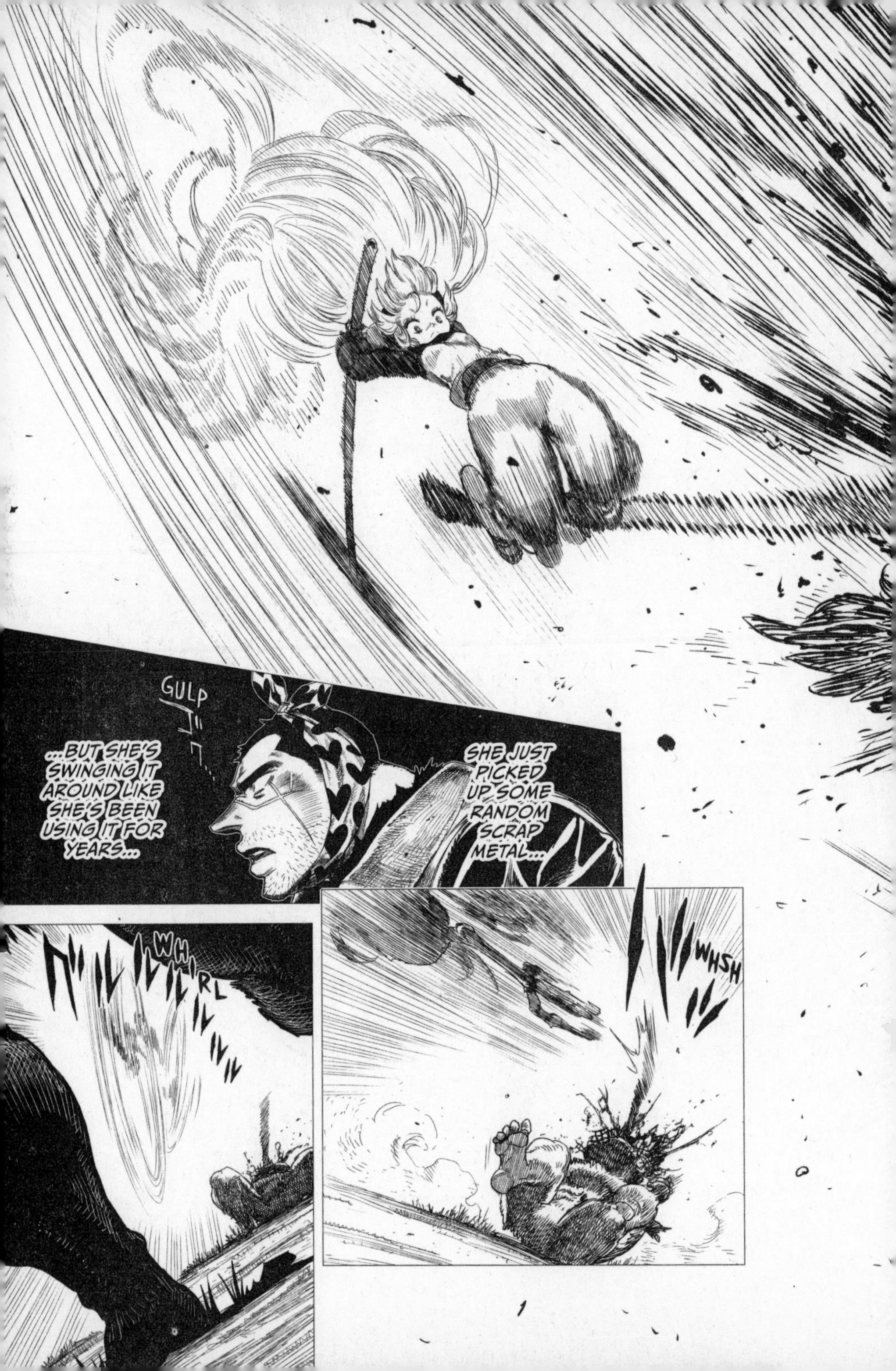
SHE JUST PICKED UP SOME RANDOM SCRAP METAL...
GULP
...BUT SHE'S SWINGING IT AROUND LIKE SHE'S BEEN USING IT FOR YEARS...
WHSH
WHIRL

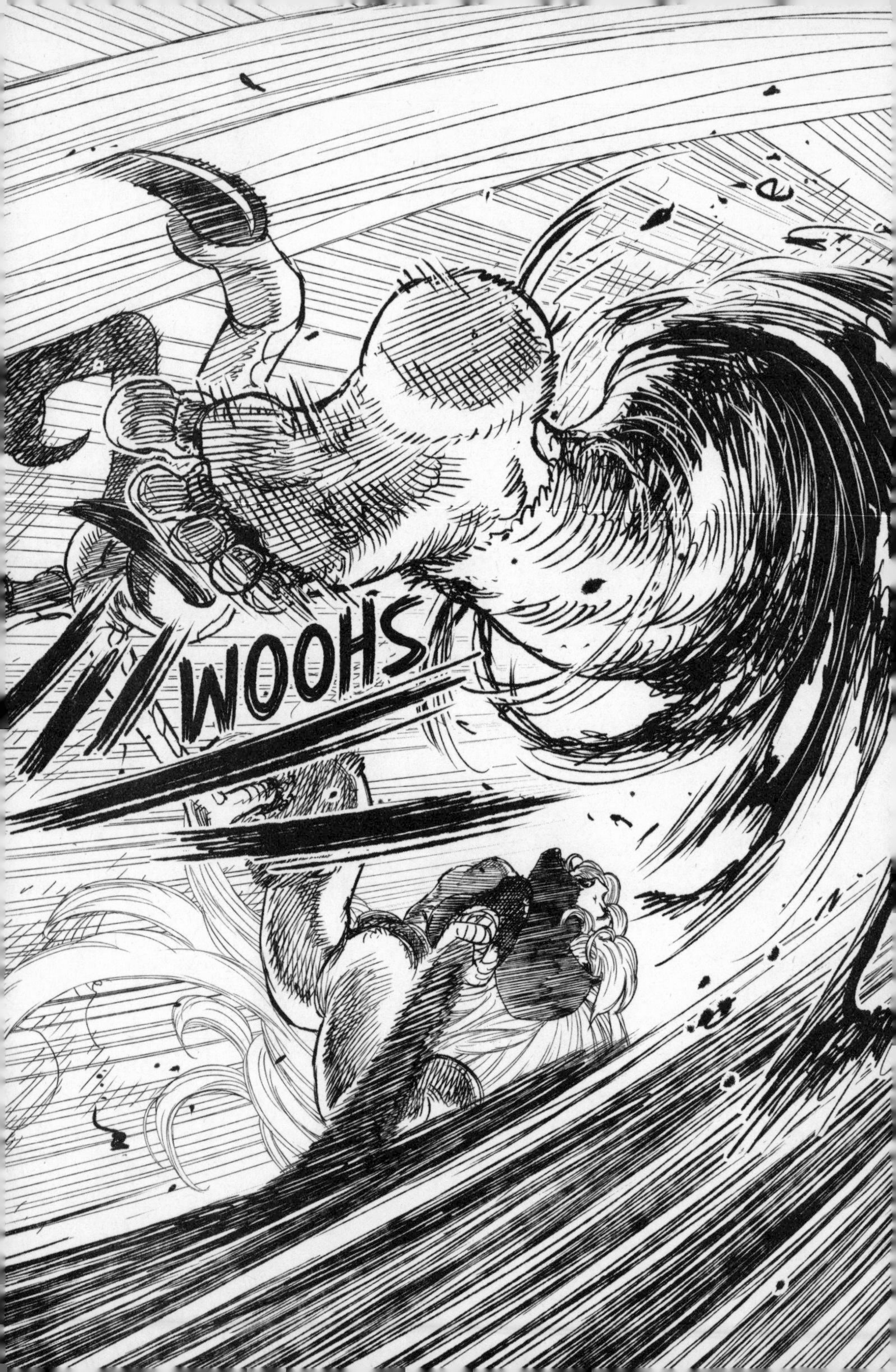
WOOHS

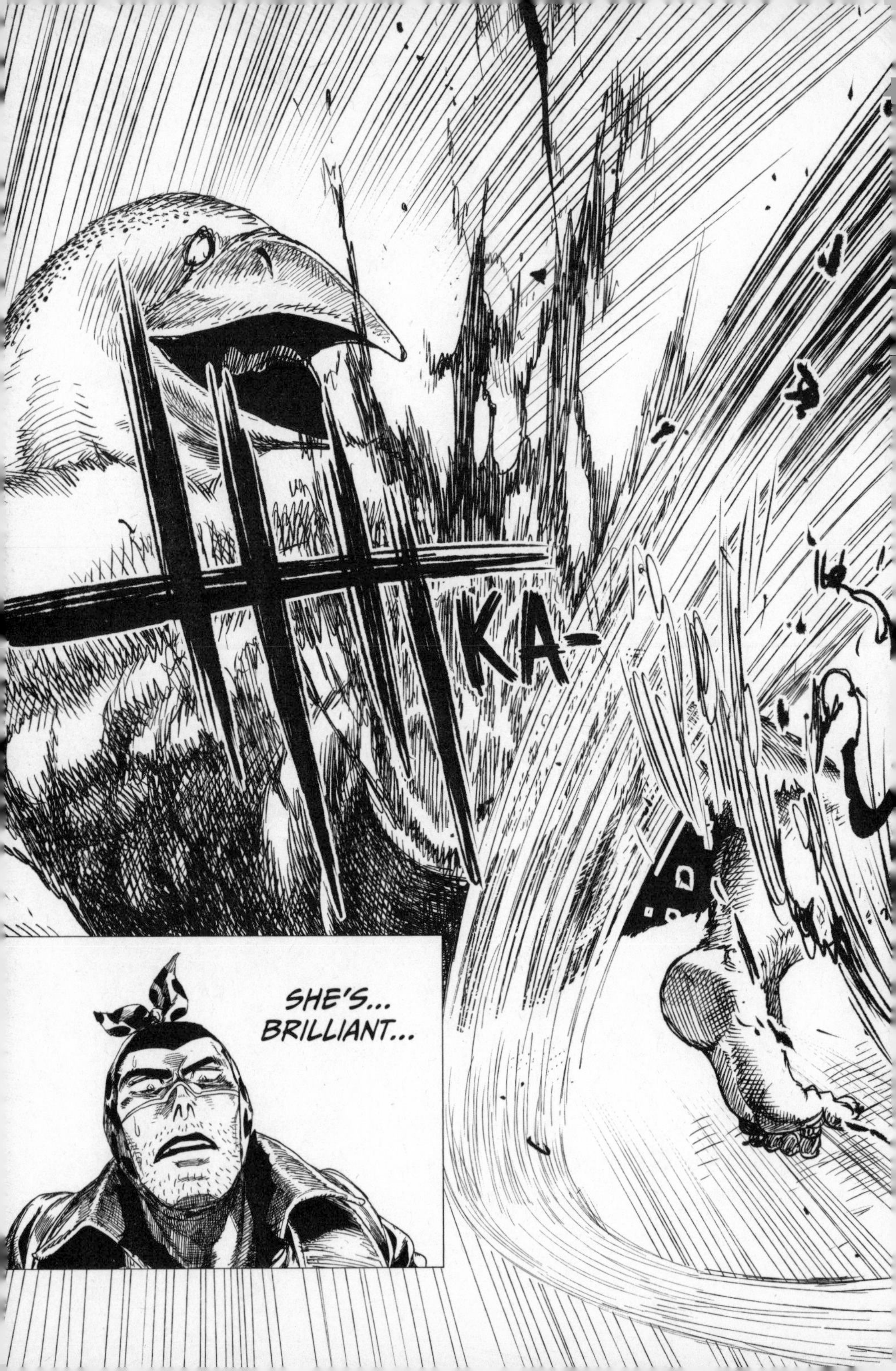
KA-
SHE'S...
BRILLIANT...

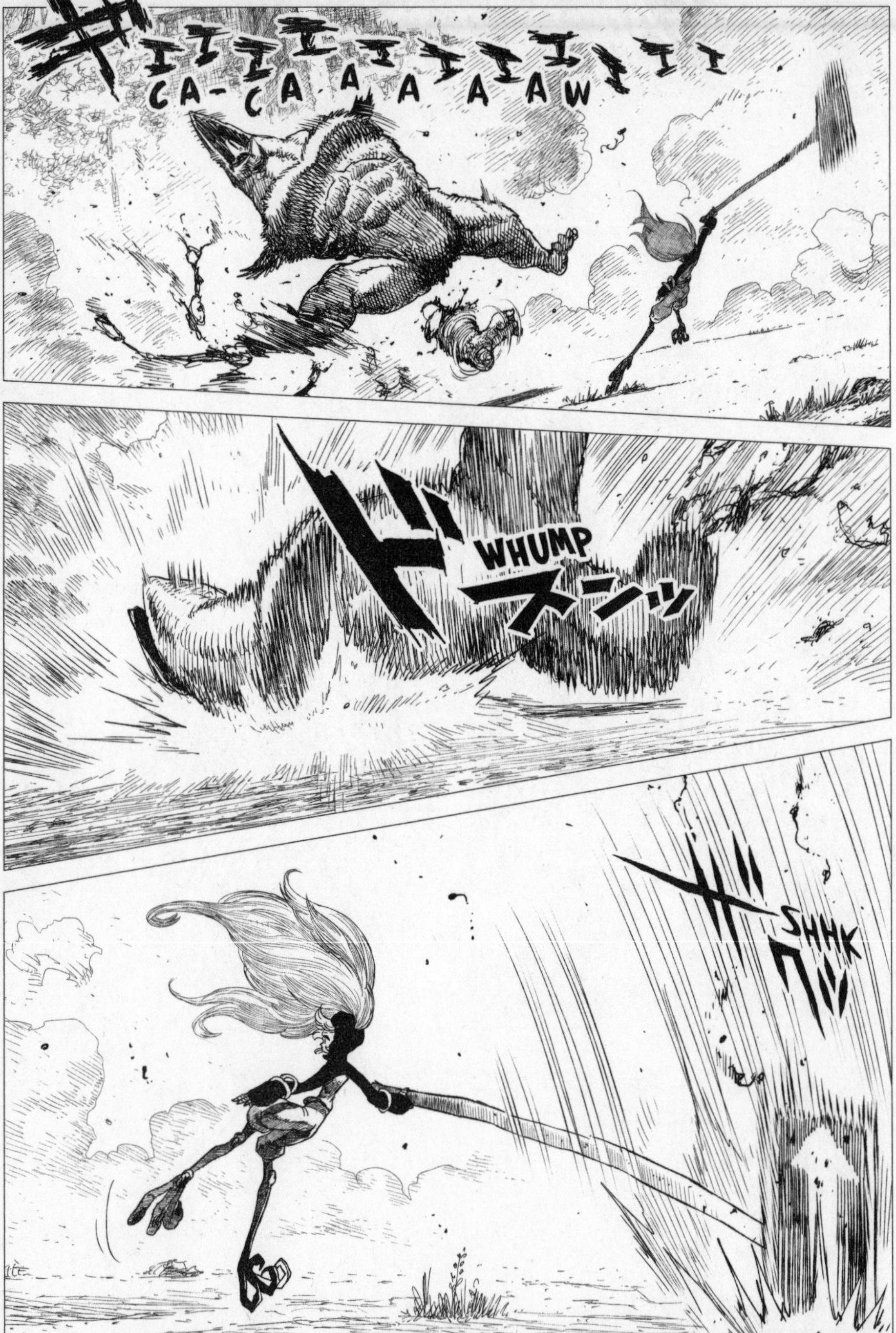
CA-CA A A AAW
WHUMP
SHHK

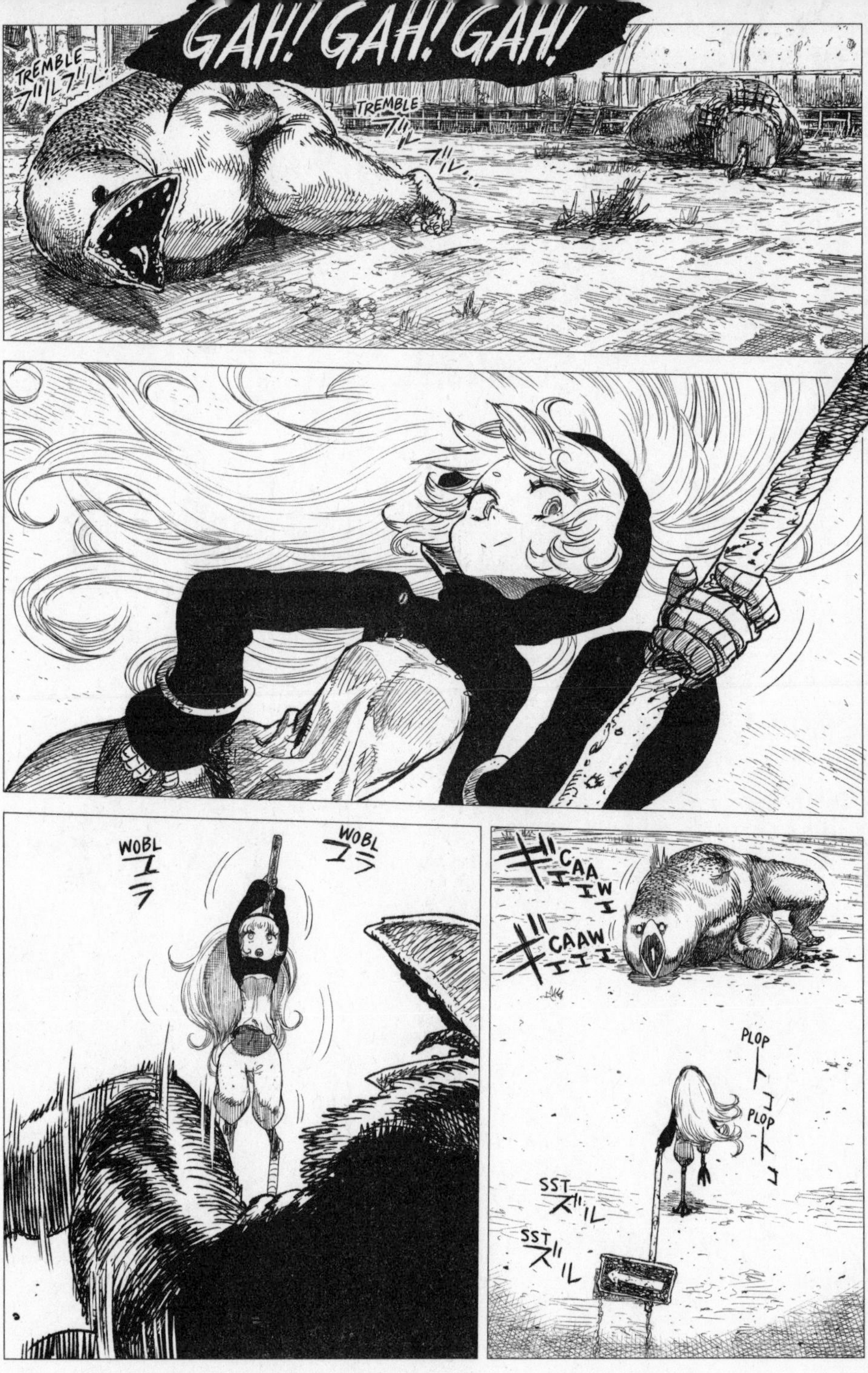
GAH! GAH! GAH!
TREMBLE
ブルブル
TREMBLE
ブル
ブル...
CAAIWI
CAAWIII
PLOP
トコ
PLOP
トコ
SST
ズル
SST
ズル
WOBL
ユラ
WOBL
ユラ

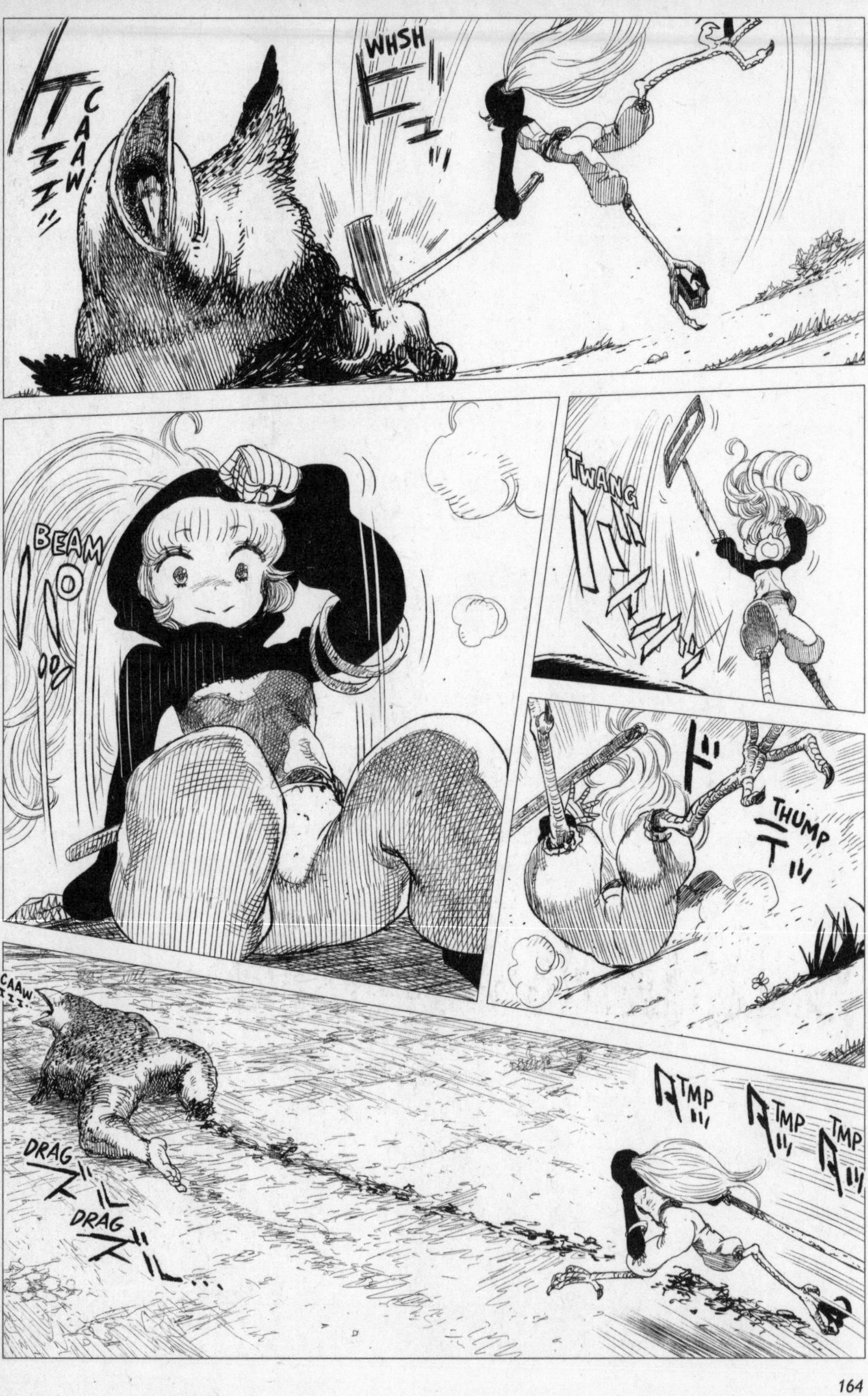
WHSH
CAAW
TWANG
THUMP
BEAM
TMP
TMP
TMP
DRAG
DRAG
CAAW

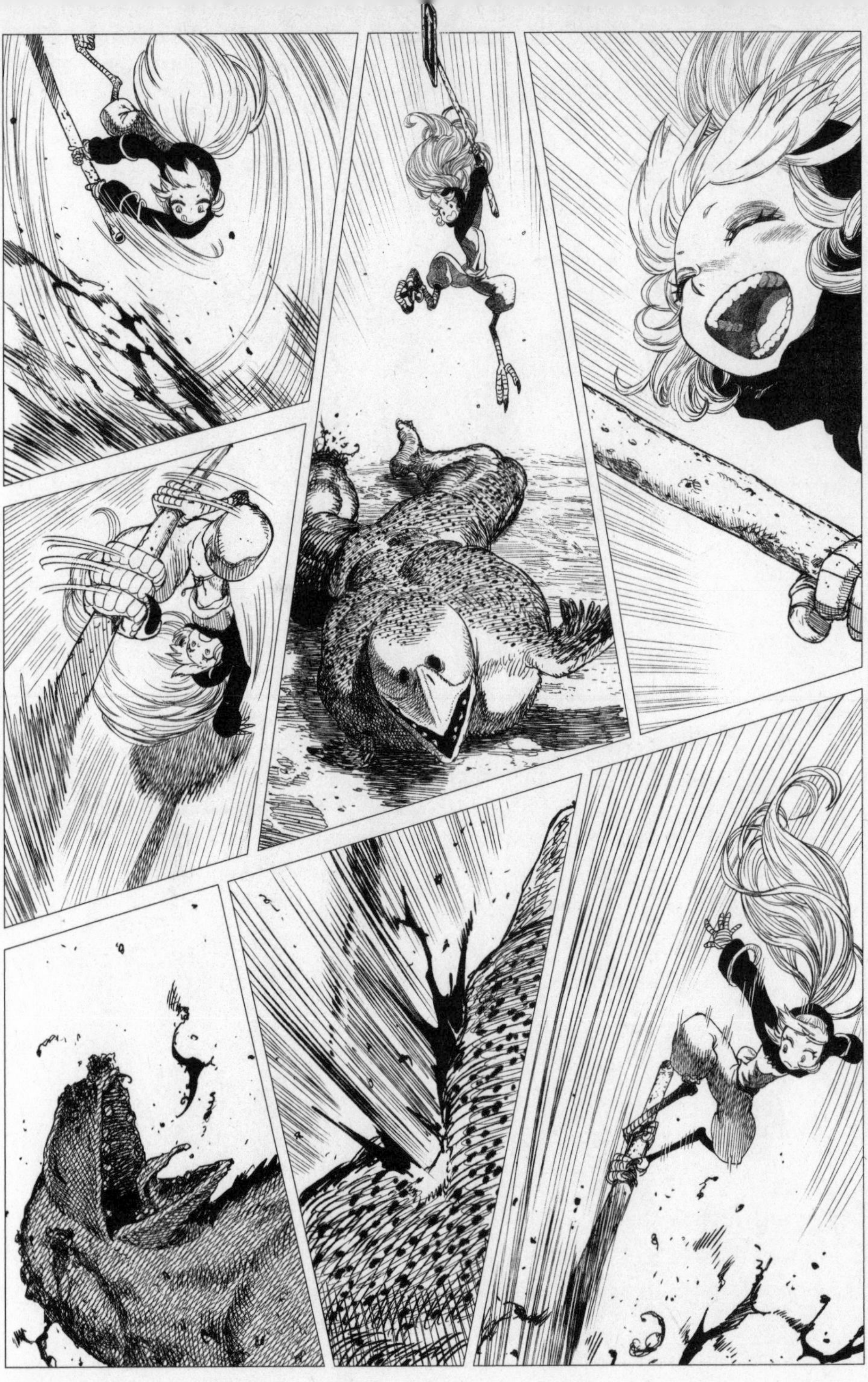

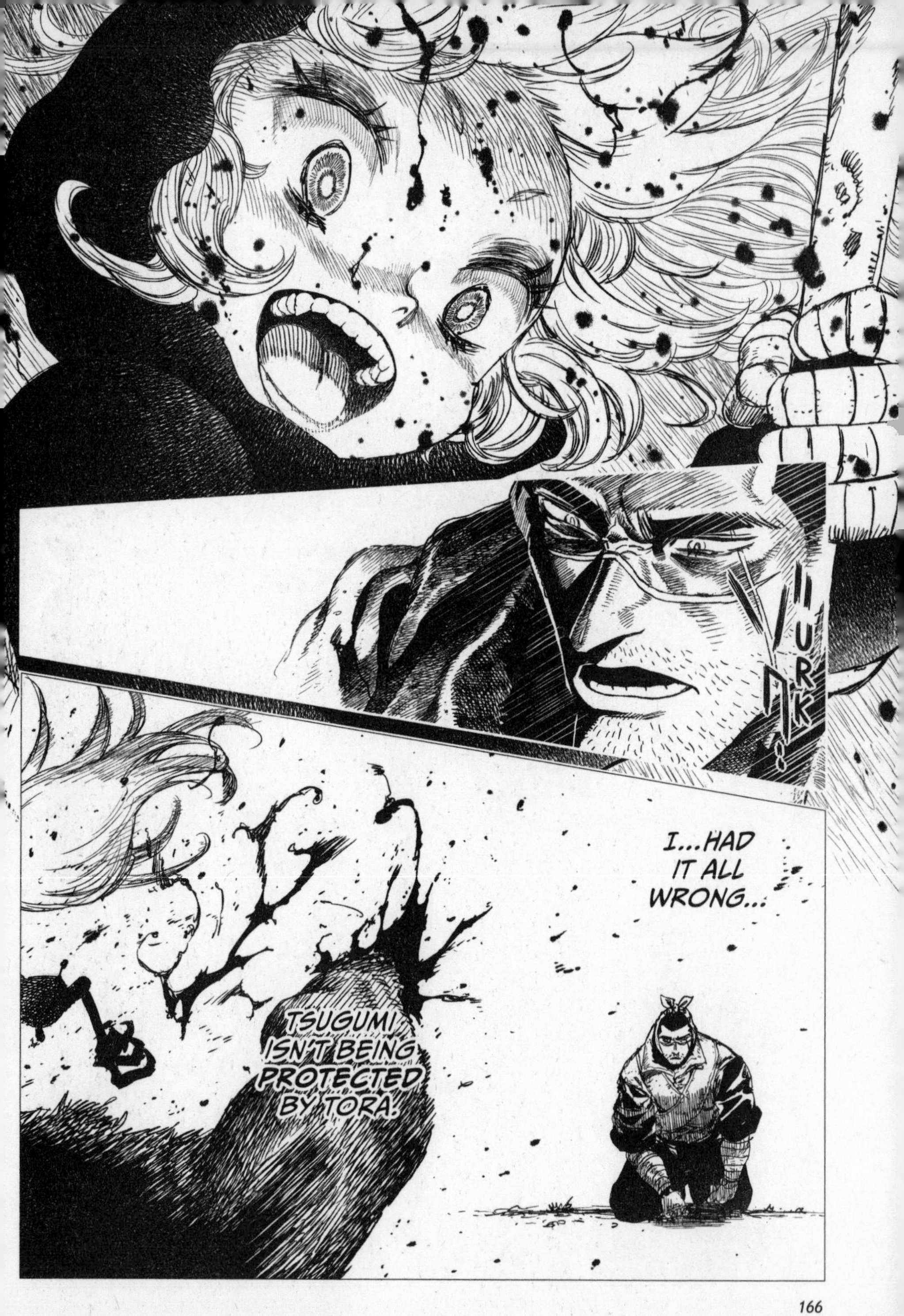
HURK
!!
I...HAD IT ALL WRONG...
TSUGUMI ISN'T BEING PROTECTED BY TORA.

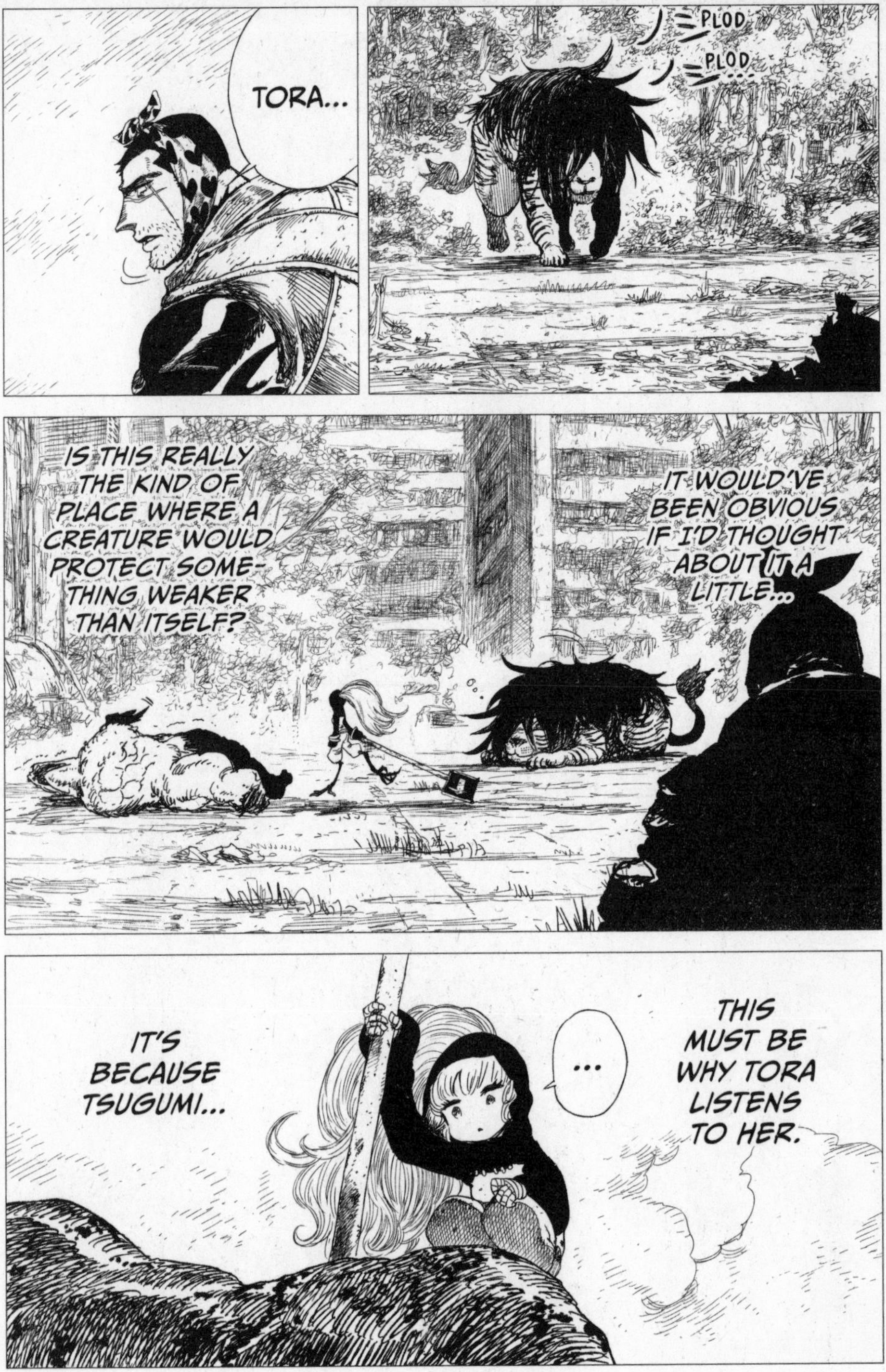
PLOD
PLOD...
TORA...
IT WOULD'VE BEEN OBVIOUS IF I'D THOUGHT ABOUT IT A LITTLE...
IS THIS REALLY THE KIND OF PLACE WHERE A CREATURE WOULD PROTECT SOME-THING WEAKER THAN ITSELF?
THIS MUST BE WHY TORA LISTENS TO HER.
...
IT'S BECAUSE TSUGUMI...

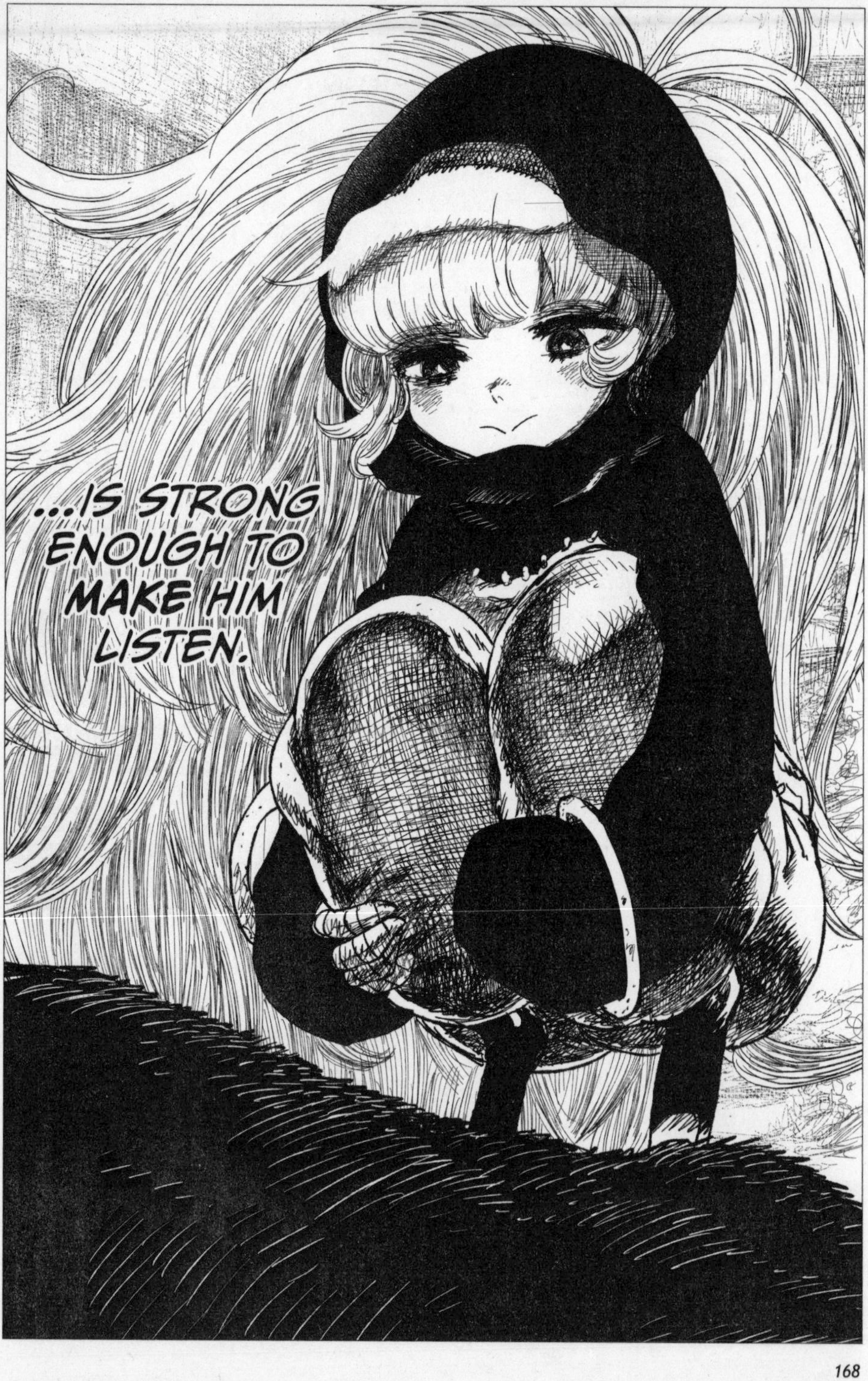
...IS STRONG ENOUGH TO MAKE HIM LISTEN.

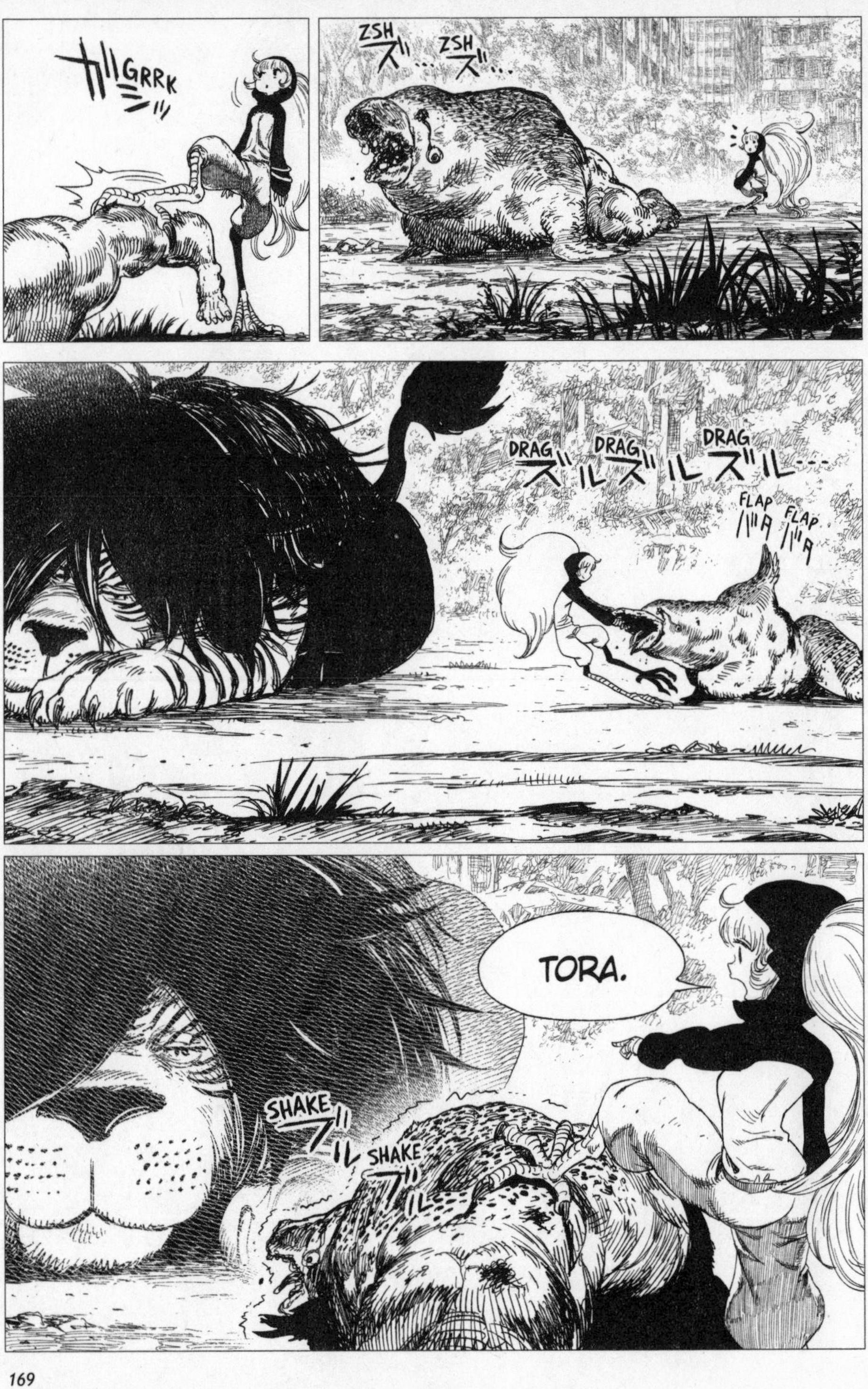

ZSH ズ… ZSH ズ…
カリ GRRK
DRAG ズル DRAG ズル DRAG ズル…
FLAP バタ FLAP バタ
TORA.
SHAKE ブル SHAKE ブル

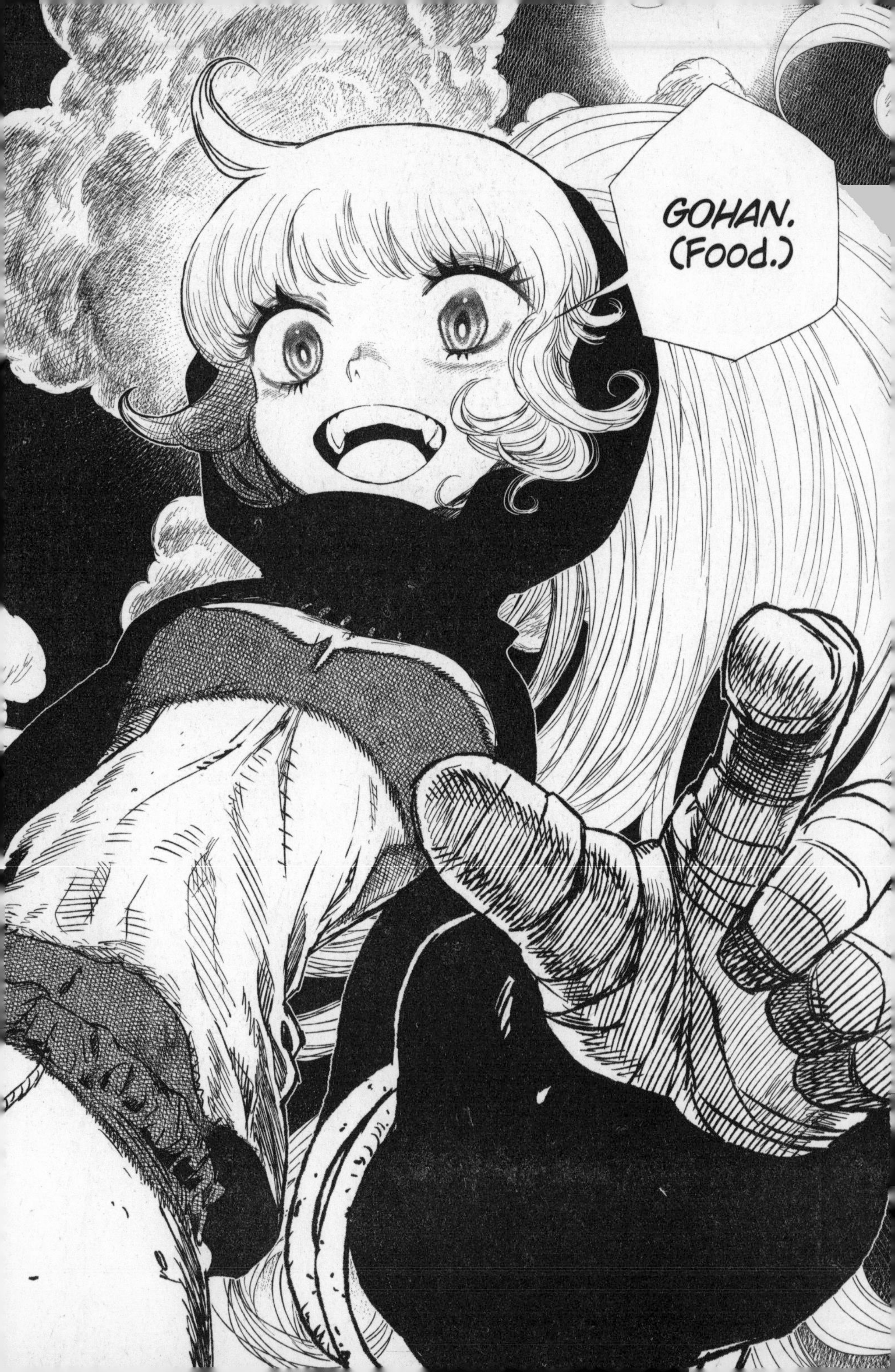
GOHAN. (Food.)

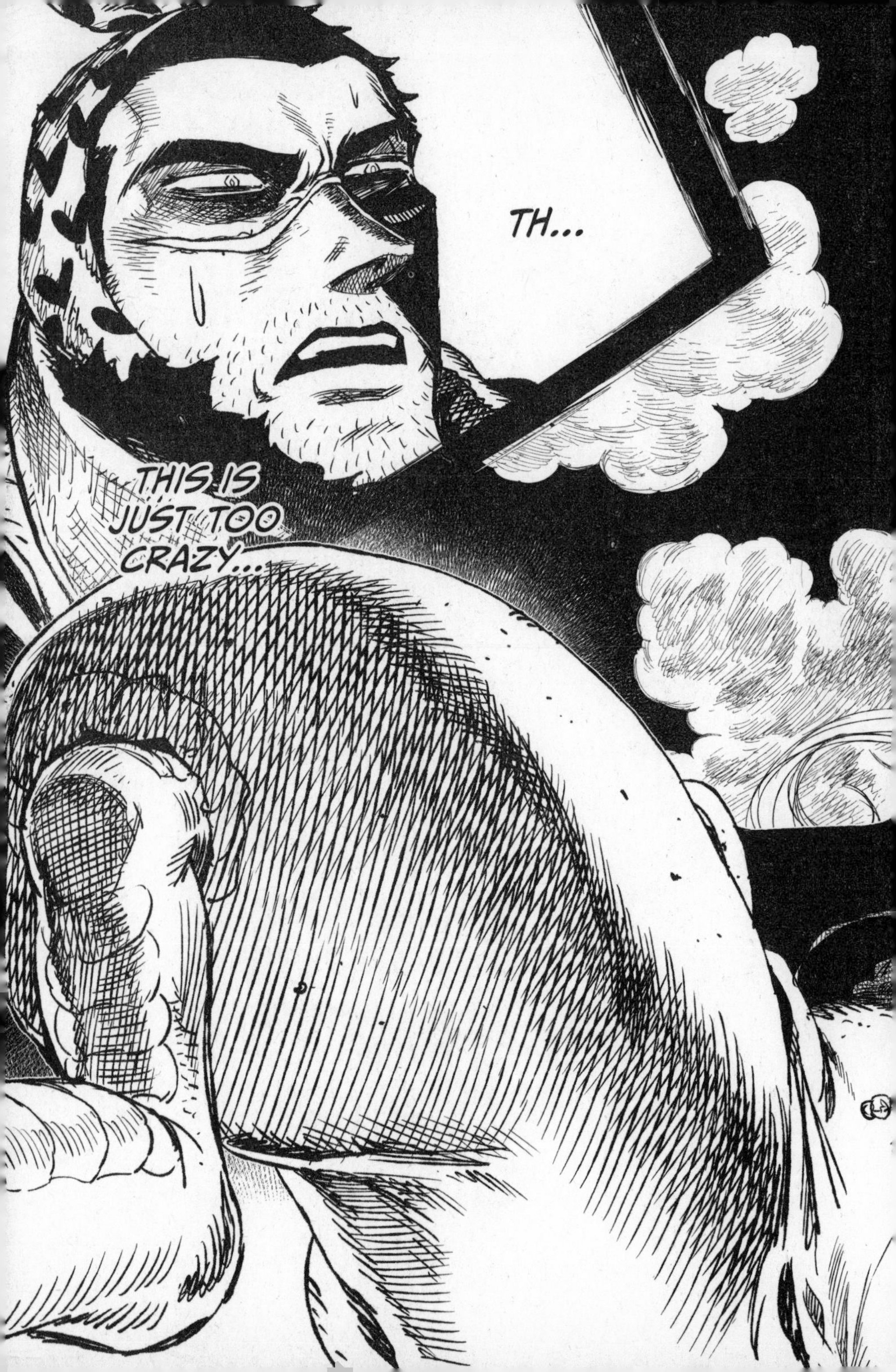
TH...
THIS IS JUST TOO CRAZY...

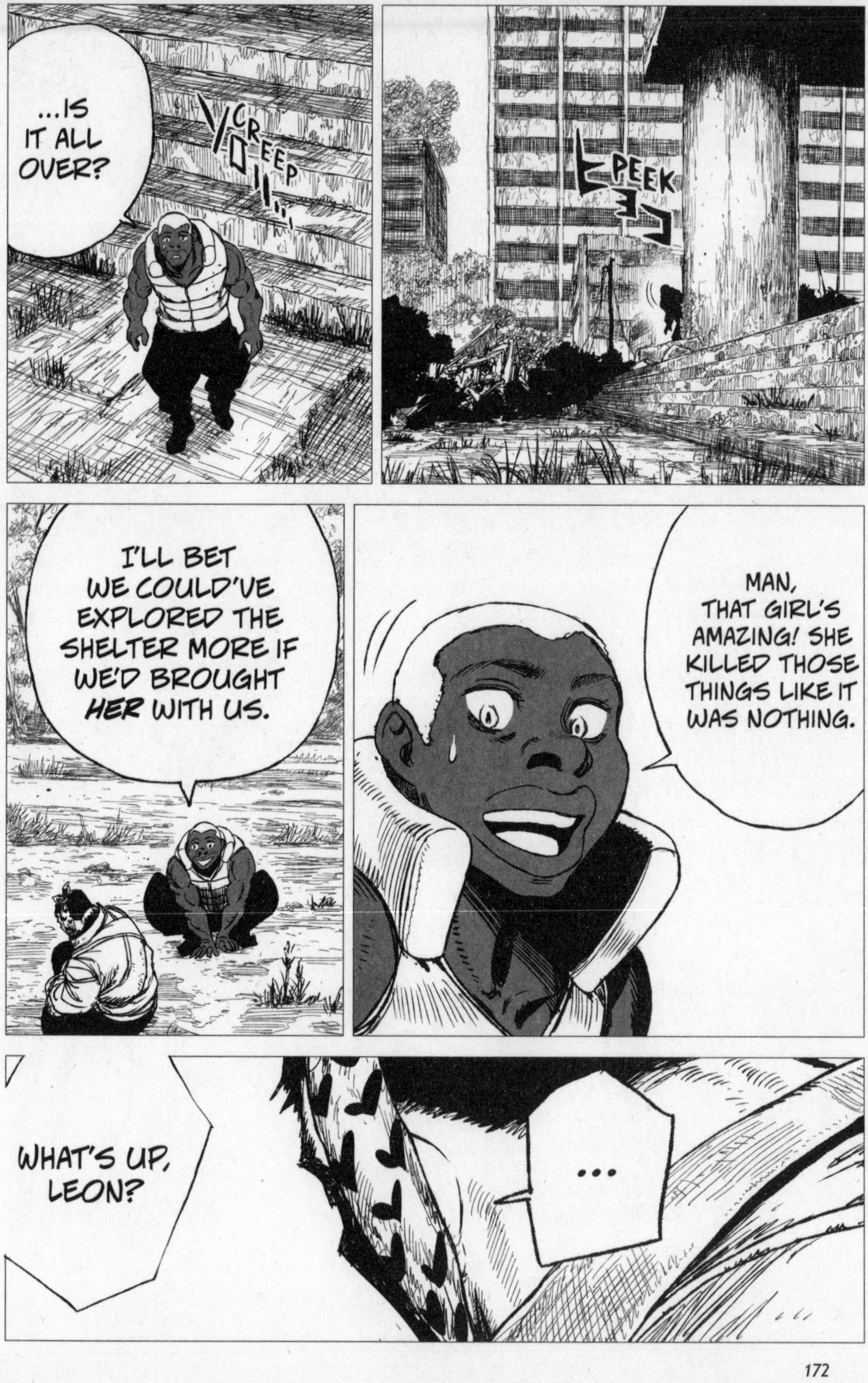
PEEK
CREEP
...IS IT ALL OVER?
MAN, THAT GIRL'S AMAZING! SHE KILLED THOSE THINGS LIKE IT WAS NOTHING.
I'LL BET WE COULD'VE EXPLORED THE SHELTER MORE IF WE'D BROUGHT **HER** WITH US.
WHAT'S UP, LEON?
...

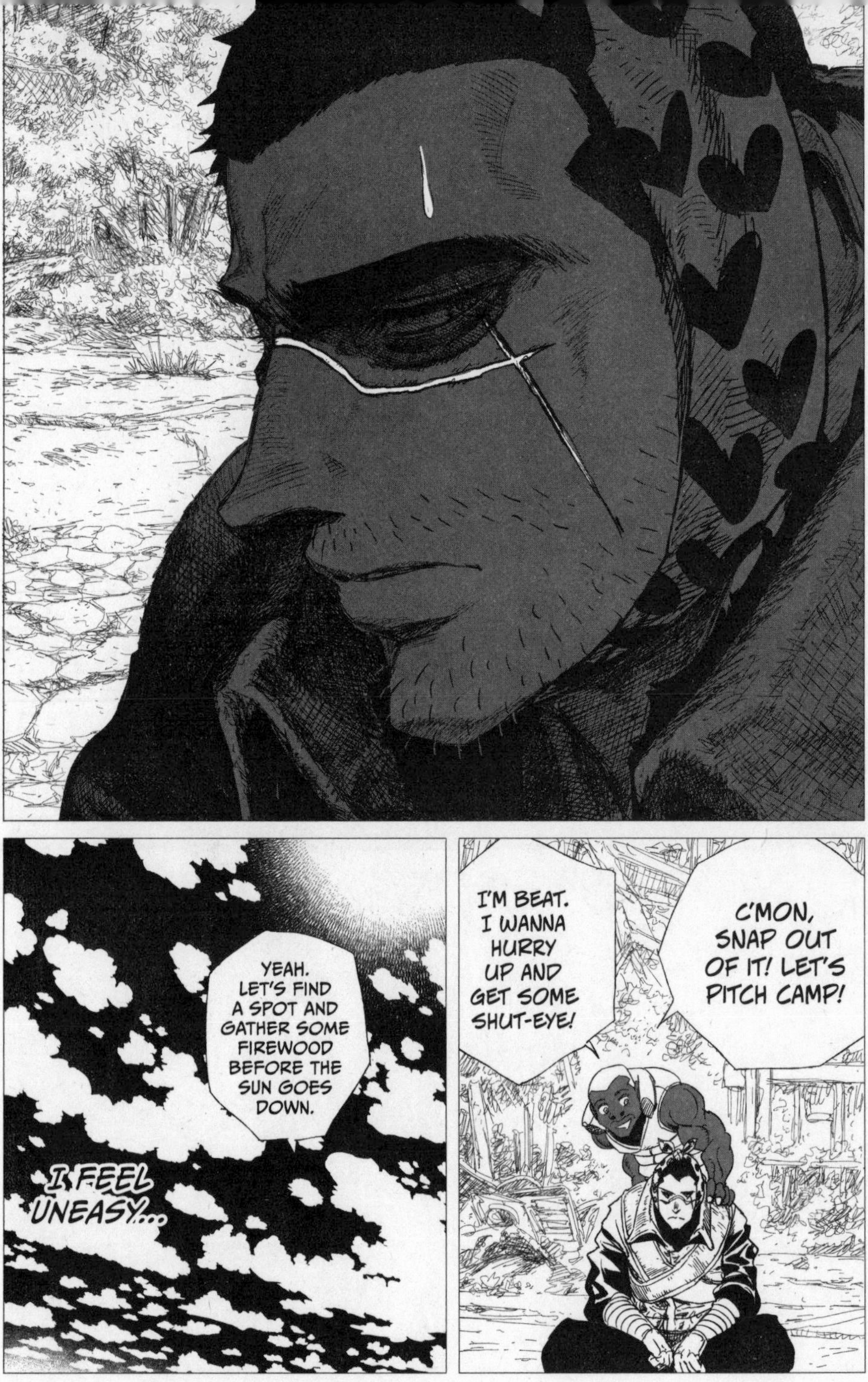
C'MON, SNAP OUT OF IT! LET'S PITCH CAMP!
I'M BEAT. I WANNA HURRY UP AND GET SOME SHUT-EYE!
YEAH. LET'S FIND A SPOT AND GATHER SOME FIREWOOD BEFORE THE SUN GOES DOWN.
I FEEL UNEASY...

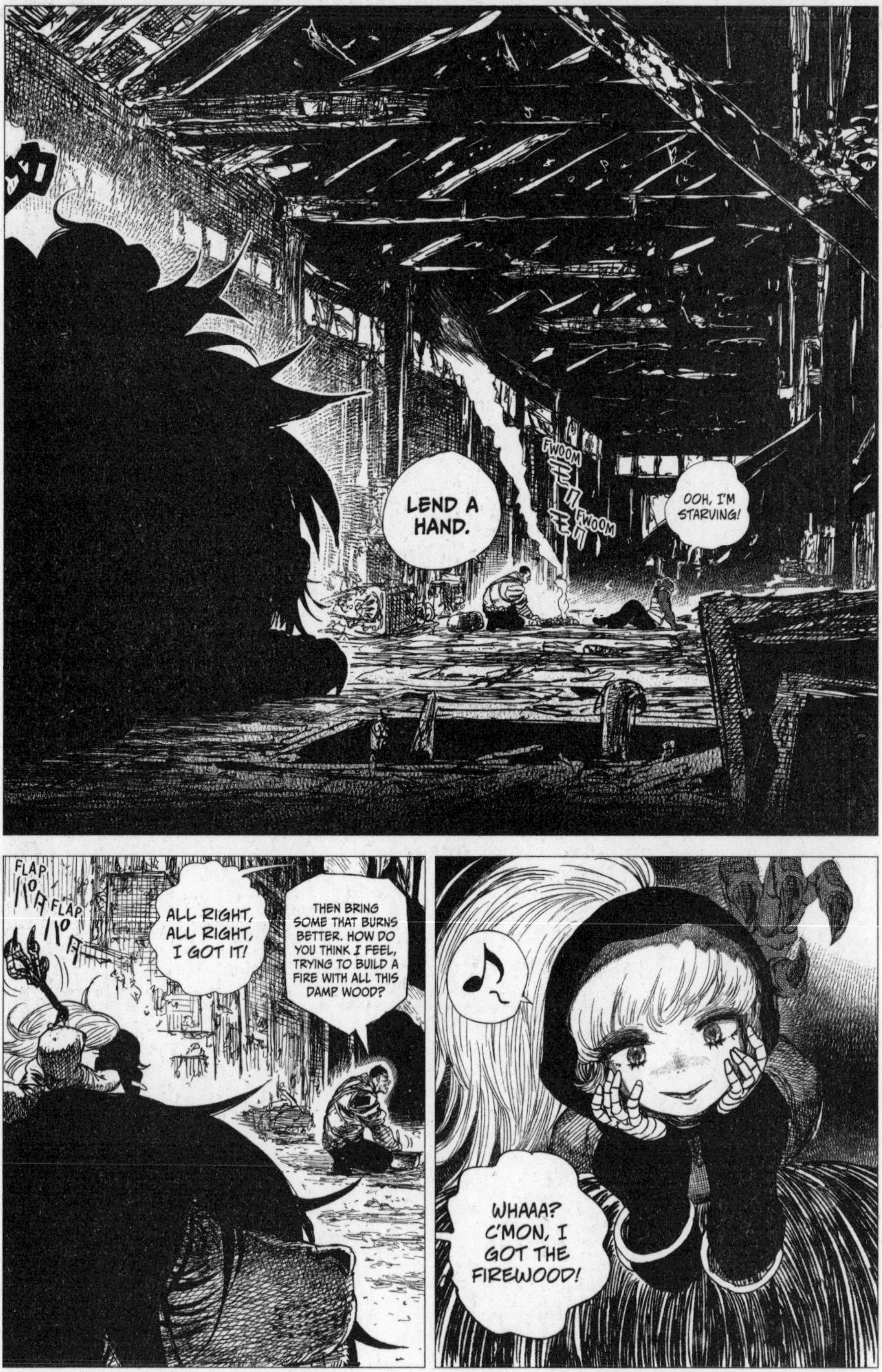
OOH, I'M STARVING!
FWOOM FWOOM
LEND A HAND.
♪~
WHAAA? C'MON, I GOT THE FIREWOOD!
THEN BRING SOME THAT BURNS BETTER. HOW DO YOU THINK I FEEL, TRYING TO BUILD A FIRE WITH ALL THIS DAMP WOOD?
ALL RIGHT, ALL RIGHT, I GOT IT!
FLAP FLAP

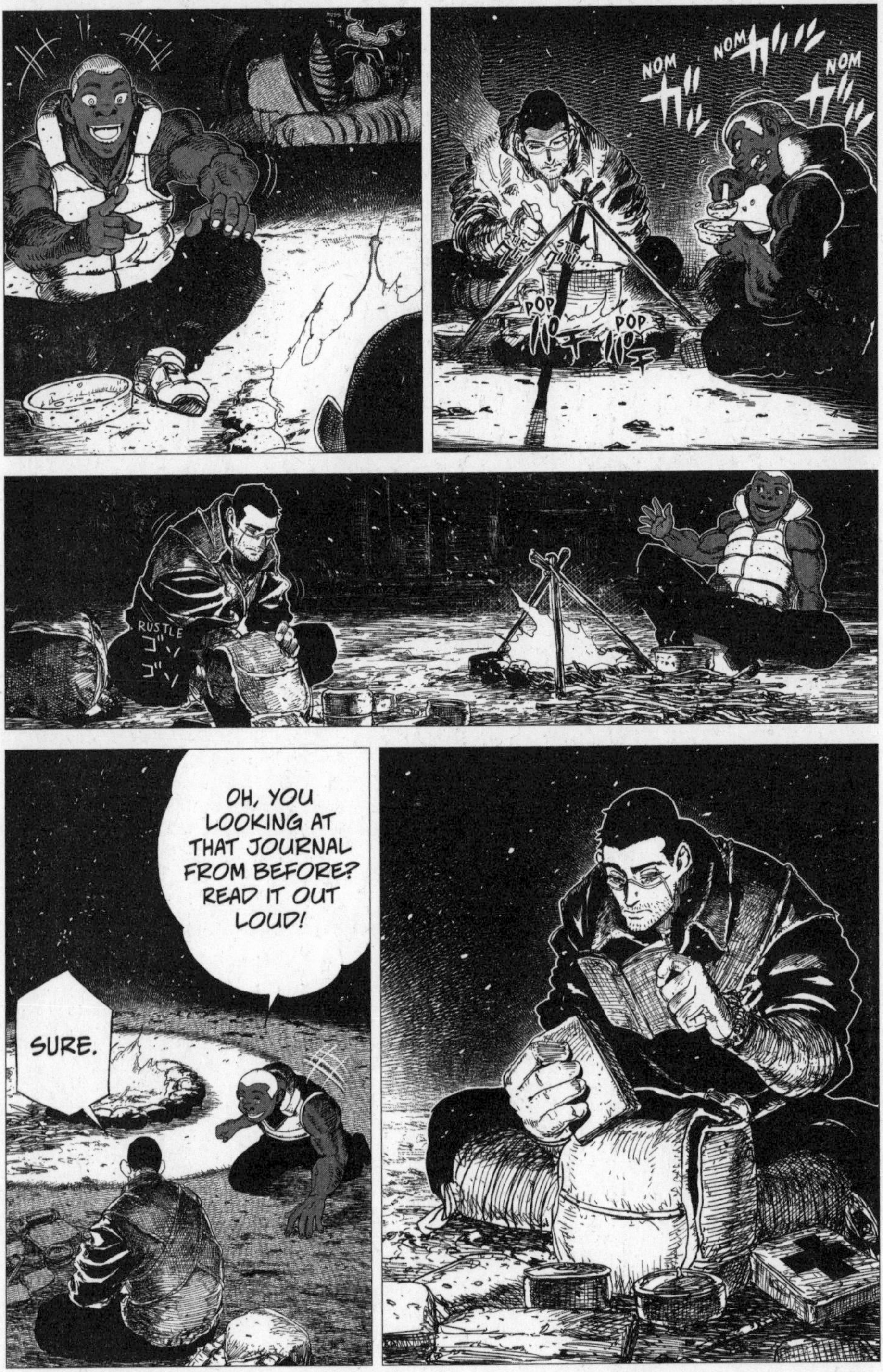
STIR
STIR
POP
POP
NOM
NOM
NOM
RUSTLE
OH, YOU LOOKING AT THAT JOURNAL FROM BEFORE? READ IT OUT LOUD!
SURE.

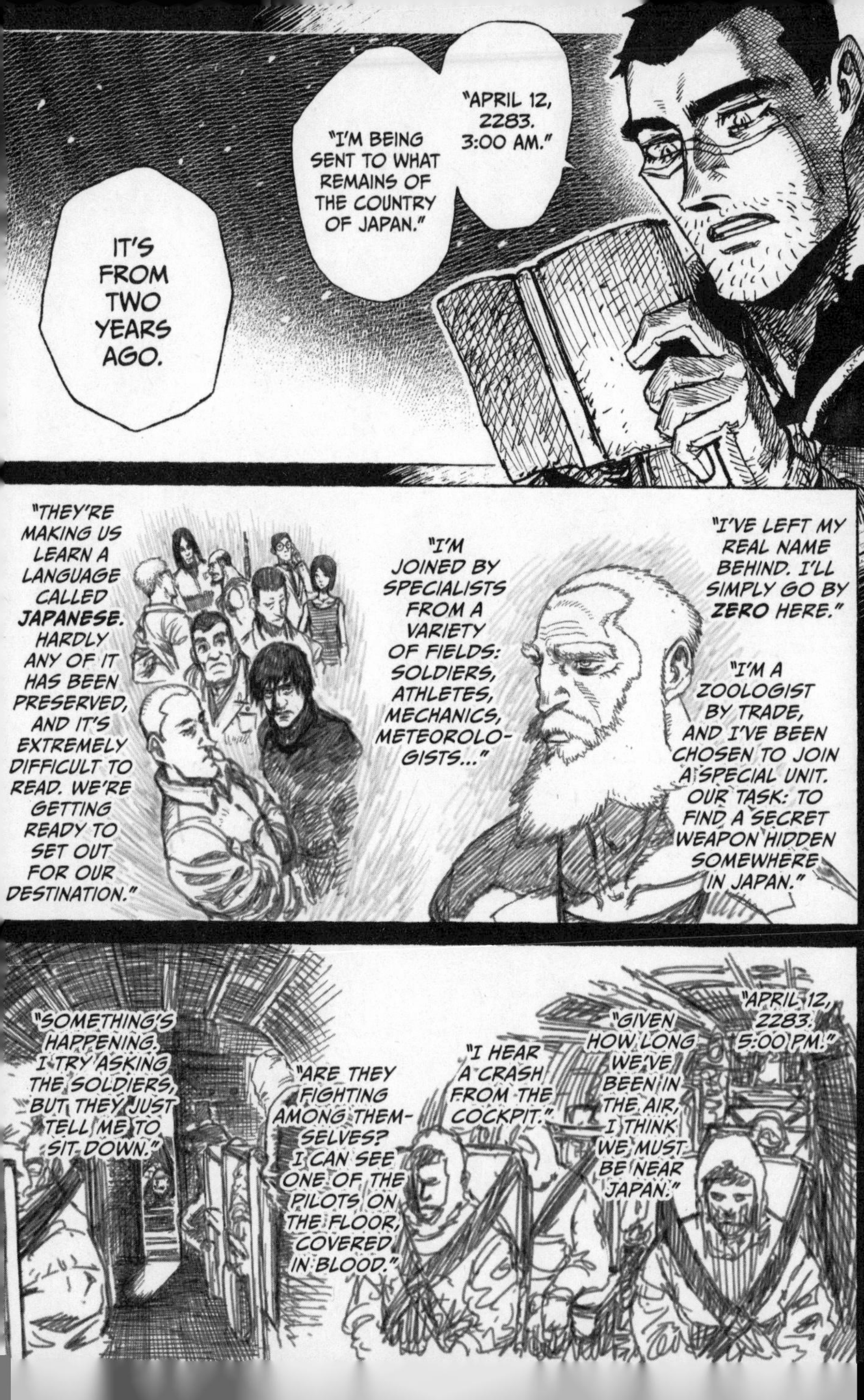
"APRIL 12, 2283. 3:00 AM."
"I'M BEING SENT TO WHAT REMAINS OF THE COUNTRY OF JAPAN."
IT'S FROM TWO YEARS AGO.
"I'VE LEFT MY REAL NAME BEHIND. I'LL SIMPLY GO BY **ZERO** HERE."
"I'M A ZOOLOGIST BY TRADE, AND I'VE BEEN CHOSEN TO JOIN A SPECIAL UNIT. OUR TASK: TO FIND A SECRET WEAPON HIDDEN SOMEWHERE IN JAPAN."
"I'M JOINED BY SPECIALISTS FROM A VARIETY OF FIELDS: SOLDIERS, ATHLETES, MECHANICS, METEOROLOGISTS..."
"THEY'RE MAKING US LEARN A LANGUAGE CALLED **JAPANESE**. HARDLY ANY OF IT HAS BEEN PRESERVED, AND IT'S EXTREMELY DIFFICULT TO READ. WE'RE GETTING READY TO SET OUT FOR OUR DESTINATION."
"APRIL 12, 2283. 5:00 PM."
"GIVEN HOW LONG WE'VE BEEN IN THE AIR, I THINK WE MUST BE NEAR JAPAN."
"I HEAR A CRASH FROM THE COCKPIT."
"ARE THEY FIGHTING AMONG THEMSELVES? I CAN SEE ONE OF THE PILOTS ON THE FLOOR, COVERED IN BLOOD."
"SOMETHING'S HAPPENING. I TRY ASKING THE SOLDIERS, BUT THEY JUST TELL ME TO SIT DOWN."

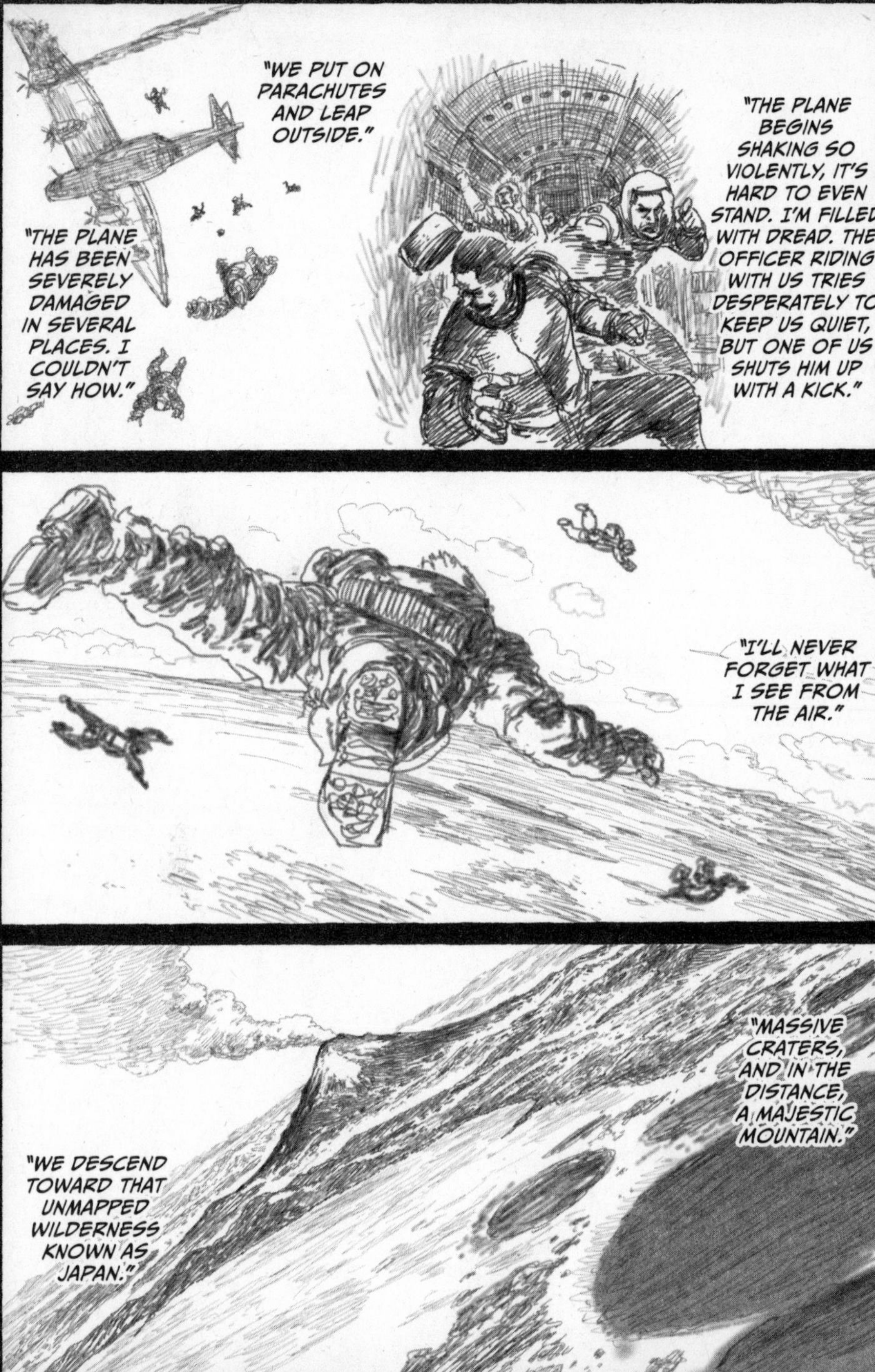
"THE PLANE BEGINS SHAKING SO VIOLENTLY, IT'S HARD TO EVEN STAND. I'M FILLED WITH DREAD. THE OFFICER RIDING WITH US TRIES DESPERATELY TO KEEP US QUIET, BUT ONE OF US SHUTS HIM UP WITH A KICK."
"WE PUT ON PARACHUTES AND LEAP OUTSIDE."
"THE PLANE HAS BEEN SEVERELY DAMAGED IN SEVERAL PLACES. I COULDN'T SAY HOW."
"I'LL NEVER FORGET WHAT I SEE FROM THE AIR."
"MASSIVE CRATERS, AND IN THE DISTANCE, A MAJESTIC MOUNTAIN."
"WE DESCEND TOWARD THAT UNMAPPED WILDERNESS KNOWN AS JAPAN."

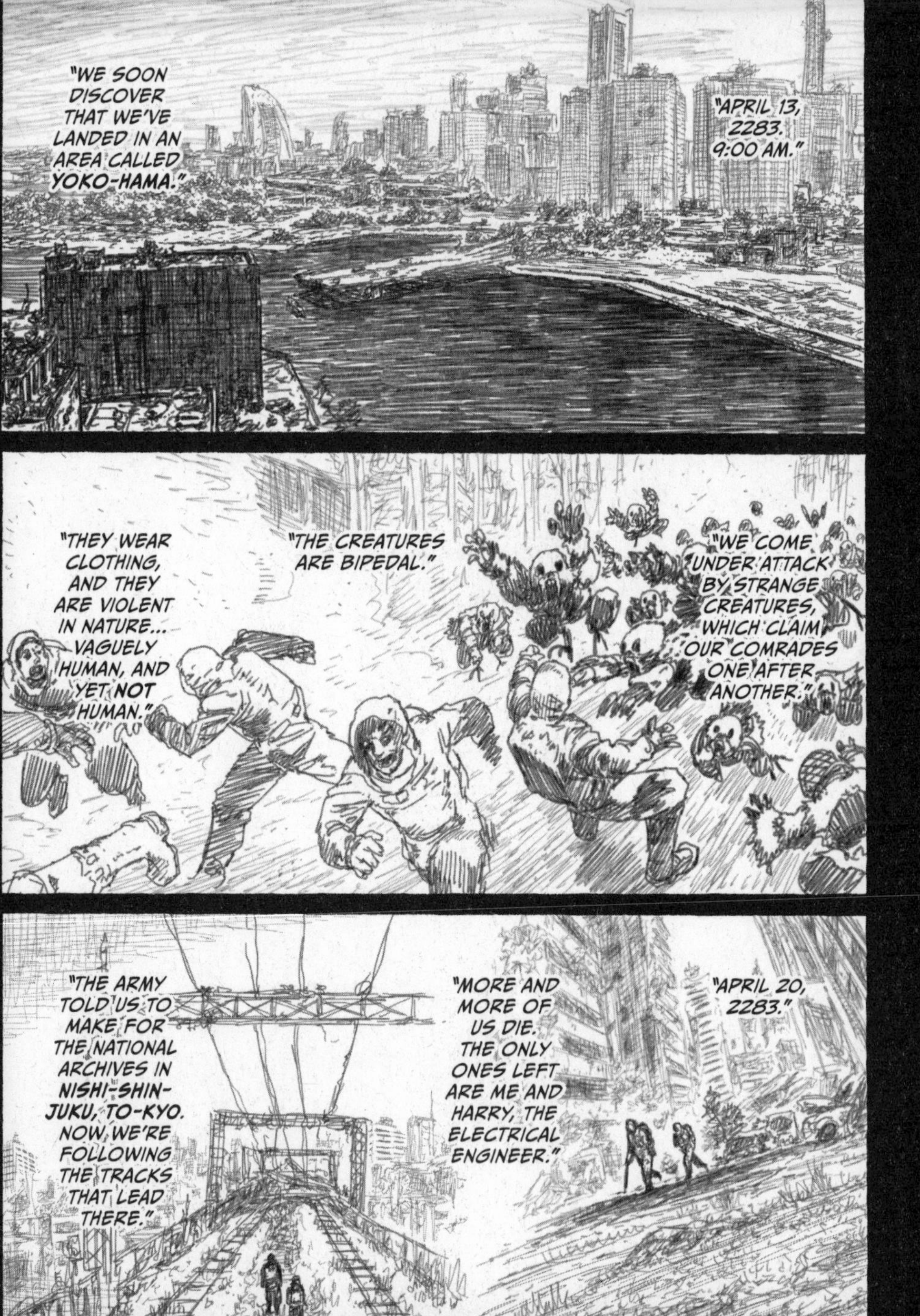
"APRIL 13, 2283. 9:00 AM."
"WE SOON DISCOVER THAT WE'VE LANDED IN AN AREA CALLED YOKO-HAMA."
"WE COME UNDER ATTACK BY STRANGE CREATURES, WHICH CLAIM OUR COMRADES ONE AFTER ANOTHER."
"THE CREATURES ARE BIPEDAL."
"THEY WEAR CLOTHING, AND THEY ARE VIOLENT IN NATURE... VAGUELY HUMAN, AND YET NOT HUMAN."
"APRIL 20, 2283."
"MORE AND MORE OF US DIE. THE ONLY ONES LEFT ARE ME AND HARRY, THE ELECTRICAL ENGINEER."
"THE ARMY TOLD US TO MAKE FOR THE NATIONAL ARCHIVES IN NISHI-SHIN-JUKU, TO-KYO. NOW WE'RE FOLLOWING THE TRACKS THAT LEAD THERE."

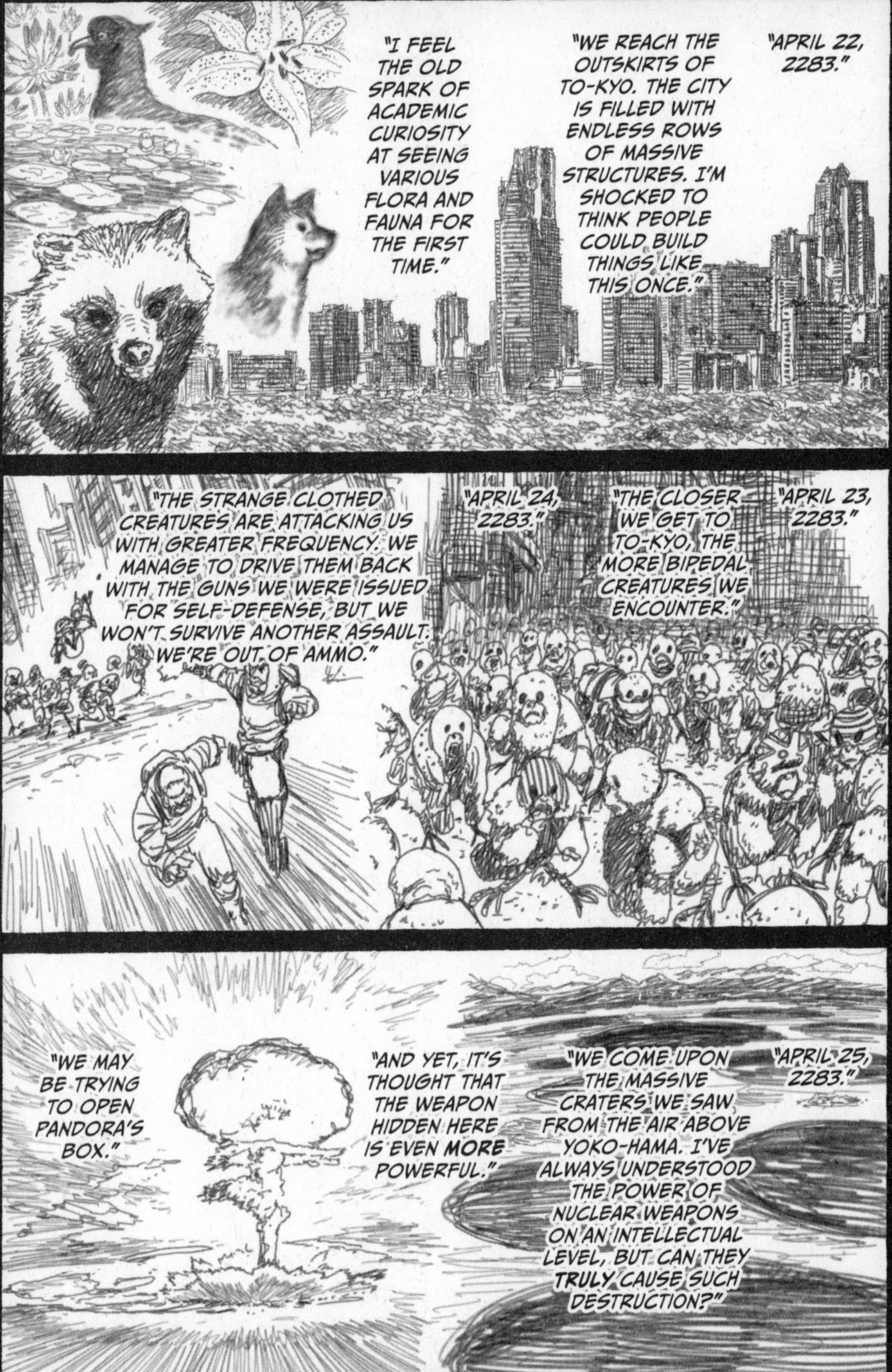
"APRIL 22, 2283."
"WE REACH THE OUTSKIRTS OF TO-KYO. THE CITY IS FILLED WITH ENDLESS ROWS OF MASSIVE STRUCTURES. I'M SHOCKED TO THINK PEOPLE COULD BUILD THINGS LIKE THIS ONCE."
"I FEEL THE OLD SPARK OF ACADEMIC CURIOSITY AT SEEING VARIOUS FLORA AND FAUNA FOR THE FIRST TIME."
"APRIL 23, 2283."
"THE CLOSER WE GET TO TO-KYO, THE MORE BIPEDAL CREATURES WE ENCOUNTER."
"APRIL 24, 2283."
"THE STRANGE CLOTHED CREATURES ARE ATTACKING US WITH GREATER FREQUENCY. WE MANAGE TO DRIVE THEM BACK WITH THE GUNS WE WERE ISSUED FOR SELF-DEFENSE, BUT WE WON'T SURVIVE ANOTHER ASSAULT. WE'RE OUT OF AMMO."
"APRIL 25, 2283."
"WE COME UPON THE MASSIVE CRATERS WE SAW FROM THE AIR ABOVE YOKO-HAMA. I'VE ALWAYS UNDERSTOOD THE POWER OF NUCLEAR WEAPONS ON AN INTELLECTUAL LEVEL, BUT CAN THEY TRULY CAUSE SUCH DESTRUCTION?"
"AND YET, IT'S THOUGHT THAT THE WEAPON HIDDEN HERE IS EVEN MORE POWERFUL."
"WE MAY BE TRYING TO OPEN PANDORA'S BOX."

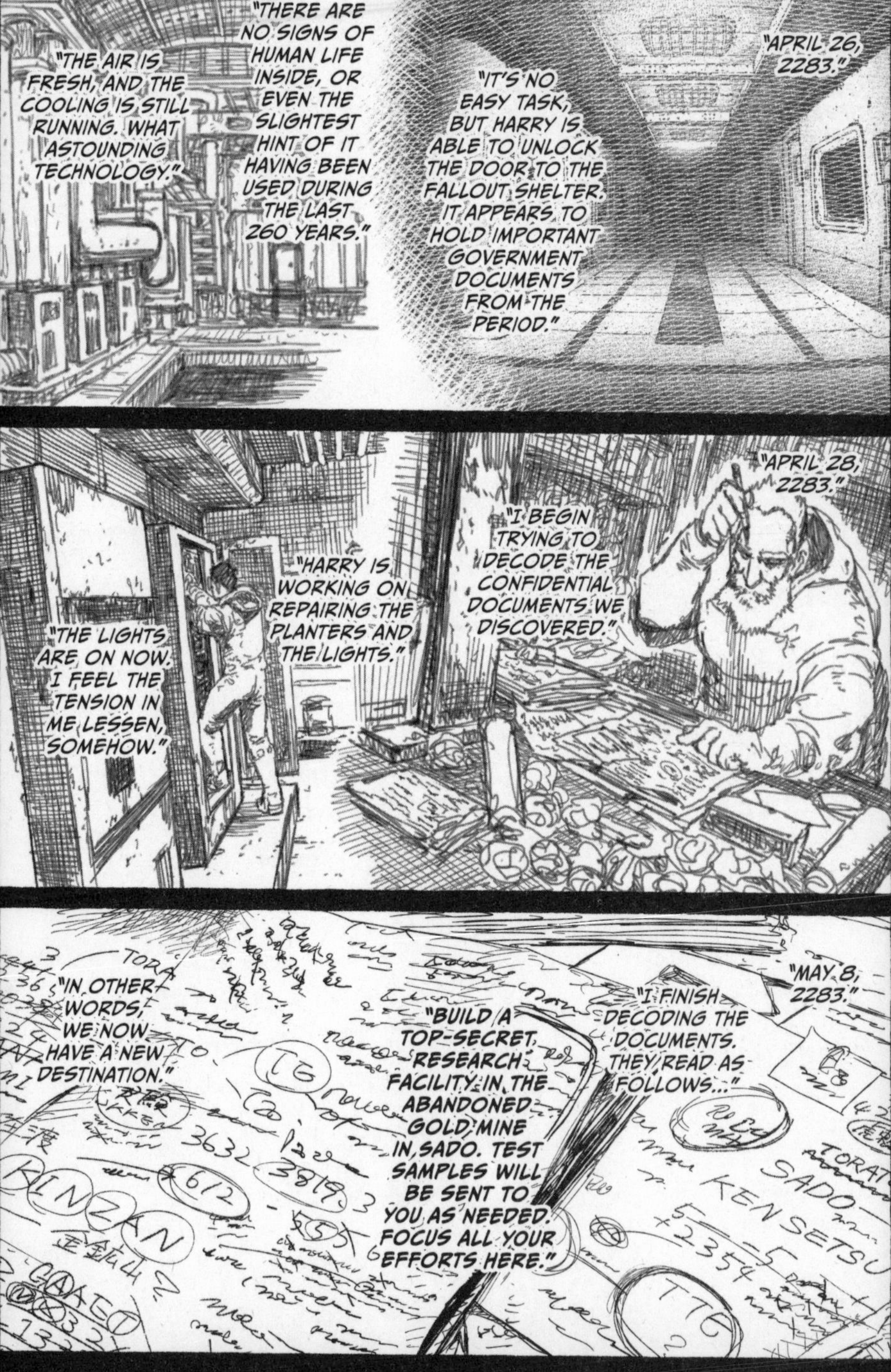
"APRIL 26, 2283."
"IT'S NO EASY TASK, BUT HARRY IS ABLE TO UNLOCK THE DOOR TO THE FALLOUT SHELTER. IT APPEARS TO HOLD IMPORTANT GOVERNMENT DOCUMENTS FROM THE PERIOD."
"THERE ARE NO SIGNS OF HUMAN LIFE INSIDE, OR EVEN THE SLIGHTEST HINT OF IT HAVING BEEN USED DURING THE LAST 260 YEARS."
"THE AIR IS FRESH, AND THE COOLING IS STILL RUNNING. WHAT ASTOUNDING TECHNOLOGY."
"APRIL 28, 2283."
"I BEGIN TRYING TO DECODE THE CONFIDENTIAL DOCUMENTS WE DISCOVERED."
"HARRY IS WORKING ON REPAIRING THE PLANTERS AND THE LIGHTS."
"THE LIGHTS ARE ON NOW. I FEEL THE TENSION IN ME LESSEN, SOMEHOW."
"MAY 8, 2283."
"I FINISH DECODING THE DOCUMENTS. THEY READ AS FOLLOWS..."
"BUILD A TOP-SECRET RESEARCH FACILITY IN THE ABANDONED GOLD MINE IN SADO. TEST SAMPLES WILL BE SENT TO YOU AS NEEDED. FOCUS ALL YOUR EFFORTS HERE."
"IN OTHER WORDS, WE NOW HAVE A NEW DESTINATION."

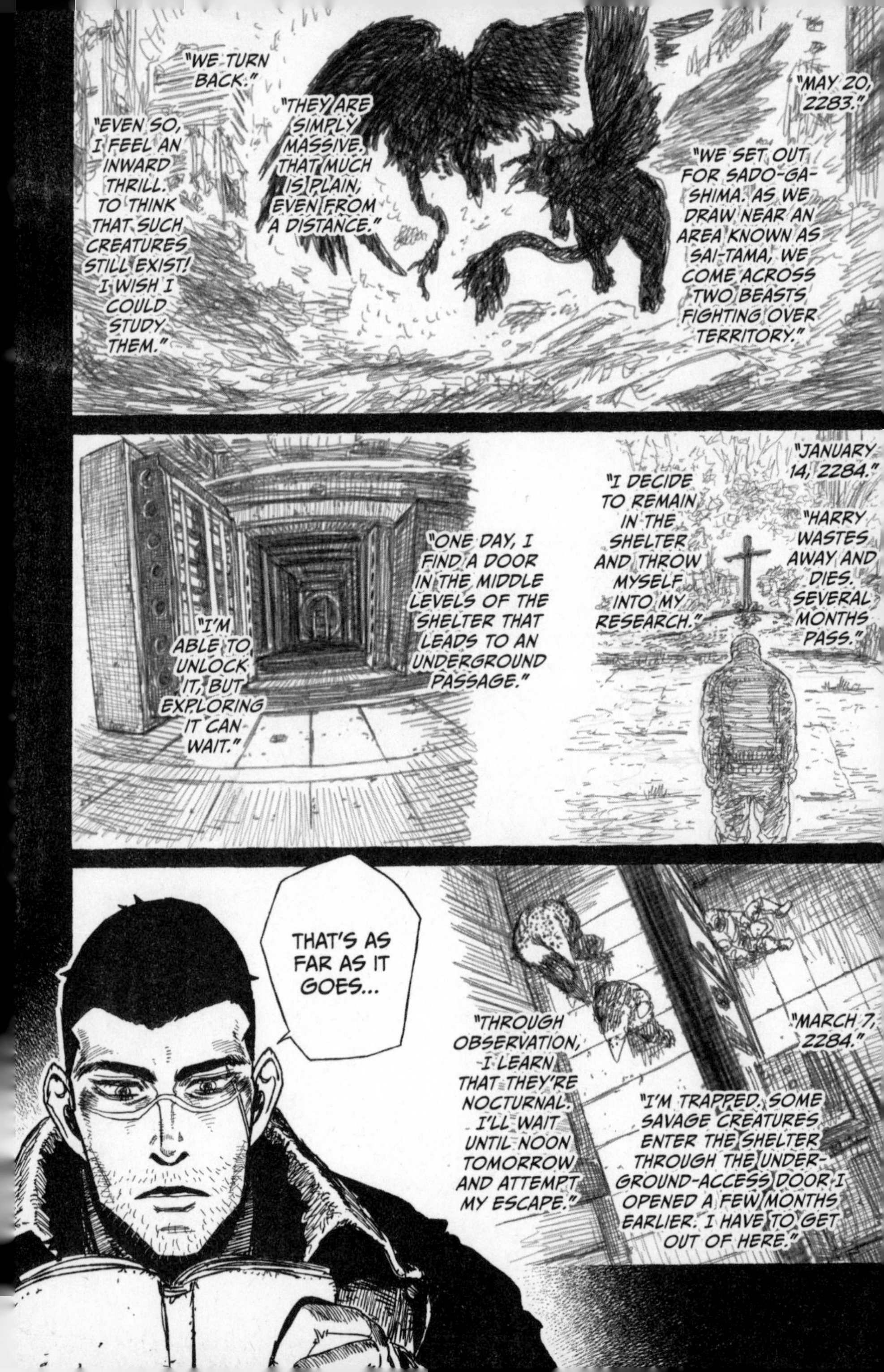
"MAY 20, 2283."
"WE SET OUT FOR SADO-GA-SHIMA. AS WE DRAW NEAR AN AREA KNOWN AS SAI-TAMA, WE COME ACROSS TWO BEASTS FIGHTING OVER TERRITORY."
"THEY ARE SIMPLY MASSIVE. THAT MUCH IS PLAIN, EVEN FROM A DISTANCE."
"EVEN SO, I FEEL AN INWARD THRILL. TO THINK THAT SUCH CREATURES STILL EXIST! I WISH I COULD STUDY THEM."
"WE TURN BACK."
"JANUARY 14, 2284."
"HARRY WASTES AWAY AND DIES. SEVERAL MONTHS PASS."
"I DECIDE TO REMAIN IN THE SHELTER AND THROW MYSELF INTO MY RESEARCH."
"ONE DAY, I FIND A DOOR IN THE MIDDLE LEVELS OF THE SHELTER THAT LEADS TO AN UNDERGROUND PASSAGE."
"I'M ABLE TO UNLOCK IT, BUT EXPLORING IT CAN WAIT."
"MARCH 7, 2284."
"I'M TRAPPED. SOME SAVAGE CREATURES ENTER THE SHELTER THROUGH THE UNDER-GROUND-ACCESS DOOR I OPENED A FEW MONTHS EARLIER. I HAVE TO GET OUT OF HERE."
"THROUGH OBSERVATION, I LEARN THAT THEY'RE NOCTURNAL. I'LL WAIT UNTIL NOON TOMORROW AND ATTEMPT MY ESCAPE."
THAT'S AS FAR AS IT GOES...

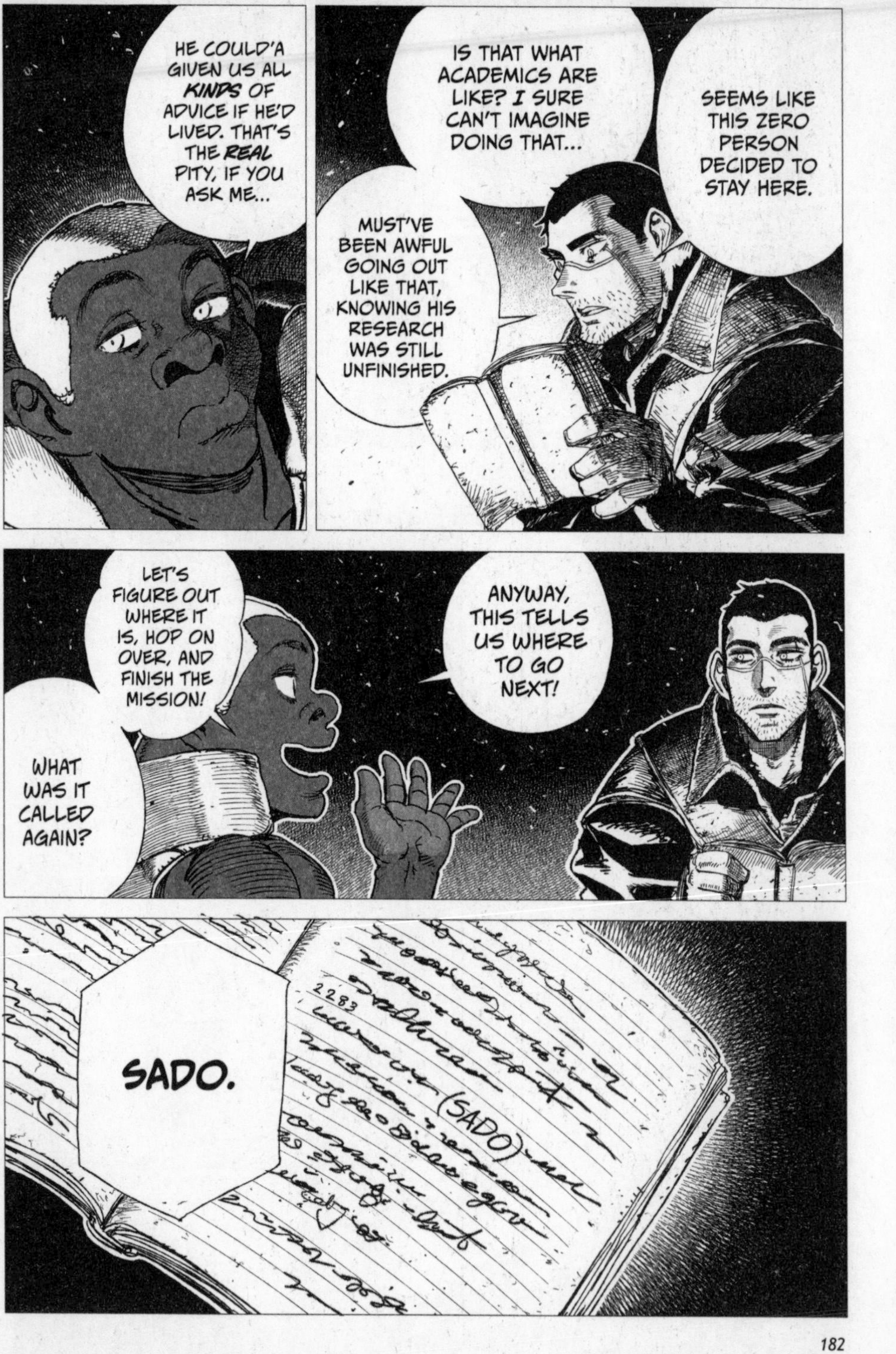
SEEMS LIKE THIS ZERO PERSON DECIDED TO STAY HERE.
IS THAT WHAT ACADEMICS ARE LIKE? *I* SURE CAN'T IMAGINE DOING THAT...
MUST'VE BEEN AWFUL GOING OUT LIKE THAT, KNOWING HIS RESEARCH WAS STILL UNFINISHED.
HE COULD'A GIVEN US ALL ***KINDS*** OF ADVICE IF HE'D LIVED. THAT'S THE ***REAL*** PITY, IF YOU ASK ME...
ANYWAY, THIS TELLS US WHERE TO GO NEXT!
LET'S FIGURE OUT WHERE IT IS, HOP ON OVER, AND FINISH THE MISSION!
WHAT WAS IT CALLED AGAIN?
SADO.
2283
(SADO)

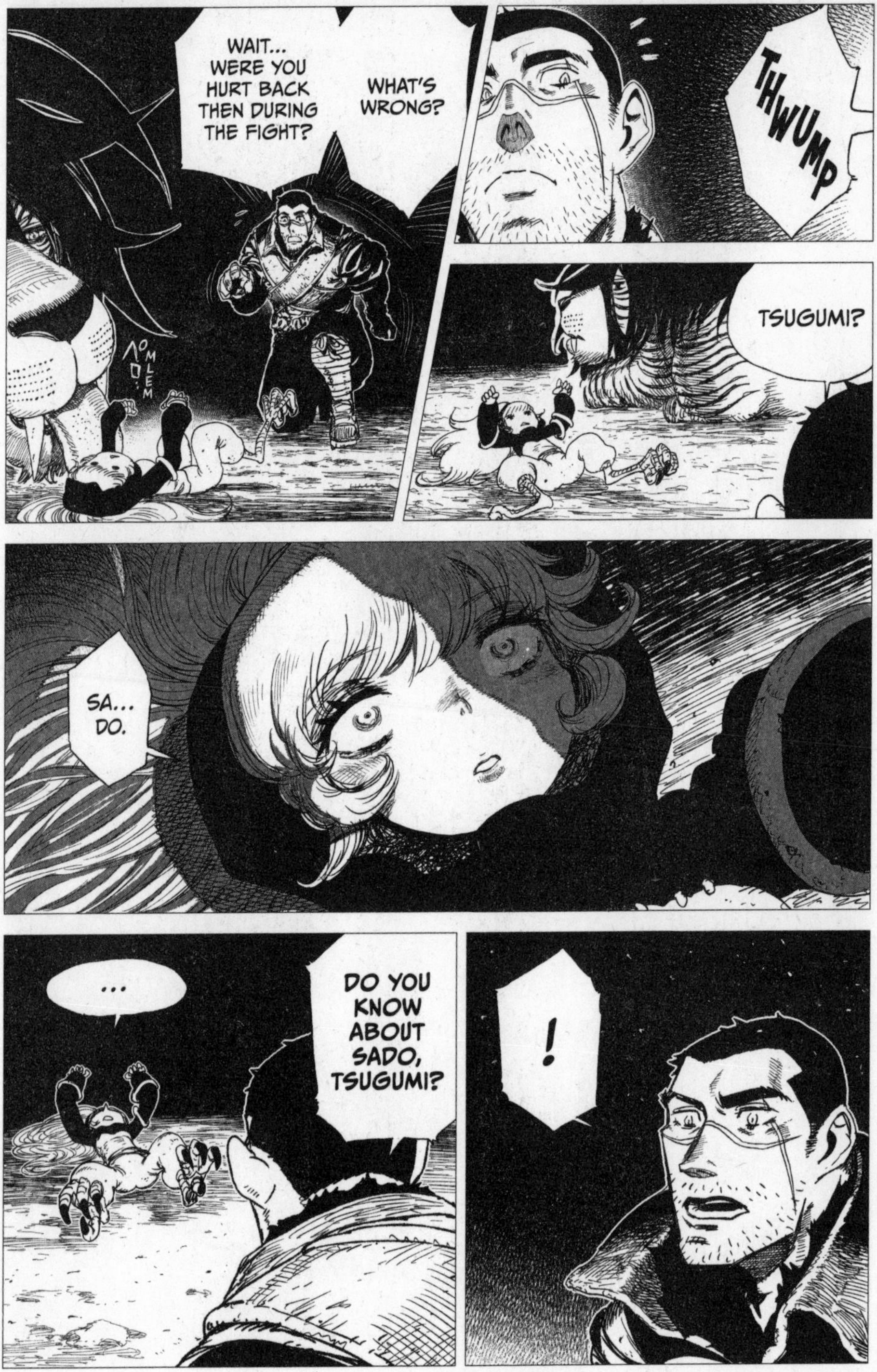
THWUMP
TSUGUMI?
WHAT'S WRONG?
WAIT... WERE YOU HURT BACK THEN DURING THE FIGHT?
MLEM
SA... DO.
!
DO YOU KNOW ABOUT SADO, TSUGUMI?
...

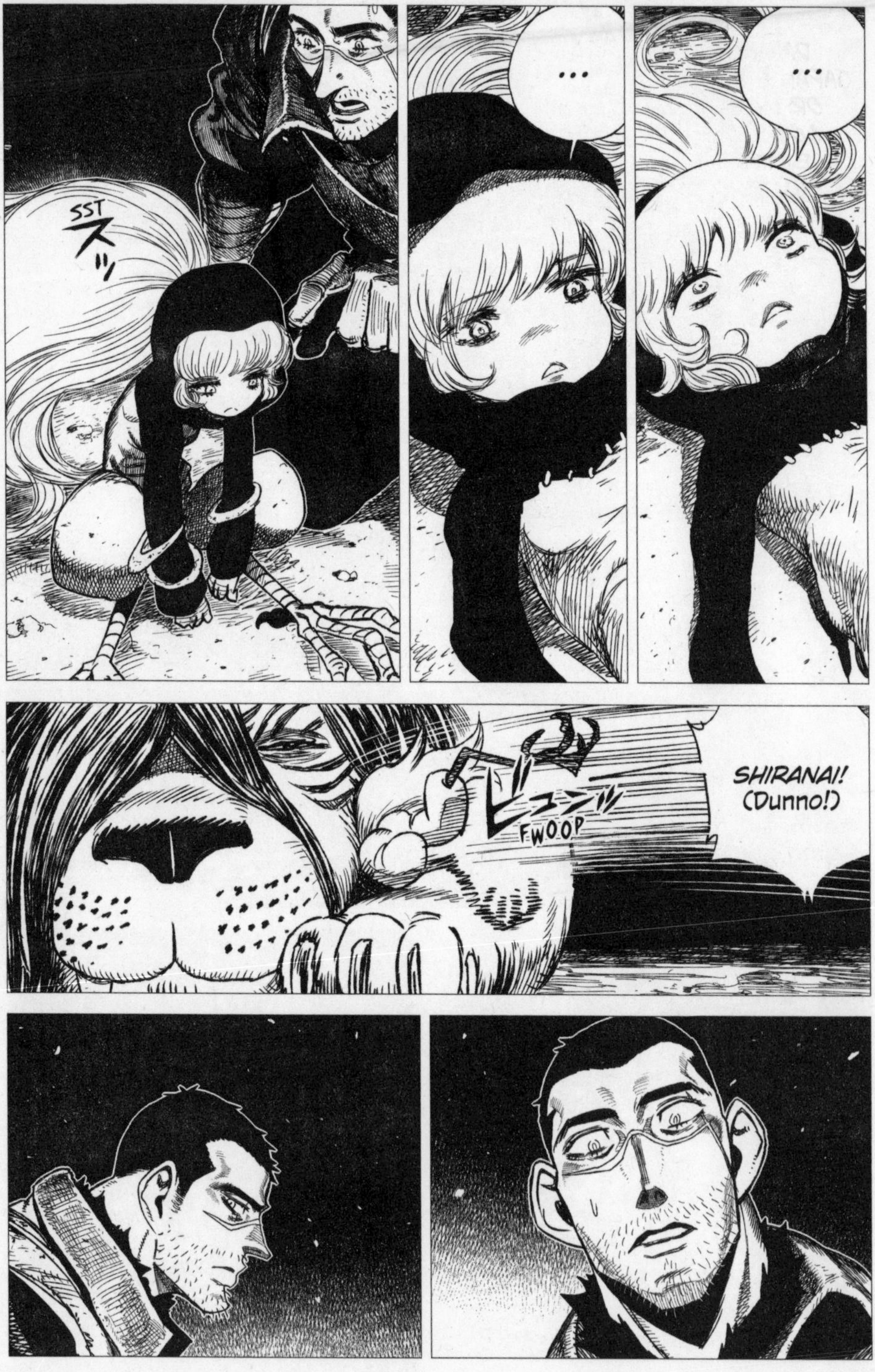
...
...
SST
スッ
SHIRANAI!
(Dunno!)
ビュンッ
FWOOP

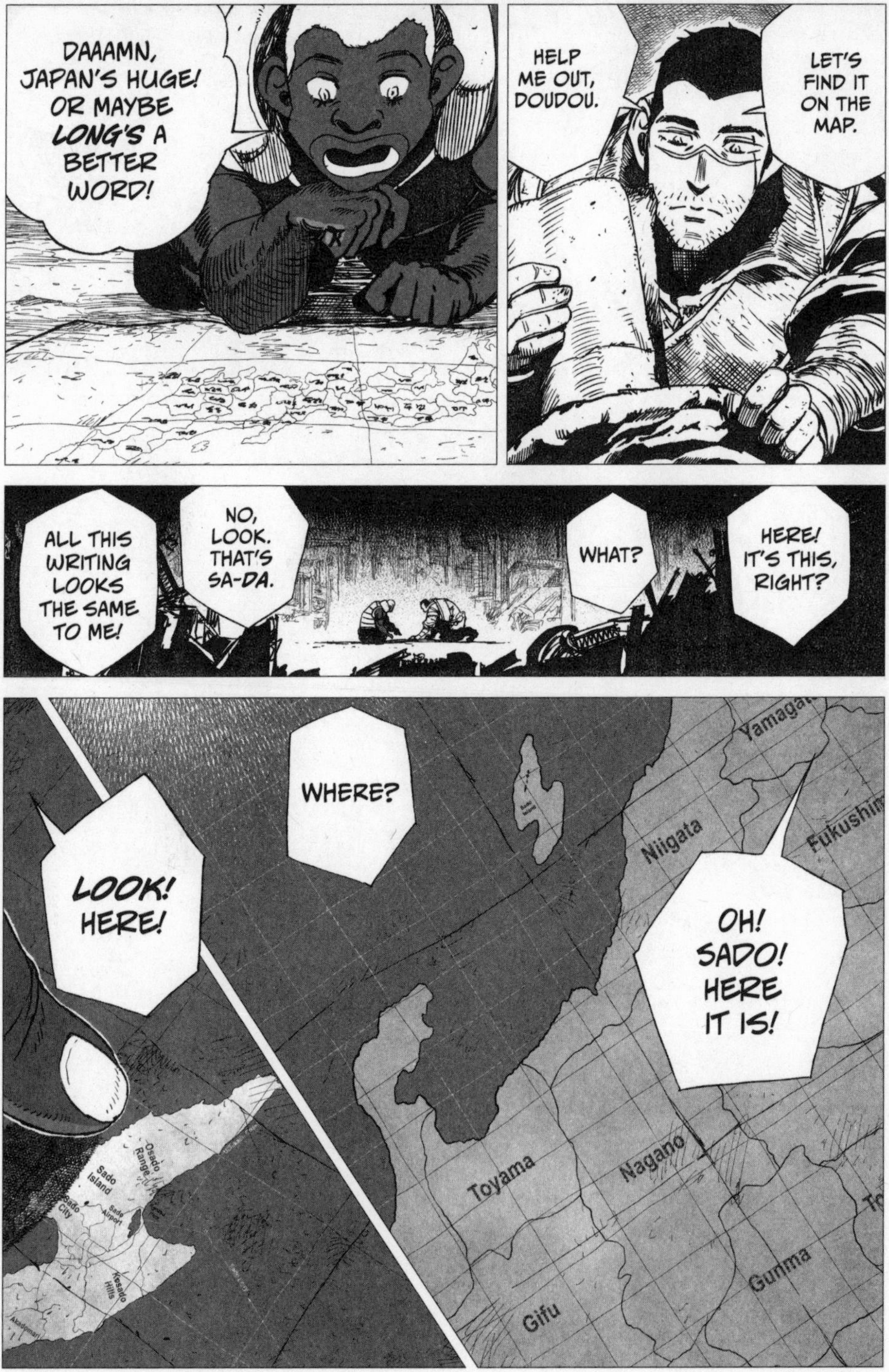
LET'S FIND IT ON THE MAP.
HELP ME OUT, DOUDOU.
DAAAMN, JAPAN'S HUGE! OR MAYBE *LONG'S* A BETTER WORD!
HERE! IT'S THIS, RIGHT?
WHAT?
NO, LOOK. THAT'S SA-*DA*.
ALL THIS WRITING LOOKS THE SAME TO ME!
OH! SADO! HERE IT IS!
Niigata
Toyama
Nagano
Gunma
Gifu
WHERE?
LOOK! HERE!
Osado Range
Sado Island
Sado City
Sado Airport
Kosado Hills

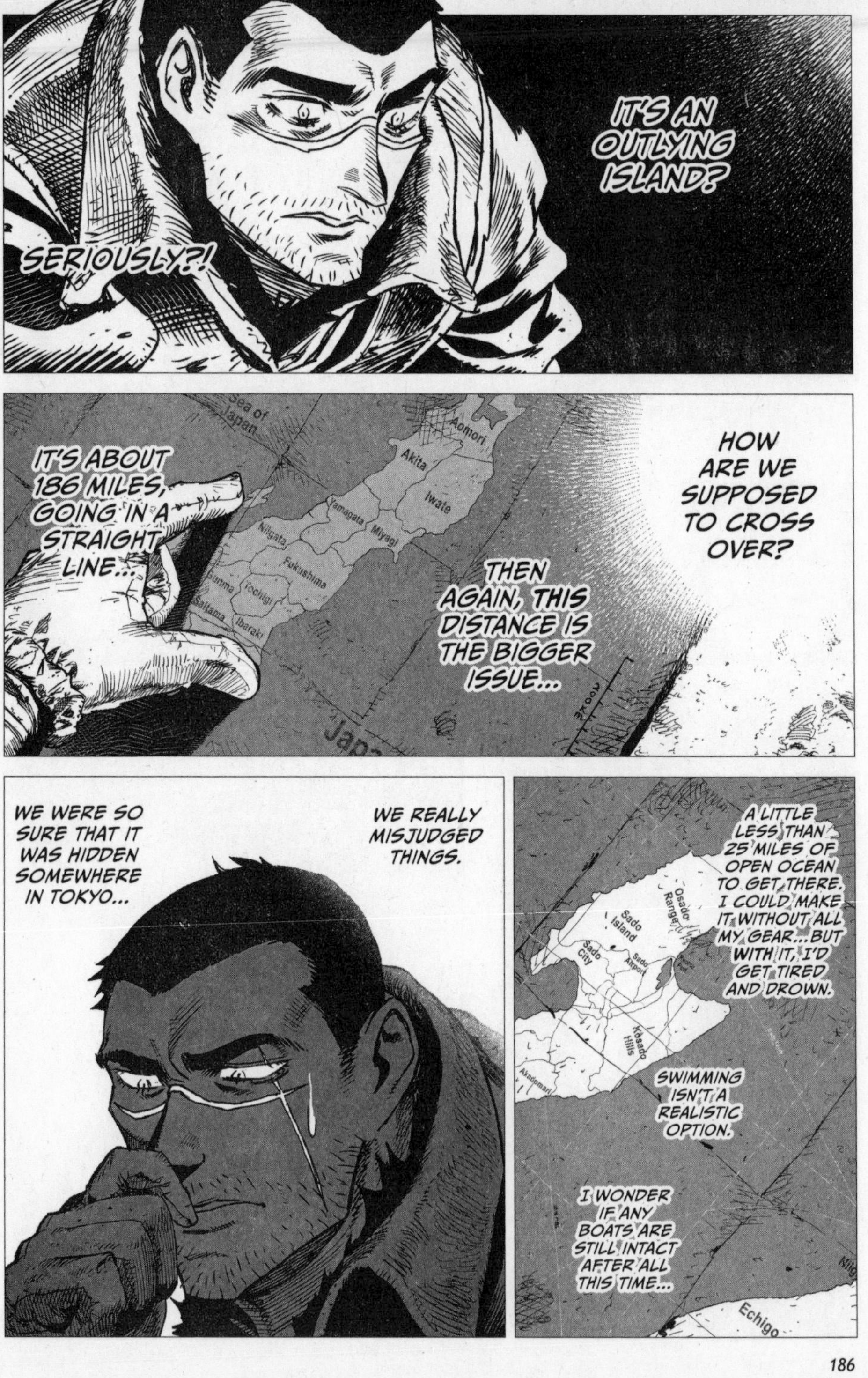
IT'S AN OUTLYING ISLAND?
SERIOUSLY?!
HOW ARE WE SUPPOSED TO CROSS OVER?
THEN AGAIN, THIS DISTANCE IS THE BIGGER ISSUE...
IT'S ABOUT 186 MILES, GOING IN A STRAIGHT LINE...
Sea of Japan
Aomori
Akita
Iwate
Yamagata
Miyagi
Niigata
Fukushima
Gunma
Tochigi
Saitama
Ibaraki
A LITTLE LESS THAN 25 MILES OF OPEN OCEAN TO GET THERE. I COULD MAKE IT WITHOUT ALL MY GEAR...BUT WITH IT, I'D GET TIRED AND DROWN.
Osado Range
Sado Island
Sado City
Sado Airport
Kosado Hills
Akadomari
SWIMMING ISN'T A REALISTIC OPTION.
I WONDER IF ANY BOATS ARE STILL INTACT AFTER ALL THIS TIME...
Echigo
WE REALLY MISJUDGED THINGS.
WE WERE SO SURE THAT IT WAS HIDDEN SOMEWHERE IN TOKYO...

IF WE SET OUT THERE NOW, WE'LL JUST WIND UP DEAD.
WE NEED TO BE AS CLOSE TO FULLY EQUIPPED AS WE CAN BE.
GLANCE
THERE'S NO GUARANTEEING THAT TSUGUMI AND TORA WILL COME WITH US THE WHOLE WAY.
THOSE CLOTHED THINGS AREN'T ATTACKING US RIGHT NOW. WE SHOULD USE THE CHANCE...
...TO GATHER AS MUCH GEAR AS POSSIBLE.
LET'S PUT TOGETHER A PLAN TO GET TO SADO.
WE'LL NEED TO FIND A ROAD MAP.
WHILE WE'RE LOOKING FOR ONE, WE'LL GATHER ANY TOOLS AND GEAR WE MIGHT NEED FOR THE JOURNEY.

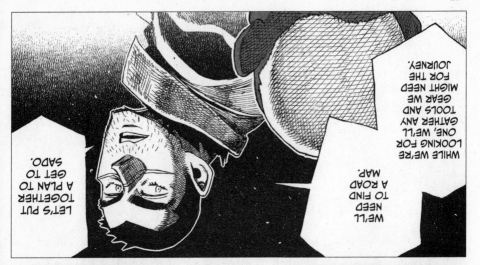

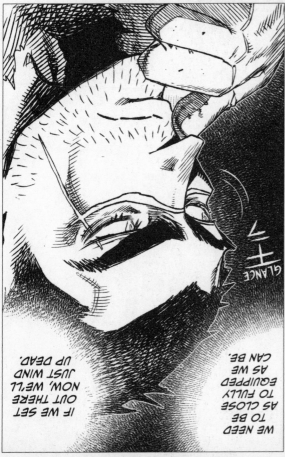

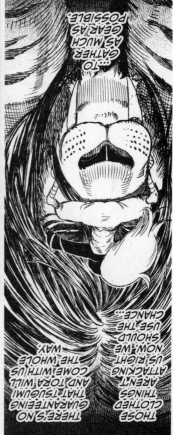

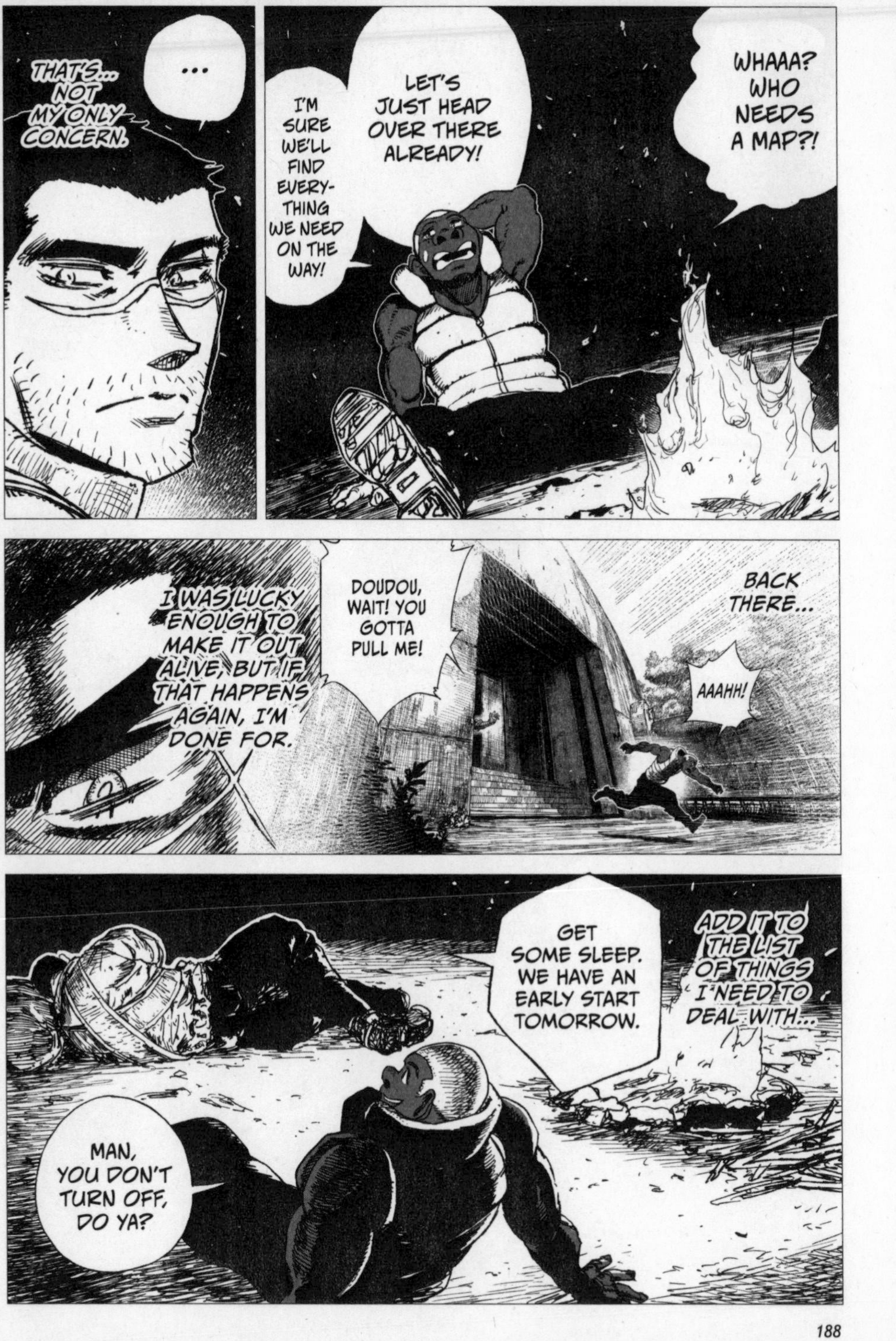
WHAAA? WHO NEEDS A MAP?!
LET'S JUST HEAD OVER THERE ALREADY!
I'M SURE WE'LL FIND EVERY-THING WE NEED ON THE WAY!
...
THAT'S... NOT MY ONLY CONCERN.
BACK THERE...
AAAHH!
DOUDOU, WAIT! YOU GOTTA PULL ME!
I WAS LUCKY ENOUGH TO MAKE IT OUT ALIVE, BUT IF THAT HAPPENS AGAIN, I'M DONE FOR.
ADD IT TO THE LIST OF THINGS I NEED TO DEAL WITH...
GET SOME SLEEP. WE HAVE AN EARLY START TOMORROW.
MAN, YOU DON'T TURN OFF, DO YA?

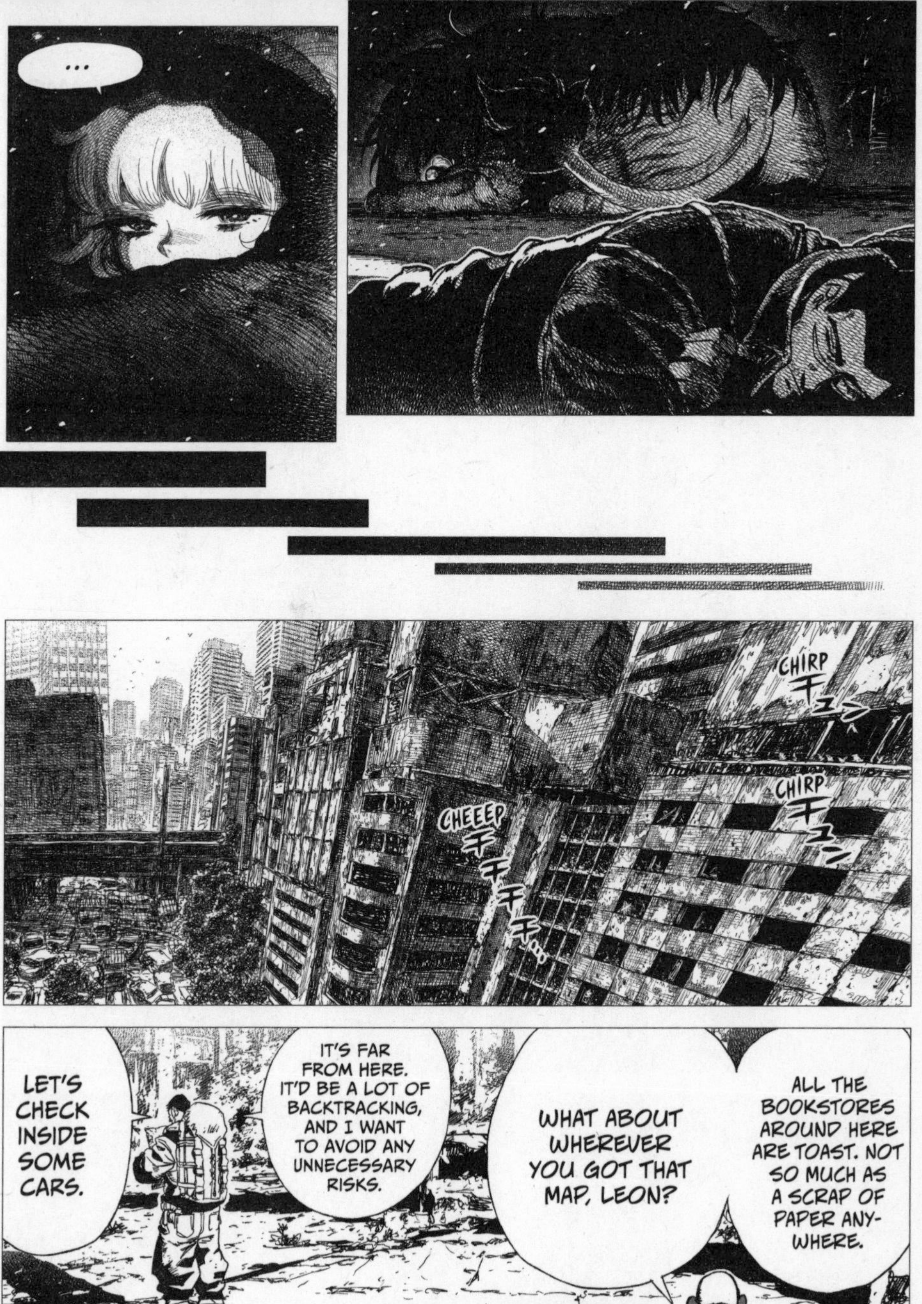
...
CHIRP
CHIRP
CHEEEP
ALL THE BOOKSTORES AROUND HERE ARE TOAST. NOT SO MUCH AS A SCRAP OF PAPER ANY-WHERE.
WHAT ABOUT WHEREVER YOU GOT THAT MAP, LEON?
IT'S FAR FROM HERE. IT'D BE A LOT OF BACKTRACKING, AND I WANT TO AVOID ANY UNNECESSARY RISKS.
LET'S CHECK INSIDE SOME CARS.

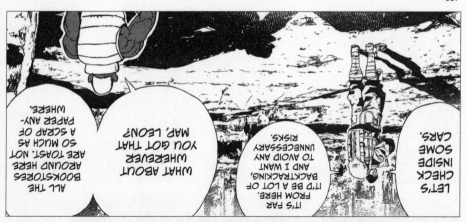

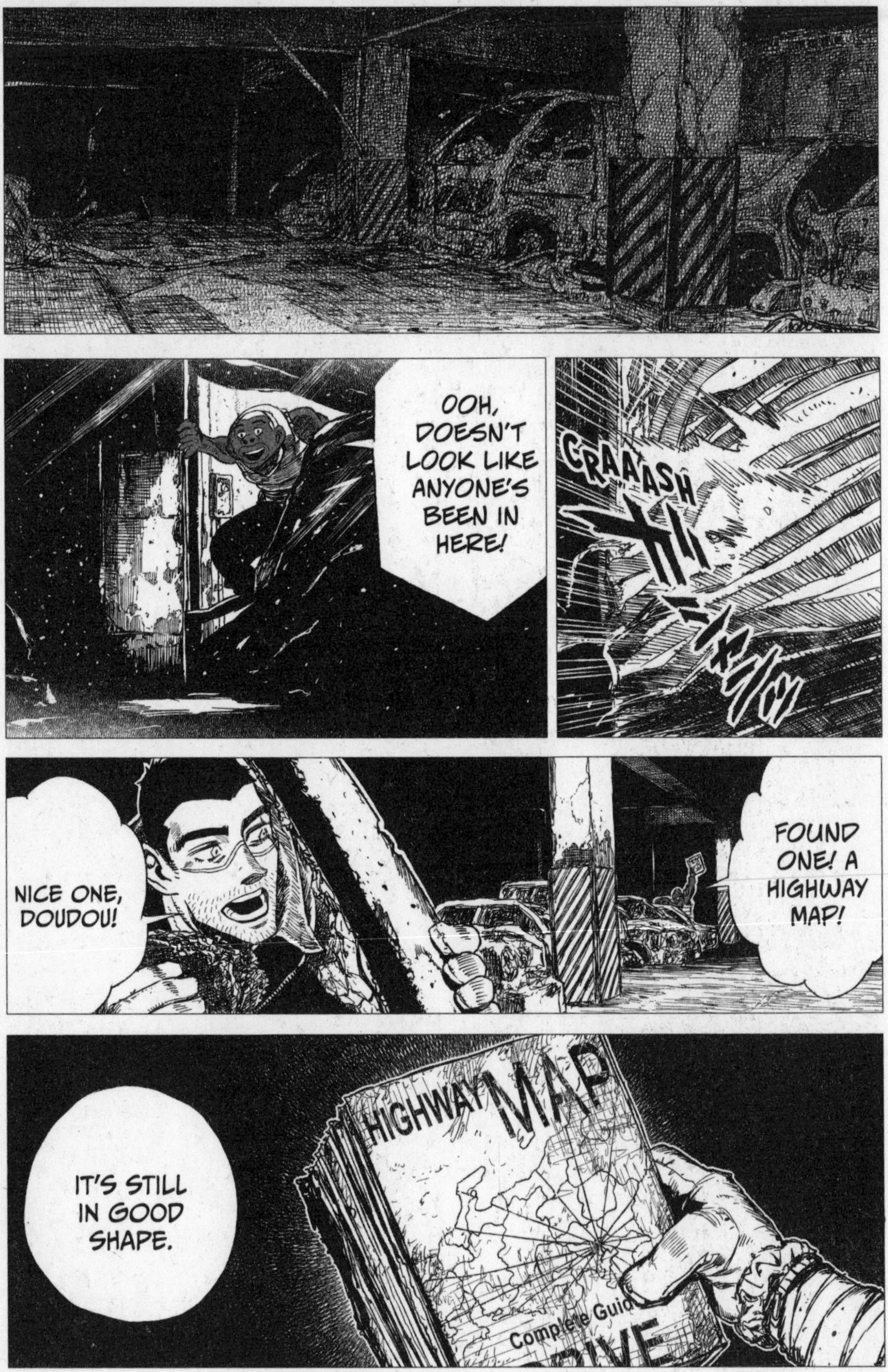
CRAAASH
OOH, DOESN'T LOOK LIKE ANYONE'S BEEN IN HERE!
FOUND ONE! A HIGHWAY MAP!
NICE ONE, DOUDOU!
HIGHWAY MAP
Complete Guid
IT'S STILL IN GOOD SHAPE.

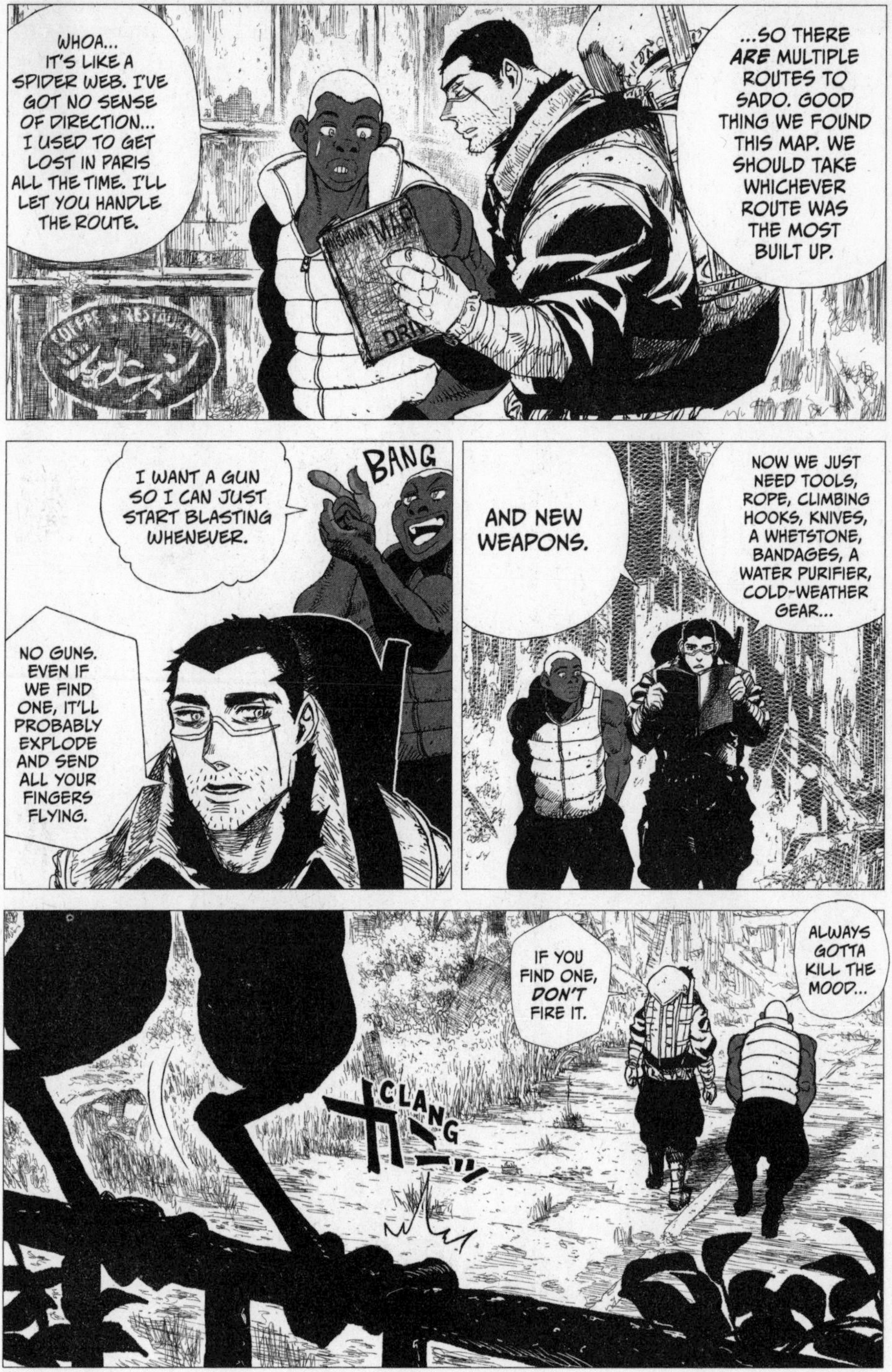
...SO THERE *ARE* MULTIPLE ROUTES TO SADO. GOOD THING WE FOUND THIS MAP. WE SHOULD TAKE WHICHEVER ROUTE WAS THE MOST BUILT UP.
WHOA... IT'S LIKE A SPIDER WEB. I'VE GOT NO SENSE OF DIRECTION... I USED TO GET LOST IN PARIS ALL THE TIME. I'LL LET YOU HANDLE THE ROUTE.
NOW WE JUST NEED TOOLS, ROPE, CLIMBING HOOKS, KNIVES, A WHETSTONE, BANDAGES, A WATER PURIFIER, COLD-WEATHER GEAR...
AND NEW WEAPONS.
BANG
I WANT A GUN SO I CAN JUST START BLASTING WHENEVER.
NO GUNS. EVEN IF WE FIND ONE, IT'LL PROBABLY EXPLODE AND SEND ALL YOUR FINGERS FLYING.
ALWAYS GOTTA KILL THE MOOD...
IF YOU FIND ONE, *DON'T* FIRE IT.
CLANG

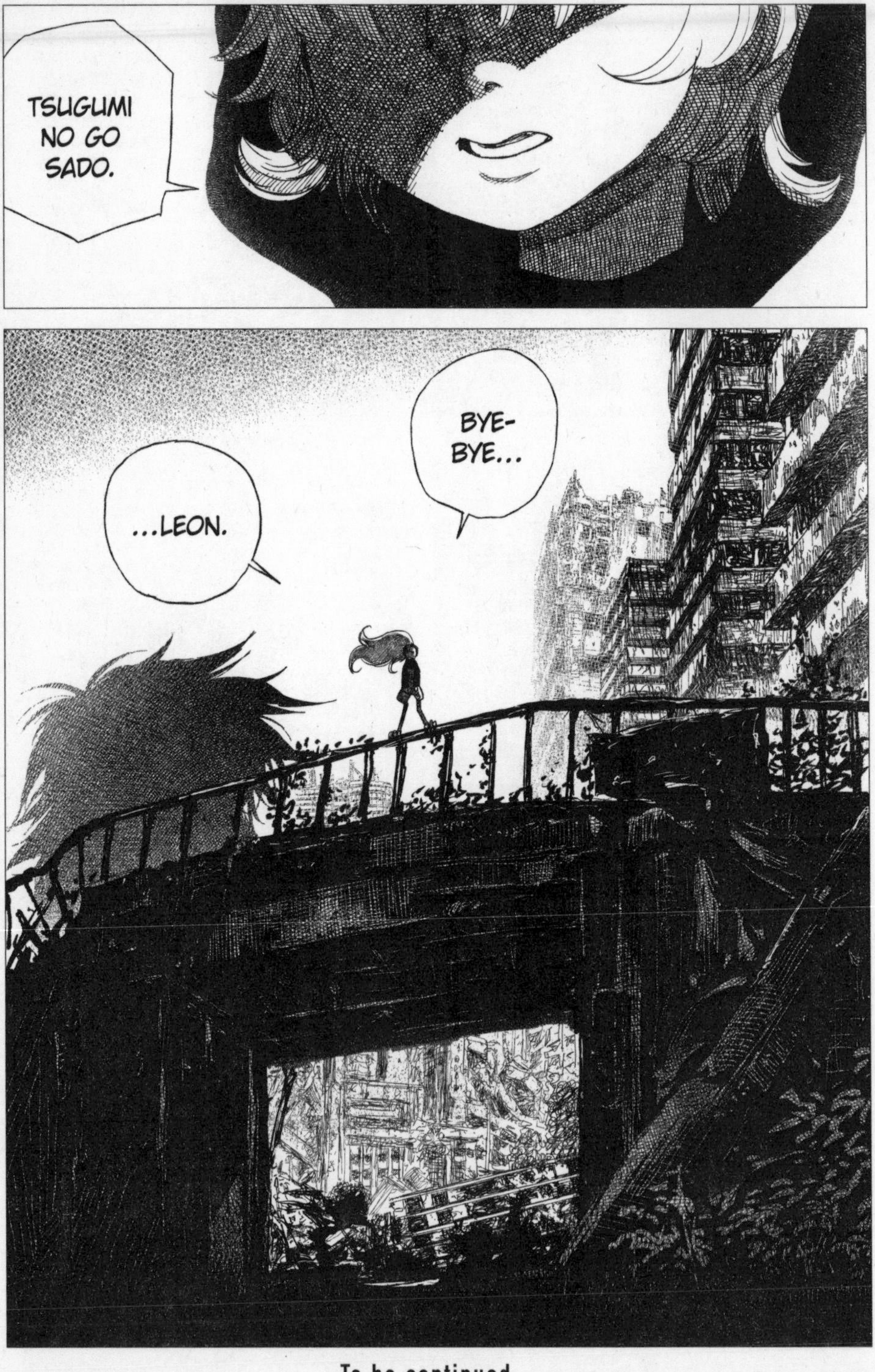
TSUGUMI NO GO SADO.
BYE-BYE...
...LEON.

To be continued...